URBAN POVERTY AND PARTY POPULISM IN AFRICAN DEMOCRACIES

When and why do the urban poor vote for opposition parties in Africa's electoral democracies? The strategies used by political parties to incorporate the urban poor into the political arena provide a key answer to this question. This book explores and defines the role of populism in Africa's urban centers and its political outcomes. In particular, it examines how a populist strategy offers greater differentiation from the multitude of African parties that are defined solely by their leader's personality, and greater policy congruence with those issues most relevant to the lives of the urban poor. These arguments are elaborated through a comparative analysis of Senegal and Zambia based on surveys with informal-sector workers and interviews with slum dwellers and politicians. The book contributes significantly to scholarship on opposition parties and elections in Africa, party linkages, populism, and democratic consolidation.

Danielle Resnick is a Research Fellow at the United Nations University–World Institute for Development Economics Research. Her work on voting behavior, political parties, and the political economy of development has appeared in *Comparative Political Studies, Party Politics, Democratization, African Affairs, World Development, Journal of Modern African Studies*, and *Development Policy Review*, as well as in chapters within edited volumes. She is also the co-editor of *Democratic Trajectories in Africa: Unraveling the Impact of Foreign Aid* (2013). She has received fellowships from the Social Science Research Council, the Council of American Overseas Research Centers, and the Mario Einaudi Center for International Studies at Cornell University. She has lived in and conducted fieldwork in a number of African countries, including Botswana, Burkina Faso, Malawi, Senegal, and Zambia. She received her PhD in government from Cornell University.

Urban Poverty and Party Populism in African Democracies

DANIELLE RESNICK
United Nations University

CAMBRIDGE
UNIVERSITY PRESS

CAMBRIDGE
UNIVERSITY PRESS

University Printing House, Cambridge CB2 8BS, United Kingdom

One Liberty Plaza, 20th Floor, New York, NY 10006, USA

477 Williamstown Road, Port Melbourne, VIC 3207, Australia

314-321, 3rd Floor, Plot 3, Splendor Forum, Jasola District Centre, New Delhi-110025, India

79 Anson Road, #06-04/06, Singapore 079906

Cambridge University Press is part of the University of Cambridge.

It furthers the University's mission by disseminating knowledge in the pursuit of
education, learning and research at the highest international levels of excellence.

www.cambridge.org
Information on this title: www.cambridge.org/9781108453165

First published 2014
First paperback edition 2018

A catalogue record for this publication is available from the British Library

Library of Congress Cataloging in Publication data
Resnick, Danielle, 1980–
Urban poverty and party populism in African democracies / Danielle Resnick,
United Nations University, Helsinki.
page cm
Includes bibliographical references and index.
ISBN 978-1-107-03680-2 (hardback)
1. Urban poor – Political activity – Africa. 2. Populism – Africa. 3. Political
participation – Africa. 4. Political parties – Africa. 5. Africa – Politics
and government – 1960– I. Title.
JQ1879.A15R47   2013
324.96–dc23   2013018647

ISBN 978-1-107-03680-2 Hardback
ISBN 978-1-108-45316-5 Paperback

For James

Contents

Figures and Maps

Figures

Maps

Tables

Acknowledgments

The intersection between politics and development has long been a source of fascination for me. After spending my early research career focusing on agricultural and rural development in sub-Saharan Africa, I became interested in the implications of rapid urbanization for the region's party systems and nascent democracies. In writing this book, I wanted to highlight the dynamism and complexity of African party strategies with diverse constituents, especially the urban poor, and to place the region's politics in a broader comparative context.

The ideas, arguments, and evidence presented in this book would not have been possible without the guidance, support, and enthusiasm of numerous individuals and institutions. First and foremost, I thank the many interviewees and survey respondents whose political perspectives fill the pages of this book. Conducting a year of fieldwork in Senegal and Zambia made me realize how incredibly giving people can be of their views and time, even when the direct benefits to them are not immediately obvious. Politicians generously fit me into their busy schedules to elaborate on campaign strategies, party platforms, and constituency bases. Market workers and residents of informal settlements kindly halted their daily activities, offered me a place to sit, and responded to my seemingly endless questions. I hope I have captured here their struggles, expectations, and political views as accurately as possible.

Much of my survey work would have proved impossible without the efforts of two diligent research assistants, Khoudia Ndiaye from the University of Cheikh Anta Diop and Agnes Mbewe from the University of Zambia. Both graciously accommodated my sometimes demanding schedule and spent long days in either stifling heat or heavy rain to assist with surveying market workers. Their own views on their respective political systems broadened my thinking and surely improved my understanding of local circumstances. Three amazing taxi drivers, Habib, Lucky, and Godfrey, helped us navigate the markets and neighborhoods of Dakar and Lusaka and patiently taught me a smattering of Wolof and Nyanja.

A number of other individuals provided access to interview contacts and research resources. In Senegal, these included Ibrahima Faye as well as Ousmane Sène and the late Mame Coumba Ndiaye of the West African Research Center (WARC). In Zambia, Phillimon Nbubani of the Institute for Economic and Social Research (INESOR), Jimmy Sabi at the National Assembly, and Brenda Zulu helped me contact key politicians and access government ministries. Guy Scott deserves special thanks for helping me gain access to debates on the floor of the Zambian National Assembly and arranging meetings on my behalf with Members of Parliament belonging to various political parties. For assisting me in finding subnational election data, I also thank Macoumba Coumé at Senegal's Ministry of the Interior and Peter Lonje at Zambia's Electoral Commission. The staff at the national archives in both countries were especially helpful at directing me to two decades of newspaper articles on each country's respective political parties.

Scholars on Senegalese and Zambian politics and urban development also deserve my thanks. Karen Tranberg Hansen shared early drafts of work she was completing on Zambia's informal sector, and Wilma Nchito offered me valuable insight into the political dimensions of Zambia's markets. Alioune Badara Diop met with me during the height of a student strike at the University of Gaston Berger in St. Louis, Senegal, to offer useful feedback on my initial research proposal. Scott Taylor encouraged my original interest in Africa as an undergraduate at Georgetown University and years later took the time to provide me with a range of useful advice before I embarked on my fieldwork, from where to live in Lusaka to whom I should contact for interviews.

This book originated as my doctoral dissertation, which I completed at Cornell University in 2010. My dissertation committee members' intellectual support undoubtedly has made this book much stronger. Nicolas van de Walle's vast expertise on African politics, development, and democratization helped me see my cases as representative of a broader trajectory within the region rather than stand-alone phenomena. He often encouraged me to marshal more convincing evidence to support my claims and provided invaluable advice on how to frame the empirical and theoretical motivations of this study. Devra Coren Moehler's high standards and keen eye for detail helped me refine the logic and implications of my arguments.

By forcing me to be transparent about theoretical assumptions and to find innovative ways to test my hypotheses, she surely has transformed me into a more critical scholar. Much of Kenneth Roberts's work on the informal sector and populism in Latin America inspired my own interest in these topics. He has not only pushed me to sharpen my definition of key concepts regarding political parties and populism, but also helped me draw parallels between Africa and other regions of the developing world. Likewise, based on his own scholarship on Western Europe, Christopher Anderson assisted me in understanding how important it is that political parties provide distinct alternatives to citizens and the implications of party differentiation for voting behavior.

A number of individuals have subsequently provided feedback on various aspects of the research presented in this book. In this regard, I am especially grateful to Nicolas Cheeseman and Lise Rakner, who have provided me with useful insights about the political scene in Zambia and the possible consequences of populism. I also thank a wide range of graduate students and academics who offered feedback on segments of this research that I presented at the American Political Science Association, Columbia University, Oxford University, and the Chr. Michelsen Institute.

At Cambridge University Press, I am grateful to Eric Crahan, who initially shepherded the manuscript through the review process. Subsequently, I have been very lucky to receive guidance and encouragement from Scott Parris, Kristin Purdy, and Abigail Zorbaugh. Two anonymous reviewers for Cambridge University Press provided incisive comments and suggestions that I believe have very much enhanced the quality and clarity of this study.

Several organizations have been instrumental in supporting this research. I am particularly appreciative of an International Dissertation Research Fellowship from the Social Science Research Council, which made my overseas fieldwork possible. In addition, I wish to thank the Council of Overseas American Research Centers for a Multi-Country Research Fellowship and the Mario Einaudi Center for International Studies at Cornell University for an international travel grant. As a Research Fellow at the United Nations University–World Institute for Development Economics Research (UNU-WIDER), I was further offered the time and collegial atmosphere needed to bring this project to completion. Some of the material in Chapters 2, 3, and 5 are drawn from articles that appeared in *Comparative Political Studies* (copyright © 2012 by SAGE/SOCIETY) and in *Journal of Modern African Studies* (copyright © 2011 by Cambridge University Press) and are reprinted here with permission.

Finally, I am indebted to my family for their constant encouragement in all my endeavors. My parents, Carol and Jim, and sister, Stephanie, further fostered my curiosity about politics and other cultures that motivated this research and stimulated my interest in international affairs more broadly. Most of all, I thank my partner and best friend, James Thurlow, who probably has been inundated with more facts about African political parties in the last five years than he ever cared to know. Yet, his own enthusiasm for this project, repeated willingness to act as a sounding board for my ideas, and a great sense of humor gave me the perspective and inspiration needed to ultimately finalize this manuscript. I dedicate this book to him.

Abbreviations

AD	Acción Democrática (Democratic Action)
ADD	Alliance for Democracy and Development
AFP	Alliance des Forces du Progrès (Alliance for the Force of Progress)
AJ/PADS	And-Jëf-Parti Africain pour la Démocratie et le Socialisme (Act Together -African Party for Democracy and Socialism)
ALDEP	Arable Lands Development Program
ANC	African National Congress
ANCYL	African National Congress Youth League
APR	Alliance pour la République (Alliance for the Republic)
ARAP	Accelerated Rainfed Arable Program
ASSOTSI	Associação dos Operadores e Trabalhadores do Sector Informal (Association of Operators and Workers of the Informal Sector)
AZIEA	Alliance for Zambia Informal Economy Associations
BAM	Botswana Alliance Movement
BBC	British Broadcasting Corporation
BDP	Botswana Democratic Party
BEE	Black Economic Empowerment
BFTU	Botswana Federation of Trade Unions
BNF	Botswana National Front
BSS	Benno Siggil Senegal (United to Boost Senegal)
CFA	Communauté financière d'Afrique (Financial Community of Africa)

CGT	Confédération Générale du Travail (General Workers' Confederation), Guinea
COPE	Congress of the People
COPEI	Comité de Organización Política Electoral Independiente (Political Electoral Independent Organization Committee)
COSATU	Confederation of South African Trade Unions
COTU	Central Organization of Trade Unions
CPA	Coalition populaire pour l'alternance (Popular Coalition for a Change)
CSO	Central Statistical Office
DA	Democratic Alliance
DP	Democratic Party
DRP	Drought Relief Program
DS	Démocratie et Solidarité (Democracy and Solidarity)
ECOWAS	Economic Community of West African States
ECZ	Electoral Commission of Zambia
EDF	European Development Fund
ESAM	*Enquête Sénégalaise auprès des Ménages* (Senegalese Household Survey)
ESPS	Enquête Suivi de la Pauvreté au Sénégal (Poverty Survey in Senegal)
FAL	Front pour l'Alternance (Front for Alternation)
FDD	Forum for Democracy and Development
FORD	Forum for the Restoration of Democracy
FPTP	First-Past-the-Post
FRA	Food Reserve Agency
FRELIMO	Frente de Libertação de Moçambique (Front for the Liberation of Mozambique)
FSD	Front pour la Socialisme et la Démocratie (Front for Socialism and Democracy)
FSP	Fertilizer Support Program
GEAR	Growth, Employment, and Redistribution
GOANA	*Grande offensive agricole pour la nourriture et l'abondance* (Great Agricultural Offensive for Food and Abundance)

HP	Heritage Party
IMF	International Monetary Fund
JCTR	Jesuit Center for Theological Reflection
JICA	Japanese International Cooperation Agency
KANU	Kenyan African National Union
LCC	Lusaka City Council
LCMS	Living Conditions Monitoring Survey
LD-MPT	Ligue-Démocratique-Mouvement pour le Parti du Travail (Democratic League–Movement for the Worker's Party)
LDP	Liberal Democratic Party
LITA	Lusaka Informal Traders Association
LOASP	*Loi d'Orientation Agro-Sylvo-Pastorale* (Agricultural, Fisheries, and Pastoral Orientation Law)
LPI	Lived Poverty Index
MAS	Movimiento al Socialismo (Socialist Movement)
MLGH	Ministry of Local Government and Housing
MMD	Movement for Multi-Party Democracy
MUFIS	Malawi Union for the Informal Sector
NARC	National Rainbow Coalition
NAREP	National Restoration Party
NCC	National Constitutional Conference
NDC	National Democratic Congress
NDP	National Democratic Party
NGO	Nongovernmental Organization
NP	National Party
NPP	New Patriotic Party
NRC	National Registration Card
ODM	Orange Democratic Movement
OECD	Organisation for Economic Cooperation and Development
PAI	Parti Africain de l'Indépendance (African Party of Independence)
PAMECAS	Partenariat pour la Mobilisation de l'Epargne et le Crédit au Sénégal (Partnership for the Mobilization of Savings and Credit in Senegal)

PDS	Parti Démocratique Sénégalais (Senegalese Democratic Party)
PF	Patriotic Front
PIT	Parti de l'Indépendance et du Travail (Party of Independence and Work), Senegal
PIT	Parti Ivoirien des Travailleurs (Ivoirian Workers' Party), Côte d'Ivoire
PNU	Party of National Unity
PR	Proportional Representation
PREG	Politically Relevant Ethnic Group
PRI	Partido Revolucionario Institucional (Institutional Revolutionary Party)
PS	Parti Socialiste (Socialist Party)
RDP	Reconstruction and Development Program
REVA	*Retour vers l'Agriculture* (Return to Agriculture)
RTS	Radio-Télévision Sénégalaise (Senegalese Radio and Television)
SACP	South African Communist Party
TGP	*Très Grands Projets* (Very Large Projects)
TRS	Two-Round System
TUC	Trades Union Congress
UDA	United Democratic Alliance
ULP	United Liberal Party
UNACOIS	Union Nationale des Commerçants et Industriels du Sénégal (National Union of Senegalese Traders and Manufacturers)
UNDP	United Nations Development Program
UNIP	United National Independence Party
UPND	United Party for National Development
UPS	Union Progressiste Sénégalaise (Senegalese Progressive Union)
ZANAMA	Zambian National Marketeers' Association
ZATMA	Zambian Traders and Marketeers Association
ZCTU	Zambian Confederation of Trade Unions

ZDC	Zambia Democratic Congress
ZED	Zambia for Empowerment and Democracy
ZMK	Zambian Kwacha
ZNCB	Zambian National Commercial Bank

ONE

Urbanization, Voting Behavior, and Party Politics in African Democracies

"No power, no votes!" was the chant hurled at politicians from Zambia's former ruling party, the Movement for Multi-Party Democracy (MMD), when they toured the shanty compound of Kanyama in the capital of Lusaka during the 2008 electoral campaign.[1] Kanyama is one of Lusaka's poorest and most populous neighborhoods and, like most other urban neighborhoods across sub-Saharan Africa in recent years, suffered from frequent electricity outages.[2] Frustrated residents were determined to leverage their one source of currency, their votes, until the problem was rectified. Ultimately, the MMD suffered a crushing electoral defeat by the opposition in both Kanyama and the rest of Lusaka. Kanyama residents therefore illustrated on a micro scale the importance of the urban poor to electoral politics and democratic consolidation in Africa.

Given that Africa is now the fastest-urbanizing region of the world, the relevance of the urban poor to the region's electoral dynamics is growing. Within the next twenty years, a majority of Africa's population will reside in urban areas (Kessides 2006). Undoubtedly then, Africa's future will be increasingly shaped by dynamics in urban areas. However, this demographic shift to the cities has been accompanied by a growing concentration of poverty, disproportionately young and unemployed populations, and a host of service delivery gaps in areas such as housing, sanitation, water, and electricity (Haddad, Ruel, and Garrett 1999; Mitlin 2004; Ravallion, Chen, and Sangraula 2007; Satterthwaite 2003). Such circumstances contribute to widespread disillusionment that should be advantageous to opposition parties. Yet, why have opposition parties in some countries benefited at the ballot box from these conditions whereas others have not?

---

[1] This vignette draws on Chilemba (2008).
[2] Hereafter, "Africa" refers to sub-Saharan Africa.

Understanding when and why the urban poor vote for opposition parties lies at the heart of this study. Viable opposition parties are pivotal to achieving democratic consolidation, including Huntington's (1991) benchmark of having at least two turnovers of political leadership following a democratic transition. Yet, many scholars have lamented that since the region's wave of democratic transitions, few countries have witnessed the ousting of the party that was victorious during the transition (e.g., Bratton 1998; Doorenspleet 2003; Nohlen, Krennerich, and Thibaut 1999; van de Walle 2003). In fact, Posner and Young (2007) note that incumbent presidents in Africa still win reelection more than 85 percent of the time. By contrast, incumbents in Latin America and the Caribbean have lost elections about 68 percent of the time in the postwar period (Molina 2001). In India, evidence also suggests that incumbents face a distinct disadvantage in elections (see Uppal 2009). Consequently, instances of both opposition success and failure in Africa are especially deserving of further attention.

I argue that the types of strategies used by political parties to incorporate the urban poor into the political arena help explain when and why this constituency votes for an opposition party in some African democracies but not in others, despite suffering equally abysmal living and working conditions. In particular, populist strategies are more likely than alternative approaches to attract the urban poor. As defined in more detail in Chapter 2, a populist strategy represents a mode of mobilization that involves an antielitist discourse, a policy message oriented around social inclusion, and a charismatic leader who professes an affinity with the underclass. Its advantage in mobilizing the urban poor is twofold. First, a populist strategy offers voters greater *differentiation* from the multitude of parties within the region that are defined solely by a party leader's personality. Secondly, it provides greater policy *congruence* with those issues most relevant to the urban poor's living and working conditions. Where an opposition party employs a populist strategy, that particular party is more likely than its competitors to garner the support of the urban poor.

A secondary concern of this study is to examine how the approach used by opposition parties to mobilize the urban poor affects the mobilization of rural voters, whose support still remains necessary to win national elections. African opposition parties traditionally are disadvantaged vis-à-vis the incumbent when trying to mobilize voters outside the city. Opposition parties reliant on populist strategies with the urban poor face the additional challenge of retaining their base in urban areas without alienating rural voters. I argue that parties that use populist strategies with the urban poor simultaneously mobilize a sizable share of rural voters through clientelistic linkages based on appeals to a politically salient identity cleavage such as ethnicity, religion, language, or race. This allows opposition parties to target only enough rural voters who, in tandem with the urban poor, help them win national office without requiring extensive campaigning in remote rural areas.

To illustrate the arguments, I focus on two countries, Senegal and Zambia, and their respective capital cities of Dakar and Lusaka. Qualitative evidence on party strategies, based on interviews with political elites and local experts, is complemented by a quantitative analysis of survey data collected from the urban poor within each city. The latter data represent a unique and novel set of information on both the voting decisions of the urban poor and their perceptions regarding the effectiveness of their country's respective political parties. This comparative case study analysis is also embedded within a broader examination of differences in urban and rural mobilization across the continent, including in countries such as Botswana, Kenya, and South Africa.

URBANIZATION, DEMOCRATIZATION, AND CONSOLIDATION

Underlying much of this study is a concern with how demographic shifts, such as urbanization, alter party competition and voting behavior. Scholars have long believed that urbanization fostered democratization through a number of mechanisms. First, urbanization signifies the existence of a host of other factors deemed relevant to democratic sustainability. Modernization theorists such as Lerner (1968) and Lipset (1959) argued that urbanization was associated with higher education and literacy, greater media participation, and increased industrialization. Similarly, Dahl (1989) believed that high levels of urbanization were accompanied by wealth, literacy, and occupational diversity, which in turn facilitated the emergence of "polyarchy." Secondly, Huntington (1991) stressed that the expansion of the urban middle classes was one of the main contributing factors to the "third wave" of democracy, particularly because this sector of society brought with it a set of values and attitudes supportive of greater liberalization. Huber, Rueschemeyer, and Stephens (1993, 1997) placed more emphasis on a third mechanism, namely that urbanization accompanied by capitalist development increases the ability of the working and middle classes to organize and therefore to reduce the power of a controlling narrow group of elites. Finally, Bates (1991) argued that more agrarian countries are exposed to more excessive taxation and expropriation, both of which help authoritarianism to thrive. By extension, then, less agrarian countries contribute to greater democratization.

In Africa, urban centers frequently have represented the locus of political contention and change. Between the 1930s and 1950s, African cities were the source of anticolonial strikes throughout the region, ranging from railway workers in Senegal to dockworkers in Kenya. A few decades later, in the struggle for political liberalization from authoritarian and one-party regimes, cities were once again where citizens and state authorities clashed. From the *villes mortes* campaign in Cameroon to the Soweto uprising in South Africa, the inability to govern the city placed political regimes in highly vulnerable positions.[3] During much of Africa's political liberalization in the 1990s, pro-democracy protests tended to occur first in the most urbanized countries in the region (Bratton and van de Walle 1997). The middle classes, including students, teachers, nurses, and civil servants, typically initiated and sustained these protests (Bratton and van de Walle 1992).

However, much of the scholarship linking urbanization with democratization assumes that urbanization accompanies industrialization and therefore proxies for economic development. Yet, urbanization in Africa increasingly is driven by "push" factors in rural areas rather than by large-scale industrial growth in urban centers (Annez, Buckley, and Kalarickal 2010; Myers and Murray 2007). Although urban areas do generate approximately 60 percent of Africa's economic growth, employment opportunities remain scarce, and incomes are either stagnant or falling (Sisk 2004).[4] For instance, the informal sector is believed to account for 61 percent of urban employment in Africa (Kessides 2006) and is estimated to be the source of more than 90 percent of additional jobs that will be created in Africa's urban areas within the next decade (UN-Habitat 2003). Moreover, approximately 72 percent of Africa's urban population lives in slum housing (UNFPA 2007), and the region's total slum population increased from 103 million to 200 million people over the last decade (UN-Habitat 2010a). This is often because most African countries have retained colonial, legal frameworks for urban development that are aimed at containing settlement instead of confronting rapid growth (Hansen and Vaa 2004).

---

[3] The *villes mortes* campaign was a general strike in the towns and cities of Cameroon during the early 1990s as a protest against President Paul Biya's opposition to constitutional reform and multiparty elections. The impetus for the 1976 Soweto uprising was opposition by South African youth to being forced by the apartheid regime to learn Afrikaans in school.

[4] This is largely because capital investment in these cities is oriented toward commercial businesses, finance, and tourism instead of industrial and manufacturing enterprises where more jobs are usually created (Myers and Murray 2007).

Recent estimates also suggest that the number of Africans in urban areas living below the dollar-a-day poverty line increased from 66 million in 1993 to 99 million by 2002 (Ravallion et al. 2007). Even based on national poverty lines, the number of the urban poor generally has increased across many African countries since the 1990s. Although comparing poverty over time is an imperfect exercise, especially because of changes in countries' measurement methodologies and poverty lines, Table 1.1 nonetheless provides suggestive evidence that urban poverty remains a very real challenge for the region.[5]

THE URBAN POOR AND POLITICAL PARTICIPATION

Conventional perceptions of the urban poor traditionally have spanned two extremes. On the one hand, "culture of poverty" studies in other regions of the world speculated that the urban poor were excessively quiescent and politically apathetic as a result of feelings of marginality and a lack of solidarity (see Lewis 1959, 1966; Moynihan 1965).[6] On the other hand lie claims that the relative deprivation experienced by the urban poor makes them especially prone to violence (e.g., Buvinić and Morrison 2000; Davis 2006; Gutkind 1973). This view was largely echoed by the United Kingdom's Commission for Africa (2005: 29) when it warned that "Africa's cities are becoming a powder keg of potential instability and discontent" as a result of the concentration of the unemployed and disaffected in the region's growing slums.

However, research suggests that rather than complete disengagement or violence, voting represents the most common form of political participation by the urban poor within developing world democracies. According to Huntington and Nelson (1976: 75), voting provides a powerful tool for eliciting responsiveness by elites: "By and large, the evidence from recent studies reinforces that from earlier ones: political participation via the ballot is a potent weapon of the urban poor in achieving higher levels of certain material benefits and thus in helping to reduce economic inequality." This in turn may explain why the urban poor are often more active in elections than their compatriots. For instance, Thornton (2000) found that workers

---

[5]   Satterthwaite (2003, 2004) further suggests that urban poverty not only is growing but also has been severely underestimated in the past because urban poverty lines are usually based on food expenditures, ignoring that non-food expenditures, such as rent, transport, and fuel, are a large source of expenditure in urban areas. In addition, even though access to certain services is greater in urban areas, few indicators measure the quality of the services, which can be lower in urban areas because of higher population densities.

[6]   Based on her work in Brazil's *favelas*, Perlman (1976) challenged this view.

Table 1.1. *Trends in the Number of the Urban Poor for Selected African Countries*

Country	1990s	2000s
Benin	602,402	829,787
Botswana	171,718	197,687
Burkina Faso	428,465	1,107,827
Burundi	151,052	244,685
Ethiopia	2,717,199	4,092,459
Gambia	275,290	320,323
Ghana	1,535,863	1,158,856
Kenya	1,387,668	2,601,458
Lesotho	76,336	184,862
Madagascar	2,318,912	2,679,905
Malawi	821,307	474,111
Mali	865,404	1,099,834
Mozambique	2,861,634	3,386,762
Namibia	146,085	119,873
Nigeria	11,779,176	26,495,940
Tanzania	1,568,541	2,240,615
Uganda	270,478	435,224

Note: Poverty data are available for countries during only specific years. The years selected for this table were as follows: Benin (1995, 2003), Botswana (1993, 2003), Burkina Faso (1998, 2009), Burundi (1990, 2006), Ethiopia (1996, 2005), Gambia (1998, 2010), Ghana (1999, 2006), Kenya (1994, 2005), Lesotho (1993, 2003), Madagascar (1997, 2005), Malawi (1998, 2004), Mali (1998, 2006), Mozambique (1997, 2008), Namibia (1994, 2004), Niger (1993, 2007), Tanzania (1991, 2004), and Uganda (1999, 2009).
Source: Calculated from urban poverty and urban population data in the World Bank's World Development Indicators (2012).

in Mexico City's small-scale informal sector were more likely to vote in elections than formal workers. In India, Yadav (1996: 96) has described a "second democratic upsurge" in which electoral participation rates are increasingly higher among low-caste, poorer, and less-well-educated citizens. Based on two rounds of Afrobarometer data, Bratton (2006) noted that by 2005, Africa's urban poor were turning out to vote more often than they had in the late 1990s and that the poor generally were more likely to vote than their wealthier compatriots. Moreover, survey research in Kenya and Côte d'Ivoire revealed that voter turnout among shantytown dwellers exceeded the national average (Kersting and Sperberg 2003).

Nevertheless, studies on the urban poor, and on class more broadly, have been largely absent in contemporary scholarship on African parties, elections, and democratization. Baker's (1974) study on the impact of urbanization on political change in Lagos provides an in-depth, historical view over fifty years, but the study ends in 1967, only shortly after Nigeria received independence from Britain. Theoretically rich and broad-sweeping analyses of political participation and party responses to the urban poor in developing regions, such as the ones by Cooper (1983), Nelson (1970, 1979), and Huntington and Nelson (1976), were conducted at the height of one-party regimes in Africa. They also preceded much of the region's adoption of structural adjustment programs, which are believed to have exacerbated the extent of urban poverty (White 1996). In Tripp's (1997) study of Tanzania, the urban poor, represented by Dar es Salaam's informal sector, are placed at the forefront of analysis. Yet, the focus is on their role in lobbying for economic and political liberalization over the course of the mid-1980s and early 1990s rather than their preferences and behavior in the country's post-transition period.

The reason for this research gap is twofold. First, the urban bias literature of the 1970s and 1980s, popularized by Bates (1981) and Lipton (1977), emphasized that African policy makers kowtowed to the wishes of urban dwellers at the expense of exploiting the agricultural sector. The belief that an urban bias in government practices still persists, and that Africa's urban dwellers remain privileged over their rural counterparts, traditionally has caused urban poverty in Africa to be sidelined as an area of study (Maxwell et al. 2000). Secondly, Africa historically has been predominantly agrarian, and therefore the urban poor have until recently comprised a relatively small sector of society.

Yet, given that they now comprise the majority of residents in African cities, and their numbers continue to grow, the urban poor can have a potentially significant impact on the region's political landscape. Consequently, the urban poor represent what Kitschelt (2000: 849) terms "vote-rich but resource-poor constituencies." In fact, despite laments of incumbent dominance at the national level, opposition parties fare better in major urban areas.[7] Table 1.2 shows the results for the most recent executive elections

---

[7] This is a major contrast from the early period of democratic transition when most African incumbents lacked a strong attachment to rural constituents (see Bienen and Herbst 1996).

in fourteen of Africa's electoral democracies.[8] Following Lindberg (2007), those countries considered electoral democracies have held at least two elections, not endured an electoral breakdown caused by a coup or other military intervention, and obtained an average rating of 4 or better on "political rights" by Freedom House over the last five years.[9] If, at the time of elections, a party belonged to the opposition and received a plurality of votes in the largest city, then the respective country is classified as "opposition party dominant." Similarly, if the incumbent party at the time of elections received a plurality of votes in the largest city, the country is categorized as "ruling party dominant." As seen, the opposition was victorious in the largest urban area for more than half of these countries.[10]

THE ARGUMENT: POPULIST STRATEGIES AND
THE URBAN POOR

Table 1.2 emphasizes that there are disparities across African countries regarding whether opposition parties are favored in major urban areas. As already noted, these urban areas are predominantly comprised of low-income residents who labor in the informal sector and often reside in slum housing. Consequently, the primary research question that this study addresses is the following: when and why do the urban poor support opposition parties in some countries, and in some elections, but not in others?

Given the dearth of literature on Africa's urban poor, addressing this question requires relying on explanations of the urban poor in other areas of the world or evaluating whether common claims about general voting behavior in Africa are easily applicable to the region's urban poor. There are at least four schools of thought in this respect, which are presented in further detail in Chapter 2. First, the literature on vote-buying claims that

---

[8] Parliamentary results are provided for non-presidential regimes, which include Botswana, Lesotho, and South Africa.

[9] Notwithstanding some criticisms of this measure (Munck and Verkuilen 2002), it offers a comparative measure of political rights that is available for a broad time period across a wide range of countries. The Freedom House scale assigns a 1 to countries that best fulfill the political rights category and a 7 to those that are the worst performers in this dimension.

[10] As a result of using these criteria, Guinea Bissau, Madagascar, and Mali were excluded because of recent democratic reversals Moreover, disaggregated election data were not available for four countries that fit these criteria – Cape Verde, Niger, São Tome e Principe, and Seychelles – and therefore urban preferences could not be discerned. In Mauritius, the national assembly and the prime minister are elected from multimember constituencies, with each voter having three votes, and thus it is not possible to determine the exact percentage of voters who supported each party.

Table 1.2. *Patterns of Political Party Support in Africa's Largest Cities*

Ruling Party Dominance, Country, *City* (Year)	Opposition Party Dominance, Country, *City* (Year)
Botswana, *Gaborone* (2009)	Benin, *Cotonou* (2011)
Ghana, *Accra* (2012)	Kenya, *Nairobi* (2007)
Malawi, *Lilongwe* (2009)	Lesotho, *Maseru* (2012)
Mozambique, *Maputo* (2009)	Liberia, *Monrovia* (2011)
Namibia, *Windhoek* (2009)	Senegal, *Dakar* (2012)
South Africa, *Johannesburg* (2009)	Sierra Leone, *Freetown* (2007)
Tanzania, *Dar es Salaam* (2010)	Zambia, *Lusaka* (2011)

Sources: Please see text for criteria on the countries included and Appendix A for details on specific election results.

political parties encourage loyalty among the urban poor by disbursing money, T-shirts, food, and other selective benefits during electoral campaigns. Voters see such handouts as an indicator of future benefits they may receive if that particular party came into office. Thus, by extension, voting disparities across Africa would be attributed to how much largesse ruling and opposition parties accordingly provided to poor communities before elections.

A second school of thought posits that ethnicity plays a powerful role in shaping electoral preferences in Africa. In a context of low education levels and indistinguishable party platforms, ethnicity can serve as an "information shortcut" for voters as to which candidate is most likely to be sympathetic to their needs. This may be particularly true in urban areas. Indeed, contrary to the claims of modernization theorists, some scholars have argued that urbanization only exacerbates the salience of ethnicity in the political, social, and economic domains of African city life (e.g., Bates 1983; Melson and Wolpe 1970). As such, this school of thought implies that the urban poor are more likely to support a particular opposition party when the ethnicity of that party's leader corresponds to their own.

Retrospective, economic voting represents a third strand of scholarship. In this view, constituents decide whether to support the incumbent based on the performance of the overall macroeconomy (e.g., Lewis-Beck 1988). The urban poor are particularly vulnerable to economic downturns because they are more dependent than their rural counterparts on monetized goods and services (Fay 2005; Kessides 2006), but they have fewer resources than the urban elite to withstand such downturns. Economic voting would therefore imply that the urban poor support the opposition in countries where macroeconomic conditions deteriorate prior to elections.

Finally, the degree of participation in associational life represents another factor that can influence voting behavior. Among Africa's urban poor, associational life is increasingly vibrant, whether in the form of self-help groups or organizations for slum dwellers and informal-sector workers. From a social capital perspective, membership in such associations may increase political activism (e.g., Putnam 1993; Woolcock and Narayan 2000). From a corporatist perspective (e.g., Schmitter 1974), political parties that cater to the demands of, or are formally aligned with, such organizations are more likely to garner the votes of those organizations' members.

For either empirical or theoretical reasons detailed in Chapter 2, all four of these explanations are incomplete on their own for explaining the disparate voting patterns among Africa's urban poor. Instead, this study focuses on the interactive relationships between political parties, the urban poor, and other groups of citizens. Specifically, the initial assumption of this study is that the urban poor want improvements to their welfare and parties want to win votes. Compared with both rural dwellers and higher-income urbanites, the urban poor face distinct challenges toward securing improved welfare. Most critically, prices tend to be higher in urban areas and access to goods and services is highly monetized, whereas in rural areas, basic goods such as shelter, fuel, and food may not be marketed but rather are self-provisioned (Bratton 2006; Mitlin 2004; Satterthwaite 2004). Most taxes are paid in cities and used to subsidize service provision in rural areas, where taxes on income are extremely rare (UN-Habitat 2003). At the same time, the urban poor enjoy fewer informal safety nets in the form of kinship and community networks than do their rural counterparts, making poor economic circumstances particularly difficult to handle (Maxwell et al. 2000). Compared to other urbanites, the urban poor are viewed as a threat to state authority by circumventing property laws and building homes on land for which they lack an official title (e.g., Centeno and Portes 2006). They also lack the resources of other urbanites to secure certain services privately, such as electricity generators and private security guards, when the state is under-providing such goods. Compared to urban professionals, such as teachers and nurses, the urban poor lack the leverage to engage in strike activity to obtain concessions from the state. Overall then, the urban poor are uniquely dependent on the state for their well-being, and therefore, choosing which party to elect to national office can hold particularly important implications for them.

Opposition parties intent on winning votes are most likely to gain the support of the urban poor by tapping into the latter's disgruntlement and marginalization. Populist strategies are especially well-suited to this task. Populist strategies represent an amalgam of Kitschelt's (2000) three types of party-voter linkages. Clientelist linkages involve the disbursement of selective benefits in exchange for votes and are usually forged with lower-income constituents. This may be in the form of money and gifts during campaigns or development projects and legal concessions only in those neighborhoods where residents showed loyalty at the ballot box. Parties that rely on programmatic linkages can map their policy programs along an ideological spectrum. In contrast to clientelist linkages, programmatic linkages imply that all constituents experience the impact, both good and bad, of those policies, rather than just those who supported the party. Personalistic linkages constitute a third category and involve appeals to constituents almost entirely via a politician's charisma.

A populist strategy combines these various linkages. Like clientelist linkages, a populist strategy relies on a constituency base of poorer, subaltern, and often unorganized groups, as well as the use of selective benefits (Roberts 1995; Weyland 2001). As with personalistic linkages, a populist strategy involves mobilization via the charisma of a party leader and fosters unmediated ties between the leader and his/her followers (Barr 2009). At the same time, a populist strategy contains key programmatic components that manifest through an antielitist discourse and a policy message that promotes social inclusion.

A populist strategy not only can help an opposition party obtain more support from the urban poor than the incumbent, but also explains why some opposition parties are more successful than others at garnering votes from the urban poor. The advantage of a populist strategy in winning the votes of the urban poor is twofold. First, in a region dominated by parties using personalistic linkages that advance vague catch-all messages intended to appeal to everyone, parties reliant on populist strategies function in a manner similar to a niche product by providing a good for which there is much demand but little supply among the urban poor. As such, parties with populist strategies offer greater differentiation from a majority of the party alternatives in Africa, creating a memorable impression on a voter's mind. Secondly, vis-à-vis both the myriad of personalistic parties and the few programmatic parties in the region, populist strategies provide a policy message with greater congruence to the concerns of the urban poor, including jobs, taxes, public services, and state harassment. Populist strategies further mobilize the urban poor by promising to engage in radical reforms and rejecting the existing political establishment (see Nelson 1979).

BUILDING A BASE BEYOND THE CITY

The second part of this study examines how the strategies used by opposition parties with the urban poor affect the mobilization of rural voters. I discuss how opposition parties traditionally possess fewer resources than incumbents to campaign extensively in remote rural areas. This is problematic because lower literacy and fewer independent media outlets in rural areas usually result in less awareness of opposition alternatives. By not being in office at the time of campaigning, opposition parties also lack credibility to implement the promises they make on the campaign trail.

When competing for a national office, such as the presidency, opposition parties reliant on populist strategies face an additional challenge, which is to retain a core constituency base while trying to expand support. Populist strategies may cause parties to lose other potential voters, such as rural constituents, by placing the urban poor at the forefront of their campaigns. As Nelson (1979: 323) suggests, few parties systematically exploit the electoral opportunities presented by the urban poor because "[p]olitical leaders must also weigh the risks of alienating established supporters by overzealous attempts to mobilize the urban poor." At the same time, employing populist strategies in rural areas reduces a party's ability to provide differentiation and congruence with the priorities of the urban poor.

To reconcile these dilemmas, opposition parties reliant on a populist strategy with the urban poor can simultaneously mobilize a sizable share of rural voters through clientelistic linkages based on appeals to a politically salient, ascriptive identity cleavage. As discussed further in Chapter 6, ascriptive identities refer to those identities over which people have relatively little ability to choose, such as ethnicity, indigenous language, race, caste, parents' nationality, and, in some cases, religion (Chandra and Metz 2002). Yet, as constructivist theory highlights, not all ascriptive identities are actually activated or relevant to an individual's own perception of his/her identity (Chandra 2012). A politically salient, ascriptive identity cleavage refers to one that has been activated and has played a historically important role among political competitors within a particular country.

There are at least three reasons why combining a populist strategy with appeals to politically salient, ascriptive identities is particularly attractive to opposition parties. First, appeals to ascriptive identities help overcome the credibility constraint by conveying to rural voters that a candidate who shares his/her identity will uphold promises to that voter once in office. Secondly, such identities tend to be geographically targeted in rural areas (Barkan 1995; Kimenyi 2006), and therefore less extensive campaigning is needed in the countryside. Thirdly, identity appeals do not require that the party dampen its urban-oriented policy appeals.

Depending on the rules for electing a president and the backgrounds of other election candidates, opposition parties ideally would target only enough rural voters through identity appeals who could, in tandem with the urban poor, help them win national office. In such circumstances, an opposition party can forge what Gibson (1997) referred to as coalitions comprising "metropolitan" and "peripheral" members. In other words, the opposition keeps its policy proposals targeted to the urban poor, who are the core of the coalition, while relying on a segment of the rural population for the necessary number of votes to win national office.

The key factor necessary for using this approach is whether politicians combine populism with inclusive, rather than exclusive, identity appeals (see Madrid 2008). Inclusive appeals imply that a party leader's tenure in office will coincide with benefits to those with similar backgrounds but do not explicitly suggest that other ethnolinguistic, religious, or racial groups will not receive those same benefits. Moreover, inclusive appeals rely on implicit overtures to a specific identity through the use of local languages, cultural symbols, and a shared history of real or imagined political and economic marginalization. This latter dimension is particularly important because perceptions of marginalization will coincide with frustrations also experienced by the urban poor about their lack of opportunities.

RESEARCH CASES AND DESIGN

These arguments are illustrated through a comparative case-study design focused on political parties and the urban poor in Senegal and Zambia. These two countries were selected for a number of key reasons relevant to better understanding when and why the urban poor prefer the opposition. First, they are full multiparty democracies, enabling opposition parties in both countries to experience a more level playing field than their counterparts in either the region's hegemonic or competitive authoritarian systems.[11] Secondly, they are among the region's more urbanized countries with equivalent levels of urban poverty. This means that, in principle, political parties would have a much greater incentive to mobilize the urban poor to bolster their electoral chances than in the region's more agrarian countries, such as

---

[11] Hegemonic authoritarian regimes allow elections but not contestation by opposition parties. Competitive authoritarian regimes allow for contestation by opposition parties, but elections are not free and fair and instead are highly skewed to the incumbent's advantage (see Howard and Roessler 2006).

Malawi. Thirdly, because they lack a history of civil conflict, partisanship is less likely to be shaped by loyalty to a former liberation or rebel movement, as in Mozambique or Namibia. Fourthly, because of the advent of multiparty competition in each country, there has been a broad range of viable opposition parties and this in turn has increased the pressure they each face to further differentiate themselves to constituents. This differs markedly from a country such as Ghana, which has essentially become a two-party system. Finally, despite these similarities, the urban poor in each country have, since 2000, displayed disparate behavior with regards to this study's main dependent variable: support for opposition parties.

More specifically, Dakar's pace of urbanization accelerated with the development of the first rail line in West Africa in 1885 (Scheld 2002). Lusaka was founded in 1905 during the building of a railroad from Cape Town to the mining areas of today's Democratic Republic of Congo (Hansen 2002). The age of both cities means that contemporary urbanization trends are driven more by urban-to-urban migration and natural population growth rather than rural-to-urban migration (ANSD 2005; CSO 2003a). Almost one-quarter of Senegal's population and 50 percent of its urban population currently resides in Dakar (ANSD 2007a; UNFPA 2007). Thirty-five percent of Zambia's population is considered urbanized and 32 percent of its urban population lives in Lusaka (UN-Habitat 2007; World Bank 2009), with other significant portions living in the country's urbanized Copperbelt region.

Income poverty rates in both countries are high but still tend to understate the level of deprivation because they are measured according to national poverty lines rather than separate urban and rural ones. In Dakar, 42 percent of the population are estimated to live below the national poverty line (Mesple-Somps 2007); 48 percent of the population in urban Lusaka Province is considered poor (Simler 2007). The degree of deprivation in Dakar is further emphasized by the fact that 76 percent of the city's population labors in the informal economy, a sector that accounted for 97 percent of employment growth between 1994 and 2005 (ANSD 2007b; World Bank 2007b). In Zambia, urban unemployment increased from 13.7 to 26 percent between 1990 and 2000 (CSO 2003a), and today, 56 percent of the country's urban population and 69 percent of Lusaka's works in the nonagricultural informal sector (CSO 2007; World Bank 2007a).

Beyond working conditions, each city's poor live in a substandard housing environment. Seventy-six percent of Senegal's urban population lives in slums, with most of Dakar's poorest residents living in vast irregular settlements in the city's suburbs of Parcelles Assainies, Pikine, and Guédiawaye.

A majority of these residents, as well as beggars, lepers, and street peddlers, were viewed by authorities as *encombrements humains,* or "human
clutter," and pushed out of Dakar's city center during the 1970s and 1980s
(Collignon 1984; Zeleza and Eyoh 2003). Conditions in these neighborhoods are dire: "In Pikine for example, an average of 20 households may
share a single water source, and many others have no access to a latrine.
The consequences of limited urban planning force suburbanites to shift
back and forth between the city center and outer areas in search of housing,
hospitals, schools, employment opportunities, and other basic resources
necessary for survival" (Scheld 2002: 86). Likewise, as a result of British
town-planning principles, the dearth of government housing initiatives,
and the lack of private-sector housing development, more than 70 percent
of Lusaka's residents live in squatter settlements on the periphery of the city
center, which are popularly referred to as "shanty compounds" or "high-
density areas" (Hansen 2002; Mulenga 2003; UN-Habitat 2007). Most of
these compounds lack proper infrastructure and key services such as internal plumbing, which in turn often forces communities to share the same
latrines and communal water taps (Taylor 2006). As Hansen (2002: 85) sur-
mises, "The health of the public is seriously at risk in Lusaka at the outset
of the 21st century due to the combined effects of overcrowding, declining
infrastructure, and insufficient services." The return of cholera in the city
during every rainy season and the large number of deaths caused by tuber-
culosis highlight the urgency of the situation.

Notwithstanding their similar living and working conditions, the urban
poor in both countries have exhibited different levels of affinity to opposition parties over the last decade and a half. Specifically, Zambia's previous
ruling party, the MMD, first entered office in 1991 with strong support in
both the country's urban areas and almost all rural provinces. Although
corruption and economic mismanagement during the 1990s under
President Frederick Chiluba significantly reduced the MMD's popularity, economic circumstances improved considerably under President Levy
Mwanawasa's tenure, which began in 2001. In fact, under Mwanawasa's
New Deal government, the country's inflation dropped to single digits and
economic growth averaged approximately 5 percent, buoyed by improved
copper prices and substantial external debt forgiveness (*Economist* 2006;
Larmer and Fraser 2007).

However, high unemployment and economic disparities persisted, and
in the October 2006 presidential elections, Mwanawasa and the MMD lost
substantially to the Patriotic Front (PF) in Zambia's major urban areas.
In Lusaka district, the PF presidential candidate, Michael Sata, obtained

58 percent of the vote compared with 21 percent for Mwanawasa. In the 2008 presidential by-elections that followed Mwanawasa's death, Sata gained 61 percent of the votes in Lusaka district compared with 27 percent for the MMD candidate Rupiah Banda. In both elections, Sata's voting shares were particularly high in urban Lusaka's poorest constituencies, such as Chawama, Kanyama, Mandevu, and Matero. Similar high results in cities within the Copperbelt Province lend credibility to Gould's (2007: 8 and 9) observation that "Michael Sata has brought real *issues* of concern to the urban poor into the political arena." By 2011, Sata not only increased his vote share in Lusaka to 63 percent but also obtained enough votes to become the country's fourth president.

In Senegal, a very different dynamic occurred. During the second round of Senegal's historic 2000 presidential elections, overwhelming support in Dakar helped Abdoulaye Wade and his Parti Démocratique Sénégalais (PDS) defeat the then-incumbent Parti Socialiste (PS) candidate, Abdou Diouf. The support of other opposition parties for Wade's *Sopi* coalition catapulted Wade to victory during those second round of elections. Critically, Wade far exceeded the number of votes obtained by any of his competitors in Dakar during the first round of the elections, indicating that Dakarois did not just want a general change of political regime but a specific change that involved Wade as leader. In particular, Galvan (2001) argues that Wade inspired hope among Dakar's economically marginal youth.

After seven years of Wade's tenure, the plight of the urban poor had not improved. In fact, high unemployment prompted thousands of Senegalese men to risk their lives and emigrate in ramshackle fishing boats (Polgreen 2007). Many of Wade's projects, such as the multilane Corniche highway along the Atlantic coast, were deemed to favor the city's wealthy few rather than the poor majority, prompting observations that life in Dakar was operating *à deux vitesses*, "at two speeds" (Meunier 2008: 38). In the 2007 elections, however, it was mostly Dakar's intellectuals who supported opposition candidates, such as Ousmane Tanor Dieng of the PS, Moustapha Niasse of the Alliance des Forces de Progrès (AFP), or Idrissa Seck of Rewmi. By contrast, many of Dakar's poor surprisingly still supported the incumbent. Indeed, in both the region of Dakar and at the national level, Wade received 56 percent of the votes in the first round of the 2007 elections, exceeding the majority needed to obviate a second round. As Galvan (2009: 5) observes, "Tellingly … angry mobs did not take to the streets to denounce the government's alleged 'theft' of the presidential election." Despite Wade's failure to deliver for the urban poor, the latter did not shift their support to the opposition.

Indeed, even when Wade violated the constitution and tried to run for a third term in 2012, the urban poor did not overwhelmingly support the opposition. Macky Sall, who is the leader of the Alliance pour la République (APR) Party, ultimately won those elections but only received 27 percent of the votes in the region of Dakar during the first round of voting; Wade obtained 25 percent of the votes and Moustapha Niasse finished a close third. Turnout in the capital was also much lower than in either the 2000 or 2007 elections, indicating a clear lack of enthusiasm for the alternatives. Thus, although Wade clearly lost his urban base by 2012, no one opposition party was able to replicate his previous success at mobilizing the urban poor.

Understanding Opposition Mobilization in Senegal and Zambia

In this study, I focus predominantly on the period from 2000 until 2008 to better understand why the urban poor consistently supported the opposition in Zambia over subsequent elections while their counterparts in Senegal remained supportive of the incumbent. In particular, I argue that growing support for the opposition by the urban poor in Zambia during this period, but not in Senegal, is due to the manner in which opposition parties in each country mobilized the urban poor, and I further substantiate this by examining changes in mobilization strategies over time. Whereas the PF used a populist strategy with Zambia's urban poor in the 2006 and 2008 elections, all of Zambia's opposition parties relied on personalistic linkages in the 2001 elections. By contrast, Senegal's opposition parties employed a mixture of personalistic and programmatic linkages with the urban poor during that country's 2007 elections, thereby failing to imitate the PDS's use of a populist strategy with this sector of society during the 2000 elections.

Specifically, in Zambia's 2001 elections, none of the main opposition parties, including the PF as well as the Forum for Democratic Development (FDD) and the United Party for National Development (UPND), obtained an overwhelming plurality of votes in Zambia's urban centers because of their reliance on personalistic linkages. After these elections, Mwanawasa increasingly steered the MMD to a more programmatic orientation and focused on free-market policies intended to attract foreign investment, particularly in the country's copper sector. At the same time however, he placed even greater restrictions on the urban poor by amending the Street Vending and Nuisances Act to include more stringent provisions and launching his Keep Lusaka Clean Campaign, which blamed informal workers for traffic congestion, littering, cholera outbreaks, and deterring business investment in the city. With the help of his Minister of Local Government and Housing, Sylvia Masebo, those living in informal housing settlements were often threatened with evictions and demolitions (see Mushinge 2007; Mwape 2007).

As a consummate political entrepreneur who was previously a major player in the MMD, Michael Sata took advantage of this disgruntlement and used a populist strategy to achieve victory among the urban poor during both the 2006 and 2008 elections. With showmanship tactics, such as arriving at the High Court in a speedboat to register the PF for the 2008 elections, Sata represents the quintessential charismatic politician. Popularly known as King Cobra, he also has a record for getting things done. For example, when he was Lusaka district governor in the 1980s, he provided affordable housing to many residents and cleaned the rubbish off the streets (Gould 2007). In cities, he appealed to the poor based on their main economic priorities, using a campaign slogan of "Lower taxes, more jobs, and more money in your pockets." By contrast, his main opposition competitor, Hakainde Hichilema of the UPND, relied on personalistic linkages with the urban poor and failed to generate much support in Lusaka or the Copperbelt.

Sata also increased his share of national votes in each subsequent election by campaigning heavily in the mainly rural Northern and Luapula Provinces, which are dominated by the country's largest ethnolinguistic group, the Bemba.[12] In those provinces, he appealed to voters on the basis of his shared Bemba identity and argued that Bembas were unfairly marginalized under the MMD. Hichilema, by contrast, could not rely on an urban support base and belongs to a numerically inferior ethnolinguistic group, the Tonga. Instead of solely targeting the Tonga in rural areas, Hichilema was therefore forced to campaign more broadly in rural areas in an attempt to gain enough support to win national office.

When Wade was in the opposition, he targeted his appeals in Senegal's urban areas to unemployed youth and members of the informal sector, relied on simplistic language and innovative campaign messages, and invented a novel form of campaigning, known as the "blue marches." Despite his failure to deliver tangible benefits for Dakar's urban poor during his first term, no one Senegalese opposition party was able to tap into the frustrations of this constituency in the 2007 elections and duplicate Wade's previous

---

[12] Although there are approximately seventy-three languages in Zambia, there are eight broad ethnolinguistic groups that encompass mutually intelligible languages. These groups, as classified by Zambia's Central Statistical Office, are Barotse, Bemba, English, Mambwe, North-western, Nyanja, Tonga, and Tumbuka.

populist strategy. Instead, a majority of the opposition parties in Senegal are perceived as being associated with Dakar's *citadins*, or the traditional urban elite, who express discontent with policies via national conferences rather than street protests. They espouse virtually indistinguishable party platforms and claim they represent all Senegalese rather than one particular constituency base. Many of their plans to improve conditions for the urban poor involve stimulating agricultural growth in the countryside and stemming migration to the city, rather than tackling the conditions of those already residing in Dakar.

The failure of any one Senegalese opposition party to employ a populist strategy with the urban poor in the 2007 elections had an impact on rural mobilization. Without being able to depend on an urban support base, those reliant on personalistic linkages with the urban poor needed to campaign broadly in rural areas rather than specifically target one of the country's main Sufi Muslim brotherhoods. Membership in these brotherhoods constitute the most politically salient identity cleavages in Senegal, with the two largest being the Tijaniyya and the Mouridiyya.[13]

In the 2000 elections, Wade combined a populist strategy to the urban poor with direct appeals to his coreligionists in rural areas. His campaigns in rural areas highlighted his own devotion to his Mouride identity and especially the Mouride Khalifa, or head of the Mouride brotherhood. As a consequence, Wade proved much more popular in Mouride rural strongholds than his main opposition competitors, who belong to the Tidiane sect. By contrast, he gained less support in Tidiane-dominated rural areas during the first round of those elections.

Yet, in the 2007 presidential elections, no opposition candidate could specifically rely on the exclusive support of one of these brotherhoods for a number of reasons. First, neither the rural Tidiane nor Mouride populations comprise a majority of the country's population on their own without the combined support from the urban poor. Secondly, three of the main candidates – Idrissa Seck, Ousmane Tanor Dieng, and Moustapha Niasse – were all from the same brotherhood, the Tidiane. Thirdly, Wade had already forged clientelistic linkages in rural areas with not only members of the Mourides but also sections of the Tidiane sect. Consequently, opposition parties such as the PS, AFP, and Rewmi campaigned widely across Senegal rather than targeting a particular region dominated by their coreligionists. Instead of using clientelistic linkages predicated on identity appeals in rural areas, they relied on personalistic linkages.

[13] The other two orders are the Qadiriyya and the Layène, which are discussed in Chapter 6.

STUDY OUTLINE

The remainder of the study is organized into seven chapters. Chapter 2 examines theories about the preferences of the urban poor and derives potential hypotheses regarding their voting decisions. In particular, I examine the role of vote buying, ethnicity, economic voting, and associational life in influencing voting decisions. I then advance this study's central argument, which is that voting decisions by the urban poor depend on the linkage strategies used by political parties to incorporate them into the political arena. A populist strategy in particular is more likely to attract the urban poor than alternative party-voter relationships because it offers greater differentiation and greater congruence. A typology of linkages is introduced that distinguishes clientelistic, personalistic, and programmatic linkages according to a party's constituency base, mode of mobilization, the role of voter participation, and implications for party organization. I then elaborate on how a populist strategy represents a fusion of these different linkages. The chapter further discusses what demographic, socioeconomic, and political factors facilitate the emergence of a populist strategy. The chapter concludes by presenting how the study will operationalize party linkages, differentiation, and congruence and discussing indicators of the success or failure of a populist strategy.

Chapters 3 and 4 delve into the contemporary political context of Zambia and Senegal, respectively, and focus on the linkage strategies that parties have used with the urban poor. In each country, I conducted semi-structured interviews with ruling and opposition political party elites, journalists, civil society members, local academics, and development experts.[14] These actors were asked about differences in the ideologies of their countries' main political parties, who comprises the main constituency base of each party, and whether parties possess any specific policy proposals aimed at the urban poor. Party manifestoes and archival materials on elections in each country supplemented these interview materials.

Based on these materials and the fact that party linkage strategies can change over time, I examine different electoral periods since 2000 in each country. In Zambia, most of the opposition parties relied on personalistic linkages in the 2001 elections and therefore none could garner a sizeable share of votes among the urban poor despite widespread disillusionment with the ruling MMD. Whereas the MMD became more programmatically oriented by the 2006 elections, Michael Sata and the PF relied on a populist

---

[14] Appendix B provides a full list of the individuals interviewed in both countries.

strategy with Lusaka's underclass to defeat both Mwanawasa and the other opposition parties competing in those elections. He was able to sustain that strategy and repeat this performance in 2008, when the MMD advanced Rupiah Banda as its presidential candidate. In Senegal, the populist strategy employed by Wade and the PDS in 2000 are compared with those used by other political parties during that election. In turn, the personalistic strategies of the PS, AFP, and Rewmi parties are examined within the context of the 2007 elections and highlighted as a reason for Wade's reelection despite his failure to noticeably improve the urban poor's welfare during his first term.

Chapter 5 introduces a survey of the voting decisions of Africa's urban poor in the capital cities of Dakar and Lusaka. In each city, a survey was conducted that consisted of 200 interviews with informal sector workers, resulting in a total of 400 interviews overall. These interviews occurred in ten different markets, which is where many informal sector workers spend most of their day vending from either stalls or on the side of the street. The ten markets in each city spanned different electoral constituencies and included both centrally located markets as well as more peripheral ones. To confirm that the views of the market workers represented those of the broader urban poor, more in-depth interviews were conducted with a total of sixty low-income households across three different neighborhoods within each city.

After discussing how these surveys were designed, Chapter 5 focuses on a series of quantitative analyses based on the survey data. These analyses are used to test both the alternative hypotheses presented in Chapter 2 as well as the degree of congruence and differentiation provided by populist strategies compared with other linkage approaches. The analyses reveal that in Zambia, disappointment with job creation under the MMD constituted the main influence on the urban poor's support for Michael Sata. In addition, most of Sata's supporters claimed they supported him because of the PF's manifesto and their belief that of all the country's political parties the PF was most interested in improving living conditions in Lusaka. By contrast, most respondents in Senegal supported Wade in 2007 not because they appreciated his policies but because he had promised to change them. Ironically, their disappointment manifested in support for the incumbent rather than any of the opposition parties. A majority of respondents further admitted to seeing no distinction among their country's parties, few understood the concept of a party platform, and most believed that no Senegalese party was particularly interested in improving Dakar's living conditions. The comparison of survey results emphasizes that an opposition party reliant on a populist strategy with the urban poor offers greater differentiation and issue congruence than existing alternatives and therefore is more likely to secure the urban poor's votes.

Chapter 6 examines how the strategies used by opposition parties with the urban poor influences their mobilization of rural voters. This chapter argues that parties reliant on a populist strategy with the urban poor can simultaneously mobilize a sizeable share of rural voters through clientelistic linkages based on appeals to a politically salient identity cleavage, such as ethnicity, religion, language, or race. The argument is then applied to the two case-study countries. Census data from each country reveals the share of the population belonging to various ethnic, linguistic, and religious categories, and demonstrates that these identities are geographically concentrated in rural areas. This data is then combined with newspaper reports of candidates' campaign stops during each country's most recent elections. Together, this information reveals whether or not candidates were concentrating their campaigns in rural regions where the population overwhelmingly belongs to one particular ethnic, linguistic, or religious group. I show that in Zambia, Sata was the only opposition candidate who could concentrate his campaigns in rural regions dominated by his co-ethnics. In Senegal, where no opposition party used a populist strategy with the urban poor in 2007, I illustrate that they all engaged in broad campaigning across rural areas.

Chapter 7 then applies the study's main arguments to other African democracies. In particular, I examine Raila Odinga and the Orange Democratic Movement (ODM) in Kenya, Kenneth Koma and the Botswana National Front (BNF) in Botswana, and Jacob Zuma and the African National Congress (ANC) in South Africa. These cases all confirm that a populist strategy is not only a winning approach for mobilizing the urban poor but also almost always complemented by appeals to a segment of rural voters along an ascriptive identity cleavage. In addition, the cases show that a populist strategy is also available to incumbent parties that are concerned with reinvigorating their image among the urban poor.

Chapter 8 summarizes the major findings and broader contributions of the entire study. In addition, it highlights how the study's main arguments have been supported by more recent events in each country, including the outcomes of the 2011 and 2012 presidential elections in Zambia and Senegal, respectively. The conclusion also suggests areas for further research, including whether leaders who use populist strategies do adhere to their campaign promises upon entering office, how the use of populist strategies in one election affects voters' expectations about a party's future campaign tactics, and what rapid urbanization implies for the voting behavior of Africa's rural poor.

STUDY CONTRIBUTIONS

In brief, the study's contributions span at least four domains. First, whereas a majority of literature on African politics focuses on voting behavior, electoral outcomes, or party systems alone, this study is one of the few that examines how parties actually interact with citizens. By recognizing intra-urban disparities and not just rural-urban cleavages, it further emphasizes the value of a subnational approach for gaining a more nuanced understanding of the variety of electoral constituencies in Africa with which parties interact. At the same time, the study does not simply examine "the opposition" as a monolithic entity but rather differentiates African opposition parties according to how they mobilize the urban poor and other constituents. This is valuable for illustrating under what conditions an opposition party will be able to not just defeat an incumbent party but why one opposition party proved more appealing than alternative competitors.

Secondly, as defined in this study, populist strategies represent a fusion of personalistic, programmatic, and clientelistic linkages. As such, contrary to Kitschelt's (2000) claims, all three linkages can be simultaneously combined to provide an especially potent means of mobilization, albeit typically for only a limited period of time. In addition, I show that parties are dynamic entities and can use disparate linkages with different constituents within the same country and over time.

Thirdly, the study embeds Africa in cross-regional discussions about populism. In many respects, the African cases presented in this study demonstrate important similarities with contemporary manifestations of populism in Latin America. These include the reliance on eclectic policy ideologies and the fusion of populist strategies in urban areas with appeals to ascriptive identities in rural areas. However, African leaders that have relied on populist strategies have much more explicitly focused on particularly mobilizing poor, urban youth, which reflects the growing importance of the region's youth bulge. Moreover, such leaders have rarely been genuine outsiders to the political establishments they claim to oppose in the same manner as their Latin American counterparts.

Finally, the study speaks to the importance of opposition parties for generating the level of contestation and citizen participation that characterizes a genuine electoral democracy. In many African countries, opposition parties consistently fail to defeat incumbent parties. Although incumbent advantages explain part of this trend, the lack of credible opposition parties is also an important factor. As will be shown in the following pages, in order to have meaningful multiparty competition, opposition parties must not just participate in elections but use such occasions to articulate citizens' preferences. By targeting the priorities of the urban poor, opposition parties using populist strategies represent a credible alternative to the status quo for this particular constituency, and their participation in elections can therefore facilitate the turnover of incumbents. Thus, how the growing ranks of the urban poor are incorporated into the political arena will prove significant not only for their own welfare but also for broader party development and democratic consolidation within the region.

TWO

Drivers of Voting Behavior among Africa's Urban Poor

Why Populist Strategies Prevail

Explanations for the motivations underlying the voting behavior of Africa's urban poor are scarce, and the broader political preferences of this group remain unexplored. This chapter therefore initially considers four strands of literature on voting behavior more broadly to derive possible hypotheses for when and why the urban poor support opposition parties. First, from findings in other regions of the developing world, the literature on clientelism postulates that the urban poor support the political party that offers the most selective benefits in exchange for votes. Secondly, scholarship squarely focused on Africa often highlights the salience of ethnic cleavages in voting decisions, and this in turn could suggest that a poor urban voter is more likely to support a co-ethnic candidate. A third school of thought suggests that voters select which party to support based on the incumbent's handling of the macroeconomy or changes in their own personal economic circumstances. Finally, both social capital and corporatist theories highlight that ties to civil society associations or work organizations may shape partisanship and political engagement more broadly.

For either empirical or theoretical reasons detailed in the rest of this chapter, I find that each hypothesis is an incomplete explanation on its own for the voting motivations of poor urban voters. Instead, I argue that the urban poor's voting decisions depend on the types of relationships established with them by political parties during election periods. Building on the work of Kitschelt (2000), the chapter proceeds to delineate three types of linkages according to not only their mode of mobilization but also their constituency base. Subsequently, I introduce the idea of populist strategies, which represent an amalgam of these three linkages. The chapter then details the logic underlying the central argument of this study: opposition parties that rely on populist strategies are more likely to obtain votes from

Africa's urban poor than parties that rely on any of the other party linkages alone. The reason for this is twofold. First, parties that employ populist strategies provide greater differentiation for voters than personalistic linkages, which tend to represent the norm in Africa. Secondly, the appeals inherent within a populist strategy offer greater congruence with the policy issues most relevant to the working and living conditions of the urban poor. The chapter further describes the conceptualization and operationalization of party linkages and populist strategies as well as the causal mechanisms of differentiation and congruence.

EXPLANATIONS OF VOTING BEHAVIOR

Clientelism

Clientelism, or the distribution of resources and promises to a select group of constituents in exchange for votes and loyalty, has often been deemed the dominant mode of interaction between political parties and the urban poor. For Walton (1998), clientelism presents the least costly means of redressing grievances that is simultaneously amenable to both the state and the urban poor. Based on research in Argentina, Stokes (2005) argues that clientelism is easiest when voters are poor enough to value private goods highly but the party values them very little. According to survey data, she found that the higher an Argentinean's income, the less likely it was that she or he would accept a gift aimed at influencing her or his vote. Dixit and Londegran (1996) and Calvo and Murillo (2004) also argue that clientelism appeals most to the poor because income has diminishing marginal utility as someone becomes richer. For Kitschelt (2000), in the absence of a welfare state, clientelism mitigates instability caused by distributional struggles because it appeases the poor without necessarily hurting the affluent and concurrently benefits the established political order.

Two types of clientelism repeatedly appear in this literature. One type, largely derived from observations in Latin America, emphasizes the importance of established vertical ties between parties and the urban poor. By becoming embedded in the neighborhoods and workplaces of the urban poor and forming long-term relationships with them, local party patrons attempt to foster loyalty among constituents and a fear of losing access to certain goods and services. For example, Auyero (1999) focuses on a pro-Peronist shantytown in Buenos Aires, and notes the installation of offices, known as *Unidades Básicas,* in such neighborhoods that operate as brokers for the party. In Mexico, Magaloni, Diaz-Cayeros, and Estevez (2007) observe that during the 1980s, the Partido Revolucionario Institucional

(PRI) tried to create clientelist links with new migrants in city slums and informal workers by offering property titles, jobs, subsidized food and housing, and licenses for vending in flea markets. Likewise, Eckstein (2001) highlights how in the wake of an earthquake in the 1980s that destroyed slum dwellers' housing in Mexico City, the PRI entered into a pact with residents to provide them with affordable housing and even a free tank of gas in exchange for their political support.

Yet, this mode of clientelism requires intermediaries. In order to disburse benefits for votes or punishments for disloyalty, parties require the ability to monitor the actions of constituents, which in turn requires an efficient means of information gathering. Auyero (1999) stresses that in order for clientelism to be effective, strong face-to-face relationships are required on an everyday basis, not just around elections. Furthermore, mass parties that have deteriorated into patronage machines can benefit from more institutionalized structures to engage in such clientelism.[1] Based on her research of Argentina's Peronist party, Stokes (2005: 322) finds that parties with a "tentacle-like organization" are most amenable to engaging in clientelist practices.

According to Stokes (2005), the monitoring necessary for this type of clientelism is more feasible in smaller communities, such as villages, where it is easier to gain knowledge about whether someone is inclined to support one party over another. Indeed, in Africa, examples of this type of institutionalized clientelism primarily exist in rural areas (Kasara 2007), and often traditional authorities perform the function of brokers. For example, Senegal's PS distributed credit, monetary benefits, and agricultural equipment to Mouride *marabouts,* who controlled production of the country's peanut sector, in order to maintain support from the rural population for agricultural policy decisions and obtain votes during elections (see Villalón 1995).

Yet, van de Walle (2007) notes that this first type of clientelism in Africa is primarily oriented to serve the needs of elites and help them build coalitions with each other that span ethnic, regional, or religious divides.[2] He observes that the weakness of African party systems and the centralization

---

[1] Mass parties originally emerged in nineteenth- and twentieth-century Europe as a result of mobilization by the working classes. Historically, they relied on trade unions and social movements to engage voters, and they established nationwide networks to expand membership and espouse the party's ideology (Gunther and Diamond 2001).

[2] Arriola (2009) confirms this, finding that across forty African countries, patronage via the expansion of cabinet appointments facilitates the accommodation of elites who are from different ethno-regional groups.

of power around individuals rather than established parties explain the dearth of mass-based patronage machines organized around vertical ties with the poor. As such, a second type of clientelism, which focuses on the distribution of gifts and promises as part of election campaigns, is the more dominant form of clientelism practiced with Africa's poor. Its manifestations are readily observable in both rural and urban communities. Hats, T-shirts, and fabric covered with candidates' faces and party symbols are standard fare during election campaigns in Africa. In many cases, free bus trips to rallies, money, meals, and even beer are provided as inducements.

For Fox (1994: 157 and 158), this is "semi-clientelism" because individuals cannot be easily punished for disloyalty at the ballot box. Instead of threatening to punish, candidates can only claim that their largesse is a precursor to even greater benefits if elected into office. In turn, such claims are "unenforceable deals" for both sides because the candidate cannot be sure the voter will support him or her and the voter cannot be sure of the candidate's future actions. Stokes (2007: 606) distinguishes this second type of clientelism as a subtype of the first and accordingly labels it "vote buying."

A burgeoning area of survey research has not only measured the vote-buying subtype of clientelism in broadly similar ways across different African countries but also concluded that its presence does not unequivocally determine electoral outcomes. In Ghana, Lindberg and Morrison (2008) classified clientelism in terms of vote buying, defining it as promises of personal favors, service, patronage, or assistance to a voter or a member of the voter's family. Their analyses revealed that such promises play a minor role in influencing outcomes in Ghanaian elections. Drawing on Afrobarometer survey data for Kenya and Zambia, Young (2009a) operationalizes clientelism in two ways: as a party representative offering a survey respondent food or a gift in return for his or her vote and how often the respondent contacts his or her member of parliament (MP) for help with a problem. Measured in this manner, the results show that clientelism does not increase the likelihood that a voter in either country will support his or her MP again at the polls. Using an experimental design approach in Benin, Wantchekon (2003) divided eight electoral districts into three subgroups, which were each exposed to different types of campaign messages. He found that the clientelist message worked well for regionally based candidates and incumbents but also discovered that such appeals are not uniformly accepted, even amongst the poorest of voters.

Indeed, Wantchekon (2003) further observes that the incumbent candidate most credibly engages in vote buying because she or he is already in office. Analyzing Nigeria's 2007 elections, Collier and Vicente (2009) also conclude that vote buying usually favors the incumbent rather than the opposition. By extension then, if vote buying is the driving factor behind voting behavior, then the opposition would rarely ever win a substantial level of votes in urban areas, contradicting current patterns across the continent.

Additional reasons cast doubt on the ability of vote buying to shape voting alignments specifically among Africa's urban poor. As noted previously, the poor in general are the most likely to be targeted by parties using vote buying because more affluent voters can afford the goods that parties disburse. At the same time, opposition parties typically possess fewer resources than incumbents and have limited geographical coverage during campaigns (see Salih and Nordlund 2007). In fact, opposition parties typically concentrate their campaigns in dense urban areas to ensure that these resources go as far as possible. Together, these two facts imply that the urban poor will be courted by many different parties, all offering material goods and promises. Because these exchanges are unenforceable deals, the urban poor can accept the generosity of all the parties and still vote for their favorite candidate, or abstain entirely. As Nugent (2007: 254) observes, "Money cannot literally buy votes under conditions of a secret ballot: at best it can buy goodwill."

In fact, Vicente (2008) uses experimental methods in São Tomé e Principe to uncover that vote buying is less effective with urban than with rural voters. He quotes an anonymous voter who notes: "We do like vote buying. It is essential. That is the only way we have to see anything good coming from the politicians. Anyway, I can vote for whoever I want" (Vicente 2008:3). Banégas (1998) likewise finds that voters in Benin accepted gifts from every party and then actually voted according to other criteria and interests. Magaloni et al. (2007) further observe that parties cannot rely exclusively on vote buying as a campaign strategy because it is both very expensive and offers few guarantees about the ultimate electoral outcome.

Thus, vote buying alone fails to provide a convincing explanation for the voting behavior of Africa's urban poor. Oriented around campaign gifts and promises, vote buying creates uncertainty about the actions of voters and future credibility of candidates' pledges. Because vote buying practiced by incumbent parties is believed to be the most credible, and presumably the most generous, we would rarely observe a majority of the urban poor in some African countries offering their support to opposition parties if this mode of mobilization represented the primary driving force behind voting decisions. In addition, precisely because vote buying by both incumbents and the opposition is widespread throughout Africa, this variable fails to provide a useful explanation on its own for variations in support by the urban poor for the opposition.

Ethnic Voting Alignments

Instead of vote buying, a large share of Africanist scholarship stresses the influence of ethnic affinities on voting behavior. Ethnicity is frequently portrayed as a tool strategically used by skilled political entrepreneurs to capture a share of the electorate. During the era of one-party rule, Zolberg (1966) highlighted how political leaders used a mantra of unity and the fear of ethnic tensions as a means of justifying the banning of opposition parties. Yet, even if political leaders publicly denounced the role of ethnicity in political affairs, many nonetheless manipulated ethnicity as a means to stay in power (Ottaway 1999). For instance, Posner (2004a) demonstrates that Malawi's Hastings Banda strategically exploited cleavages between the Chewa and Tumbuka groups as a means of holding on to political power. In the multiparty era, Ottaway (1999) claims that ethnicity remains a salient feature in electoral politics because the swiftness of democratic transitions gave parties little time to develop their policy programs, and the concurrent discrediting of socialism increased the difficulty for parties to define themselves in ideological terms.

Why would ethnic appeals attract voters? According to van de Walle (2007), in the absence of programmatic parties, individuals may resort to ethnic voting in the expectation that they are more likely to receive certain goods and services from a co-ethnic than a politician with a different background. Such "cognitive shortcuts" are particularly useful for those with minimal education and few other means to distinguish political parties (Ferree 2011; Norris and Mattes 2003). Kimenyi (2006) further claims that ethnic groups are akin to interest groups with high exit and entry barriers, and ethnic diversity precludes a socially optimal distribution of public goods by increasing the transaction costs of cross-ethnic collective action. By contrast, because collective-action problems can be addressed more efficiently within an ethnic group and ethnic groups tend to be geographically concentrated, intra-ethnic cooperation facilitates the acquisition of local public goods, which can materialize when a co-ethnic is in power. In addition to these material benefits, Chandra (2004) also suggests that voters may experience "psychic benefits" from seeing a co-ethnic occupy an elected office.

However, empirical research provides ambiguous evidence about the impact of ethnicity on voting behavior. For instance, Norris and Mattes

(2003) examined whether a link exists between ethnolinguistic identification and party identification. Although they find that there is a significant relationship between the two variables, they concede that other structural factors and government performance also influence party support in most countries. Lindberg and Morrison (2008) also find that ethnicity was not an overriding determinant of voting decisions in Ghana's 1996 and 2000 national elections. Wantchekon's (2003) field experiment in Benin likewise reveals that voting decisions are far from determined by a candidate's ethnic affiliation.

These studies, however, do not explicitly distinguish between rural and urban voters. In the specific context of urban Africa, the salience of ethnicity and its implications for the political arena have undergone at least three generations of debate. The first generation of theorists argued that urbanization reduces the salience of ethnicity via a variety of mechanisms, including through socioeconomic development, the exacerbation of inequality within ethnic groups, or exposure to greater diversity. In particular, scholars of the modernization school proposed that urbanization contributes to more progressive and cosmopolitan world views that erode parochial forms of identification (e.g., Lerner 1968; Lipset 1959; Parsons 1975). A few case studies support this perspective in the African context. In Bamako, Meillassoux (1968) found that the Muslim religion and availability of Bambara as a lingua franca contributed to the creation of a new urban identity that transcended rural ethnic affinities. Crowder (1962: 83) likewise claimed that "tribal" identities were difficult to maintain in Dakar, where he noted that a "new community of Dakarois" were emerging. For others, the expansion of education and media that accompanies such socioeconomic and demographic processes tends to increase inequalities within ethnic groups, also creating a basis for shared interests and experiences that foster new solidarities across ethnic groups (e.g., Beteille 1970; Hardgrave 1970). Proponents of the "contact hypothesis," such as Allport (1954), also argued that prolonged interaction with others reduces barriers to communication and thereby increases mutual awareness of shared characteristics, whereas infrequent contact can reinforce hostile stereotyping. Cities in particular provide more of a forum for such interaction than dispersed rural areas.

In contrast to the modernization school, a second generation of scholars argued that urbanization can foster interethnic competition over scarce resources and opportunities within the city. For Bates (1983: 164–165), the benefits of modernization are limited but also highly visible and desired by many in an urban setting, and ethnic groups therefore compete with each other to obtain them. For him, competition occurs along ethnic lines because ethnic groups constitute a "minimum winning coalition," meaning they are large enough to gain benefits from the interethnic competition for resources but small enough to maximize the per capita value of these benefits, as they are only distributed to members of the group. Based on an analysis of Nigeria, Melson and Wolpe (1970: 1115) likewise argued that urban areas create conditions for zero-sum conflict amongst different ethnic groups:

> Nowhere is the reality of "modern scarcity" experienced more intensely than in the cities, wherein the rate of population growth invariably exceeds the rate of economic development and the availability of new jobs. It is here that the various elements of the mobilized population are thrown into direct, and very personal, competition with one another – for positions within governmental agencies and commercial concerns, for the control of local markets, for admission to crowded schools, for induction into the army, and for control of political parties.

In his study of the Democratic Republic of Congo, Young (1965) concurs that urban ethnic tensions could be linked to a strong demand for resources that outstrip supply as well as the tendency for social status to overlap with ethnic divisions. He further observes that the coexistence of ethnic groups in urban areas contributed to a heightened sense of cultural identity. For the urban poor in particular, Nelson (1979) argues that ethnic ties are the main source of information, employment opportunities, and political participation in Africa. In addition, she believes that the inability of the urban poor to forge cross-ethnic linkages inhibits their ability to act as a unified political class, and therefore she concludes that voting, along with other forms of participation, would occur along ethnic rather than socioeconomic lines.

More recently, constructivist views of ethnicity emphasize that the urban milieu may cause identities to be constantly redefined and ethnic groups are not necessarily cohesive or monolithic. Indeed, rather than ethnicity becoming transplanted to the city or modernization eroding such affinities, Ferguson (1999) finds an overlapping duality in urban identities that were both "localist" and "cosmopolitan" in his study of mineworkers in Zambia's Copperbelt. Eyoh (2007) echoes this sentiment, noting that cities contribute to the creation of distinct urban identities that are highly heterogeneous and shaped by transnational cultural influences, youth, religion, class, locality, gender, and ethnicity. The mutability of ethnicity may be even further enhanced by changing demographic patterns because fewer urbanites today are retiring to their rural villages and most urbanization in Africa is increasingly fueled by natural population growth in cities or urban-to-urban, rather than rural-to-urban, migration (Freund 2007; Tacoli 2001).[3]

In addition to this constructivist viewpoint, there are additional theoretical reasons for questioning whether ethnicity trumps all other considerations for the urban poor when they go to the polls. First, it is not clear that ethnicity serves the same political function in urban areas as it does in rural ones. For rural dwellers with less access to media and divergent views, a candidate's ethnicity may be interpreted as a sign of a credible commitment to deliver goods and services. However, given the higher population density of urban areas, opposition parties in particular are likely to concentrate a majority of campaign efforts in cities to ensure that their limited resources go as far as possible. As a result, urban residents are more likely than their rural counterparts to learn about the various party options available and make their voting decisions accordingly.

Secondly, even if ethnic attachments remain strong for urbanites and the urban poor, political parties cannot feasibly take advantage of such affinities in their election campaigns without alienating other groups. According to Eyoh (2007), ethnic residential segregation is less of a reality today than in the past precisely because of the rapid growth of African cities and the attendant expansion of both poor and mixed-income neighborhoods. Moreover, in cities, parties do not know ex ante the ethnicity of those attending political rallies to hear the party message. Thus, in cities, political parties cannot target their campaign messages easily along ethnic lines.

Given the prominence of ethnicity in studies on Africa, the impact of this variable on voting behavior cannot be dismissed entirely. Yet, as discussed later in Chapter 6, its influence may vary across urban and rural areas. Because rural areas have less access to the media, encounter fewer opposition candidates because of the latter's resource constraints, and tend to possess more homogeneous and geographically concentrated identities, ethnicity may hold greater symbolic power of a candidate's commitments. By contrast, urbanites encounter greater ethnic diversity on a daily basis and more information about alternative political options. Although the urban poor in particular may not necessarily possess a clear class consciousness, the urban setting offers more axes for unity, including the need for quality public services and job opportunities, than division. Furthermore, both the inconclusive nature of the literature and lack of voting data on this

---

[3] Tacoli (2001) notes that although rural-to-urban migration accounted for more than 40 percent of urban growth in the 1960s and 1970s, it only accounted for about 25 percent during the 1980s and 1990s.

particular issue cast doubt that ethnicity is the dominant factor driving the urban poor's choice of political party.

Economic Voting

Whereas the ethnic voting literature portrays voters as intransigently loyal to co-ethnics, the traditional economic voting literature implies more fickle citizens who will automatically switch allegiances if government performance on the economy proves unsatisfactory. Retrospective, sociotropic economic voting assumes that voters support a candidate based on the incumbent's past performance in managing the macroeconomy (e.g., Lewis-Beck 1988; Tufte 1978).[4] Based on indicators such as gross domestic product (GDP) growth and inflation, studies in both the developed and developing world have found that voters tend to blame incumbents when macroeconomic conditions deteriorate (e.g., Hibbs 1987; Remmer 1991; Roberts and Wibbels 1999; Wilkin, Haller, and Norpoth 1997). In developing countries in particular, Pacek and Radcliff (1995) conclude that economic conditions, especially when times are bad, are even more important determinants of voting behavior than in industrialized countries. Because the urban poor are especially susceptible to macroeconomic shocks due to their dependence on monetized goods and services (Fay 2005; Kessides 2006), economic voting theories are particularly relevant to this sector of society.

More recently, however, scholars have questioned whether voters can draw a clear chain of accountability between economic performance and incumbent actions. Rather, as Anderson (2007) argues, there are a number

---

[4]　Another approach considers how prospective assessments of the economy impact voting behavior or, in MacKuen, Erikson, and Stimson's (1992) language, whether voters think more like "bankers" rather than "peasants." However, even though prospective expectations can be important drivers of voting decisions, Lewis-Beck and Paldam (2000) conclude that they rarely vary from retrospective evaluations. Based on public opinion data for forty-one countries, including ten in Africa, Cohen (2004) further argues that in developing countries in particular, uncertainty about the future is often too high for respondents to feel that they can provide accurate, prospective assessments. As noted in Chapter 5, survey respondents for the present study predominantly could not answer whether they believed economic conditions would improve within the next year.

One key problem that particularly hampers research on prospective economic voting is that it often contains a large degree of measurement error. Indeed, as Michelitch et al. (forthcoming) observe, it is unclear whether respondents' prospective assessments are dependent on whether they believe a new party will enter office in the interim. In such cases, future assessments of the economy become endogenous to the prospects of the incumbent party's continuation in office rather than a determinant of it.

of contingencies that can inhibit economic performance from directly influencing voting decisions. Key among these is the nature of party systems and political institutions. For example, Samuels (2004) finds that presidential systems increase the clarity of partisan responsibility for economic performance compared with parliamentary ones, and this is particularly true if executive and legislative elections are held concurrently. Powell and Whitten (1993) observe that attributing accountability to incumbents for the economy is more difficult in coalition governments, especially minority ones, or where the opposition possesses high levels of control over the second house of the legislature. Cognitively, voters may be uncertain whether economic downturns are primarily due to government failure or global recessions (Stokes 2001). Moreover, economic hardships in the wake of reforms may convince voters that better times lie ahead, leading to continued support for incumbents (Stokes 2001).

In addition, this literature says very little about when opposition parties will prevail. The opposition can defeat the incumbent even during economic booms (Geddes 1999; Smith 2005). Then again, voters may still support incumbents in adverse economic circumstances because they do not believe the opposition can do any better (Radcliff 1994). Alternatively, negative retrospective assessments of the macroeconomy could result in abstention rather than choosing an opposition party (Posner and Simon 2002).

Pacek and Radcliff (1995) further suggest that it is not aggregate growth per se but inclusion in the growth process that determines whether constituents vote against the incumbent. Indeed, the urban poor in particular may judge a government more on its failure to abide by promises regarding service delivery, job creation, affordable education, and better health care than about only the state of GDP and inflation, which are the most common indicators used in this literature. Finally, the economic voting literature does not recognize the ability of parties to shift the locus of accountability for the macroeconomy: ruling parties may convincingly justify poor performance, and opposition parties may be able to persuade voters of an incumbent's culpability.

Thus, although economic conditions may be a source of discontent, what this implies for the opposition is unclear. Even if the opposition benefits from an incumbent's poor management of economic circumstances, the question remains as to why one opposition party is favored by voters over another. This in turn hints that economic considerations are secondary to the way in which parties market themselves and foster ties to various constituencies.

Associational Ties

A fourth school of thought posits that the involvement of voters in neighborhood, civil society, and work associations influences political participation and partisanship. Participation in civic associations can foster trust and cooperation as well as encourage citizens to become more engaged in their political communities (e.g., Putnam 1993), and this may be particularly true among the poor (see Woolcock and Narayan 2000). A corporatist perspective goes even further to suggest that members of some associations can actually possess explicit ties to specific political parties. Based on observations of Western Europe and Latin America, Schmitter (1974: 93–94) defined the concept of *corporatism* as "a system of interest representation," dominated by a small number of interest-group organizations that are "recognized or licensed (if not created) by the state and granted a deliberate representational monopoly within their respective categories in exchange for observing certain controls on their selection of leaders and articulation of demands and support." In other words, such organizations are notable for their degree of "encompassment," containing not only a large, concentrated membership base but also a high degree of authority over their members' actions (Olson 1971). In turn, this provides them with the leverage to engage in a process of concertation with the state in order to design relevant economic and social policies and help with their implementation. By extension, members of such organizations are most likely to support the ruling party in charge of the state apparatus when their interests are taken into account and filtered into the policy process.

Africa's associational life is vibrant and historically has proved highly politicized. Strike activities by labor and trade unions during the 1940s and 1950s were pivotal to ending colonial rule. In fact, one of Africa's most vocal anticolonial leaders, Guinea's Sékou Touré, was the leader of the Confédération Générale du Travail (CGT), and he gained notoriety by leading a series of strikes against French colonial rule in the early 1950s (Cooper 2002). The withdrawal of the state during periods of economic liberalization in the 1980s and 1990s was expected to provide even greater political space to foster the growth of civic associations and labor unions (see Bratton 1989). During the 1990s, labor unions were indeed key players in a number of countries' pro-democratization movements, including those in Benin, Malawi, Nigeria, and Zambia (see Bratton 1994; Cooper 2002; Decalo 1997; Ihonvbere 1997). In Zambia, the leader of the Zambian Confederation of Trade Unions (ZCTU), Frederick Chiluba, became the country's first democratically elected leader in 1991.

Yet, outside of South Africa, unions have rarely retained a corporatist relationship with political parties after democratic transitions occurred. For instance, internal divisions over economic reforms caused the ZCTU to splinter, and it was rarely consulted by the government on issues of economic policy (Rakner 2003). The growth of the informal sector and loss of formal jobs has also weakened union membership throughout Africa (Olukoshi 1998), further reducing the power of unions to exert influence over political parties. For instance, in Senegal, only 7 percent of those formally employed are members of a union (Lawrence and Ishikawa 2005).

Admittedly, some traditional labor unions are broadening their mandate to incorporate informal sector workers. In Ghana, the Trades Union Congress (TUC) has established an informal economy desk that has been assisting informal sector workers for over a decade (Croucher 2007). The example of Senegal's Union Nationale des Commerçants et Industriels du Sénégal (UNACOIS), which is an organization of informal sector workers that originally emerged in 1989 to protest the role of state monopolies in the country's economy (Thioub, Diop, and Boone 1998), also hints at the potential for informal sector workers to unionize in their own right. In Southern Africa, there exists the Malawi Union for the Informal Sector (MUFIS) as well as Mozambique's Associação dos Operadores e Trabalhadores do Sector Informal (ASSOTSI). Likewise, Zambia contains a multitude of such organizations, ranging from the Zambian National Marketeers' Association (ZANAMA), the Zambian Traders and Marketeers Association (ZATMA), and the Lusaka Informal Traders Association (LITA).

Similar organizations exist to improve the urban poor's living conditions. One of South Africa's most active organizations is Durban's Abahlali baseMjondolo (shack dwellers) movement, which was founded in 2005 during a protest over the dearth of toilets, land, and suitable housing within the city. Abahlali baseMjondolo was particularly vocal about not wanting its members to support the ruling ANC in elections until such services materialized (Pithouse 2006). Along with the Western Cape Anti-Eviction Campaign and the Landless People's Movement in Gauteng, Abahlali baseMjondolo remains quite active in contesting that country's anti-slum and squatter legislation (see Tolsi 2008, 2009). Other comparable organizations include Ghana's Homeless People's Federation and the Shack Dwellers Federation of Namibia.

Nevertheless, such organizations may not represent the interests of a broad segment of the urban poor. For Nelson (1979), large-scale organization of the urban poor is hampered by both the heterogeneous nature of their interests and their lack of resources. Amis (2004) offers some confirmation of such sentiments by observing that informal traders in Johannesburg and Kumasi were too poorly organized and not sufficiently well connected to prevent their forcible relocation from markets in their respective cities. Dietz (1998) concurs that the urban poor rarely possess enough money and time to engage in associational activities. A study of street vendors in South Africa found that informal sector workers were also loath to join organizations claiming to represent their interests due to a belief that the required membership fees fueled corrupt practices (Lund and Skinner 1999). For precisely all of these reasons, Tostensen et al. (2001) question whether associational life includes the poorest elements of Africa's urban population.

Without a sizable membership base amongst the urban poor, it is therefore doubtful that such organizations possess the qualities of encompassment needed to function in a corporatist mode. In addition to their small size, Widner (1997) adds that such types of associations may be too transient or numerous to represent a dependable source of votes for a party. According to a report by the International Labor Organization (2002), most informal sector organizations are in fact very short-lived and disband after their objectives are achieved, rarely becoming more institutionalized structures able to pursue long-term development objectives. At least in the case of Zambia, Rakner (2003) further confirms that a large number of economic interest associations precludes any single one from gaining adequate attention by the broader public, and weak membership reduces the government's incentive to consider the concerns of any single one. In addition, many of these organizations, especially those supported by nongovernmental organizations (NGOs), may be loath to form close relationships with parties for fear of co-optation into coalitions that ultimately implement policies antagonistic to the urban poor. Such fears are not without precedent: both the ZCTU and the South African Confederation of Trade Unions (COSATU) became handmaidens to neoliberal policies directly antithetical to their own interests through their close relationships with the MMD and ANC, respectively. In other words, organizations representing the urban poor may be unable or unwilling to perform the delicate act of balancing autonomy from party forces with influence over party policies.

Associational life in Africa is therefore eclectic and vibrant, at least among a small segment of the urban poor. Yet it remains unclear whether and how membership in such associations affects voting behavior. Moreover, as Hagopian (2007) notes, there is little evidence to suggest that a dense associational life reduces the salience of political parties as citizens' main source of interest representation.

PARTY LINKAGES AND POPULIST STRATEGIES

Given the incomplete nature of existing explanations for the voting behavior of Africa's urban poor, this study advances an interactive approach that focuses on the relationships between parties and constituents. In particular, the study examines the linkages, or mode of connection, used by parties with voters. As Barr (2009: 34) specifies, the term *linkages* refers to the manner in which support and influence is exchanged by parties and voters. Differentiating amongst various forms of linkage requires understanding who the voters targeted by a party are, how they are mobilized, and the ultimate aim of their participation.

Kitschelt (2000) delineates three types of linkages: personalistic, clientelist, and programmatic. Drawing on Max Weber's notion of charismatic authority, *personalistic linkages* depend on appealing to constituents almost entirely by showcasing a politician's individual qualities. A party reliant on such linkages is virtually reduced to its leader's agenda rather than representative of a particular ideology or broader mandate. *Clientelist linkages* revolve around the disbursement of selective benefits, both before and after elections, in exchange for votes. As noted earlier, clientelist linkages with Africa's poor tend to manifest through the distribution of money, gifts, and promises during campaigns. Kitschelt (2000) further classifies appeals made to citizens based on ethnic or other identity factors as a type of clientelist linkage because such appeals delimit who should receive future benefits in exchange for votes. Parties establish *programmatic linkages* with citizens when they offer a set of policies that they would implement if elected into office. In contrast to clientelist linkages, programmatic linkages imply that all constituents experience the impact, both good and bad, of those policies rather than just those who supported the party. From Kitschelt's (2000: 850) perspective, "Political parties offer packages (programs) of policies that they promise to pursue if elected into office. They compensate voters only indirectly, without selective incentives."

Yet Kitschelt's categorization does not actually define different linkage strategies but rather focuses predominantly on how voters are mobilized (i.e., through charisma, selective benefits, or policy proposals). Table 2.1 elaborates on other aspects of these linkages beyond mobilization. As already discussed, poorer voters typically represent the main constituents for clientelist linkages because they are more likely to value the benefits received from parties than better-off voters (e.g., Stokes 2005). The main intention of the linkage is to garner votes rather than for the poor to exercise any influence over policy orientation, contributing to a vertical and

Table 2.1. *Typology of Party Linkages*

Dimension	Clientelist	Personalistic	Programmatic
Who is the core constituent base?	The poor	Any societal group	Any societal group
How are they mobilized?	Particularistic benefits	Charisma	Policies and ideological program
What is the aim of targeting the constituent base?	Votes	Votes	Participation in shaping policy agenda
Mode of interaction with constituents?	Direct, vertical ties between leader and voters	Direct, vertical ties between leader and voters	Indirect, horizontal ties between leader and voters

asymmetrical relationship between the party and voters. A hierarchical party structure facilitates this relationship (Gunther and Diamond 2001) and encourages direct ties between a leader and voters.

For personalistic linkages, obtaining votes is also the primary aim of a party. However, any particular sector of society may comprise the constituent base. Because the party leader's charisma is the main mode of mobilization, vertical ties likewise exist between the leader and his or her followers. Party organization is therefore shallow, and dependent on the leader (Gunther and Diamond 2001).

Programmatic linkages can also be formed with any socioeconomic group but, crucially, they have participatory aims. Relationships are forged with voters in order for them to help shape the policy agenda and become incorporated into the political process (Lawson 1980).[5] Horizontal ties may be formed with civil society organizations to expand influence. This in turn causes accountability to be more indirect and dispersed amongst different actors and institutions rather than solely attributable to the party leader.

Elements of a Populist Strategy

Party *strategies* combine different types of linkages in various proportions, and I argue that parties that employ *populist strategies* in particular fuse aspects of all three of the above linkages in order to obtain votes. The concept of populism has proved contentious, and often associated with

[5]   Roberts (Forthcoming) further distinguishes between participatory and programmatic linkages, usefully noting that although programmatic linkages tend to encourage participation, participation can also exist in tandem with more eclectic ideologies.

disparate characteristics in various regions of the world. For the purposes of this study, I draw on characteristics of populism that have featured prominently in another developing region, Latin America.[6] In that part of the world, scholars often distinguish between the "classical" populism that dominated during the 1930s and 1940s, typified by Argentina's Juan Péron and Brazil's Getulio Vargas, and more recent "neo-populism" represented by Venezuela's Hugo Chávez, Bolivia's Evo Morales, Peru's Alberto Fujimori, or Ecuador's Rafael Correa.

Classical populism occurred during a period of mass industrialization that eroded the strength of land-based oligarchic orders and coincided with growing citizen enfranchisement, thereby creating a new constituency ripe for incorporation into the political system. The urban working classes often comprised the main constituency base of populist movements, and their relationship with political parties was usually mediated by grassroots organizations, especially labor unions (see Conniff 1982). Such populism often coincided with a commitment to workers' rights and state intervention in the economy (Roberts 2007).

Neo-populism emerged during the 1980s and 1990s in the wake of Latin America's debt crises, growing unemployment, falling wages, and increasing urban migration. With many pushed into the informal sector, once-important intermediaries, such as labor unions, began to dwindle in membership and influence, and a window of opportunity emerged for neo-populist leaders (e.g., Demmers, Fernández, and Hogenboom 2001; Weyland 1999). One of its key distinctions from classical populism therefore is that it is less dependent on intermediary organizations and more likely to use eclectic policy appeals that defy neat classification along a left-right ideological spectrum (see Roberts 2006, 2007).

For reasons elaborated on in the following section, core aspects of neo-populism are more relevant to contemporary Africa. One of the key aspects of this type of populism is not just an appeal to "the people" but specifically to poorer, subaltern, diverse, and often unorganized groups (Roberts 1995; Weyland 2001). In some contexts, populism can exacerbate polarization among classes; in others, populism can easily thrive on a multi-class coalition (see Cameron 1991; Gibson 1997; Mudde and Kaltwasser 2012; Roberts and Arce 1998). Nevertheless, in developing countries with small middle classes and a majority of citizens belonging to low-income groups, the poor will constitute the core of a populist strategy. As such, there is a

---

[6] For a comparative assessment of populism in developing and developed regions, the volume edited by Mudde and Kaltwasser (2012) is a valuable resource.

similarity in constituency base to those parties that rely more exclusively on clientelist linkages.

Much of the literature further stresses that populism relies on antielitist rhetoric that criticizes established institutions and aims to rectify the exclusion of marginalized constituencies (e.g., Canovan 1999; Ionescu and Gellner 1969). According to Canovan (1981: 294), "All forms of populism without exception involve some kind of exaltation of and appeal to 'the people,' and all are in one sense or another anti-elitist." This rhetoric always involves denouncing the domestic political and economic elite, who are believed to be detached from the needs of the majority. Yet, depending on the nature of a country's political economy and the role of foreigners within it, such rhetoric can sometimes also adopt strongly nationalistic and even xenophobic overtones.[7]

Much like programmatic linkages, this antielitist rhetoric is often intertwined with a policy discourse. Although these policies may not necessarily fall along a traditional left-right ideological continuum, they are focused on a program of social inclusion oriented around providing goods, services, and recognition to those who have been excluded from the economic and political status quo. In the case of the urban poor, these policies may involve decisions about practices deemed legal and illegal, formal and informal. For instance, are shanty homes upgraded or demolished? Are street hawkers removed from streets or relocated? Are basic services provided to settlements deemed illegal by the state? To achieve these policies and gain support, populist strategies can also involve some selective benefits to supporters in the form of economic redistribution or material incentives (Roberts 1995), much like the mode of mobilization central to clientelist linkages.

In addition to an antielitist policy discourse to rectify exclusion, a charismatic leader is usually a sine qua non of a populist strategy (e.g., Canovan 1999; Conniff 1982; Mouzelis 1985). This leader often professes an affinity with the underclass, or a "closeness with the common people" (Weyland 2001:14), which is reinforced by the leader's self-portrayal as an outsider to the political establishment against which she or he protests (e.g., Barr 2009: 38). By relying on "nonmediated rapport between the leader and 'his people'" (Mouzelis 1985, 334), populism is essentially plebiscitarian, "vesting a single individual with the task of representing 'the people'" (Barr 2009: 36). As with clientelistic linkages, populism tends to involve vertical forms of incorporation of the lower classes (Mouzelis 1985). Both Barr (2009)

---

[7] Conceptually, the use of antiforeigner discourse can be considered a feature of a certain subtype of populist strategies rather than a defining feature of all populist strategies.

Table 2.2. *Elements of a Populist Strategy in Developing Regions*

Dimension	Populist
Who is the core constituent base?	The poor
How are they mobilized?	Policies, charisma, particularistic benefits
What is the aim of targeting the constituent base?	Votes
Mode of interaction with constituent base?	Direct, vertical ties between leader and voters

and Nelson (1979) further emphasize that citizens are not seen as agents of social reform by populist parties but rather as objects for providing votes and a popular legitimacy for the leader and/or party.

Table 2.2 summarizes these characteristics and stresses that populist strategies fuse together key aspects of the three voter-citizen linkages. They share the same constituency base as clientelist linkages. Moreover, they share the same internal party organization, direct ties with voters, and aims of personalistic and clientelist linkages. However, they also incorporate the modes of mobilization of all three linkages, with policy discourse playing a major role. As such, in contrast to some Latin American scholars such as Weyland (2001), who believe that the essence of populism is its plebiscitarian organization, this study instead emphasizes that in the African case, programmatic content around issues of social inclusion is critical to populist strategies.

FACTORS ACCOUNTING FOR THE EMERGENCE OF POPULIST STRATEGIES

What accounts for the emergence of populist strategies in some countries and in certain time periods but not in others? First and foremost, the decision of a politician to use a populist strategy is somewhat idiosyncratic. Such a politician must not only possess the requisite charisma and recognize the opportunities of such a strategy but also accept the risk, elaborated in more detail in Chapter 6, that populism can alienate certain constituencies. Secondly, as Roberts (Forthcoming) suggests, democracies provide a much more conducive environment for the emergence of populist strategies than autocracies. In the latter, repressive measures often limit opposition mobilization and reduce the space for antielitist rhetoric aimed at the masses. By contrast, democracies are supposed to provide institutions of accountability and responsiveness that, when ineffective, spawn disaffection and create fertile ground for populists.

Beyond this, Kaltwasser (Forthcoming) stresses the importance of considering both demand- and supply-side drivers, which do not guarantee that populist strategies will emerge but certainly increase the propensity that they will. On the demand side, consideration must be given to factors that create the foundations for popular discontent that can be seized upon by savvy politicians. Demographic and socioeconomic shifts in particular represent a key driver for generating new grievances. Certainly, there are examples of primarily rural-oriented populist movements, such as the U.S. Populist Party and the Russian Narodniki in the nineteenth century (see Hofstadter 1969; Walicki 1969). However, in developing regions, rapid urbanization has played a significant role by increasing demands for jobs and basic services in geographic areas where political and economic power are also concentrated. As Kaufman and Stallings (1991) observe, populism usually thrives where inequality is high because these circumstances are conducive to redistributive demands by citizens. With wealthy elites dwelling in proximity to slum dwellers, urban areas in developing countries often magnify socioeconomic inequalities.

Indeed, in Latin America, populism has been predominantly, albeit not exclusively, an urban phenomenon (Canovan 1981; Conniff 1982; Drake 1982). Dietz (1998: 33) observes that rapid migration to Latin American cities at the end of World War II led to an exploding demand for jobs, housing, and other services: "Such services might not be essential in rural areas, but in an urban setting, low-income inhabitants-migrants or otherwise-came to expect such services and to react in politically sensitive ways if they were not delivered." More recent incarnations of populism have also been oriented toward an urban base, although they may also incorporate other sectors of society as well (see Madrid 2008; Weyland 1999; 2001). In Peru, for example, Cameron (1994) notes that the state's inability to provide public services led urban masses to increasingly focus on individual modes of advancement that corresponded well to self-styled leaders, such as Alberto Fujimori. In Venezuela, Canache (2004) highlights that the urban poor were most affected by economic austerity measures in the 1980s, leading to large-scale riots, a rejection of the established party system, and an affinity to the individualism of Hugo Chávez.

The existence of grievances alone, however, does not automatically result in the emergence of a populist strategy. Instead, supply-side explanations emphasize that the structure of the party system plays an equally critical role. Specifically, where there is growing convergence in the positions and appeals of mainstream parties that fail to align with the concerns of a majority of the population there exists a crisis in representation that facilitates the rise of a populist strategy (see Kaltwasser Forthcoming).

The responsiveness of the party system can sometimes be affected by the same demographic and socioeconomic shifts already discussed. For instance, growing unemployment and informalization of the workforce in Europe since the 1970s created a class of "outsiders" whose preferences were largely ignored by Western Europe's traditional leftist parties (Rueda 2005). Ignazi (1992) argues that the rise of populist right parties in Europe therefore reflected a new set of issues, such as the perceived perils of immigration, that were not being adequately addressed by existing parties. Likewise, during the 1980s and 1990s, processes of urbanization and informalization in Latin America further eroded organizational ties between laborers and parties, thereby generating greater fluidity in cleavage structures and higher electoral volatility (Roberts and Wibbels 1999). In Venezuela, for example, the rise of Chávez has been viewed as a consequence of the weak ties between the two long-standing political parties, the Acción Democrática and the Comité de Organización Política Electoral Independiente, and the growing urban poor and informal sector (see Canache 2004; Morgan 2007; Roberts 2012).

Indeed, as Coppedge (1997) notes, when a particular cleavage is absent from the political sphere, political entrepreneurs face a window of opportunity to form new parties to reflect new social conflicts. Huntington and Nelson (1976: 29) observe that this is particularly true when such entrepreneurs belong to the opposition: "Political elites out of power are more likely to be interested in expanding political participation, changing its bases, and, at times developing new forms of participation. Bringing new actors into the political arena is a classic way of altering the balance of power in that arena." A populist strategy aimed at incorporating the urban poor into the political arena is therefore one means for an opposition party to augment its political power.

Relatedly, critical junctures for the party system can be an important driving feature regarding the timing at which a populist strategy emerges. Such critical junctures can be a crisis of confidence in the configuration of existing parties, leading to fluid systems that cause partisan affinities to become volatile. Alternatively, another critical juncture occurs when entrenched, dominant party regimes lose substantial voter support over time because they are increasingly viewed as ineffectual and self-serving (see Roberts 2014).

These demand- and supply-side factors are equally important for explaining the emergence of populist strategies in the African context. As highlighted in Chapter 1, the region's rapid urbanization has been accompanied by a growing informalization of the labor force and substandard housing and services for city dwellers. Although development challenges exist equally in rural areas, the realities of political campaigning in Africa mean that for opposition parties in particular, populist strategies are most feasible in urban areas. Indeed, given the limited resources of African opposition parties, it is unrealistic for them to engage in widespread campaigning in vast, low-populated rural areas to mobilize via a populist strategy a mass, agrarian support base. In fact, the two notable examples of an agrarian, populist project in Africa during the 1980s, led by Jerry Rawlings in Ghana and Thomas Sankara in Burkina Faso, occurred after such leaders came to power via military coups rather than as a strategy for garnering popular legitimacy in the voting booth.[8] Thus, it remains questionable how much these leaders' vision of society coincided with the grievances of those they claimed to represent. In today's African democracies, populist strategies for mobilizing votes, particularly by opposition parties, are much more likely in countries with a sizable share of the population concentrated in urban areas where inequalities remain most pronounced. By extension, we would also expect that populist strategies are less likely to emerge in the near future in democracies such as Malawi, which is highly agrarian and contains only 16 percent of its total population living in urban areas (see UN-DESA 2011).

On the supply side, many of Africa's political parties either exhibit too much verisimilitude or fail to demonstrate much relevance to the concerns of the urban poor. In fact, parties reliant on purely programmatic linkages that advance a clear ideology along a left-right continuum are relatively rare (e.g., Manning 2005; Ottaway 1999; Randall and Svåsand 2002; van de Walle and Butler 1999). Instead of a vehicle for class grievances, many established African political parties emerged as a result of anticolonial protest and relied on a nationalist discourse that emphasized unity over division. Africa is also similar to many other developing regions in that industrialization

---

[8] Relying on slogans such as "power to the people," both leaders advocated a radical restructuring of society by empowering a broad coalition of citizens, including the peasantry, workers, and women. Both leaders also denounced imperialism and neocolonial influences, establishing grassroots party cells, ostensibly aimed at promoting the peoples' interests by reducing the strength of "corrupt" traditional leaders but clearly serving to institutionalize their own party's power at the local level (see Le Vine 2004; Rothchild and Gyimah-Boadi 1989).

occurred after independence, therefore weakening the autonomy of trade unions vis-à-vis the state and dampening the impact of class-based interest groups in political debates (see Mouzelis 1985). Moreover, foreign aid can constitute one-quarter to two-thirds of central government expenditures in many African countries, resulting in a heavy dependence on international donors whose conditionalities limit the degree of freedom for parties to define their own political programs (Manning 2005).

This is not to claim that Africa is entirely devoid of programmatic parties. The long-ruling Botswana Democratic Party (BDP) is well recognized as a conservative, free market-oriented party whose policies have favored the creation of an enabling institutional environment targeted at attracting investment (Molomo 2000). According to Good and Taylor (2008), the fact that the BDP ruling elite emerged from wealthy cattlemen and was never particularly anticolonialist or African nationalist contributed to its orientation. Under Thabo Mbeki, South Africa's ANC became decidedly more neoliberal, particularly through the implementation of the Growth, Employment, and Redistribution (GEAR) plan (Lodge 2002). Neoliberal parties, however, have often implemented policies that have not necessarily improved the circumstances of the urban poor.[9]

Traditional leftist parties are uncompetitive in contemporary Africa due to either the discrediting of socialism in other regions of the world (Randall and Svåsand 2002) or the absence of a viable constituency base. Without adapting their electoral strategies to incorporate Africa's vast nonunionized informal sector, such leftist parties as Senegal's Parti de l'Indépendance et du Travail (PIT) or Côte d'Ivoire's Parti Ivoirien des Travailleurs cannot gain much support in urban areas beyond working-class professionals. In turn, attempting to appeal to the heterogeneous and unorganized informal sector requires a more amorphous message and a shift in party organization that may reduce the programmatic nature of a traditionally leftist opposition party.

Ghana is unique in Africa because of the gradual institutionalization of a two-party system there that revolves around the National Democratic Congress (NDC) and the New Patriotic Party (NPP). The NPP is perceived to be a center-right party that supports individual liberty and free-market principles; the NDC is considered a more leftist party (Daddieh 2009). Because both parties have been in government at some point, Bleck and van de Walle (Forthcoming) argue that this has reduced their uncertainty

---

[9] This is highlighted in more detail in Chapter 7 when I examine these parties and their policies in more detail.

about their electoral prospects and in turn motivated both parties to "own" various issues rather than simply rely on valence messages. Consequently, the two parties have alternated in gaining a plurality of support in major urban areas, especially in the capital of Accra, over the last four elections.[10]

Notwithstanding these exceptions, personalistic linkages are the norm in most of Africa, and parties that forge such linkages tend to advance vague platforms and valence goods, offering to improve everything for everyone. Voters in turn cannot clearly articulate what distinguishes the party's agenda from the leader's personality. There are a number of reasons for this. First, many new parties in Africa either emerge as or transition into a vehicle for one individual's personal ambitions. Secondly, the financing of most political parties in Africa depends on the personal resources of the party leader rather than contributions from citizens or public funding (Bryan and Baer 2005; Salih and Nordlund 2007). This reinforces both the control of the party leader over the internal workings of the party as well as increases the tendency for political leaders and parties to become synonymous in the eyes of the voters. Thirdly, political institutions in many African countries foster a high degree of centralization around the office of the presidency, resulting in vast powers awarded to the executive (van de Walle 2003). The fusion of the executive office with a person filters over into the electoral sphere, causing campaigns to revolve around a presidential contender's personal qualities rather than his or her policy beliefs.

Moreover, in some countries, the systems within which these parties operate have faced important junctures in recent years that have led to increasing party fluidity. For instance, attempts to change constitutional term limits for presidents have been widespread in Africa (Posner and Young 2007), often leading to fissions within ruling parties, the formation of new parties, and a realignment of alliances among opposition parties (e.g., Rakner, Svåsand, and Khembo 2007). This was certainly an important factor for Zambia's political scene in the wake of Frederick Chiluba's efforts to amend the constitution (see Chapter 3). Just as significant have been broader constitutional changes related to strengthening executive powers, such as the failed constitutional referendum in Kenya that divided the National Rainbow Coalition (NARC) and created new party alignments (see Chapter 7).

---

[10] In 2000 and 2004, the NPP received a plurality of votes from residents of the Greater Accra region. In 2008 and 2012, this pattern shifted and the NDC was more popular in the region. In almost all cases, however, the difference in vote shares accorded to the two parties from Accra's residents was relatively small.

In other countries, one particular party has long been dominant, characterized by both holding an absolute majority of legislative seats and consistently winning presidential elections (see Bogaards 2004). The ability of some dominant parties to retain large vote shares in major urban agglomerations often stems from the fact that such parties were originally liberation movements that maintain deep roots in specific geographical regions. This is especially true of the South West Africa People's Organization in Namibia, which derived its historical support from the Ovambo people who exist in large proportions in the urban region of Khomas, and Frente de Libertação de Moçambique in Mozambique, which has a long-standing stronghold in the southern part of the country and around the capital of Maputo (Lemon 2007). At least in the very near future, it will be difficult for a populist strategy, especially one launched by the opposition, to emerge and gain salience in these countries.

Yet, there are other instances of dominant parties in Africa that have been increasingly perceived as corrupt and ineffectual at addressing key public grievances. Consequently, declining voter turnout and diminishing levels of partisanship to the incumbent have ensued. As highlighted in Chapter 4, this dynamic created an important window of opportunity for Abdoulaye Wade in Senegal. Likewise, Chapter 7 illustrates that a similar trend contributed to the foundations for populist strategies by the opposition in Botswana and within the ruling party in South Africa.

THE APPEAL OF POPULIST STRATEGIES TO AFRICA'S URBAN POOR

When populist strategies do emerge, I argue that they exhibit greater appeal to the urban poor than the individual party linkages presented in Table 2.1 on their own. As noted earlier, clientelist linkages in the form of vote buying are a common practice in urban areas by both incumbent and opposition parties alike. As such, there is nothing to prevent urban citizens from accepting material incentives from all parties and then voting according to other preferences. Pure programmatic linkages are either rare or often irrelevant to the needs of the urban poor, and personalist linkages are abundant but often not specifically targeted at the priorities of this particular constituency.

Thus, an opposition party that relies on a populist strategy is more likely to achieve the support of the urban poor at the ballot box for at least two reasons. First, because most opposition parties campaign in urban areas to conserve scarce resources, the urban poor are inundated by political contenders. A party that engages in a populist strategy functions in a manner similar to a niche product, in effect choosing an area of specialization for which there is a demand that no other party is addressing. Populist strategies therefore offer a degree of *differentiation* for a party operating in a political milieu crowded by purely personalistic linkages. In fact, scholars focused on industrialized democracies have also argued that the clarity and differentiation of party choices offered to voters influences their decision to vote in the first place (see Aarts and Wessels 2005; Dalton 2008). The availability of meaningful and differentiated party alternatives increases voters' motivation to invest time and energy in making electoral decisions (Klingemann and Wessels 2009).

However, the likelihood of voting for a particular party is higher when a voter not only has a clear choice among parties but also has preferences that are closest to one of those parties (see Brockington 2009; Zipp 1985). Thus, greater issue congruence with poor urban voters represents the second advantage of populist strategies. *Congruence* is defined as the degree of distance between policies advocated by parties and voters' own preferences (see Dalton 1985; Huber and Powell 1994). Naturally, individuals weigh some electoral issues more heavily than others, and they therefore evaluate candidates' positions on those issues when they decide how to vote (Fournier et al. 2003). By definition, populist strategies rely on mobilization through an antielitist discourse, which appeals more to marginalized groups. Beyond this, however, a policy discourse by populist parties that addresses the distinct challenges faced by the urban poor, vis-à-vis their rural counterparts and more affluent urbanites, further enhances congruence.

What are some of the distinct challenges faced by the urban poor? Most critically, prices tend to be higher in urban areas, particularly in large cities where costs are affected by those with higher incomes. In African cities, access to goods and services is highly monetized, whereas in rural areas basic goods such as shelter, fuel, and food are more likely to be self-provisioned (Bratton 2006; Mitlin 2004; Satterthwaite 2004).[11] Compared with their rural counterparts, the urban poor are more likely to be tenants rather than owners of their homes, increasing their vulnerability to rent increases and evictions by landlords (see Mitlin 2007). Unlike rural areas, the urban poor face daily expenditures on public transport to reach labor markets

---

[11] For instance, Ruel et al. (2010: 171) noted that city dwellers across a wide range of metropolitan regions of the developing world buy about 90 percent of their food. The corresponding level for rural residents is between 29 and 58 percent.

(Mitlin 2004). Moreover, research in other regions indicates that the urban poor are more exposed to media stimuli as well as the actions of political parties, civil society organizations, and neighbors (e.g., Dietz 1998). This means that they are more likely to be aware of the nature of their economic circumstances and the potential political alternatives to address their situation. All of this suggests that although absolute poverty remains higher in Africa's rural areas, relative poverty and inequality may be more acutely felt in urban areas where gleaming shopping malls compete with street vendors for space and residents tend to be more politically mobilized.

Table 2.3 further suggests that in some regards, urban and rural Africans possess different priorities. Drawing on Round 4 of Afrobarometer's public opinion survey data, this table reveals survey responses to a question asking what the most important problem was in a respondent's country.[12] Almost 30 percent of urban Africans identified unemployment, wages, and salary levels as their primary concern. By contrast, issues related to agricultural production including farming, agricultural marketing, food shortages, drought, and land tenure were most important for rural Africans. A survey by Gallup of 18,000 respondents across 18 African countries likewise found that jobs were viewed as the top issue in urban areas and agriculture was most important in rural areas (see Tortora and Marlar 2010).

The urban poor also experience a dissimilar relationship with the state than more affluent urbanites. The urban poor threaten the authority of the state by circumventing property laws and building homes on land for which they lack an official title (e.g., Centeno and Portes 2006). In addition, African states have rarely supported the informal activities in which the urban poor engage (e.g., Potts 2007). As Cooper (1983: 42) observes:

In African cities, people are more likely to be buffered from the harshness of poverty and unemployment by social ties rooted in illegal space and the nonregulated economy, which only emphasize the impotence of the state. This in turn may draw the state into gestures of control that, whether effective or not, show the state's hostility to the poor's efforts at survival.

Despite such attitudes, the urban poor must depend on the state for service delivery much more than other urbanites. For instance, more affluent urbanites can buy generators when electricity provision is erratic or hire private security guards if the police are not adequately tackling crime. Urban professionals such as doctors, nurses, and teachers also have more leverage for obtaining concessions to their demands through strike activity

---

[12] Retrieved from www.afrobarometer.org. The relevant question is Q56PT1.

Table 2.3. *Differences in Priorities between Urban and Rural Africans*

What is the top problem facing your country?	Urban Residents (N = 10,081)	Rural Residents (N = 16,432)
Unemployment, wages, taxes, and salary levels	29.3	18.4
Agricultural production challenges (farming, agricultural marketing, drought, food shortages, and land tenure)	13.5	22
Management of the economy	12.7	7.5
Poverty and destitution	11.2	13.5
Crime and security	4.3	2.7
Roads	2.9	5.9
Health and HIV/AIDS	4.3	4.6
Education	3.3	3.5
Corruption	3.0	1.6
Housing	1.1	0.5
Water and electricity	4.8	11.5
Don't know/nothing	1.3	1.5
Others	8.3	6.8
Total	100	100

Chi^2 = 1691.59; p = 0.000

Notes: These proportions are based on the within-country weighting variable, which adjusts the distribution of the sample based on individual selection probabilities.

Source: Afrobarometer, Round 4.

than those in the informal sector. Indeed, the degree of competition in the saturated informal sector and inability to forfeit even a day's wages contributes to the urban poor's incapacity to use such tactics to place pressure on the state. Simultaneously though, the degree of desperation amongst this group may contribute to shorter time horizons as their impatience grows for some means to ameliorate their plight.

Thus, the urban poor lack the ability of other urbanites to procure private services or elicit government responsiveness. At the same time, they possess fewer options to engage in self-provision of goods and services in the same manner as rural dwellers. When they do try to build makeshift homes or sell goods in the street as a survival strategy they often face harassment by the ruling regime. Their combination of deprivation, dependence, and neglect by the government makes them particularly ripe for populist opposition

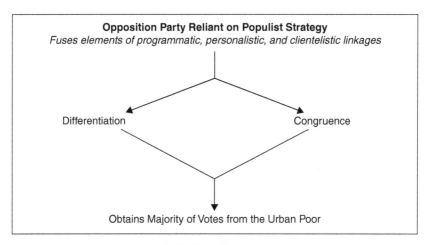

Figure 2.1 Outline of key mechanisms.

parties that espouse radical reforms over a short period of time that are intended to address the existing establishment's nonresponsiveness to their demands. As such, through both the content of their messages and their claim to deliver fast rewards, parties engaged in populist strategies provide a close degree of congruence with this group's needs.

Overall then, as highlighted in Figure 2.1, this study argues that populist strategies are a key explanatory variable for understanding when and why the urban poor support opposition parties. Such strategies are more likely to generate support from the urban poor because they offer greater congruence with the issues relevant to the urban underclass and provide greater differentiation from parties reliant on purely personalistic linkages, which tend to mobilize all types of voters with the same catchall messages. But they are also superior to parties with programmatic linkages oriented around a left-right ideological spectrum, which are, as already discussed, relatively rare. Those that do exist are either oriented toward salaried workers by dwindling leftist opposition parties or espouse neoliberal policies that have not demonstrated much benefit to Africa's urban poor. In other words, traditional programmatic linkages may offer greater differentiation than those of personalistic parties but less congruence than populist strategies that focus on policies relevant to the everyday realities of the urban poor.

Importantly, the two main benefits of a populist strategy do not require the urban poor to collectively experience a sense of class consciousness that binds them together. Rather, the urban poor collectively face certain challenges as a result of their living and working conditions, and these may constitute the basis for common grievances that are instrumental for parties' electoral fortunes. For instance, Cameron's (1991) study of Peru's expanding informal sector revealed that although this group was neither cohesive nor a unified social force, its collective emergence profoundly influenced that country's party dynamics.

Moreover, because parties are dynamic entities, they will shift their interaction with voters as a result of both structural factors that change voter preferences and a means of responding to modifications of other parties' electoral strategies. As Hagopian (2007) observes, political parties may mix their electoral strategies with different types of constituents. Consequently, opposition parties may rely on a populist strategy with the urban poor but purely personalistic linkages with rural dwellers. At the same time, ruling parties may craft programmatic linkages with elites that espouse a free-market ideology, resorting to clientelist linkages to maintain the support of the rural poor. As seen in studies of India and Brazil (Chhibber 1999; Hagopian, Gervasoni, and Moraes 2009), parties can also alter their electoral strategies over time. Likewise, opposition parties in Africa may transition both toward and away from populist strategies with the urban poor over time.

OPERATIONALIZING KEY CONCEPTS

To test this study's main argument, the key concepts discussed in this chapter require operationalization. This study provides a dual approach to operationalization by examining these concepts from the standpoints of both parties and voters. In addition to drawing on secondary materials about political parties in Senegal and Zambia, interviews with political party members and local governance experts are complemented by the views of the urban poor regarding the political scene in their respective countries.

From the view of political parties, a comparison of party manifestoes, responses from semi-structured interviews, and party activities documented in local newspapers help characterize the linkages they forge with both the urban poor and other constituencies. Based on these resources, personalistic linkages dominate if opposition parties cannot define the ideological differences that distinguish them from their competitors and instead each espouses a commitment to the same values and goals. Other indicators include a party's claim that it broadly represents all citizens and cannot define a clear constituency base. Moreover, if voters define their motivation for supporting a presidential candidate only in terms of his or her personal characteristics rather than policies, then personalistic linkages prevail.

As already noted, clientelist linkages can sometimes prove difficult to identify. But for the purposes of this study, clientelist linkages as conceptualized in Table 2.1 involve systematized handouts to a certain constituency base, namely the poor. Although such handouts may persist during normal times as part of an effort toward fostering more long-term relationships between a party and the poor, it was argued earlier that vote buying around elections is the most common manifestation of clientelist linkages in Africa. In such cases, handouts usually involve the disbursement of money, clothing, food, and/or drinks during election campaigns. From the incumbent party, they may also involve localized infrastructure and/or development initiatives that are timed right before elections. The nature, degree, and timing of such handouts will be uncovered through the use of interviews with observers of election campaigns, newspaper reports, and the claims of survey respondents.

For programmatic linkages, this study draws on some of the suggestions offered by Kitschelt and Wilkinson (2007: 323). As such, I classify a party as purely programmatic if the following conditions are met: 1) parties' positions on relevant issues systematically diverge; 2) politicians within the same party demonstrate less variance on key issues than those belonging to different parties; and 3) politicians can map their party positions on a left-right scale ranging from more to less government intervention, respectively.

A populist strategy can be discerned according to the dimensions presented in Table 2.2. In order to be populist, the party needs to be firmly oriented around a constituency comprising lower-class groups. Although electoral support amongst this group is an indicator of a party's popularity, it does not necessarily mean that a party is populist. Rather, the party needs to center most of its electoral campaigns in the neighborhoods and working areas of the urban poor, potentially even establishing party offices in such areas. At the same time, a charismatic leader is an essential element of a populist strategy, and such charisma may manifest through publicity stunts and controversial claims that stir up attention. Unmediated ties between a charismatic leader and the underclass can emerge when the leader attempts to identify himself as a common man, using a form of language, repertoire of campaign tactics, or selection of personal experiences that resonate with the masses. Most significantly, given that a populist strategy involves a programmatic component focused on social inclusion, parties using this strategy should offer policy promises targeted to the distinct challenges faced by the urban poor and aimed at rectifying their exclusion from the economy. Simultaneously, given that the populist strategy described here is especially focused on the urban poor, a party using this strategy should have a much weaker policy message toward other constituencies, including rural dwellers and the urban elite.

The two intervening variables central to this study, differentiation and congruence, can be uncovered by focusing more on a voter's perspective in the manner delineated in Table 2.4. Survey data collected from market workers and residents of low-income neighborhoods in Dakar and Lusaka provide such viewpoints. Voters were asked if they viewed any distinction among their country's political parties and, if so, were asked to identify how that party was different. If they acknowledged distinctions and could articulate what they were, this provided an indicator that parties did not simply merge together in a voter's mind. A secondary indicator of differentiation relied on how much support opposition parties received as measured by who survey respondents voted for and according to official election results in low-income urban areas. If two or more opposition parties received equivalent support, this implies that voters did not discern a major difference among them. However, if one opposition party received overwhelming support, then it clearly stood out among its competitors.[13]

Traditional measures of congruence require mapping a median voter's positions on key issues along a left-right scale, estimating the positions of politicians on the same issues, and then measuring the distance between the median citizen and median legislator according to the width of scale positions (see Huber and Powell 1994; Powell and Vanberg 2000). The smaller the distance is the greater the congruence. Yet such techniques are usually applied to studying industrialized countries where the assumption that parties and voters possess views along a left-right scale rarely proves problematic. As noted earlier, such an assumption is not always valid in the African context.

Nevertheless, certain parties can still offer policy prescriptions that are more aligned with a particular constituency base than others. The policy priorities of the urban poor were uncovered through the surveys as well as secondary resources on low-income populations in Dakar and Lusaka. If survey respondents voted for a presidential candidate who promised to

---

[13] The focus on comparing opposition parties is more meaningful because voters would be expected to be more likely to see a difference between the incumbent and opposition than among opposition parties alone.

Table 2.4. *Indicators of Differentiation and Congruence from Surveys of the Urban Poor*

Dimension	Degree	
	More	Less
Differentiation	- Respondents report observing a difference among parties along key dimension (e.g., policies) - One particular opposition party received significantly more support than any other	- Respondents report they cannot see a difference among country's parties - No opposition party received significantly more support than any other
Congruence	- Majority of respondents articulated that a specific policy was the main motivation for supporting a particular opposition candidate *and* that candidate also expressed that particular policy message in his/her campaign - One opposition party repeatedly identified as interested in improving urban living conditions	- Majority of respondents voted for incumbent despite registering disappointment with the status quo - No opposition party identified as interested in improving urban living conditions

address these priorities, which often included the provision of jobs and basic services, and the respondent reported that the policies of the candidate rather than his or her personality or campaign handouts were the primary motivation for support, then this is an indication that such a party offered more congruence to the demands of the urban poor than the existing alternatives. In turn, those who voted for another candidate should not have identified party policies as the main motivation for support because this would then imply that different segments of the urban poor support various parties due to their respective policies, thereby meaning that no one party provides more congruence with this constituency base than any other. In the same manner, if a majority of respondents repeatedly identified the same party as being most likely to improve living conditions in either Dakar or Lusaka, then that party was deemed to have greater congruence with the urban poor's demands. Lastly, if a respondent reported disappointment with the status quo but nevertheless voted for the incumbent, this highlights that none of the existing opposition parties offered greater congruence to the needs of the urban poor than the incumbent.[14]

SUMMARY

This chapter considered four possible hypotheses for the urban poor's voting behavior and found each incomplete on its own. The institutional requirements and party discipline for monitoring voter actions renders clientelist party machines that exist in other developing regions quite rare in Africa's urban context. Moreover, empirical findings in a set of African cases show that a subtype of clientelism, vote buying, does not entirely influence voters' decisions. From a theoretical standpoint, it is conceivable that the urban poor may accept handouts from all parties but ultimately vote in accordance with their own conscience. The influence of ethnolinguistic identity on political behavior has long occupied a large body of the literature on Africa. However, the evidence is far from conclusive that ethnolinguistic cleavages overwhelmingly determine who a voter supports. Economic decline often provides a key motivation for voters to reject an incumbent, but whether this manifests as a vote for the opposition or through abstention remains less clear. Cases where Africa's urban poor support an opposition party even when macroeconomic conditions are improving implies that such factors cannot entirely account for voting behavior. Associations for the urban poor, whether in the form of slum-dwellers movements or informal-sector work organizations, are growing fast throughout Africa. But how many Africans actually belong to these associations and what influence they actually exert on members' voting preferences remain questionable.

Due to the limitations of these alternative explanations, this study focuses on the role of political parties and their interactions with constituents. This chapter presented the study's main argument, which is that opposition parties that employ a populist strategy are more likely to obtain support from this group than parties reliant on personalistic, clientelist, or programmatic linkages alone. A populist strategy fuses key elements of these distinct linkages, including their modes of mobilization. Like programmatic linkages, a populist strategy relies on a policy discourse, but one focused on social inclusion rather than a left-right ideology. Similar to personalistic linkages,

---

[14] If a respondent was not disappointed with the incumbent's performance, it would not be surprising if she or he proceeded to vote for the incumbent. Indeed, as described, a populist strategy relies on incorporating those who feel alienated by the status quo. By extension then, a member of the urban poor who does not feel that way would be less likely to support an opposition party espousing such a message.

a populist strategy depends on a charismatic leader. In the same manner as clientelist linkages, a populist strategy may also involve the selective disbursement of material incentives, and its constituency base is firmly focused on the poor.

The advantage of a populist strategy is that its policy message can exhibit greater congruence to those issues relevant to the urban poor, and in turn it can increase a party's differentiation from the multitude of other competitors that are dependent on purely personalistic linkages with the urban poor. A populist strategy therefore enables a party to fuse the charisma of its party leader with a specific policy agenda oriented toward the excluded, creating a memorable impression on the mind of a poor urban voter when she or he goes to the polls.

THREE

The Bite of "King Cobra"

Populist Strategies in the Zambian Context

Chapter 2 delineated criteria for identifying the disparate linkages used by political parties with their country's citizens, and introduced the concept of populist strategies. This chapter focuses on different strategies used by Zambian political parties to mobilize the urban poor. Predominant attention is given to political developments between 2001 and 2008 because this period characterized the rise of the PF and its metamorphosis from a party reliant on personalistic linkages to one that employed a populist strategy.

Briefly, in Zambia's 2001 elections, when the PF and all of the country's other political parties relied on personalistic linkages, the urban poor divided their support amongst four political parties rather than overwhelmingly supporting just one. This symbolized the inability of the urban poor to discern any clear differentiation or congruence among these party alternatives. However, during both the 2006 and 2008 elections, the PF's pursuit of a populist strategy resulted in overwhelming support in Zambia's major urban centers, including Lusaka and the Copperbelt. The leader of the PF, Michael Sata, targeted his campaigns in shanty compounds and mobilized the urban poor not only with his charismatic style but also with a bundle of policy promises that collectively aimed to rectify this constituency's economic exclusion and lack of political voice. His campaign messages were reinforced by the use of tactics intended to portray himself as a common man who understood the plight of the marginalized.

To contextualize these developments, the chapter first provides an overview of the party landscape in Zambia and discusses the emergence of the PF. This is then followed by an analysis of demographic and socioeconomic factors that contributed to the growth of the country's urban poor. The MMD's response to these dynamics, particularly under President Mwanawasa, was a crackdown on the activities of the urban poor. Even though Mwanawasa presided over a period of positive macroeconomic growth, living and working conditions for the urban poor deteriorated. I subsequently illustrate how Sata took advantage of these circumstances in the 2006 and 2008 elections to craft his populist strategy. The fact that the other opposition parties were much less successful at mobilizing the urban poor demonstrates that this constituency was not simply demonstrating an anti-incumbent bias. Instead, as the chapter proceeds to show, the PF's main opposition competitors, including the UPND and Heritage Party (HP), articulated broad-sweeping messages intended to hold national appeal but that demonstrated little congruence with the concerns of the urban poor.

ZAMBIA'S POLITICAL PARTY LANDSCAPE

Zambia's peaceful transition to multiparty democracy in 1991 heralded the beginning of greater political liberalization in a number of countries throughout the continent.[1] With the slogan "The Hour Has Come," the MMD and its then-leader, Frederick Chiluba, successfully defeated Kenneth Kaunda and the United National Independence Party (UNIP), which had ruled Zambia for twenty-seven years.[2] Formed from an eclectic mix of labor union officials, civil society members, and career politicians, the MMD originally emerged in urban areas. However, its victory in 1991 was due to support in both the country's urban and rural provinces.[3]

Yet corruption, mismanagement, and electoral maneuvering by the MMD ultimately generated friction within the party, leading to many defections and the creation of new parties, such as the National Party in 1993 and the Zambia Democratic Congress in 1996. Two years later, Zambia's managing director at Anglo-American, Anderson Mazoka, formed the UPND. A second round of parties mushroomed in 2001 after Chiluba's failed bid to alter the constitution to secure a third term as president. Notable amongst these were the FDD, HP, and PF.

Unlike the leaders of the FDD and HP, who both left the MMD because they disagreed with Chiluba's third-term bid, Michael Sata's motivations were

---

[1] Benin, which abolished an eighteen-year military-authoritarian regime through a national conference in 1990, is often seen as representing an equivalent symbol of democratization, especially for francophone Africa.

[2] Previous to the 1991 elections, Zambia had experienced a brief period of multiparty democracy from 1964 to 1972.

[3] The only province the MMD did not win in the 1991 elections was Eastern Province, the stronghold of UNIP (Bratton 1994).

Table 3.1. *Overview of Zambia's Main Political Parties*

Party Name	Leader (as of 2011)	Year Founded
Forum for Democracy and Development (FDD)	Edith Nawakwi	2001
Heritage Party (HP)	Godfrey Miyanda	2001
Movement for Multi-Party Democracy (MMD)	Rupiah Banda	1990
Patriotic Front (PF)	Michael Sata	2001
United Liberal Party (ULP)	Sakwiba Sikota	2006
United National Independence Party (UNIP)	Tilyenji Kaunda	1958
United Party for National Development (UPND)	Hakainde Hichilema	1998

quite different.[4] Nicknamed "King Cobra" because he is allegedly venomous toward his political enemies, Sata originally served as the Lusaka district governor, an MP for Lusaka's Kabwata constituency, and minister of state for decentralization under the UNIP regime. When he foresaw UNIP's waning popularity, he defected to the MMD. Under the latter party, he obtained prominent positions as the minister of local government and housing, minister of labor and social security, minister of health, minister without portfolio, and MMD national secretary. After the failure of Chiluba's third-term bid, Sata expected to be chosen as Chiluba's successor. When Levy Mwanawasa was chosen instead, Sata decided to found the PF. Today, there are approximately twenty-eight officially registered political parties in the country (Matlosa 2007), with the most competitive ones presented in Table 3.1.[5]

URBANIZATION CHALLENGES

Zambia's proliferation of parties occurred in tandem with an economic liberalization program that impoverished the urban population and simultaneously increased its ranks. Chiluba's tenure was characterized by the adoption of vast reforms under the auspices of a structural adjustment

[4] Sata had supported the attempt to change the constitution. In fact, during the May 2001 conventions during which MMD party members voted on Chiluba's proposition, Sata pressured fellow party members to wear third-term T-shirts (Malupenga 2001).

[5] For the 2011 elections a number of new parties were formed, including the Alliance for Democracy and Development, the National Restoration Party, and Zambia for Empowerment and Democracy.

program. As has been documented elsewhere (e.g., Tacoli 2001; Myers and Murray 2007), structural adjustment often hurt urban consumers by ending currency controls and price subsidies on staple foods. Simultaneously, greater economic austerity reduced available public spending for urban infrastructure, health, and education, and privatization and trade liberalization forced uncompetitive domestic industries to either shed workers or impose wage freezes. As a result of these latter measures, between 30,000 and 50,000 formal sector workers in Zambia lost their jobs between 1992 and 1996 (Rakner 2003). Moreover, poverty in Lusaka increased from 25 to 39 percent in only two years between 1991 and 1993 (United Nations Development Program [UNDP] 1998: 59). Consequently, so many Zambians resorted to laboring in the urban informal sector that by the mid-1990s, middle-class Lusakans were complaining about the lack of walking space on city sidewalks due to the predominance of street vendors and the growth of *tuntembas*, or makeshift market stalls crafted out of wood and plastic (see Chilaizya 1993; Mwiinga 1993). As Hansen (2004: 62) notes, street vending in the capital had reached "anarchic proportions" by Christmas 1998: "Main streets, alleyways, and shop corridors in the city centre, and many other spots besides, had turned into one huge outdoor shopping mall where thousands of street vendors were selling all manner of goods."

At the same time, Lusaka experienced an increase in population. The city's population growth rate over the 1990s was 3.3 percent, more than twice the rate for Zambia overall (CSO 2003a). The impetus for this demographic shift was twofold. First, migrants arrived from Zambia's other main urban area, the Copperbelt province, which is the source of the country's main export commodity. A prolonged decline in copper prices and production, along with privatization of the mines, caused more than 25,000 workers in the mining sector to lose their jobs over the 1990s (McCulloch, Baulch, Cherel-Robson 2000). Most migrated to Lusaka in the hope that the city's more diversified industrial base would provide alternative employment opportunities. In fact, the capital city received approximately 133,000 residents from the Copperbelt during the 1990–2000 period (CSO 2003a). Secondly, Lusaka contained a higher concentration of young people than the rest of the country, meaning that the city experienced higher natural population growth than other areas of Zambia (Mulenga 2003).

Such demographic pressures placed constraints on housing availability within Lusaka. Due to British town-planning principles, many African residents of Lusaka lived in housing on the outskirts of the city during colonial times, and because permanent settlement was discouraged, housing options for Africans generally were limited (Taylor 2006). With successive waves of migration to the city in the 1990s, coupled with the dearth of government housing initiatives or private sector development, this housing became characterized by vast, unorganized shanty compounds (Hansen 2002; Mulenga 2003). According to the director and deputy directors of housing and social services for the Lusaka City Council, approximately thirty-five such compounds exist in Lusaka, seven of which are considered illegal and therefore not eligible to receive infrastructure investments from the government (interview with Phiri and Matawe, 2009).[6] In all, such settlements contain the highest density of the city's population, and are home to 70 percent of Lusaka's residents (UN-Habitat 2007). Tellingly, although the government refuses to recognize illegal shanty compounds because this implies an onus of service provision, it nonetheless has designated some of them as official political wards for the purpose of elections (interview with Phiri, 2009).

Throughout the 1990s, the MMD actively alienated the urban poor through housing demolitions and crackdowns on vendors. In his role as the MMD's Minister of Local Government and Housing, Michael Sata razed the homes of 500 families living in Kanyama's shanty compounds in 1991 (*Weekly Post* 1992).[7] Illegal homes in the compounds of John Laing and Misisi were also threatened with demolition in 1992 (F. Chibuye 1992). One year later, approximately forty shacks in Kamwala Township were targeted by bulldozers to make way for more modern houses (Chitenje 1993). By the end of the decade, John Laing and Misisi were threatened yet again with demolition (Mumbati 2000; Kabuswe 2000), and the deputy minister of Lusaka Province requested the eviction of squatters in Lusaka's Ibex Hill neighborhood. This prompted one affected resident to exclaim, "My husband is a policeman and he gets very little money so, where do you want us to go? It seems the ruling MMD is for the rich" (cited in Hampande 2000: 3). Map 3.1 illustrates the location of these and other major neighborhoods within the capital city.

With respect to street vendors, a particularly violent crackdown in 1993 by the Lusaka City Council (LCC) led to riots and prompted Chiluba to intervene on the vendors' behalf (Hansen 2004: 65). In 1996, Chiluba established a Vendors' Desk at State House and appointed a deputy minister in charge of street and market vendors' affairs (War on Want n.d.). By 1999, however, traders recognized the limits of their protection when the LCC engaged in a massive sweep across Lusaka that resulted in the destruction

---

[6] Hickey (2005) echoes that the Zambian government is not responsible for investing in basic services within those settlements deemed "illegal."

[7] Apparently, just a few years later, residents whose homes were destroyed had already rebuilt on the same site (Nampito and Gina 1995).

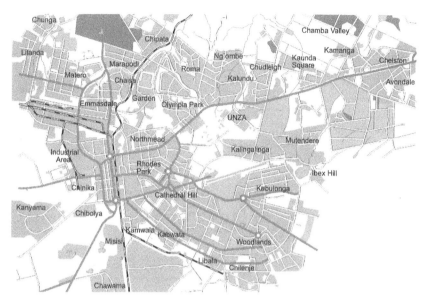

Map 3.1 Map of Lusaka. Copyright © 2007 Streetwise Limited.

of hundreds of tuntembas in the city center and within the residential town-ships on the periphery (Hansen 2004: 66). According to Hansen (2007b: 10), Chiluba did not intervene on this occasion because the MMD realized that few vendors were actually registered voters and therefore did not need to be co-opted in exchange for electoral support.

THE 2001 ELECTIONS: PERSONALISTIC
LINKAGES FAIL THE URBAN POOR

Poor living circumstances, harassment, and Chiluba's attempts to alter the constitution collectively presented an opportunity for the opposition in the 2001 elections. However, the use of personalistic linkages to mobilize the urban poor failed to deliver electoral majorities in urban areas to any major opposition party. In fact, only 2.5 million of a potential 4.6 million eligible Zambians even registered to vote in 2001 (Venter 2003), implying a significant lack of enthusiasm with the possible candidates.

Although the MMD's candidate, Levy Mwanawasa, obtained the presidency with only 29 percent of the national vote, the opposition did not perform much better. In fact, the second-place finisher at the national level, the UPND's Mazoka, only received a quarter of the votes. As seen by the boldfaced numbers in Table 3.2, the UPND and FDD split votes in Lusaka's

Table 3.2. *Results from Zambia's 2001 Presidential Elections in Selected Urban Areas (%)*

Urban Constituencies	Poverty Rates	Main Candidates (Party)			
		Levy Mwanawasa (MMD)	Andrew Mazoka (UPND)	Christon Tembo (FDD)	Godfrey Miyanda (HP)
Lusaka Province					
Chawama	0.61	21.4	27.3	**29.2**	3.8
Kabwata	0.25	15.0	**34.5**	21.8	9.8
Kanyama	0.57	14.5	**41.4**	19.9	4.5
Lusaka Central	0.26	12.4	**34.7**	21.9	13.5
Mandevu	0.52	16.5	18.7	**30.5**	7.4
Matero	0.42	19.4	20.1	**25.1**	9.2
Munali	0.58	12.5	**31.7**	24.6	12.9
Copperbelt Province					
Kitwe	0.45	30.0	15.9	4.9	**30.1**
Ndola Central	0.56	**26.1**	15.6	12.2	22.1

Sources: Election data from the Electoral Commission of Zambia; Poverty data from Simler (2007), based on the 2000 Census and 2002–2003 LCMS.

poorest constituencies, with the UPND more popular in Kanyama and Munali and the FDD prevailing in Chawama and Mandevu. Within the Copperbelt, the HP received the most votes in the country's second-largest city, Kitwe; the MMD proved victorious in the third-largest city of Ndola. Thus, despite a decline in urban living standards, no one party was able to overwhelmingly capture the imaginations of the urban poor.

Based on some of the criteria discussed in Chapter 2, the fact that the urban vote was split among four parties indicates that the opposition parties exhibited very little differentiation. Indeed, analysts of these elections agree that although the MMD certainly engaged in some techniques to hinder the opposition, the opposition parties themselves were largely to blame for failing to mobilize greater support.[8] For instance, Rakner (2003: 124) notes

---

[8] Some of the MMD's tactics involved harassment of the media, physical violence against opposition party members, and scheduling the elections immediately after Christmas, when most people would be away from the constituency in which they registered to vote (Simon 2005).

that all the parties contesting those elections shared the following traits: emerged from the MMD; were formed behind a strong leader who contributed the majority of the party's finances; and lacked any programmatic or ideological leanings. Momba (2005: 33) observed that "the lack of significant differences in terms of policies due to similar ideologies and general outlooks raises questions about the meaningfulness of alternative choices presented to voters at election time." Burnell (2001) noted that the opposition had failed not only to craft a policy agenda targeted at key issues but also to mobilize grassroots support. He further claimed that the state of the opposition helped qualify Zambia as an example of Mkandawire's (1999) "choiceless democracies."

A closer examination of the opposition parties' promises indicates that no single one advanced a message with a large degree of congruence with the priorities of the urban poor. The FDD focused on the need for institutional reforms such as curbing executive powers, but economic concerns and food security were more urgent issues for the electorate (Burnell 2002). Whereas the HP campaigned on a vague message of "national renewal," both UNIP and the UPND offered to introduce free health care and education (Burnell 2002). The UPND also announced that agriculture would receive priority if Mazoka was voted into presidential office (Chifuwe 2000). None of the parties offered different economic policies than the MMD, but promised to implement them with greater oversight and transparency (Rakner 2003).

The PF only obtained between 2 to 4 percent of the vote across Lusaka's urban constituencies. The party certainly was disadvantaged by time constraints, having decided to compete in the elections only fifty-nine days after it had been established. But Sata's poor showing was also due to his close association with Chiluba, and therefore with the rampant corruption and economic policies that typified the MMD's first decade in power (Larmer and Fraser 2007). At the time of the 2001 elections, Sata's populist strategy had yet to take shape.

The "New Deal" Gets Old

Mwanawasa entered office proclaiming a "New Deal" administration, which resulted in greater commitment to economic liberalization and increased harassment of the urban poor. Specifically, by furthering many of the privatizations initiated by Chiluba and courting foreign investors, the MMD retained a pro-capitalist, free-market stance, emphasizing the importance of entrepreneurship. According to the party's manifesto, prepared for the 2006 elections, during his first term Mwanawasa's government had pursued "macroeconomic policies aimed at arresting economic decline, stabilizing the economy and further entrenching a liberal economic environment" (MMD 2006: 6). During his second term, the MMD's priorities were to create a climate attractive to private-sector investors, who were anticipated to invest in the mining, agriculture, tourism, and manufacturing sectors (see MMD 2006).

Guided by these objectives, Mwanawasa considerably improved Zambia's economic circumstances and governance environment during his tenure. The country's inflation dropped to single digits and economic growth averaged approximately 5 percent, buoyed by improved copper prices and substantial external debt forgiveness (*Economist* 2006; Larmer and Fraser 2007). Mwanawasa also engaged in a concerted effort to combat corruption, including establishing a corruption task force and controversially removing Chiluba's immunity from prosecution on corruption charges (Mthembu-Salter 2007). Compared with Chiluba's presidency, Mwanawasa's tenure also coincided with greater tolerance of the independent press, such as *The Post* newspaper, even though it offered more favorable coverage to the opposition (interview with Chifuwe, 2009).

Mwanawasa's Policies toward the Urban Poor

But life for the urban poor did not necessarily improve under Mwanawasa. A rebound in copper prices benefitted foreign investors more than local residents, especially because foreign-owned mining companies were only taxed 0.6 percent of their profits (Larmer and Fraser 2007). Other growth came from the country's tourism and construction industries (EIU 2008), neither of which had significant employment spillover effects. One outcome was an observable rise in inequality. In fact, urban inequality measured according to the Gini coefficient is an alarming 0.66 in Zambia (UN-Habitat 2010b).[9] As Larmer and Fraser (2007: 618) observe, "Popular resentment regarding liberalization has been strengthened by visible signs of rising inequality.... Liberalization's winners ostentatiously display their wealth in Lusaka's new shopping centres, their car parks full of luxury vehicles." A related outcome, highlighted in Figure 3.1, was only a marginal decline in the number of poor people living in Lusaka despite relatively stable growth during Mwanawasa's first term.

Other data also attests to the persistence of urban poverty despite economic growth during this period. By 2004, formal-sector employment

[9]   The Gini coefficient is the most common indicator of inequality and represents an index ranging from 0 to 1. A value of 0 indicates no inequality, a 1 implies complete inequality.

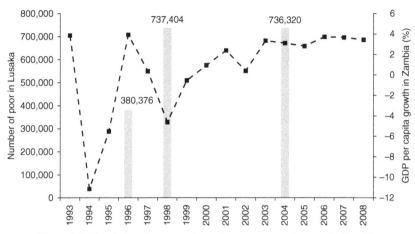

Figure 3.1 Trends in urban poverty and macroeconomic growth, Zambia.

had declined by 24 percent from its 1992 level (Larmer and Fraser 2007). Approximately 56 percent of Zambia's urban population and 69 percent of Lusaka's worked in the nonagricultural informal sector (CSO 2007; World Bank 2007a). Today, unemployment is estimated at 33 percent in urban areas compared with 6 percent in rural ones (EIU 2011). As seen in Table 3.3, urban Zambians surveyed in the country's 2006 Living Conditions Monitoring Survey (LCMS) highlighted that the lack of jobs and low wages represented the top reason for their poverty, compared with lack of agricultural inputs for rural Zambians.[10]

Moreover, the cost of living and service delivery remained expensive in urban areas. For instance, the monthly cost of basic food staples and essential nonfood items for a family of six living in Lusaka increased from 829,250 to 1,421,650 Kwacha between 2002 and August 2006. This exceeded by more than double the average monthly income of 645,326 Kwacha found in most of Lusaka's low-income neighborhoods (JCTR 2006). The average cost of electricity and water for a family of four living in Lusaka steadily increased during Mwanawasa's tenure (see Figure 3.2). Given the frequency of long water and power outages, the quality of such services was also low. In the area of housing, the urban poor were likewise disadvantaged. Whereas the government's National Housing Authority focused on houses for middle-class Lusakans, the Low-Cost Housing

---

[10] The urban poverty data from the 2006 LCMS has been widely contested (see Chibuye 2011), which is why it is excluded from Figure 3.2. The 2010 LCMS was not publicly available at the time of writing.

Table 3.3. *Different Perceived Causes of Poverty across Urban and Rural Zambia*

What do you believe is the main reason you have become poor?	Urban, % (N = 7,825)	Rural, % (N = 8,507)
Lack of employment and/or low wages	**37.7**	8.3
Lack of agricultural inputs	10.0	**39.2**
Low agricultural production	1.3	5.0
Weather	0.5	3.6
Lack of land	4.6	3.7
Low prices	0.6	2.5
Lack of market	0.4	1.9
Lack of cattle	0.8	9.0
Lack of capital	15.4	11.2
Lack of credit	2.7	2.6
Pension too little	1.1	0.2
Retrenchment	0.6	0.1
High price of commodities	4.5	1.7
Hard economic times	8.2	3.3
Business not doing well	3.7	0.9
Too much competition	1.2	0.2
Disability	0.3	0.6
Death of breadwinner	4.4	4.4
Debts	0.1	0.1
Other	1.8	1.5
Total	100	100

Notes: These are the responses of those who rated themselves "moderately" or "extremely poor," as opposed to "not poor," in the survey.
Source: LCMS 2006.

Development Foundation within the Ministry of Local Government con-centrated most of its projects on the poor in rural areas (interview with Ncube, 2009).

In addition, the harassment of the urban poor prevalent during the Chiluba era grew even more pronounced under Mwanawasa. Those living in illegal squatter settlements were consistently threatened with demoli-tions. In late 2002, a campaign of squatter-compound demolitions occurred throughout the city at the height of the rainy season, causing more than 700

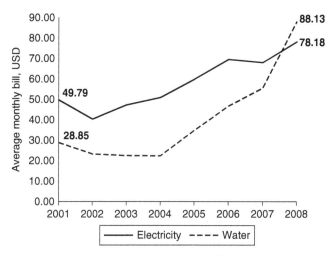

Figure 3.2 Trend in average cost of utilities in Lusaka.

families to become homeless and placed in refugee tents, where dysentery and cholera ensued (Myers 2005). In March 2007, the Mwanawasa government announced full backing from the president's cabinet to proceed with plans to demolish illegal shanty compounds in Lusaka, some of which were in existence for decades. Under the protection of antiriot police, the government proceeded to destroy 100 homes in the Kalikiliki compound alone (Mwanangombe 2007).

President Mwanawasa also invested 200 million kwacha into the "Keep Zambia Clean" campaign (*Times of Zambia* 2007a). Designed to improve cleanliness and hygiene around the city, the campaign involved adding more stringent provisions to Zambia's Street Vending and Nuisances Act, which levies fees on those who are engaged in street vending or who purchase from vendors (*Times of Zambia* 2007a). Crackdowns on street vendors and illegal marketeers ensued because they supposedly worsened traffic congestion and street littering and contributed to cholera outbreaks. For example, in mid-2007, the four-lane Freedom Way in downtown Lusaka was cleared of street vendors whose activities had made the road virtually impassable (interview with Henriot, 2009).

Tellingly, the former MMD National Secretary, Dr. Katele Kalumba, has since lamented the harassment perpetuated by the former ruling party:

And I realized that we were really hurting a lot of our people by the approach that we were taking in enforcing the public hygiene measures. It touches upon whether the street or the town is the privilege of a certain group of people.

Whose town is it? It appears that if you live in Woodlands, Kabulonga, and so on, you are *the* town owners, and if you live in Kaunda Square or Kalingalinga or places like this, you are simply strangers in the city who can be moved and resettled somewhere.... Before, in the colonial times, it was a white man's city, a white man's town. The natives were brought in from outside, they were kept away and at night, after 17 hours, you are not expected to be seen anywhere near the neighborhoods. So, this time, it's just a different configuration, from race to class. The new sort of *nouveaux riches,* the new economic leaders and players think that they have the power to define who occupies what space. (Interview with Kalumba, 2009)[11]

Likewise, the ZCTU decried the government's actions, stating that the informal sector was being treated as "a nuisance merely tolerated for cheap political propaganda, electioneering and even financial extortion" (ZCTU 2006: 17). For Hansen (2007a: 2) though, such harassment was consistent with the government's perception of the "free market," which means attracting foreign investors to a clean city free of vendors.

ELECTION RESULTS IN 2006 AND 2008

The MMD's treatment of the urban poor proved detrimental to its subsequent electoral fortunes in Lusaka and other urban areas. Overall, the 2006 elections were characterized by much higher voter registration than in the 2001 elections. Four million Zambians registered (Wines 2006), and the Electoral Commission of Zambia reported that 70 percent of these registered voters actually turned out to vote, indicating less voter apathy at the choice of candidates or outcome.[12]

At the national level, Mwanawasa received a larger mandate than in 2001, gaining 43 percent of the vote compared to Sata's 29 percent. The MMD obtained most of its votes in majority rural areas, such as Eastern, Western, Northwestern, and Central provinces, but only 22 percent of the votes in Lusaka. In the wake of Andrew Mazoka's death, Hakainde Hichilema took over leadership of the UPND and entered into a coalition for the 2006 elections with UNIP and the FDD, which was called the United Democratic Alliance (UDA). Despite hoping to reverse the 2001 results when these three parties split each other's votes by running separately, Hichilema only received 20 percent of the votes in Lusaka. However, Michael Sata obtained about 58 percent of the vote in Lusaka and obtained the majority of votes

---

[11] Woodlands and Kabulonga are affluent neighborhoods in Lusaka., Kaunda Square and Kalingalinga are shanty compounds.
[12] See "2008 Elections," retrieved from http://www.elections.org.zm/.

in all of Zambia's major urban constituencies.[13] Such an outcome indicated that urbanites did not simply want a change from the MMD but rather chose a specific opposition party that was believed to be most likely to implement the exact change they wanted.

A similar pattern occurred in the October 2008 by-elections that followed Mwanawasa's death.[14] Rupiah Banda beat Sata by only two percentage points at the national level, obtaining 40 percent of the vote compared with his competitor's 38 percent. Simultaneously, Sata's vote shares actually increased in all of Lusaka's constituencies, as well as in country's second- and third-largest cities on the Copperbelt (see Table 3.4). By contrast, Hichilema and his UPND actually lost some ground. Although the national turnout rate was 69 and 45 percent in the 2006 and 2008 elections, respectively, the comparative rates for urban Lusaka were 71 and 58 percent.

The importance of Sata's victory across both Lusaka and cities in the Copperbelt is even more remarkable considering the ethnic composition of the two regions of the country. Whereas the Copperbelt is primarily Bemba speaking, Lusaka's population is highly heterogeneous. Although migrants from the Copperbelt and Northern provinces have arrived more recently, most migrants are from Eastern and Southern provinces (Hansen 2002). Nyanja speakers are in the majority, representing almost 53 percent of the population as of 2000 (CSO 2004). Thus, even though Sata is Bemba, he was still highly popular in a city dominated by Nyanja speakers.

THE POPULIST STRATEGY OF "KING COBRA"

By employing a populist strategy, rather than the personalistic linkages of his opposition competitors, Sata was able to tap into the frustrations of the urban poor more effectively in the 2006 and 2008 elections than the opposition had done during the 2001 elections. His strategy was threefold. First, he relied on a careful targeting of his campaign rallies within key areas of Lusaka. Secondly, he mobilized constituents via a combination of charisma and a programmatic message around issues of social inclusion and antielitism, with some distribution of selective benefits to potential supporters.

---

[13] All of the election results for Lusaka refer to those for Lusaka district, which consists of seven constituencies. Lusaka Province, of which Lusaka district is one component, contains three additional districts (Chongwe, Kafue, and Luangwa). These districts are overwhelmingly rural and consistently supported the MMD.

[14] The Zambian constitution stipulates that in the case where a president dies in office, a new president needs to be elected within ninety days. The vice president, Rupiah Banda, became the interim president and endorsed as the MMD's candidate. Ironically, Banda was an official member of UNIP until only a few years earlier.

Table 3.4. *Results from 2008 Zambian Presidential Elections in Major Urban Areas*

Main Urban Constituencies	Poverty Rates	Presidential Candidates (Party), % of Votes			
		Rupiah Banda (MMD)	Michael Sata (PF)	Hakainde Hichilema (UPND)	Godfrey Miyanda (HP)
Lusaka Province					
Chawama	0.61	25.5	**60.3**	13.9	0.3
Kabwata	0.25	20.2	**63.3**	15.8	0.7
Kanyama	0.57	26.1	**52.2**	21.3	0.4
Lusaka Central	0.26	24.7	**58.6**	15.9	0.8
Mandevu	0.52	28.8	**63.2**	7.5	0.5
Matero	0.42	25.0	**66.5**	8.1	0.4
Munali	0.58	27.1	**58.5**	13.7	0.6
Copperbelt Province					
Kitwe	0.45	18.5	**75.2**	5.6	0.6
Ndola Central	0.56	30.4	**60.8**	7.6	1.3

Sources: Election data calculated from the ECZ (http://www.elections.org.zm/). Poverty data from Simler (2007), based on the 2000 Census and 2002–2003 LCMS.

Thirdly, he relied on simplistic language and an open-door policy, as well as magnifying his own lack of education in order to foster the image of a paternalistic benefactor who understands the plight of the common man. This, in turn, fostered vertical ties between Sata and his constituents and translated into an autocratic and hierarchical management of the PF by him.

Geographically Targeted Campaigns

Sata spent a majority of his time campaigning amongst street vendors, marketeers, bus and taxi drivers, and the 66 percent of Lusaka's population who are twenty-four years old or younger (CSO 2004). In the run-up to the 2006 elections, Sata held the final rally of his presidential campaign in Mandevu compound (Larmer and Fraser 2007), which is among the poorest in Lusaka. In the 2008 elections, he launched his campaign from the Matero market, where the PF contains an office (Kalaluka and Noyoo 2008). By contrast, Banda launched his campaign from Lusaka's plush Inter-Continental Hotel (*Times of Zambia* 2008c), and Hichilema began at the Mulungushi Conference Center, a site traditionally reserved for meetings amongst politicians.[15] Shanty compounds are specifically targeted by the PF during election campaigns because, as mentioned earlier, these neighborhoods have the highest density of residents, where many potential votes can be obtained (interview with Chibamba, 2009). In fact, it was in the compounds of Mandevu, Matero, Garden, and Chipata where riots spread out in the aftermath of the 2006 elections, when many urbanites were surprised that Sata did not win the presidency.

Targeting the urban poor is strategic given not only the size of this constituency but also their greater propensity to appear at the polls than other socioeconomic classes. In fact, the leader of the UPND, Hakainde Hichilema, observed the following: "First, you must understand who votes in the city. It is the people living in squalor, mainly. The people in these big offices that you see hardly go into the queue to vote, they don't even register" (interview with Hichilema, 2009). A journalist with the main independent paper, *The Post,* echoed this claim, noting that in urban areas, those with formal jobs will not be able to spare adequate time to stand in long voting queues (interview with Chifuwe, 2009). The director of policy and research for the UPND, Dr. Choolwe Beyani, despaired at these circumstances: "Unfortunately, the unemployed are the majority of the voters. The so-called middle-class is insignificant. Even the working classes, who have certain levels of education, have become insignificant in voting patterns" (interview with Beyani, 2009).

Mixed Modes of Mobilization

As a consummate political entrepreneur, Sata grabbed the attention of this constituency by crafting a charismatic and controversial image that has helped distance himself from his previous image as Chiluba's right-hand man. Most notably, he engaged in theatrical antics during his campaigning to grab attention. In 2006, his campaigns featured broken clocks because the clock is the MMD's symbol (Wines 2006). The implication was that the MMD's time had expired. The PF's own symbol is Noah's Ark, and its rallying cry of *Pabwato* translates as "get on the boat," implying that Zambians should join the party to escape the country's deluge of economic hardships.[16] Playing on the theme, Sata arrived at the Zambian High Court to register his party for the 2008 elections standing in a speedboat towed by a truck.

[15] See Hichilema's campaign website: http://www.hakainde.com/, accessed October 1, 2009.
[16] The MMD joked that if too many people got on the boat though, it was bound to sink like the Titanic (*Africa Confidential* 2006).

Importantly, he sustained this image outside of election periods. In 2005, more than a year before the 2006 elections, he addressed a huge rally in Matero compound to denounce the MMD's performance and argued that Zambians needed a respite from power outages, high taxes, and the lack of clean water (*The Post* 2005). In January 2007, he organized a mass procession in the streets of Lusaka to protest the privatization of Zambian National Commercial Bank and the International Monetary Fund's (IMF) suggestion that the government place higher valued-added taxes on food and agricultural products (Larmer and Fraser 2007). Moreover, he exerted great effort to remain in the eye of the media and was featured on the front cover of *The Post* newspaper practically every day. The PF's Vice President, Dr. Guy Scott, noted that Sata purposely held press conferences on Sunday, when there is often less for journalists to report, so that he would be guaranteed to appear in the Monday paper (interview with Scott, 2009). He often intentionally created large crowds by hiring buses to bring people to his rallies, which in turn is intended to convince others that he has legitimacy as the people's representative. In fact, when he went to the High Court in January 2009 to demand a recount of the 2008 election results, fifteen busloads of supposed supporters were brought in to cheer in his favor (interview with Simutanyi, 2009).

Coupled with this charisma is a package of policy promises that resonate with the priorities of the urban poor and aim to rectify their relegation, both figuratively and literally, to a marginal place in Zambian society. Collectively, Sata's promises challenged the MMD's rigid definitions of legality and illegality as well as highlighted that support for a free-market economy need not require the state to abrogate its responsibilities to provide basic goods and services. In the words of the PF's vice president, "The growth of the elite and elite-led kind of policy-making, or elites serving-their-own policy-making, coupled with dreadful poverty, both urban and rural, it's a serious apartheid kind of problem. I think Michael [Sata] grasps that, verbalized that better than anybody, the inequality" (interview with Scott, 2009). A respected Zambian political analyst, Dr. Neo Simutanyi, concurs:

> He [Sata] has been able to package his message in a way that resonates well with the majority of the poor, especially in urban areas. He seems to understand the problems of the poor, the problems of the working people, especially you know those who have lost jobs and so forth. And having worked as Minister of Local Government, he seems to understand the local issues, the issues of water, the issues of services, and these are some of things that he is able to talk about in a language that the local people actually understand. (Interview with Simutanyi, 2009)

He articulated this message most vocally through the PF's slogan of "Lower taxes, more jobs, more money in your pockets." Although vague, this slogan offered more substantive policy commitments than the slogans of the other parties. The MMD exhorted Zambians to support it "For Growth and Empowerment" (MMD 2006) and the UPND encouraged voters to "Realize the dream of a better Zambia through real change" (UPND 2008). Growth, empowerment, and a better Zambia essentially represent valence goods against which no one would argue. By contrast, low wages, high prices, and few job opportunities were cited among residents in Zambia's informal urban settlements as the top causes of poverty (see World Bank 2007a).

Lubinda who is the PF's former spokesman as well as an MP for Lusaka's Kabwata constituency – recognized that the message was particularly effective in urban areas rather than rural ones: "We talk about lower taxes, we talk about jobs for people. Now, that appeals to the people in the urban areas because they're the ones who are looking for jobs, they're the ones whose incomes are overtaxed. So, we appeal to them more than to rural dwellers. We haven't articulated issues of agriculture that strongly" (interview with Lubinda, 2009). Others echoed the same claim, noting that people living in rural areas are less likely to understand the concept of tax and more inclined to want to hear campaign promises about farming inputs than jobs (interview with Zulu and Chiwama, 2009).

On the surface, promising more jobs and lower taxes may also appear devoid of any programmatic content. However, tax rates are particularly contentious in Zambia, where the MMD government privatized the mines and only requires foreign investors to pay 0.6 percent of royalties on their profits (Lungu 2008). Many low-income Zambians in formal jobs believe that they should not have to pay taxes on their meager incomes when wealthy investors could do so more easily. Informal workers who do not pay income tax are still forced to pay monthly or daily fees for using a market stall or setting up a tuntemba (interview with Nchito, 2009). The urban poor are also more likely to have a higher share of their incomes going to pay value-added taxes on consumer goods (interview with Palale, 2009). With respect to jobs, the PF argued that creating more employment required diversifying the economy away from copper and requiring foreign investors, particularly the Chinese, to use local labor rather than importing workers from overseas (interviews with Mulenga, 2009; Lubinda, 2009). For those who remain unemployed, Sata also advocated the provision of unemployment benefits until a job was found (interview with Simutanyi, 2009).

In addition, improved water, sanitation, electricity, and housing were among the top promises offered by the PF during its campaigns. The PF's Director of Research, Chileshe Mulenga, claimed that the PF's advantage was the adoption of a "human rights approach" to these issues. When a clean water supply, for example, is portrayed as a basic need, then it becomes inexcusable for a government not to provide it (interview with Mulenga, 2009). This emphasis on a human rights approach is not necessarily uncontroversial when one considers that the MMD will not provide such services to compounds considered illegal.

A comprehensive housing development program was the main pillar of the PF's party manifesto in 2008, and stressed the need to provide low-cost, decent housing to those individuals currently residing in squatter settlements.[17] Upgrading shanty housing by providing the proper infrastructure, rather than demolishing them, was stressed throughout the PF's last two electoral campaigns (interviews with Chibamba and Henriot, 2009). In addition, after the March 2007 housing demolitions, Sata proclaimed that he would sue the state on behalf of the people who lost their homes (Mwape 2007). When asked about the housing situation, Sata personally replied that illegal housing should be upgraded, and added, "But, you don't demolish for the sake of demolishing. The people must come first. People must come first. The laws are made for people, laws are made to protect the people. We're going to do that" (interview with Sata, 2009).

Part of the PF's message was also to deride the MMD's harassment of street vendors as both counterproductive and inhumane and instead advocate that more adequate places be found for them to sell. In fact, Sata noted:

The MMD, they don't know anything about how to deal with anything because ... when it comes to the vote, they [MMD members] don't run in the streets where they [vendors] vote and they don't provide them [vendors] with employment. They [MMD members] don't provide them with more space. You can't force them [vendors] out of the streets.... If you crack down on them [vendors], where are you going to take them? What I'm saying is, if you fail to provide for them, don't bring punitive measures against them. (Interview with Sata, 2009)

Such a claim is surprising from someone who, as minister of local government and housing under Chiluba, engaged in wide-ranging crackdowns on informal sector workers and was even the architect of the Street Vending and Public Nuisances Act. However, for Edward Chisenga of the Street Vendors' Association, Sata's past behavior is forgotten, and King Cobra's more recent interventions on their behalf are appreciated. In choosing a presidential candidate, Chisenga added that treatment of street vendors

---

[17] The PF also adopted the same position for the 2011 elections. See "Patriotic Front Manifesto," retrieved from.

is more important to him than other issues, such as health or education (interview with Chisenga, 2009). PF Vice President, Guy Scott, further added that his party, which controlled the Lusaka City Council but received orders from the MMD-controlled Ministry of Local Government, tried to sabotage the crackdowns on street vendors and market workers as much as possible (interview with Scott, 2009).

Importantly, this package of messages around social inclusion remained constant across the two elections. But some of Sata's more extreme xenophobic rhetoric disappeared in 2008 without hurting his support among the urban poor. Most notably, Sata had been extremely critical of the predominance of foreign investors, or in his words, "infestors," in the Zambian economy. In the Copperbelt, Sata criticized the presence of Chinese and Indian companies, who own many of the region's copper mines in the wake of the MMD's privatization policies. He likewise decried that most of Lusaka's shops were owned by Chinese and South Asians (Wines 2006) and vowed to deport foreign business owners if elected into office. At his final rally in Mandevu in 2006, he stated, "The markets are for Zambians ... if you want to remain poor and if you want all good things to go to foreigners, vote for Mwanawasa" (cited in Chellah and Mwilu 2006).

However, in the run-up to the 2008 elections, he toned down his antiforeigner rhetoric noticeably (interviews with Simutanyi and Chibamba, 2009). In fact, in the September 30, 2008, edition of *The Post* newspaper, the PF sponsored a full-page campaign advertisement with the following message, which was personally signed by Sata:

> We started our journey in 2001, we have come a long way. I would like on behalf of the Central Committee, Provincial Committees, District Committees, Constituencies, Wards, Branches, Sections, the General Membership of our Party and indeed on my own behalf pay tribute and *sincerely thank our Asian community for the tremendous support and contribution rendered to the Patriotic Front.* Without it, we would not have reached this far. (Emphasis added)

He also reversed direction and pledged that if elected into office, he would actually protect all investment deals signed under the MMD administration (EIU 2008). The fact that his vote shares were actually slightly higher in urban areas despite a reduction in xenophobic claims suggests that his message on social inclusion had been the constant factor in attracting the urban poor.[18]

---

[18] I further test the appeal of xenophobic rhetoric to the urban poor in Chapter 5 when I look at the urban poor's attitudes toward Chinese involvement in the economy and whether any relationship existed between those attitudes and the party they ultimately chose to support.

Although the various components of Sata's populist strategy have endeared him to the urban poor, his appeal to other urbanites appears mixed. Certainly, some of Sata's xenophobic claims in the 2006 elections and his outspoken admiration for Zimbabwe's dictatorial leader, Robert Mugabe, frightened away intellectuals and the middle classes (Schatz 2007). Larmer and Fraser (2007: 631) claim that civil society leaders are largely distrustful of Sata's "street politics." Big business elites also tended to shy away from the PF and favor the MMD, through votes and/or campaign contributions, specifically because they preferred the certainty that comes from supporting the status quo (interview with Kabimba, 2009).

Whereas Sata's charisma and programmatic message around social inclusion were his primary mobilizing tactics, he may have relied on selective benefits to a small extent, as well. Specifically, there was some speculation that the PF distributed money to bus and taxi drivers before both elections in order to encourage them to generate support for the party among their customers (interview with Simutanyi, 2009). But many believe that vote buying does not necessarily influence urban voting behavior to the same extent it might in rural areas. For instance, Cheikh Chifuwe of *The Post* newspaper claimed that urban voters who receive handouts still tend to vote according to their consciences: "Urban voters get those things [handouts] but, at the end of the day, they make an independent decision, choice. I think over time, there has been greater awareness in the urban areas so it doesn't matter what you really give them" (interview with Chifuwe, 2009). As noted in Chapter 2, one reason for this is that due to resource constraints, opposition parties will concentrate campaigns in urban areas so they can all offer handouts, but urbanites can in turn vote as they choose.

Vertical Ties

The third key element of Sata's populist strategy was the use of language, symbols, and party-management tactics that brought him closer to the people. In turn, these actions reinforced his vertical ties and plebiscitarian relationship with the urban poor while emphasizing the lack of autonomous civil society organizations mediating the PF's interaction with this constituency. For instance, Sata spoke in the vernacular during his campaign speeches; Mwanawasa gave his speeches in English and then had a staff member translate them into local languages (Wines 2006). According to a PF MP from the Copperbelt, Sata portrayed himself as a common man who understood the travails of low-income urbanites: "He [Sata] talks about people eating a meal in the compound. He talks about what affects a person in the compound and they understand that this man knows what he's talking about" (interview with Simuusa, 2009). According to the PF's vice president, Sata purposely highlighted his own lack of education and refinement because it elicited claims from the opposition that one needs to be educated to run a country: "He [Sata] likes the image that he's uneducated. It brings out the worst in the educated elite. They say, 'Honestly, a man with grade 4 [education], how can he run a country?' I mean, 99 percent of the voters are grade 4 [educated]. What's their problem? What a stupid thing to say" (interview with Scott, 2009).

Likewise, the PF tried to discredit the leader of the UPND by calling him "calculator boy" as a reference to Hichilema's former background working in the accounting multinational Grant Thornton. Hichilema, although somewhat insultingly, admits that the PF's style of leadership is effective given the nature of the urban poor:

It is the circumstances that they [the urban poor] have found themselves in that they are looking for someone who can – well, their perception is that the one who shouts a lot, the one who threatens to beat up everyone else is the one who is macho enough and maybe is the one who should rule the country. And you can't blame them because they have been denied education. They've been denied jobs. So, they tend to be on the riotous side and obviously somebody who is closer to the riotous behavior is someone who they will think is their savior. (Interview with Hichilema, 2009)

In the same manner, Dr. Chitala of the MMD candidly acknowledged that his party has less success with the urban poor because his party is perceived as aloof and intellectualistic (interview with Chitala, 2009).

Another tactic used by Sata was to show that unlike other politicians, he was directly accessible to the people. In the mid-1990s, when he was minister of local government and housing, dozens of people regularly queued up to speak with him directly about their problems (Mwiinga 1994). Anyone who visited the PF headquarters in Farmer's House off Cairo Road witnessed that this open-door policy continued until Sata's election as president in 2011, with constituents constantly lined up to meet with him. Furthermore, the PF's Vice President, Dr. Scott, acknowledged that Sata publicly lambasted the performance of PF councillors and MPs to purposely bring himself closer to the voters (interview with Scott, 2009). By criticizing his own party members for not effectively responding to the peoples' demands, Sata created a paternal image that only he cared for the people and could accordingly provide for them.

On the other hand, the PF does not forge horizontal relationships with civic organizations representing the urban poor, debunking the possibility that a corporatist arrangement between associations of the urban poor and this opposition party have been responsible for the PF's success. Leaders of the largest umbrella organization for informal workers, known as the Alliance for Zambia Informal Economy Associations, have been angry about the targeting of its members by all political parties during election times (see Katasefa 2008).

The country's main alliance of labor unions, the ZCTU, has become increasingly involved in advocating rights for informal sector workers. Although the ZCTU formerly possessed a corporatist relationship with the MMD during the party's early years under Chiluba, the party's privatization practices alienated much of the labor movement. By the 1996 elections, the ZCTU openly announced that it no longer supported the MMD (Rakner 2003), and since then the union movement has abstained from endorsing any parties, including the PF (Larmer and Fraser 2007). This lack of horizontal ties resonates with contemporary populist movements in Latin America, where leaders have sought to mobilize atomized, unorganized urban masses not represented by any organizational intermediaries, such as unions (e.g., Roberts 1995; Roberts and Arce 1998).

Not surprisingly, Sata's reliance on strong, vertical ties with the voters has manifested in a party organization firmly oriented around him. Thus far, Sata has demonstrated little tolerance for internal dissent. Tellingly, the PF did not hold internal party elections until 2011, a full decade after the party was first established. Consequently, the party lacks institutionalization and would likely lose momentum if Sata was not at the helm. The authoritarian nature of the party was clear when Sata forbade PF MPs from participating in Zambia's National Constitutional Conference, an initiative aimed at revising the constitution, because he believed that the other invited stakeholders were too partisan. When twenty-seven PF MPs contravened his order and nonetheless participated, he attempted to expel them from the party (*Times of Zambia* 2007b).

OTHER OPPOSITION PARTY ALTERNATIVES IN ZAMBIA

The contribution of a populist strategy to Sata's success among the urban poor during the 2006 and 2008 elections contrasts markedly with the purely personalistic linkages employed by the two other main opposition parties, the UPND and the HP. The UPND finished third in the 2008 elections; the HP probably achieved its greatest popularity in the 2001 elections, and has since then failed to gain more than 2 percent of the vote in Zambia's urban constituencies.

The ideologies of each party remain relatively similar, offering a wide-ranging agenda intended to appeal to all Zambians. Larmer and Fraser

(2007: 623) observe that in the 2006 elections, the UPND-led UDA co-alition proved unappealing to the electorate because it failed to offer any substantive policy differences with the MMD. Likewise, in 2008, the UPND proposed running a "mixed economy" that aimed to increase and proper-ly structure "private/public local and foreign investments in sectors such as agriculture, mining, construction, energy, tourism, manufacturing, in-frastructure, telecommunications, pensions, insurance, financial and other services, many of which have in the past decades been neglected" (UPND 2008: 1). However, these objectives are not a dramatic deviation from those articulated in the MMD manifesto but rather convey a commitment to improve and intensify investments in a broad range of sectors. In fact, con-trary to the PF, whose rallying cry of Pabwato conjured an image of radical departure from the status quo, the UPND's motto of *Pa Kuboko Chabe* translates as "let's shake hands" and implies a conciliatory stance.

In terms of substantive policy areas, education, health, and agriculture represented the UPND's three main foci. According to the party's research director, Dr. Beyani, the party advocates the introduction of free educa-tion, reform of the health care system, irrigation, agro-processing, effective agricultural marketing arrangements, and improved road infrastructure (interview with Beyani, 2009). But as the governance advisor with the UNDP observes, the party is not specific about how they will achieve these improvements, particularly with respect to how they will pay for them. Moreover, because no Zambian political party opposes more education, better health care, and a revived agricultural sector, it is unclear how these goals differentiate the UPND from its competitors.

Both the UPND and HP emphasized rural development as the key to improving urban challenges. For Hichilema, stopping the tide of rural-to-urban migration would help "decongest" the cities: "So, if we made the conditions better for them out there [in rural areas], by making agriculture viable through subsidies and other programs, you will reduce the pres-sure of influx of street vendors coming in and looking for a better life" (interview with Hichilema, 2009). Likewise, the "Village Concept" lies at the heart of the Heritage Party's manifesto, advocating that Zambia return to the way of life before the country was colonized. Such a life involves ownership of a wealth-generating investment (e.g., land or business), food security, incorruptible leadership, productivity, and a social safety net to protect the destitute (Heritage Party n.d.). According to Wazziah Phiri, the party's spokesman, the Village Concept emphasizes that improving prod-uctivity in rural areas will decrease rural-urban drift because Zambians would no longer only find opportunities in the cities (interview with Phiri, 2009).

Although certainly not ignorant of the challenges of urban poverty, both UPND members – such as Dr. Beyani – and MMD representatives – including Dr. Kalumba – claimed that the UPND's constituency base predominantly spans middle-class, urban intellectuals as well as rural dwellers in Hichilema's stronghold of Southern Province (interviews with Beyani and Kalumba, 2009). This is partly due to the way in which the young Hichilema markets himself. He alternately claims, "I'm a villager," "I'm a rancher," and "I come from a business background" (interview with Hichilema, 2009). His rhetoric does not seem to be relevant for the urban poor, however. For instance, he advocated in his 2008 campaign that Zambians should more actively read the auditor general's reports, which show how poorly citizens' money has been spent under the MMD (Noyoo 2008). He also widely advertised that his party has written acerbic critiques of the MMD's budget proposals (interview with Hichilema, 2009). But given the low education levels of most of the urban poor, delving into such esoteric reading did not hold the same appeal as attending Michael Sata's raucous rallies.

Zambia's other main opposition parties do share a party organization with the PF that centers on their leaders. This problem is especially acute for the Heritage Party, which has no members in parliament and therefore fails to convey that the party is more widely representative beyond Miyanda. In the same manner, the UPND revolves around Hichilema, as it previously did around his predecessor, Mazoka. Transition of leadership from Mazoka to Hichilema did occur in 2006 on the basis of intraparty elections, but Hichilema was widely perceived as Mazoka's protégé (Banks, Muller, and Overstreet 2008). Since then, there have been no further elections for the UPND leadership during Hichilema's tenure.

Thus, although Zambia's two other main opposition parties share a party organization largely centered on their leaders, they deviate from the PF in a number of other key respects. First, they advance messages that are oriented around goods that all Zambians would prefer, such as improved health and education, rather than specific issues that are priorities for the urban poor. Secondly, their tactics for addressing urban poverty often focus on nebulous promises to invest in rural areas to prevent overcrowding in the cities rather than new solutions for helping those already settled in the cities. Thirdly, for the UPND in particular, the tactic of emphasizing agricultural production while advocating a thorough analysis of auditor's reports may appeal to a vast constituency of rural dwellers and well-educated urbanites, but creates little resonance with the urban underclasses. Such characteristics explain why in both the 2006 and 2008 elections the PF defeated not only the MMD amongst constituencies largely comprised of the urban poor, but also other

Table 3.5. *Summarizing Interactions of Zambian Parties with the Urban Poor*

Election Years	Incumbent Party (*Leader*)	Opposition Party (*Leader*)	Interaction by Opposition Party	Outcome
2001	MMD (*Mwanawasa*)	UPND (*Mazoka*), FDD (*Tembo*), Heritage (*Miyanda*)	Personalistic linkages	Vote is split among UPND, FDD, HP, and MMD in Lusaka, Kitwe, and Ndola
		PF (*Sata*)	Personalistic linkages	
2006 and 2008	MMD (*Mwanawasa* in 2006; *Banda* in 2008)	UPND (*Hichilema*), Heritage (*Miyanda*)	Personalistic linkages	The PF obtains an overwhelming majority of support in Lusaka, Kitwe, and Ndola
		PF (*Sata*)	Populist strategy	

opposition parties. The urban poor's support for the PF therefore should be viewed as a consequence of the party's ability to craft a populist strategy to address exclusion and harassment by the MMD and thereby become more distinguishable than the rest of the opposition, which predominantly relied on personalistic linkages with this constituency.

CONCLUSION

This chapter examined how various political parties in Zambia mobilized urban constituents between 2001 and 2008. Due to Zambia's capital-intensive growth trajectory and attendant demographic shifts, Zambia's major cities are categorized by a large number of the urban poor living in peripheral shanty compounds and relying on the low-wage informal sector. Given these circumstances, three key points emerged by comparing parties over time. First, even when the incumbent MMD engaged in harassment and failed to provide jobs, decent housing, and basic public services, the opposition proved unable to capture the imagination of the urban poor in the 2001 elections. Secondly, such dire circumstances created the fodder for the resonance of a populist strategy implemented by the PF. Thirdly, this strategy prevailed because other key opposition parties, including the UPND and the HP, relied on personalistic linkages that reduced their degree of differentiation and level of congruence with the policy priorities of the urban poor. These trends are summarized in Table 3.5.

The PF's populist strategy relied on geographically targeted campaigns in deprived areas of Lusaka and the cities on the Copperbelt. The charismatic Sata employed a policy message of social inclusion that manifested through promises to provide jobs, end harassment of informal workers, and improve housing and service delivery. The PF's policies often involved an eclectic mixture of liberal and leftist norms that privileged both individual preroga- tive and government intervention. Despite the fact that Sata was a long-time MMD loyalist, he relied on the use of the vernacular and theatrical antics during campaign rallies to reinvent himself as an antiestablishment outsider and established direct, vertical ties with the urban poor. Although the strat- egy was not particularly endearing to the urban middle class, it enabled the PF to clearly differentiate itself from other opposition competitors and win over a whole subset of voters who were historically treated as a blight on the city's landscape rather than citizens with a genuine electoral advantage.

FOUR

Gorgui's Gamble

The Rise and Fall of Populist Strategies in Senegal

Similar to Chapter 3, this chapter examines the various linkages used by political parties to mobilize the urban poor in Senegal during the period from 2000 to 2007. This time frame provides the opportunity to highlight variation across different political parties as well as within parties over time. Specifically, in the run-up to Senegal's historic 2000 elections, Abdoulaye Wade relied on a populist strategy similar to Michael Sata's in order to mobilize Dakar's excluded and disgruntled masses, particularly the youth. He defeated not only the ruling PS but also his other opposition competitors in the first and second rounds of voting.

By contrast, no single opposition party obtained significant support from the urban poor during Senegal's 2007 presidential elections. Wade, an octogenarian who is often referred to as Gorgui, or the "old one," retained the presidency despite having accomplished very little for the urban poor during his first term. His victory was assisted by Senegal's lackluster opposition in those elections. Amongst these opposition parties were those reliant on purely personalistic linkages that espouse vague, indistinguishable platforms. A smaller set of programmatic opposition parties with strong ties to the country's dwindling labor unions offered more distinct appeals around socialism, workers' rights, and economic nationalism. However, the comprehension of such messages remains limited to only a small segment of unionized urbanites and salaried professionals rather than the mass of the urban poor.

To illustrate this pattern, the chapter first reviews the political party system in Senegal, focusing on the country's main parties up through 2007. Subsequently, the country's urbanization challenges are elaborated and the development priorities of the urban poor are highlighted. This is followed by a discussion outlining components of Wade's populist strategy in the 2000 election and why this strategy was so successful. Even though Wade subsequently deviated from his populist strategy after winning elections, no one opposition party was able to mobilize the urban poor in the country's 2007 elections. Through interviews with various opposition parties and political observers, I show that the main reason for this lack of appeal is the absence of distinguishable policy messages that demonstrate congruence with the priorities of the urban poor.

SENEGAL'S POLITICAL PARTY LANDSCAPE

Like Zambia, Senegal did not experience substantive political liberalization until the early 1990s. From 1966 to 1976, the country was a single-party system under Léopold Sédar Senghor's Union Progressiste Sénégalaise (UPS), which espoused a form of democratic African socialism (Nohlen et al. 1999). In 1976, Senghor amended the constitution and introduced the "law of three trends," which legalized three political parties as long as they adhered to an acceptable ideological position: liberal democracy, social democracy, and communism/Marxism. At the same time, the UPS changed its name to the PS and staked claims on the centrist, social democratic position (Diaw and Diouf 1998). The liberal democratic orientation was foisted upon the PDS. Founded in 1974, the PDS was led by Abdoulaye Wade, who was trained as an economist, mathematician, and lawyer. The Parti Africain de l'Indépendance (PAI) accepted the Marxist designation.

When Senghor resigned in 1980 as leader of the PS, he was replaced by his prime minister, Abdou Diouf, and restrictions on party registration were subsequently removed. In both 1991 and 1995, the PDS joined the PS government during brief periods of cohabitation. These periods helped create the foundation for a more competitive political environment. The PS consulted with the opposition about the creation of a new electoral code, guaranteed a secret ballot, lowered the voting age from twenty-one to eighteen, expanded voter registration, and permitted foreign election monitors (Creevey, Ngomo, and Vengroff 2005; Kanté 1994). By 2000, an opposition coalition called Alternance 2000 was formed. Along with the PDS, this coalition included a number of leftist parties, such as the Ligue-Démocratique-Mouvement pour le Parti du Travail (LD-MPT), And-Jëf/ Parti Africain pour la Démocratie et le Socialisme (AJ/PADS), and the PIT. Between 2000 and 2007, the number of officially registered political parties in Senegal increased from fifty-seven to seventy-seven (Camara 2000; Adejumobi 2007). Table 4.1 presents only the country's most competitive parties at the time of the 2007 elections.

Table 4.1. *Overview of Main Senegalese Political Parties*

Party Name	Leader	Year Founded
Parti Socialiste (Socialist Party, PS)	Ousmane Tanor Dieng	1959
Parti Démocratique du Sénégal (Democratic Party of Senegal, PDS)	Abdoulaye Wade	1974
Ligue Démocratique-Mouvement pour le Parti du Travail (Democratic League-Labor Party Movement, LD-MPT)	Abdoulaye Bathily	1981
Parti de l'Indépendance et du Travail (Party of Independence and Work, PIT)	Amath Dansokho	1981
And-Jëf-Parti Africaine pour la Démocratie et la Socialisme (Act Together –African Party for Democracy and Socialism, AJ/PADS)	Landing Savané	1991
Alliance des Forces de Progrès (Alliance of Forces for Progress, AFP)	Moustapha Niasse	1999
Rewmi (The Nation)	Idrissa Seck	2006
Démocratie-Solidarité (Democracy-Solidarity, DS)	Robert Sagna	2006

URBANIZATION CHALLENGES

This political liberalization coincided with rapid urbanization and growing primacy of the capital of Dakar. At independence in 1960, Dakar was already becoming West Africa's most urbanized city, with 14 percent of Senegal's population living in the capital (DPS 1993). By 2002, almost one-quarter of the population lived in the city of Dakar and its main suburbs of Pikine and Guédiawaye (ANSD 2006). Dakar's high population density presents major challenges, prompting it to be described as a place "invaded by poverty, offering today the face of a city knocked to pieces, anarchic and polluted. An urban monster" (Ghorbal 2001: 15).

At least three factors have contributed to the city's growth and impoverishment during the postindependence period. First, the agricultural sector collapsed in the early 1980s as a result of drought in the peanut basin and the adoption of a structural adjustment agreement that reduced fertilizer subsidies (Mbow 1993; Pison et al. 1995). This stimulated a massive rural exodus to Dakar. Secondly, structural adjustment also resulted in extensive job retrenchments and fewer civil service positions for university students upon graduation (Graham 1994). Both trends resulted in a city increasingly crowded with job seekers at a time when the state could not afford to create more employment. At the start of the 1990s, open unemployment in Dakar was estimated at 24 percent, with underemployment much higher (Graham 1994). The devaluation of the currency, the CFA, in 1994 also reduced the purchasing power of Dakarois.[1]

More recently, however, the city has grappled with a third trend, which is that the country's birth rate peaked in the 1980s; therefore, a surfeit of young people is now on the job market (*Oxford Analytica* 2007). For the youth, the rule of the day therefore has become *débrouille*, meaning "to cope" or "manage to get by," which usually involves accepting a low-paid apprenticeship, attempting to emigrate overseas, or most likely entering the already-saturated informal sector (M. Diop 2002). In fact, 76 percent of Dakar's population labors in the informal economy, a sector that accounted for 97 percent of employment growth between 1994 and 2005 (ANSD 2007b: 48; World Bank 2007b).

Consequently, jobs for the youth are repeatedly identified as a major priority by the urban poor. For instance, Table 4.2 highlights the top development priorities identified by those Senegalese interviewed for the country's most recent poverty survey in 2005/2006, the Enquête de Suivi de la Pauvreté au Sénégal (ESPS). Among the poorest Dakarois, who are found in the first income quartile, 24 percent stated that youth employment was the biggest challenge facing their community. Potable water and proper sanitation follow as the next two most important issues for this constituency. Although the rural poor share the desire for potable water, they differ markedly on the other priorities for their communities. In fact, youth employment and sanitation are viewed as a major challenge by only 8 and 1 percent of the rural poor, respectively. Instead, the ESPS (2005) found that the construction of a medical dispensary was the second biggest priority for rural Senegalese.

Map 4.1 illustrates many of Dakar's main neighborhoods. As in Lusaka, Dakar's most densely populated areas also tend to be its poorest and are predominantly located outside of the city center. These include the Médina neighborhood, which emerged during the colonial era when African inhabitants were expelled from the central Plateau quarter, which is the center of government administration (Mehretu and Mutambirwa 2003; Scheld 2002). Likewise, the vast irregular settlements of Parcelles-Assainies, Pikine, and

---

[1]   The CFA was pegged to the French franc until 2000, when it was then pegged to the Euro. In January 1994, France decided to devalue the CFA by 50 percent, which meant that the value of Senegalese exports was halved at the same time that the cost of international imports doubled.

Table 4.2. *Top Development Priorities in Senegal (% of Respondents)*

Zone/ Income Quartile	Youth Employment	Sanitation	Provision of Potable Water	Construction of Dispensary
Dakar				
1st	24.3	15.4	15.9	8
2nd	19.1	16.1	2.6	10.9
3rd	15.6	12.9	2.5	9.4
4th	18.8	8.9	3.7	8.1
Other Urban				
1st	26.6	7.3	18.6	6.6
2nd	18	10.3	6.6	8.4
3rd	17.4	11.4	5.1	8.3
4th	18.2	11	4.4	6.4
Rural				
1st	7.7	1.2	38.0	14.8
2nd	7.8	2.5	10.8	22.6
3rd	9.7	3.4	7.2	18.2
4th	15	3.8	4.6	10

Source: ANSD (2007a).

Guédiawaye originated from forced removals of slum dwellers from the city center between the 1970s and 1980s because they were perceived as encombrements humains, or "human clutter," who tarnished the city's image (Collignon 1984; Vernière 1977; Zeleza and Eyoh 2003). A majority of the shantytowns on the city's periphery, particularly in Pikine and Guédiawaye, were built on marshlands. Thus, every year during the rainy season these neighborhoods become flood zones and in turn become breeding grounds for malaria and cholera (Fall, Guèye, and Tall 2005).

THE TRIUMPH OF A POPULIST STRATEGY IN 2000

Although historically Dakar's poor were physically marginalized, they became an attractive source of votes as the country began to liberalize politically. During his time in opposition, Wade did not always acknowledge the importance of the urban vote. For instance, Diop and Diouf (1990: 80) note that in 1990, the urban youth in particular were "in search of a framework for social and political contestation of the government, a framework which

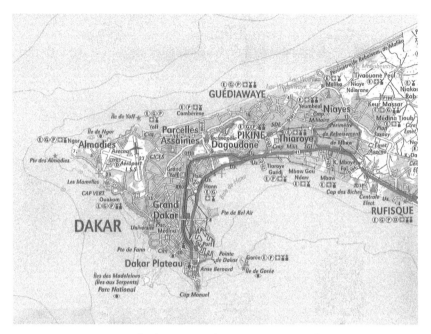

Map 4.1 Map of Dakar. Copyright © 2008, Direction des Travaux
Géographiques et Cartographiques, Dakar, Senegal.

the opposition parties did not seem capable of offering them." But as the
2000 presidential elections approached, Wade increasingly recognized the
relevance of courting the urban poor. Consequently, he relied on a populist
strategy specifically targeted at Dakar's unemployed and underemployed
youth, which consisted of a mixture of charisma and programmatic appeals
aimed at giving hope to the excluded. The manner in which he delivered
his messages signified an important deviation from the traditionally elitist
nature of Senegalese politics and fostered direct, vertical ties between him
and the broader populace.

Vertical Ties, Youth, and Informality

Wade's campaign for the 2000 elections was influenced by the growth of a
new urban identity that privileged individual initiative in the face of an unre-
sponsive state. Two trends contributed to this identity. First, disappointed
urban youth became more vocal about their living and working conditions.
In the late 1980s and early 1990s, unemployed youth and students engaged
in a series of riots, strikes, and demonstrations targeted against symbols of

power in the affluent Plateau area of Dakar (Diouf 1996). Shortly thereafter, the *Set Setal* movement was launched, which aimed to improve poor sanitation on the city's rubbish-strewn streets and protest against the corruption and bad governance under the PS (Scheld 2002; Diaw and Diouf 1998).[2] Participating youth responded to the state's incompetence by organizing volunteer neighborhood groups to clean streets, dispose of litter, and paint wall murals. The movement was an assault on the nonresponsive ruling class and an attempt to reclaim public space for the entrepreneurial activities associated with la débrouille (Mamadou Diouf 1996). McLaughlin (2001) further argues that Set Setal essentially signified the emergence of an eclectic new urban identity, exemplified by the spread of urban Wolof, which is a mixture of French and Wolof.

Secondly, this period coincided with the emergence of a class of individuals called *moodu-moodu,* which refers predominantly to uneducated, male Wolof rural migrants to the city who followed what is known as the *Baol-Baol* model of socioeconomic advancement. This model relies on the informal sector and transnational opportunities to accumulate wealth, often through contacts via the Mouride Sufi brotherhood (Magrin 2007). The moodu-moodu popularized the notion amongst the urban masses that the informal sector, not white-collar jobs, represented the easiest means to acquire social mobility and affluence (Ndiaye 1996).

In the run-up to the 2000 presidential elections, Wade's method of campaigning accorded priority to this new urban identity around youth and informality, thereby generating a sense of direct responsiveness between Gorgui and the alienated masses. Specifically, he invented an entirely new formula of political campaigning in Senegal known as "blue marches." Historically, Senegalese parties relied on elaborate, stationary performances set up around tents and chairs, complete with dancers and praise singers who would espouse the virtues of party candidates. The gathered audience would receive a meal as well as T-shirts and hats with party slogans and pictures of candidates' faces. Critically, these traditional meetings would involve the leader speaking in French to his audience, with a translator interpreting the meaning into local languages. Moreover, candidates often devoted their time to talking with small groups of older attendees; the youth were often sent away to separate mass rallies (Foucher 2007).

Whereas the PS continued in this vein for the 2000 elections, the PDS chose a cheaper but more dynamic mode of campaigning. Specifically, PDS representatives toured city streets in their own cars, waving flags and

---

[2] *Set Setal* is a Wolof phrase for "clean up."

banners colored blue, which is the color of the PDS. Instead of the suits favored by Diouf, Wade donned the typical Senegalese *boubou*. His security guards wore blue denim, a symbol of American values that favor the personal initiative of the *débrouillard* or a migrant returning from overseas, rather than the ideals of a French civil servant (Foucher 2007). Large amplifiers would blast the Senegalese pop music and Ivorian reggae favored by the young. When the music was interrupted for Wade's speeches, he used urban Wolof rather than French to directly communicate to voters.

In contrast to the PS, which launched its 2000 campaign in the rural Tambacounda region in the southeast of the country, Wade initiated his blue marches in the main thoroughfares of Dakar where informal workers typically peddle their goods. This was an important sign of who he identified as his main constituency base. He moved from the Médina to the markets of Guele Tapée and Soumbédioune and down the main thoroughfares of Cheikh Anta Diop and Avenue Blaise Diagne (Foucher 2007). By effectively marching through Dakar, Wade was using a mode of campaigning that resonated with the notion of informality. As Ibrahima Thioub, a Senegalese history professor at the University of Cheikh Anta Diop, observed, "The PS has static meetings while the PDS marches, like the street peddlers and hawkers. The PDS carries an indigenous discourse that is very understandable for the rural migrants who arrive in the city. I believe that the group that has the most difficulty with the PDS is the descendants of the citadins of the 19th century" (interview with Thioub, 2008).[3]

Such an approach helped Wade convey that he was a leader who differed from his two predecessors: "Far from the intellectual elitism of Senghor or the technocratic rigidity of Abdou Diouf, Wade's populism represented a politically effective synthesis between pride for Senegal's achievements and the triumph of the Baol Baol model" (Magrin 2007: 9). In turn, Coulibaly (2003: 128) notes that "this populism gave the appearance that he [Wade] remained an ordinary man. A leader who listened to his people. A leader who consulted them and was devoted to them" (Coulibaly 2003: 128). Indeed, despite his high level of education, he proved capable of portraying himself as a man of the people.

A "Political Animal" with a Popular Message

Beyond his blue marches, Wade's populist strategy involved a combination of charisma and a relevant policy message. Léopold Senghor had long

---

[3] *Citadins* is a term for city dwellers.

ago characterized Wade as an *ndiombor¸* or "hare," which symbolized a remarkable and shrewd political animal (Breuillac 2000b). For Diop, Diouf, and Diaw (2002: 176), one of Wade's major advantages was a talented oratory and deep knowledge of the Senegalese people. His facility with words tapped into the disillusionment of the times. Most critically, he brought the term *Sopi*, meaning "change" in Wolof, into the political sphere long before this now commonplace rallying cry became a feature of political campaigns in Africa. He would also draw on well-known fables to make parallels between literary villains and the incompetence of the PS (Breuillac 2000b). Like Michael Sata, Wade also ensured that he always remained in the public eye through deft use of the burgeoning private media. In fact, he would often hold several press conferences a day; Diouf would only agree to interviews during the week preceding the 2000 elections (McKenzie 2000).

Even Wade's own party cadres admit that Gorgui's charisma was the main allure of the PDS. When asked what attracted him to the PDS over all of Senegal's other political parties, Babacar Gaye, a former PDS spokesman and director of the Cabinet of Political Affairs responded:

I was fascinated by the man [Wade]. It wasn't his party [that attracted me] at the time because I wasn't looking for his doctrine, philosophy, method, organization. No, that didn't interest me. What interested me was that I was convinced that Abdoulaye Wade could change this country, that's all.... So, I joined the PDS more for Wade than for the philosophy or ideology of the party. Maybe if he was a fascist, I would support him. If he was a communist, I would support him. Even if he was someone who believed in savage liberalism, I would support him. (Interview with Gaye, 2008)

Beyond charisma, Wade mobilized the urban poor with promises on those issues most relevant to their everyday lives. Notably, these promises were focused on social inclusion but combined aspects of both liberal and leftist appeals, consistent with Sata's promises and observations that contemporary variants of populism adhere to an eclectic ideology (see Roberts 1995). Whereas Diouf highlighted his regime's success at reducing inflation to 3 percent and increasing growth by 5 percent annually, jobs were at the forefront of Wade's agenda. He critiqued Diouf's poor performance in this domain during his campaign launch on February 8, 2000: "Seven years ago he [Diouf] had promised 20,000 jobs. Actually he lost 100,000" (cited in Panafrican News Agency 2000). He made a ritual of asking at campaign rallies who in the audience possessed a job, anticipating only a few individuals to respond. By contrast, a sea of hands always rose up when he subsequently questioned who was unemployed (Breuillac 2000b). The technique was effective in reinforcing the PS's lackluster record on employment and highlighted that Wade "embodies the spirit of a better tomorrow for the number of those who have been excluded from economic growth" (Breuillac 2000a). Drawing on his party's characterization as a liberal party, Wade promised to provide jobs via the diversification of the economy away from peanut production and attracting foreign investment (Sixtine 2003).

Beyond jobs, Wade also focused on the need to improve the water supply in urban areas and provide relief for victims of flooding in the suburbs (EIU 2000). In addition, he vowed to end the forced removals practiced under the PS regime (interview with Thioub, 2008). Instead of demolishing unsuitable or illegal housing, the new logic was either to relocate people into better housing or compensate them if the state required them to move elsewhere (interview with Abdoul and Guèye, 2008). Finally, he stressed his commitment to improving sanitation and toilet facilities by repeatedly using the catchphrase "Sanitation is a matter of dignity" (see WSP 2011).

Overall, Diaw and Diouf (1998: 134) characterized the PDS as a "populist party which the population could believe in." Above all, Graham (1994: 126) claims that Wade's optimism was an important antidote to growing complacency with the status quo: "Usually the only way this 'culture of poverty' can be reversed is by severe economic shock or by some kind of external influence. The *Sopi* movement, which broke with years of uninterrupted political stability, may have temporarily provided such an influence."

The 2000 Elections

The 2000 election results highlighted the success of Wade's populist strategy. In the first round of the February 27, 2000, elections, Wade competed against six other opposition candidates as well as the PS, but the only other truly competitive opposition candidate was Moustapha Niasse.[4] Niasse was a former minister of foreign affairs and the United Nations envoy to the Great Lakes region. Only eight months before the 2000 elections, Niasse defected from the PS, a party that he had helped found and to which he had belonged for forty years. Immediately prior to his departure from the PS, he published a document criticizing Diouf's policies and accusing many PS members of corruption. He subsequently formed the AFP to contest the 2000 elections and, as a successful businessman, he was able to almost entirely finance the party (Diop et al. 2002).

Although Niasse was a virulent critic of Diouf during the election campaign, he focused mostly on mismanagement by the ruling party, and

---

[4]   In addition to Niasse, the other opposition candidates were Djibo Leïty Kâ, Iba Der Thiam, Ousseynou Fall, Cheikh Abdoulaye Dièye, and Mademba Sock.

opposed Diouf's termination of presidential term limits. In announcing the launch of his campaign, Niasse noted, "A quick end must be put to the system of making the state and public weal a heritage in an unbridled search for prebend. In that direction, the presidential term must be constitutionally limited to two terms, not for a seven-year period, but a five-year period at most" (BBC 1999). Rather than Dakar, Niasse launched his campaign in the southern city of Ziguinchor within Casamance, which is a region that has been grappling with a secessionist movement since the early 1980s. There, he emphasized the need for peace, noting that he wanted a "united Senegal living and moving to the tune of solidarity between all its sons and daughters" (cited in Panafrican News Agency 2000). He then proceeded to his home region of rural Kaolack, where he aimed to gain support from PS dissidents and religious figures (EIU 1999).

Ultimately, Niasse's campaign only succeeded in taking away votes from the PS rather than from the PDS, and this was particularly true in Kaolack (see Vengroff and Magala 2001). Within the departments of Dakar and Pikine, neither Niasse nor Diouf obtained more than 23 percent of the vote. By contrast, Wade won 48 and 54 percent of the vote in these two departments, respectively.[5] Although an eloquent speaker, Niasse's tactics were vastly different from Wade's populist strategy, evidenced by his lack of a targeted discourse and campaigning among the urban poor.

At the national level, Wade secured a total of approximately 31 percent of the vote compared with Diouf's 41 percent. Niasse came in third with just 17 percent of the votes, illustrating that the first round of elections amounted to a contest between the PS and the PDS rather than between the PS and the opposition more broadly. Having received enough votes to advance to a second round of elections, Wade needed to convince the unsuccessful opposition candidates to rally around him. Promising that he would install a coalition government if he won, Wade was able to convince the AFP, along with other smaller parties, to join his original Alternance coalition, which was in turn renamed the Front pour l'Alternance (FAL).

Recognizing that winning over Dakar was critical to a national victory in the second round of the 2000 elections, the PS hurriedly launched a "charm offensive" in the city and its suburbs (Diop et al. 2002: 173). But this tactic failed to have the desired outcome for the PS, which ultimately lost the second round to the PDS. In Dakar especially, the PDS garnered

[5]   At the time, Pikine and Guédiawaye were part of the same department. Since 2000, they became separate administrative entities. Data for the first and second round of the 2000 elections was graciously provided by Macoumba Coumé at the Ministry of the Interior on Oct. 2, 2008.

76 percent of the votes compared with 23 percent for the PS (Diop et al. 2002). According to one of the spokespeople for the PS, its major failure was ignoring both the plight and electoral potential of Senegal's urban poor: "This is why the PS lost in 2000, because it lost its electorate, which had shifted and become poorer and more urban and the conditions of life were very difficult. And these people sanctioned us in 2000" (interview with Tall Sall, 2008).

SOPI BECOMES NOPI

After Wade's electoral victory, his populist strategy dissipated and more purely personalistic linkages began to characterize his relationship with the urban poor.[6] Admittedly, he continued to rely on his blue marches for the campaign for the 2001 legislative elections, which allowed the PDS to obtain a parliamentary majority (Thomas 2001). In general though, the PDS retreated from a populist strategy with the urban poor and relied more on a vague platform around valence issues as well as large-scale projects that proved most beneficial for Dakar's more affluent citizens.

The seven years preceding the 2007 elections were characterized by a series of high-profile construction projects, which Wade labeled as his Très Grands Projets (TGP). These projects included luxury oceanfront hotels and shopping centers, such as Dakar City in the posh Les Almadies neighborhood. He further promised to build a new $400 million international airport and a new capital (*Oxford Analytica* 2007). According to a former minister of urbanization, Seydou Sy Sall, this general emphasis on large-scale infrastructure undermined investments in much-needed basic infrastructure within Dakar's peri-urban zones (interview with Sy Sall, 2008). Many began claiming that the acronym TGP stood for nothing else than a *Très Grand Piège*, or a "very large waste of money" (Thiobane 2008).

One of the more controversial projects was a new highway along Dakar's corniche, hugging the road parallel to the Atlantic Ocean. Given that the many thousands of poor Dakarois cannot afford a car and instead depend on dangerous, communal vehicles known as *Ndiaga Ndiayes*, according priority to building the highway seemed misplaced. According to the director for UN-Habitat in Senegal, "The relationship between the amount of money that was invested [into the highway] and the impact on the population is relatively weak because the *Corniche* only benefits a few of the privileged in Dakar and encompasses the rich neighborhoods and those who have their

---

[6] *Nopi* means "to fall silent" in Wolof. I borrowed this phrase from Havard (2004).

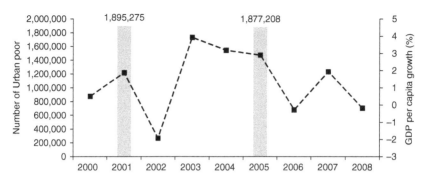

Figure 4.1 Trends in urban poverty and macroeconomic growth, Senegal.

own cars, which is a very small percentage of the population" (interview with Sy Sall, 2008).

In the meantime, life for the urban poor did not notably improve. As seen by the dashed line in Figure 4.1, growth was somewhat erratic during Wade's first term, and the number of urban poor only decreased marginally between 2001 and 2005. Moreover, Wade's 2000 campaign promises to tackle unemployment remained largely unfulfilled. In all of Senegal, the formal sector was employing only 214,700 people as of 2006 compared with 3,422,700 people working in the informal sector (IMF 2010). In fact, 22 percent of Dakar's population under the age of twenty remained completely unemployed (ANSD 2007a; ANSD 2007b). A rapper named Xuman popular amongst the youth captured disillusionment with Wade on the eve of the 2007 elections when he said, "All of the youth, we were disappointed after seven years of reign. There were a lot of promises that we are going to get jobs and life is going to be cheaper. But in seven years, we've seen these two things get worse" (cited in Dixon 2007: A3).

Early on in his first term, Wade also rescinded on his earlier promise not to demolish slum housing, and instead his government engaged in forced evictions in among other places Dakar's Baraka and Capatage slums, claiming that residents were illegally occupying state-controlled land (COHRE 2004). His one high-profile housing project was the 84 million dollar Plan Jaxaay, which aimed to assist the victims of yearly flooding in Pikine and Guédiawaye by re-locating residents of water-logged shantytowns to higher land nearby (AFP 2005).[7] But the Plan Jaxaay was poorly planned and mismanaged. Only a few months before the 2007 elections, most of the affected families were still homeless and living in tents on the outskirts of

---

[7] *Jaxaay* means "eagle" in Wolof.

Dakar, having endured yet another rainy season in even more crowded and unsanitary conditions. Furthermore, flood victims were still being required to pay 35 percent of the cost of the new housing once they were finally resettled (UN-IRIN 2006).

Furthermore, although the PDS regime began improving rural electrification, urban electrification did not receive the same degree of investment (interview with Sy Sall, 2008). Due to the government's failure to finance sufficient fuel to run its electricity generators, unrelenting blackouts began to plague Dakar beginning in March 2006 (*Oxford Analytica* 2007). Electricity cuts lasting up to twelve hours a day could be particularly aggravating for poor households that had allocated scarce resources to pay their monthly bills and could not afford the private generators on which affluent Dakarois began to depend. Similar to Zambia, Figure 4.2 highlights that the average monthly cost of both electricity and water in Dakar for a family of four people increased during Wade's first term as president.

The desperation of the urban poor was most clearly manifested by the large-scale emigration of young, Senegalese men to Europe. The trip in fragile, open wooden canoes resulted in one in six migrants perishing on the high seas (Ba 2007). But desperation made many Senegalese fatalistic, leading to the popular slogan of "Barça ou Barsakh," which means that one either makes it to Barcelona or goes on to the next life. Given the risks involved and the fact that overseas remittances can contribute 30 to 80 percent of household budgets in Senegal (Faubert 2008), many poor migrants blamed Wade directly for a massive deportation campaign led by Spain and France in late 2006. Wade's main response to this outpouring of anger only a few months before the 2007 elections was to launch a new program to address urban unemployment, which was called Retour vers l'Agriculture (Return to Agriculture, REVA) and intended to grant would-be migrants plots for farming. Playing on the title of this program, many concluded that REVA was invented by *rêveurs,* or "dreamers," who unrealistically believed that city dwellers would be enticed to move back to the countryside (interview with Guèye, 2008).

Le PDS, c'est Wade

Not unlike other political parties with personalistic linkages, Wade also engaged in excessive displays of executive power and a highly hierarchical management of the PDS. As a result, he created a rift between urban intellectuals and the PDS, contributing to the impression that the many affluent intellectuals who rallied around Wade's cause in 2000 no longer supported him (interview with Faye, 2008). Specifically, Wade began

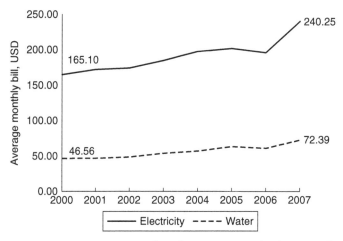

Figure 4.2 Trends in the average cost of utilities in Dakar.

purging representatives from other opposition parties who had backed him in the FAL coalition. In December 2000, he dismissed his Minister of Urbanization, Amath Dansokho, who is the leader of PIT. Moustapha Niasse of the AFP lost his job as prime minister in March 2001, and two cabinet members from the LD-MPT were fired in March 2005. Furthermore, after an initial referendum in 2001 that eliminated the upper-legislative chamber – the Sénat – for financial reasons, the National Assembly approved the reestablishment of this body in January 2007 and stipulated that 65 of its 100 members would be appointed by the president (Englebert 2008).

Within the PDS, Wade ultimately controls the career track of his party members. The clearest evidence of this occurred when Idrissa Seck, the prime minister from 2002 until 2004, was fired from this post under allegations of corruption. A long-time protégé of Wade and the director of the PDS's presidential campaign in the historic 2000 elections, Seck was widely perceived to harbor presidential ambitions. He was expelled from the party and spent seven months in prison under the charge that, as mayor of the town of Thiès, he had misappropriated funds intended for road construction projects (see M. Diop 2006).[8] Many mayors who were PDS members but considered close to Seck were also removed from their posts and replaced with Wade loyalists (interview with Fall, 2008). Once freed from jail, Seck formed his own political party, Rewmi.[9]

---

[8] A similar fate befell Seck's successor and director of the 2007 presidential election campaign, Macky Sall.
[9] *Rewmi* means "the nation" in Wolof.

The hierarchical nature of the PDS's management was only reinforced by the party's lack of horizontal relationships with civic organizations, including those representing members of the urban poor. One such organization is the UNACOIS, which was established in 1990 to fight against government monopolies. UNACOIS consists of a variety of informal sector workers, ranging from small-scale traders and service providers to large-scale importer-exporters. Defending the interests of informal sector workers and protecting them from tax levies constitute the main goals of the organization (Thioub, Diop, and Boone 1998). According to UNACOIS's Secretary General, Mame Bou Diop, the organization contains about 50,000 members in Dakar and 150,000 nationwide (interview with Bou Diop, 2008). Headquartered in Dakar's Sandaga market, the members are linked to UNACOIS's leaders through a series of hierarchical business, credit, family, and religious relations (Thioub et al. 1998), giving UNACOIS a degree of encompassment that theoretically would be conducive to a corporatist arrangement with the PDS. But in reality, it retains an independent political base. Mame Bou Diop claims that although a UNACOIS member can be a member of any political party, the organization does not subscribe to any formal political affiliations. In fact, although many presidential candidates came to discuss their programs with the UNACOIS leadership before the 2007 elections, the PDS was notably absent. Despite Wade claiming an affinity with the informal sector, Bou Diop notes that Wade did not improve conditions for informal workers and that the government's interest in taxing such workers necessarily creates antagonistic relations with UNACOIS (interview with Bou Diop, 2008).

THE 2007 SENEGALESE ELECTION

Despite Wade's inability to fulfill the needs of the urban poor during his first term, he nonetheless proved victorious in the 2007 presidential elections. He campaigned on a message of "The best is yet to come," which implied that his large-scale construction projects were just a small sample of the larger plans he intended. At the national level, Wade secured 56 percent of the vote, meaning that a second round of elections proved unnecessary. As seen in Table 4.3, he also obtained more than 50 percent of the vote in all three urban departments of the Dakar region, including the poorer suburbs of Pikine and Guédiawaye. Turnout in the region was high and estimated at around 72 percent. Moreover, his closest competitor, Seck, was between 30 to 40 percentage points behind. Thus, even if these opposition parties had entered into a coalition, as Wade himself did in 2000, they would not have defeated him in Dakar.

Table 4.3. *Vote Shares in the Region of Dakar in 2007 Presidential Elections (%)*

Main Candidates (Party)	Urban Departments in the Region of Dakar		
	Dakar	*Pikine*	*Guédiawaye*
Abdoulaye Wade (PDS)	52.5	60.4	61.0
Idrissa Seck (Rewmi)	17.7	20.0	17.8
Ousmane Tanor Dieng (PS)	16.3	10.4	11.6
Moustapha Niasse (AFP)	5.3	3.2	3.7
Robert Sagna (DS)	1.9	1.1	0.9
Landing Savané (AJ-PADS)	1.2	1.3	1.0
Abdoulaye Bathily (LD-MPT)	1.7	1.0	1.5

Notes: This table includes only the top seven performing candidates of the total fifteen that competed in this election. The fourth department in Dakar region is Rufisque, which is predominantly rural.
Source: *Sud Quotidien* (2007).

Table 4.4 focuses within the department of Dakar and highlights that Wade's success was less pronounced in middle- and upper-class neighborhoods, such as Mermoz-Sacre Coeur and Fann-Point E. This coincides with observations that upper-class intellectuals became alienated by his autocratic rule. In these neighborhoods, his support was less than or equivalent to that obtained by all opposition parties combined. At the same time, however, Table 4.4 illustrates that no one opposition party proved a favorite among the Dakarois. Instead, Idrissa Seck and Ousmane Tanor Dieng split their support, often equally, within most neighborhoods.

Most opposition parties decried Wade's victory as fraudulent and boycotted the June 2007 legislative elections. However, sixty independent observers from the Economic Community of West African States declared that the election had been "sufficiently free and transparent" and noted that although some discrepancies had occurred, they were not enough to cast doubt on the results (EIU 2007c). Moreover, Galvan (2009) notes that most Senegalese appeared to accept the vote's legitimacy because unlike during the 1980s and 1990s, no mobs of angry, unemployed youth emptied onto the streets to denounce the results. RADDHO, which is a Dakar-based NGO dedicated to promoting human rights in Africa and helped monitor the 2007 elections, concurred that the elections occurred in a general atmosphere of peace and tranquility (RADDHO 2007).

Table 4.4. *Vote Shares in Dakar's Communes in 2007 Presidential Elections (%)*

Communes d'Arrondisements	Wade	Opposition Candidates					
		Seck	Dieng	Niasse	Sagna	Savane	Bathily
Biscuiterie	55.3	16.4	17.6	3.9	1.0	1.1	1.9
Camberene	47.2	25.3	13.2	9.2	0.5	0.9	0.9
Dieuppeul-Derklé	48.7	18.8	17.3	6.2	1.8	1.1	1.8
Fann-Point E-Amité	44.3	18.1	17.5	7.6	2.1	1.4	2.5
Gorée	46.0	18.7	19.6	4.9	1.6	1.0	1.8
Grand Dakar	57.1	17.8	13.0	4.1	2.5	1.3	1.5
Grand Yoff	54.6	16.0	15.9	4.8	3.0	1.6	1.8
Guele Tapee-Fass	55.5	17.9	15.8	3.0	1.5	1.2	1.7
HLM	49.7	17.6	20.3	5.1	0.7	0.9	1.9
Hann Bel Air	51.4	21.4	18.3	4.2	1.1	1.3	1.8
Medina	56.0	16.1	16.4	3.8	0.6	1.1	1.9
Mermoz-Sacre Coeur	43.5	16.7	24.4	8.5	3.2	1.5	3.0
Ngor	66.1	12.1	11.8	3.7	0.8	1.0	1.3
Ouakam	54.8	17.7	14.6	5.1	2.4	1.1	2.1
Parcelles Assainies	52.3	18.6	13.2	7.6	2.8	1.1	1.2
Patte d'Oie	50.2	20.4	16.1	5.1	1.6	1.0	1.5
Plateau	57.8	13.2	16.8	3.9	1.2	1.7	1.4
SICAP Liberté	47.6	16.4	19.1	6.1	3.0	1.7	1.3
Yoff	53.9	19.6	15.8	4.6	0.9	1.0	1.3

Source: Data provided by the Ministry of the Interior, Republic of Senegal.

"THE LIVING ROOM OPPOSITION"

Instead of massive fraud on behalf of the PDS, Wade's ability to win a majority of votes in Dakar and other urban areas during the 2007 elections was predominantly due to the lackluster performance of Senegal's main opposition parties. Although Wade achieved very little for the urban poor, no one opposition party was able to generate the necessary level of momentum required to transform widespread urban disgruntlement with the status quo into an electoral advantage. As Galvan (2009: 5) observes, "Divided and demoralized, the opposition has no real platform from which to criticize President Wade and his party." Likewise, Magrin (2007) claimed that the vacuum created by the opposition was one of the key factors in this election. Instead of the populist strategy employed by Wade in 2000, personalistic linkages characterized the PS, AFP, and Rewmi and thereby caused a split in votes amongst these parties, which all appeared relatively similar to the electorate. The programmatic linkages used by the traditional leftist parties, such as LD-MPT, PIT, and AJ/PADS, relied on an outdated socialist message that exhibited a low level of congruence with the urban poor's everyday priorities.

Three main qualities characterize all of the opposition parties and reduce their appeal to the urban poor. First, although they consistently criticize Wade's performance, they offer no indication of what distinct policy alternatives they would offer if voted into office. In the view of a local political analyst, Ebrima Sall, "Personalities of the leaders have come to crystallize the whole identities of these parties. . . . It's been a serious indictment of the political class to say that the politicians are all the same" (interview with Sall, 2008).

Secondly, in the seven years preceding the 2007 elections, Senegal's opposition parties predominantly relied on civilized discourse as the main means of attacking the failings of the PDS. Mamador Thior, editor in chief at Radio-Télévision Sénégalaise, therefore labels this as the tendency to be an *opposition de salon*, or a "living room opposition" (interview with Thior, 2008). Instead of descending into the streets with other angry Dakarois when the cost-of-living increases or blackouts become intolerable, the opposition frequently chose to issue joint statements decrying Wade's policies. For example, in 2002 the opposition formed the Assises politiques de l'Alternance to critique the direction Wade was taking the country after only two years in office (Sow 2002). Three years later, political parties joined civil society groups, journalists, and concerned academics in the Pacte Républicain, which intended to demonstrate commitment to the democratic principles of the Republic and social peace. In the wake of the 2007 elections, about eighty organizations, including the opposition parties and civil society organizations, came together in nationwide political consultations known as the Assises Nationales. This initiative aimed to debate the main social, economic, and political issues affecting the country.

The overall impression of such activities is that the opposition rarely makes genuine sacrifices when poor Senegalese are marching in the streets. An editorial published in the traditionally pro-opposition newspaper, *Le Quotidien*, decried the opposition's lack of imagination: "The opposition is content with issuing incendiary communiqués to the police office, noisily intervening on the radio, and diplomatic visits" (Aziz Tall 2008: 9). By remaining the reserve of educated elites, such undertakings fail to incorporate the broader urban population, who may be too uneducated or busy laboring in the informal sector to even know that the opposition is involved in such efforts.[10] At the same time, precisely because so many opposition parties are involved in the same initiatives, they become virtually indistinguishable.

Thirdly, despite the fact that three opposition leaders were formerly ministers of urbanization, most of the opposition parties accord very little priority to addressing urban poverty.[11] During an opposition roundtable in March 2003, opposition parties such as the PS, AFP, and PIT published a declaration concluding that the poor performance of agriculture constituted the PDS's greatest failure (*Le Soleil* 2003). In the run-up to the 2007 elections, a number of opposition parties joined in a coalition known as the Coalition populaire pour l'alternance (CPA) and lobbied for greater attention to rural poverty (interview with Faye, 2008). During the 2007 campaigns, no opposition party addressed urban poverty and urban development:

> During the [2007] electoral campaign, some journalists asked the different parties what were their policies for addressing urban poverty. They [the opposition parties] spoke a lot about rural poverty but not about urban poverty.... I have never seen an [opposition] candidate that has elaborated in a clear manner the need to address urban poverty. They talk more about national issues, especially for presidential elections. (Interview with Tall, 2008)

The following two subsections further illustrate these characteristics by first focusing on the three opposition parties that obtained the highest results in Dakar during the 2007 elections: Rewmi, PS, and AFP. In order to emphasize that these opposition parties rely on personalistic linkages, I focus on their espoused ideology, who represents their main constituency base, and their views on urban poverty and the poor. Then, I highlight the lack of congruence between the urban poor and messages espoused by three of Senegal's most established leftist parties: AJ-PADS, LD-MPT, and PIT. Both types of opposition parties largely confirm Antoine Tine's (2005: 129) observation that Senegalese political parties "are within the hands of political elites who are most often accused of being incapable of thinking about the social realities of the most deprived classes and of proposing adequate social projects."

---

[10] For example, Chapter 5 highlights that a majority of the urban poor had never even heard about the Assises Nationales.

[11] Moustapha Niasse (AFP) and Robert Sagna (DS) were urbanization ministers under the PS. Amath Dansokho (PIT) was urbanization minister once under the PS and again briefly in the early period of cohabitation with the PDS in 2000.

The Heavyweight Contenders: Rewmi, PS, and AFP

Internal party rivalries led to the emergence of many of Senegal's current opposition parties. For instance, in 1996, Abdou Diouf appointed Ousmane Tanor Dieng as the PS secretary general. Along with other grievances mentioned earlier, this decision was one of the motivations for Moustapha Niasse to leave the PS and form the AFP in 1999. Idrissa Seck followed a similar trajectory by staunchly supporting the PDS for his entire career and then establishing Rewmi in 2006 after he was released from jail. Consequently, both AFP and Rewmi represent vehicles for the personal ambitions of their leaders rather than institutions established to address genuine societal grievances.

The personal nature of these political parties is reflected in their lack of specific platforms. Hélène Tine, the official representative for the AFP, notes that social democracy characterizes her party, which campaigned on a nebulous motto of "Faith, patriotism, and solidarity" (interview with Tine, 2008). In declaring his candidacy in 2007 for the presidency, Moustapha Niasse made ten promises to Senegalese citizens: (1) restoring the credibility of the state; (2) employment creation; (3) lowering the price of staple goods; (4) reinvigorating agricultural production; (5) improving the country's road system; (6) a more judicious allocation of resources to health, education, research, culture, and sport; (7) creating integrated management and development zones to improve service delivery in every region of the country; (8) restoring peace in Casamance; (9) reestablishing security on both Senegal's borders and within its urban areas; and (10) employing diplomacy to improve development, security, peace, and good relations with its neighbors (Niasse 2007). Although some of these promises are relevant to the urban poor, the focus on agricultural production and improving the road system is more applicable to rural residents, and many of the other pledges are targeted to more middle-class voters concerned with diplomacy, security, and the credibility of the state. In other words, the AFP's promises were all-encompassing, pledging to provide a set of valence goods that would appeal to everyone. In this way, they failed to differentiate Niasse from the other opposition parties.

Indeed, the AFP's goals are not particularly different from those of Rewmi, which campaigned on a message to "Restore Hope." According to Rewmi's representative, Omar Sarr, the party promotes education, training, health, and agriculture (interview with Sarr, 2008). His colleague Waly Fall adds that a party ideology is not particularly necessary for Rewmi:

Rewmi is not a leftist party, it's not a liberal party. The only ideology that is viable here and in all countries in the world is how to improve the lives of the population.

What are the efforts that the state should engage in? What are the sacrifices that the population should engage in? And a system of management that is fair and equitable and which allows a majority of the population to get out of their current living conditions. (Interview with Fall, 2008)

Although the PS possessed much stronger historical and ideological foundations, its party platform became even further muddled in the aftermath of the 2000 elections. In fact, when the PDS originally entered office in 2000, a number of PS cadres defected to it, in a process known as *transhumance,* which facetiously refers to the predictable movement of goats to better grazing lands (Galvan 2009). If ideological affinities were more pronounced, such a shifting of party affiliations would presumably be less feasible.

Ousmane Tanor Dieng of the PS ran on the vague slogan of "A sure president." According to Abdoulaye Vilane, a PS spokesman, the party follows the AFP in professing a social democratic orientation. But what this means in terms of practicalities remains unclear. For him, the PS platform is "socialist in the terms of humanity, justice, democracy, and progress and liberty in the fullest sense" (interview with Vilane, 2008). When asked the policy goals of the PS, Vilane explained, "We want law and order to prevail, for democracy to prevail, the separation of powers to prevail, justice to prevail, legality to prevail, solidarity to prevail, transparency to prevail, and good governance to prevail" (interview with Vilane, 2008). For Ibrahima Sall, a former minister of planning under Diouf and a counselor for the PS, the party is distinguished by the fact that it is the most committed to fighting against Wade. However, what exactly the PS is fighting for remains unclear: "It [the PS] fights for justice, equality, *things like that.* But, it doesn't have a precise, specific program" (interview with Sall, 2008).[12]

Given these generalities, differentiating among the parties is difficult, which is acknowledged by all of the parties' representatives. Aissata Tall Sall, who is the chargé of communication for the PS, admitted that because they are all committed to social democracy, there is no true philosophical difference between her party and the rest of the opposition. She recognized that the party's challenge remains distinguishing its policy projects from those of the PDS and communicating this difference more clearly to the Senegalese people (interview with Tall Sall, 2008). The AFP's Tine concurred that there is no substantial ideological difference among the opposition parties because they are all more or less "social democratic" (interview with Tine, 2008). Abdou Latif Coulibaly, a well-known journalist and fierce critic of Wade, clarifies that "the AFP is made up of people

---

12 Emphasis in italics added.

who left the PS. At their base, they have the same ideology and approach, theory, and doctrine. The area of difference that distinguishes one from the other is the experience of the people who lead the parties" (interview with Coulibaly, 2008).

None of these opposition parties specifically targets the urban poor as a key constituency base. Because the AFP was formed by elites who previously worked in civil society organizations, the party's main constituency base consists of intellectuals and university professors, as well as residents in the region of Kaolack, which is where the party began its 2007 campaign (interview with Tine, 2008). According to Coulibaly, "Moustapha Niasse is the best of all of them but the people said 'no.' But, he's also responsible for that. He is a great man but he's detached from the reality of the true Senegalese. He spent a lot of his time overseas" (interview with Coulibaly, 2008). Indeed, during the year prior to the 2007 elections, Niasse was a member of the United Nations team negotiating peace in the Democratic Republic of the Congo and the Great Lakes region, spending much of his time outside of the country (Diongue, Thiobane, and Dione 2007). This certainly did not help his party become better known to the Senegalese in general and the urban poor in particular.

Both the PS and Rewmi claim to focus on a very broad range of constituents, but not specifically the urban poor. At its founding, peasants, pastoralists, and fishermen comprised the PS's main source of votes (interview with Tall Sall, 2008). However, since its defeat in 2000, the PS's Abdoulaye Vilane claims that his party's discourse now "addresses all the Senegalese," including youth, women, and the middle classes. As for the poor in Dakar, Vilane adopts a more disparaging tone, noting that "there are a lot of people there but people live as though they are in a village. Their mentality, their treatment of the environment, etcetera, it's always anarchic" (interview with Vilane, 2008). Similarly, the former PS Minister of Planning, Ibrahima Sall, claims that Dakar's urban poor are simply rural migrants with an "anti-citizen" and "antidemocratic" mentality (interview with Sall, 2008). Both sentiments hint at the old PS elitism that Wade steered to his advantage in 2000 when he rallied the urban poor with a populist strategy. Instead of focusing on urban areas, the PS launched its 2007 campaign in the rural province of Louga (interview with Faye, 2008).

Rewmi launched its 2007 campaign in Thiès, which, as noted earlier, is where Idrissa Seck is mayor. In fact, Thiès was the one region where Wade did not obtain an outright majority in 2007 and where Remwi obtained 33 percent of the votes (*Sud Quotidien* 2007). In general however, Sarr states that "Senegal as a whole" represents Rewmi's constituency base (interview with Sarr, 2008). His colleague, Waly Fall, concurs: "Rewmi has a panoramic ambition. We traverse issues that appeal to all.... We are all Senegalese" (interview with Fall, 2008).

These three parties also share a similar outlook to Zambia's personalistic parties regarding the best way to help the urban poor: improve rural areas. For instance, the PS emphasizes that to prevent people from coming to the cities, the conditions for success need to be established in the countryside (interview with Vilane, 2008). Sarr is even blunter about Rewmi's approach: "You know, urban poverty is due to extreme poverty in the rural areas so I think we should attack the problem at its roots, going to the rural areas and finding solutions for the rural populations so that they can have local solutions to their development problems" (interview with Sarr, 2008). The AFP's Tine likewise claims that greater investment is needed in individuals' home localities so that they are not convinced to migrate to the city (interview with Tine, 2008).

All three parties' perspectives tend to contradict the contemporary realities of Senegal's urbanization process. Although the country's rate of urbanization has increased, this is no longer primarily due to rural-to-urban migration but more to natural population growth (ANSD 2005). Furthermore, augmenting the attractiveness of rural areas in the hopes of discouraging urban migration is no different than many of Wade's own policies in this domain, including REVA. As such, these opposition parties not only fail to provide concrete details for combating existing urban poverty but also advocate the same emphasis on rural development as the incumbent they all oppose.

Finally, the personalistic nature of all these parties manifests through a party organization centered on its leaders. In the view of P. Mbow (2008: 167), "Parties never turn out their own leaderships, and that needs to change. Most of those who currently run Senegal's parties are incapable of practicing democracy." Indeed, the inability of cadres to advance within their own party structure contributes to the country's proliferation of parties. For instance, Robert Sagna left the PS and formed the party Démocratie et solidarité (DS) in order to compete as a presidential candidate in 2007 because it was not possible to challenge Dieng. M. Diop (2006) notes that Dieng is deft at resisting attacks by adversaries who try to reduce his power, and he firmly controls which candidates run on the PS ticket. A similar pattern hampers the AFP. In fact, individuals such as Massokhna Kane, Cheikh Mouhamadou, and Mamoune Niasse all quit to create their own parties or join the PDS (interview with Badara Diop, 2008). Rewmi is effectively synonymous with Seck and would most likely not survive without him at the helm.

Thus, the three main opposition parties in Senegal at the time of the 2007 elections possessed relatively vague platforms and ideologies, with few ideas for addressing urban poverty. Moreover, the urban poor in particular were not specified as a constituency base and all three parties launched their campaigns outside of Dakar. Consequently, the main distinction among these parties is the personalities of their leaders, who in turn exercise a firm grip on their parties' internal power structures.

Le Pôle de Gauche

The parties of the *pôle de gauche*, or the traditional left, include AJ-PADS, LD-MPT, and PIT, and none have ever possessed much support outside of Dakar. Led by Landing Savané, the AJ/PADS emerged in 1991 from a merger of socialist and Maoist groups. PIT was formed in 1981 by dissidents of PAI and recognized by the Soviet Union as Senegal's official Communist party. The LD-MPT was also legally recognized in 1981 and was originally a self-proclaimed Marxist-Leninist group whose leader, Abdoulaye Bathily, vehemently opposed Senegal's interaction with the World Bank and IMF during the height of structural adjustment (Banks et al. 2008).

As more programmatic parties, leaders play a more muted role than they do in the PS, AFP, or Rewmi. For example, when Savané accepted a series of ministerial roles in Wade's government after the 2000 elections, the party began splintering because many party stalwarts argued that he was betraying the party's ideology by allying with an avowedly liberal party (interview with Badara Diop, 2008). Importantly, defectors left not because they could not obtain adequate power within the party but because of their commitment to its ideology. PIT did not present its leader, Amath Dansokho, as a candidate in the last presidential elections but rather participated in the CPA coalition. Ibrahima Sène, the representative in charge of PIT's social and economic affairs, emphasized that this was done to underscore that the party does not exist to serve its leader but rather a larger purpose, which is to enhance "the consciousness of salaried workers" (interview with Sène, 2008).

Historically, these leftist parties possessed strong ties to the country's unions, which hold implications for their contemporary constituency base. The LD-MPT, for instance, retains links with Senegal's main teachers' union and, according to the party's spokeswoman, originated as an elitist party vested in organizing teachers and students (interview with Wade, 2008). AJ/PADS largely consists of the same social base, including left-of-center academics, students, and professionals (Galvan 2009). Sène claims that 80 percent of PIT's members are "salaried workers," who labor in the formal sector and predominantly belong to unions. From his perspective, salaried workers are more involved in a "modern" system of production and communication, understand and fight for their rights and obligations in the workplace, and experience a sense of solidarity that manifests through organization in unions. In turn, union participation helps raise their social and political consciousness (interview with Sène, 2008). Such views largely confirm Graham's (1994: 127) observation that "most of the [Senegalese] Marxist parties, which in theory should represent the interests of the poor … are not particularly attuned to needs of the poor, whom they consider the *lumpenproletariat.*"

The abstract nature of the messages espoused by these leftist parties precludes their comprehension by the urban poor. For example, during its previous incarnation as PAI, PIT's goals included achieving political independence from France and transforming Senegal into a Communist society. Today, PIT lobbies for regional integration and economic nationalism within West Africa as a means of achieving Senegal's economic independence. Furthermore, the party aims for a fair legal system that protects the rights of workers, as according to Sène, the conditions for achieving socialism can only be attained if the rights of workers are respected (interview with Sène, 2008). Given that many of the urban poor lack education and work outside the formal sector, these issues are not priorities, and concepts such as "socialism" and "liberalism" demonstrate little resonance (interview with Thior, 2008).

Consequently, the PDS largely discounts these parties as real challengers. For example, the PDS deputy proclaimed that "the ideology of Bathily doesn't work" (interview with Gaye, 2008). Successive presidential election results support this observation. In Dakar, which is the core base of these parties, neither Bathily nor Savané obtained more than 2 percent of the vote in the 2007 presidential elections. According to Galvan's (2009: 3) analysis of those elections, "Neither [Bathily nor Savané] represented serious challengers to Wade; both hoped to be the 'dark horse' whose meticulously articulated and *largely irrelevant ideological message* would finally, somehow, catch fire with the voters" (emphasis added).

The future of these leftist parties remains unclear. On the one hand, Aiwa Wade of the LD-MPT admits that "the population does not really understand the message of the left and its meaning for them" and therefore hopes her party can "find a message to convince the masses." She further recognizes that although the LD-MPT was formerly well situated in Dakar because that was where the intelligentsia concentrated, the changing "physiognomy" of the city, including the growth of the informal sector, means that the party can no longer simply focus on intellectuals and hope to win votes (interview with Wade, 2008). On the other hand, if these traditional leftist parties, with shrinking union membership bases and an outdated message, try to amend their approach, it remains unclear how they would remain distinct from their better performing but less ideologically oriented counterparts.

CONCLUSION

By comparing the strategy of the PDS over time with the various linkages used by today's opposition parties in Senegal, this chapter again highlighted the advantages of a populist strategy for mobilizing the urban poor. Like Zambia, rapid urbanization in Senegal and economic contraction in the 1990s explains why more than a quarter of the country's population currently resides in Dakar and labors in the low-wage informal sector. Through his charisma and policy discourse focused on providing jobs, sanitation, water, and better housing, Abdoulaye Wade successfully targeted an increasingly disgruntled and impoverished urban population in the 2000 elections. Despite his age and high level of education, Wade privileged the role of the youth and the Baol Baol model of socioeconomic advancement through his use of urban Wolof and a peripatetic mode of campaigning in Dakar's streets. Despite previous periods of cohabitation with the PS, Wade portrayed himself as an outsider fighting against the technocratic and intellectualistic political establishment in order to finally address the unmet needs of Dakar's poor.

As seen in Table 4.5, this approach was much more successful than the technique used by subsequent opposition parties during the 2007 presidential elections. In those elections, Wade was theoretically at an electoral disadvantage. Many of his promises on jobs and housing failed to materialize during his first term, and he instead concentrated on large-scale construction projects with few spillovers for the poor. At the same time, the cost of living rose, especially on key utilities such as electricity and water, and the number of urban poor only decreased marginally.

But the country's main opposition parties failed to copy Wade's previous populist strategy and instead employed two types of linkages. Parties such as Rewmi, PS, and AFP relied on personalistic linkages and therefore emphasized the role of their leaders as their main axis of differentiation. With vague promises intended to appeal to all Senegalese and no clear

Table 4.5. *Summarizing Interactions of Opposition Parties with the Urban Poor*

Election Year	Incumbent Party (*Leader*)	Opposition Party (*Leader*)	Interaction	Outcome
2000	PS (*Diouf*)	PDS (*Wade*)	Populist strategy	The PDS wins overwhelmingly in Dakar in both 1st and 2nd rounds of elections
		AFP (*Niasse*)	Personalistic linkages	
		LD-MPT (*Bathily*), PIT (*Dansokho*), AJ-PADS (*Savané*)	Programmatic linkages	
2007	PDS (*Wade*)	AFP (*Niasse*), PS (*Dieng*), Rewmi (*Seck*)	Personalistic linkages	The PDS wins more than 50 percent of the vote in the Dakar metropolitan areas; no 2nd round of elections is needed
		LD-MPT (*Bathily*), PIT (*Dansokho*), AJ-PADS (*Savané*)	Programmatic linkages	

messages directly targeted at the urban poor, not one of these three parties was able to garner a majority of votes among Dakarois in those elections. The few neighborhoods of Dakar where the opposition did collectively outperform Wade tended to be more affluent and therefore not where the city's low-wage, informal-sector workers reside. More programmatic linkages were used by the PIT, AJ-PADS, and LD-MPT, which advocated messages aimed at enhancing the rights of salaried workers and achieving economic nationalism. Because these parties' constituencies are found among unionized workers within the professional classes, they demonstrated a negligible ability to capture votes from Dakar's poor. Thus, many voters turned to the paternalistic Gorgui rather than stake their faith on the opposition.

FIVE

The View from Below

How the Urban Poor React to Political Party Strategies

Chapters 3 and 4 relied on interviews with political elites and other key informants to illustrate the relationships between political parties and the urban poor in Zambia and Senegal, respectively. However, the perspective of the urban poor was largely missing from this narrative. Therefore, this chapter utilizes a novel set of primary data collected from a total of 400 market workers in the cities of Dakar and Lusaka to illustrate how the urban poor view their respective country's political parties and understand why they voted for a particular candidate in the last elections. The two surveys are supplemented with more in-depth interviews, with a total of sixty individuals in slum and shanty settlements whose responses are used to provide qualitative details on each country's party landscape.[1]

The benefits of the survey findings from the market workers are twofold. First, they help test the four models of voting behavior presented in Chapter 2, which were vote buying, ethnic alignments, retrospective economic voting, and associational membership. Secondly, the survey responses allow me to examine the two causal mechanisms that previous chapters have argued facilitate the appeal of populist strategies: congruence and differentiation.

As specified in Chapter 2, congruence refers to the distance between a party's campaign messages and the issues most important to voters. Because typical measures of congruence (see Powell 2009) are not available in the African context, this study measures congruence in a number of ways. Greater congruence occurs when a particular party is repeatedly identified by voters as concerned with the policy priorities specific to the urban poor.

---

[1] This data was collected in Dakar from August to December 2008 and in Lusaka between January and April 2009. In Dakar, interviews were conducted in French, Wolof, and Pulaar and in Lusaka, they occurred in English, Bemba, and Nyanja.

Moreover, congruence exists when a majority of respondents claim they supported a specific candidate first and foremost because of his or her policy proposals rather than the candidate's personality, region of origin, or influences of family members and friends. Chapters 3 and 4 described the campaign messages that various political parties in both Zambia and Senegal espoused to the urban poor. If those variables that most influenced a voter's choice of candidate correspond with the campaign promises offered by a particular party, then this represents another indication of congruence.

Differentiation refers to the perception of substantive distinctions among political parties, especially with regards to policy. Again, there are two ways to measure differentiation. If one opposition party receives considerably more votes than any other, then that indicates that one party significantly stands out in the minds of the urban poor. However, if parties split votes among respondents, then that reveals no particular party stood out for the urban poor. In addition, if survey respondents directly report observing variation across parties with respect to policy, rather than simply with respect to the personal backgrounds of party leaders, then greater differentiation exists.

If the argument central to this study is correct, then survey respondents in Zambia would not overwhelmingly just support the opposition but specifically support the PF, which has relied on a populist strategy. In other words, the urban poor would not simply be attracted to any opposition party but to the opposition party that espoused a message focused on their priorities. The PF would be identified as a party interested in improving living conditions for the urban poor as well as one that is distinguished by its social and economic policies. Those variables that are significantly correlated with support for Sata will encapsulate issues, such as service delivery and employment, which the urban poor themselves have identified as areas of concern and Sata in turn focused on during his campaign. At the same time, in Senegal, where the opposition did not use a populist strategy in the 2007 elections, no opposition party should receive a substantial share of votes. Even though services and jobs are equally important for the urban poor in Dakar, they will not be issues that significantly influence support for the opposition because these are not issues on which the Senegalese opposition parties exclusively focused during their electoral campaigns. Little differentiation will exist among the opposition parties, and no one party will be viewed as extensively interested in improving living conditions for the poor. The incumbent, Abdoulaye Wade, will not be chosen because of his policy achievements on behalf of the urban poor but due to the lack of alternative options.

The results confirm that Lusaka's urban poor overwhelmingly voted for Sata, and a majority did so because of the PF's policy manifesto. At the same time, Dakar's urban poor acknowledge that Senegal's opposition parties, which relied on either personalistic or programmatic linkages, were relatively indistinguishable. Few voted for the opposition and those who did spread their votes across a number of different candidates. The rest of the chapter describes how the surveys were conducted and then presents the specific findings in each city.

SURVEY METHODOLOGY

The two surveys used for this chapter relied on an emic-etic approach whereby a common set of questions were asked in both countries and supplemented by country-specific questions. In general, the surveys asked about respondents' demographic and educational backgrounds, working and living conditions, perspectives on the ruling party's performance, whether they voted in the most recent presidential elections, who they supported and why, whether and how candidates campaigned in their neighborhoods, and how they perceived their country's opposition parties. A full copy of the questionnaire used in each city can be found in Appendix C.

Traditionally, cross-national surveys pose certain difficulties. Cultural norms can dictate what questions are appropriate in some countries are not in others (Johnson and van de Vijver 2003). Interpretation of the features that constitute abstract concepts, such as "democracy" or "freedom," may vary significantly across countries (King et al. 2004). Ordinal response categories, such as those common with Likert scales, can be biased across countries when some groups have higher standards about what constitutes, for example, the definition of "strongly agree" or "strongly disagree" (King and Wand 2007).

In the present study, many of these issues were not problematic. For instance, although direct inquiries about voting can sometimes engender suspicion by respondents, the relatively democratic environment in both countries, and the fact that such questions were posed after rather than before the elections, resulted in very few refusals to answer questions about this topic. The only abstract concept used in the surveys was "party manifesto" in Zambia and "party platform" in Senegal.[2] In both cases, respondents were asked to describe their understanding of these concepts

---

[2] Manifesto is more a common term in Zambia; platform is more often found in the political discourse in Senegal.

in an open-ended fashion so that differences in interpretation could be readily uncovered. Likert scales were employed, but the responses to such questions were applied to understand voting behavior in separate statistical analyses for each country rather than in a cross-country statistical analysis. In other words, the analyses capture the political preferences and behavior of Dakarois and Lusakans according to their own culturally specific understandings.

Other challenges posed by survey research include a respondent's inability to remember relevant information or a propensity to provide biased answers (see Tourangeau et al. 2000). The latter circumstances can be particularly problematic for surveys that ask about political participation, including whether one voted in a prior election, because of the respondent's assumption that there is a socially desirable response (see Karp and Brockington 2005). However, although experimental research is also valuable for uncovering voting inclinations and political values (e.g., Wantchekon 2003; Vicente and Wantchekon 2009), surveys still remain one of the main tools for uncovering individuals' past political participation and the decisions that informed that participation (see Bratton et al. 2010; Dalton and Anderson 2011; Peffley and Rohrschneider 2003). Moreover, in each city, I oversaw the administration of each and every interview, which helped to minimize any potential biases within each sample that could be otherwise caused by variation in the enumerators.

Survey Sampling Technique

The sampling frame for this study included individuals who were eligible to vote based on age and citizenship and labored as informal sector workers in the markets of Lusaka and Dakar. An alternative approach, which would involve sampling households, was not possible for two reasons. First, household-level poverty data disaggregated to the neighborhood level is not available for these two cities, thereby precluding identification ex ante of a sampling frame of poor households. Secondly, a majority of those who constitute the urban poor spend most days away from home in order to earn a living. Focusing on households can therefore lead to an oversampling of those who are too old or too sick to work as well as women taking care of children and housework.[3]

---

[3]   The Afrobarometer public opinion survey project has also noted that in urban areas, household surveys during the week can lead to an undersampling of men (see "Sampling Methods" at http://www.afrobarometer.org/sampling.html).

Dakar and Lusaka are the largest agglomerations in their respective countries, meaning that a sample selected within them, rather than in secondary towns and cities, should be broadly representative of the general urban poor. Moreover, the informal sector comprises a large share of employment in these two cities. In Lusaka province, 69 percent of the population depends on the nonagricultural informal sector, which is higher than any other province in the country (CSO 2007: 46). According to the Senegalese statistical agency, the informal sector is by far the largest employer in Dakar, with 76 percent of the city's population dependent upon it (ANSD 2007b: 48).[4]

Markets represent an appropriate location for sampling informal workers because they are almost entirely comprised of such individuals. The prime occupation of those in the markets is vending, including retail goods such as clothing and house wares, agricultural products, and self-made foods and beverages. In Zambia, a huge proportion of retail trade occurs in *salauala* or secondhand clothing. However, one can also find tailors, carpenters, butchers, hairdressers, shoe shiners, and those providing nontraditional services, such as charging mobile phones, within the markets. In addition, sometimes within this diverse setting are students assisting a family member's business, unregistered taxi drivers, and a few unemployed.

This working population was surveyed according to a two-stage, clustered sampling procedure. In the first stage, ten markets were selected throughout each city. Cluster sampling is an appropriate technique when the working population is so large that it would be prohibitively costly and time intensive to randomly survey all of it (Rea and Parker 2005), and subsampling through multiple stages is a common approach under circumstances where a list of the population is completely lacking (Groves et al. 2004). Due to the limited size of the survey samples, clusters (i.e., markets) were deliberately, rather than randomly, chosen. Lindberg and Morrison (2008) also adopt this approach, arguing that when working with relatively small sample sizes, deliberately selecting clusters can ensure a representative level of coverage that cannot be guaranteed through random selection.

The chosen markets in each city are presented in Table 5.1 and reflect diversity in terms of geographical coverage and market type. In Lusaka, there are four classifications of markets, ranging from urban markets that

---

[4] Both countries share a similar definition of the informal sector. In Zambia, it refers to employed persons who "were not entitled to paid leave, pension, gratuity and social security, and worked in an establishment employing 5 persons or less" (CSO 2006: 18). In Senegal, it refers to those who lack written accounts; are not registered as a business; and face precarious working conditions that lack water, electricity, or a telephone, and social security (DPS 2003: 1, 3, 8–10).

Table 5.1. *Summary of Selected Markets in Each City*

Dakar, Senegal

Market	Arrondissement	Market Specialty	Share of Market's Workers who Live in the same Arrondissement (%)[b]
Grand Yoff	Parcelles Assainies	Multiple products	50
Gueule Tapée	Parcelles Assainies	Multiple products	90
HLM	Grand Dakar	Fabric	35
Kermel	Plateau	Artwork	30
Marche Zinc	Pikine Dagoudane	Multiple products	85
Ouakam	Almadies	Multiple products	90
Sandaga	Plateau	Multiple products	10
Syndicat	Pikine Dagoudane	Fruits and nuts	70
Thiaroye	Thiaroye	Multiple products	35
Tilène	Plateau	Food products	45

Lusaka, Zambia

Market	Constituency	Market Type[a]	Share of Market's Workers who Live in the same Constituency (%)[b]
Chawama	Chawama	District	90
Chelstone	Munali	Subdistrict	100
Chilenje	Kabwata	District	90
Chipata	Mandevu	Subdistrict	95
Kabwata	Kabwata	Inter-area	60
Kanyama	Kanyama	District	95
Kaunda Square	Munali	District	90
Mandevu	Mandevu	District	85
Matero	Matero	District	100
Soweto	Kanyama	Urban	35

Sources: [a] These market types are derived from the European Development Fund (1996).
[b] These shares are derived from the author's survey results.

attract vendors from all corners of the city to subdistrict markets that only cater to residents in a specific neighborhood. Most of Lusaka's markets are found on the periphery of the city, located near unplanned, high-density and low-income areas (Nchito 2006). In Dakar, those markets sampled included ones in the poorer suburb of Pikine, more residential markets in key neighborhoods, and a few major markets in the center of the city. Moreover, Dakar contains a number of specialized markets in which a majority of vendors focus on selling a certain type of merchandise, such as artwork, fabric, and food. These were purposely included because studies elsewhere in Africa have demonstrated that different subsectors of the informal economy can both attract particular ethnolinguistic groups and engender disparate responses by the state (see Macharia 1997).[5]

Cluster sampling can be problematic because those within a cluster may be more homogeneous, and therefore less statistically independent, than those across clusters. One way to mitigate any possible "design effect" variance between clusters is to only sample a small but fixed number of respondents over a wider number of clusters (Groves et al. 2004). As such, during the second stage of sampling, twenty respondents were interviewed in each market, and they were chosen according to a random sampling technique stratified by gender.[6] Research in other areas of the world highlights that gender plays an important role in voting behavior and that female voters can have different preferences for candidates or policy proposals than male voters (e.g., Inglehart and Norris 2000). Moreover, in the markets, there tends to be a form of gender segregation such that women dominate vending in the food and fabric sector and men concentrate on selling cheap manufactured goods or work as shoe shiners, carpenters, and tailors. Stratifying on gender therefore ensured that a diversity of occupations was covered. Unlike other variables, such as ethnolinguistic identity or even age, gender is also the easiest marker for stratification without asking respondents questions ex ante.

In-Depth Interviews with Slum Dwellers

Surveying market workers potentially results in "coverage error" by excluding other groups who should also be considered the urban poor but do not work in the markets. This can potentially create a major bias if those excluded are significantly different from market workers in a way that affects

---

[5]   Clusters should be chosen according to "probability proportional to size" in order to make generalizations about the working population. This means that each cluster's probability of being selected into a sample should be proportional to some known variable (Groves et al. 2004). Because the total populations of markets are unknown and change on a daily basis, the variation in market types and constituencies highlighted in Table 5.1 are characteristics that can be leveraged to ensure a representative sample of market workers.

[6]   Specifically, every other chosen respondent was a woman. According to Levy and Lemeshow (1999), stratified sampling incorporates the simplicity of random sampling as well as greater precision by reducing standard errors in estimation.

their voting behavior (Braun 2003). Consequently, three slums or squatter settlements were selected for in-depth interviews in each city to help detect and adjust for potential bias. Although the settlements all contained low-income residents, they varied in that: a) they were located in different electoral constituencies of their respective city; b) some had a contentious relationship with the state authorities; and c) some had been prime targets for NGO and service-delivery projects supported by international donors. The latter two criteria could potentially influence residents' perceptions of the ruling party's performance. Ten respondents in each settlement were asked similar questions to those of the market workers, for a total of thirty respondents in each city and sixty for the overall study. Where available, descriptions of their responses are included to provide at least illustrative evidence that coverage error did not pose a major problem in the survey with market workers. Furthermore, these interviews were more in-depth and open-ended than those with market workers, offering a qualitative understanding of political beliefs and voting behavior. Table 5.2 provides a brief description of the selected settlements.

CHARACTERISTICS OF SURVEY RESPONDENTS IN ZAMBIA

This section examines key characteristics of the survey respondents in each country. In Zambia, the availability of the 2000 census provides the opportunity to compare characteristics captured in the survey sample with those of the broader population of self-employed vendors within Lusaka.[7] Because 61 percent of those in Lusaka's informal sector concentrate on trade (CSO 2006), vending represents the dominant occupation. Thus, the census was disaggregated into self-employed vendors and sales assistants who live in the district of Lusaka and are both Zambian citizens and eighteen years of age or older.[8]

A number of observations emerge from Table 5.3. First, the survey over-sampled those whose first language falls into the Bemba group and under-sampled those in the Nyanja group. Similarly, with respect to education, it appears that the survey under-sampled those without any education at all.

---

[7] At the time of writing, the 2010 Zambian census had yet to be publicly released.

[8] More specifically, the base data for the calculations are the 2000 census data for Lusaka Province (Province 5). Observations for eligible voters in Lusaka District were isolated and the proportions calculated correspond to individuals who are self-employed in occupations classified as "Salesmen, shop assistants and demonstrators," "Street vendors, canvassers, and newsvendors," and "Sales workers not elsewhere classified." These are occupation codes 451, 452, and 490, respectively, in the census.

Table 5.2. *Summary of Selected Informal Settlements in Each City*

Dakar, Senegal	
Cité Bissap	Located in the Biscuiterie commune, most of Cité Bissap's residents are illegally squatting on land. In March 2008, 24 homes in Cité Bissap were destroyed by a fire, leaving 325 people homeless (Faye 2008).
HLM Montagne	Located in the HLM commune, HLM Montagne's housing consists of cinder-block walls with roofs of cardboard and corrugated steel. Montagne has received some support from the NGO ENDA-*Tiers Monde*.
Baraka	Baraka is situated behind affluent housing in the Liberté 6 extension of the Liberté commune. The residents were evicted from their former location in February 2001 (COHRE 2004).
Lusaka, Zambia	
Chaisa	Chaisa is located in the constituency of Mandevu. In 1987, the Ministry of Local Government and Housing declared Chaisa an Improvement Area, which allowed occupancy licenses to be given as security of tenure to some of the households (Nordin 2004). In recent years, the Japanese donor agency has helped install communal water taps in the compound.
Misisi	Misisi is an illegal, informal settlement located in Chawama constituency and has been consistently threatened with demolition by the government. Misisi has been identified as one of the five worst slums in sub-Saharan Africa and experiences frequent cholera outbreaks.
Kalikiliki	Kalikiliki is an informal settlement located in Munali constituency, in the eastern part of the city and next to the Kalikiliki Dam. In 2002, the Lusaka City Council tried demolishing a number of illegal homes within this compound, and ensuing clashes with the police resulted in the deaths of two teenagers (Myers 2005).

In order to correct for these two design errors, proportional weights are applied to the regressions presented later in this section.[9] Secondly, only an extremely small share of respondents belongs to any type of associations,

---

[9]   Survey weights are commonly applied to inferential statistics in order to address disproportionate sampling (see Hahs-Vaughn 2005; Pfefferman et al. 1998). Without applying weights, parameter estimates will be biased and nonrepresentative of the population of interest, which in this case is informal-sector workers in urban Dakar and Lusaka. The weights applied for the Zambian case were calculated by first determining from the 2000 census what share of the informal sector population in urban Lusaka jointly belongs to a specific education and ethnolinguistic category. These population shares were then divided by the sample shares of respondents who fell into each of these schooling-linguistic categories.

Table 5.3. *Summary of Survey Respondents in Lusaka Markets*

Descriptive Variable	Sample Percentage	Population Percentage from 2000 Census
Gender		
Female	48	45.5
Male	52	54.5
Age		
18–24 years	17.5	22.9
25–30 years	23.5	33.2
31–35 years	20	14.7
36–40 years	17	12.5
More than 40 years	22	16.8
Language Group		
Barotse	4	1.4
Bemba	37.5	24.3
English	0.5	3.3
Mambwe	6.5	1.5
Northwestern	5	1.1
Nyanja	32	63.3
Tonga	8.5	3.8
Tumbuka	5	1.0
Other	1	0.2
Education		
No schooling	2	13
Primary	24	15.3
Secondary	67	68
Post-secondary and vocational	7	3.7
Born in Lusaka?		
Yes	40.5	35.4
No	59.5	64.6
Belong to any association?		
Yes	8.0	–
No	91.9	–

Notes: N = 200 for the sample percentage. The designation of the ethnolinguistic groups follows the procedure used by Zambia's Central Statistical Office.

Table 5.4. *Summary of Voting Behavior in 2008 Presidential Elections*

Did you vote in the presidential elections? (N = 200)	Percentage of all Respondents (2008)
Yes	62.5
No	37.5

Party supported (N = 123)	Percentage who voted (2008)
Movement for Multi-Party Democracy (MMD)	30.9
Patriotic Front (PF)	61.8
United Party for National Development (UPND)	7.3
Heritage Party (HP)	0

Primary reason for not voting (N=77)	Percentage of nonvoters (2008)
No appealing candidates	1.3
Lack of time	22.7
Elections wouldn't be fair	6.7
Favorite candidate wouldn't win	2.7
No matter who wins, nothing will change	6.7
Lacked NRC, voter's card, or both	48.0
Too young	0.0
Jehovah's Witness[a]	5.3
Other[b]	6.7

Source: Author's survey data.
Notes: [a] Jehovah's Witnesses in Zambia are not allowed to vote.
[b] "Other" usually referred to those who were sick, pregnant, or hospitalized.

either work related, religious, neighborhood, or micro-finance.[10] All of this suggests that associational affiliation cannot be a major driving force behind respondents' voting decisions in Zambia.

According to Table 5.4, a majority of respondents voted in the last two presidential elections. In fact, the turnout rates reported by these respondents for both elections exceeded the rates reported by the Electoral Commission of Zambia for Lusaka District as a whole.[11] Of those who did vote, Sata was overwhelmingly the favorite, reflecting the general results

[10] Importantly, respondents were not asked about church attendance, which is quite high in Zambia.
[11] As noted in Chapter 3, the turnout rates for Lusaka District in the 2006 and 2008 elections were 71 and 58 percent, respectively.

for Lusaka as a whole. Although Sata's share of votes was more than double those for the MMD, the MMD still outperformed the UPND by more than threefold. This, along with electoral data presented in Chapter 3, suggests that support for the PF is not simply motivated by an anti-incumbent bias amongst the urban poor. Rather, it is spurred by this constituency's particular attraction to Sata and his party's message.

Of those who did not vote, the main procedural problem was that respondents lacked the requisite identification documents to vote, including a National Registration Card (NRC) and a voter's card.[12] This was particularly problematic in the 2008 elections because the Electoral Commission of Zambia claimed that it was logistically impossible to reopen the electoral register, and therefore those who were not registered in the 2006 elections were effectively disenfranchised in 2008 (Chibamba 2009). Moreover, those who had lost their voting cards in the interim were given only five days to replace them (ECZ 2008). The second reason cited by respondents for not voting was lack of time due to either the fact that they were working or were out of town and could not return in time to cast their vote in Lusaka, where they were registered.

CHARACTERISTICS OF SURVEY RESPONDENTS IN SENEGAL

In Senegal, data from the 2001 Senegalese Household Survey (Enquête Sénégalaise auprès des Ménages-ESAM II) illustrates how the small sample of marketeers compares to the broader population of informal sector workers in Dakar.[13] The right-hand column of Table 5.5 therefore provides characteristics on those Senegalese citizens who are at least eighteen years old, live in the urban region of Dakar, and classified as independently employed or family help and working for an individual or household.[14] This is how the Senegalese Ministry of the Economy and Finance defined members of the informal sector based on findings from the ESAM-II (see DPS 2004: 40 and 94).

---

[12] A Zambian is supposed to receive an NRC at the age of sixteen, which is in turn necessary to obtain a voter's card at the age of eighteen.

[13] The ESAM-II used a multistage stratified random sampling procedure that included 6,624 households and 64,679 individuals. The sampling was designed to allow for population estimates for regions and according to rural/urban distinctions. For more details on the ESAM-II survey, see the Central Survey Catalog at http://www.surveynetwork.org/home.

[14] Specifically, the calculations are based on the individual-level data for observations within the urban region of Dakar for those eighteen years and older and actively working (acthb = 1), independently employed or family help (sitprofp = 2 or sitprofp = 5), and work for an individual or a household (sectactp = 1).

Table 5.5. *Overview of Senegalese Survey Respondents*

Variable	Sample Percentage	2001 ESAM-II
Gender		
Female	48.0	47.0
Male	52.0	53.0
Age		
18–24 years	21.1	17.3
25–30 years	19.6	16.0
31–35 years	10.6	13.7
36–40 years	16.1	12.7
More than 40 years	32.7	40.0
Language Group		
Jola/Diola	0.5	4.0
Mandinka	2.5	4.0
Pulaar	14.5	18.7
Serer	9.0	10.9
Soninke	0.5	1.5
Wolof	71.0	54.9
Other	2.00	6.1
Education		
No schooling	43.7	57.1
Koranic/Language School	18	–
Primary	23.5	26.7
Secondary	13.1	12.1
Postsecondary, including vocational	2.0	3.2
Born in Dakar?		
Yes	37.0	–
No	63.0	–
Belong to any association?		
Yes	25.5	–
No	74.5	–

Notes: N = 200 for the sample percentage.

There are key similarities and differences between the Senegalese and Zambian samples. First, a higher share of Dakar's marketeers lacks any type of education, with about 44 percent of the sample never having attended school. Because a majority of the Senegalese population is Muslim, a share of the survey sample attended Koranic or language schools, which are informal modes of education. Students may begin Koranic school as young as the age of three, with the aim of learning to read and write Koranic verses by rote as well as to internalize the values of obedience, respect, and submission (André and Demonsant 2009). A majority of those who attended language schools did so to learn Arabic. As these informal schools teach a minimum degree of literacy but no numeracy, they offer less education than a formal primary school. Students sometimes attend Koranic or language schools in parallel with their formal education. If a respondent fell into this latter category, then his or her education was coded according to the formal education level. If, however, she or he only attended language school or obtained training in a Koranic school, known as a *daara*, then this was the type of education level assigned to the respondent.

Secondly, the marketplace tends to be concentrated among the young and those more than forty years of age, reflecting that the markets tend to be predominantly occupied by young men vending retail goods and older women selling foodstuffs. Thirdly, the Dakar respondents have a higher rate of participation in associations than their counterparts in Lusaka. A majority of those involved in work associations belonged to UNACOIS, an organization whose history and objectives were discussed in Chapter 4. But most respondents claimed they were not involved in work associations but rather community-based, rotating micro-credit groups, known as *tontines*, or micro-finance organizations such as Partenariat pour la Mobilisation de l'Epargne et du Crédit au Sénégal (PAMECAS) or Credit Mutuel. Just as in the Zambian sample, a little over one-third of these respondents were born in the capital city of Dakar.

The calculations indicate that the survey sample of marketeers is relatively representative of Dakar's informal sector. However, there was an over-sampling of those belonging to the Wolof ethnolinguistic group. Even though the Wolof are the majority in both Dakar and in Senegal overall, they may have been over-sampled to the detriment of other ethnolinguistic groups. Again, a language weight is used to compensate for this in the regressions presented later in this chapter.[15]

Contrary to the protests of many opposition parties, who claimed that the election results must have been manipulated, the voting patterns of these respondents largely emphasize that the urban poor were indeed

---

[15] The language weights were derived by dividing the population share of a language group indicated in the ESAM-II by a sample share of each language grouping provided in Table 5.5.

Table 5.6. *Voting Behavior in the 2007 Elections*

Did you vote in the presidential elections? (N = 200)	Percentage of all respondents
Yes	78.5
No	21.5
Party supported[a] (N = 149)	Percentage of those who voted
Parti Démocratique Sénégalais (PDS)	79.9
Rewmi	11.4
Alliance des Forces des Progrès (AFP)	4.0
Parti Socialiste (PS)	2.7
And-Jëf-Parti Africaine pour la Démocratie et la Socialisme (AJ-PADS)	0.7
Front pour la Socialisme et la Démocratie (FSD)	0.7
War Wi	0.7
Ligue Démocratique Mouvement pour le Parti du Travail (LD-MPT)	0
Primary reason for not voting (N = 43)	Percentage of nonvoters
No appealing candidates	14.0
Lack of time	9.3
Elections wouldn't be fair	0
Favorite candidate wouldn't win	2.3
No matter who wins, nothing will change	4.7
Lacked identity piece, voter's card, or both	34.9
Too young	7.0
Other[b]	27.9

Source: Author's survey data.

Notes: [a] Eight respondents who voted refused to admit who they supported. As such, they are excluded from these calculations.

[b] "Other" referred to those who were sick or professed a lack of interest in politics.

enthusiastic supporters of Wade. Table 5.6 shows that an overwhelming 78 percent of respondents claim to have turned up at the polls. This even exceeds the 72 percent turnout rate for Dakar reported by the official election data. For those who did vote, almost 80 percent were PDS supporters, exceeding the 55 percent who voted for Gorgui in Dakar as a whole (see Chapter 4). This indicates that Wade was particularly popular among this low-income group, and his shares at the city level may have been dampened by the preference of more affluent Dakarois for opposition candidates. Idrissa Seck's Rewmi was the second-most popular choice among the market workers, largely reflecting the broader order of party preferences in both Dakar and the rest of Senegal. Other heavy-contender parties, such as the AFP and the PS, fared less well. Parties belonging to the pôle de gauche, such as Landing Savané's AJ-PADS and Abdoulaye Bathily's LD-MPT, received negligible support, once again confirming that their leftist discourse holds little appeal for subaltern groups. Importantly, among those who did not vote, 14 percent noted they were deterred by the lack of appealing candidates.

REGRESSION SPECIFICATION

In order to analyze voter motivations, a series of multinomial logit regressions were conducted on the survey data described. In the case of Zambia, regressions were conducted on voting decisions in the October 2008 presidential elections. For Senegal, the analysis focused on voting behavior in the February 2007 presidential elections.

Both analyses examined the likelihood of a survey respondent to engage in one of three outcomes: abstention, voting for the incumbent, and voting for the opposition. In addition, each incorporates independent variables that proxy for the alternative schools of thought on voting behavior as well as important confounding factors.

Zambia

In particular, the model for Zambia relies on the following specification:

$$\Pr\left(V_i = 1 \mid Z_i\right)$$
$$\Pr\left(V_i = 2 \mid Z_i\right)$$
$$\Pr\left(V_i = 0 \mid Z_i\right) \text{ base category}$$

where V_i is the polychotomous dependent variable that is equal to 1 if the individual voted for the incumbent at the time, the MMD's Rupiah Banda; equal to 2 if the individual abstained; and the base category is set to those who voted for the PF's Michael Sata. Because only nine respondents, or 7 percent of the sample, voted for the UPND, this third party clearly lacked large-scale appeal and could not be examined statistically as a separate outcome category.

The independent variables included within the vector Z_i capture whether a respondent is thirty years old or younger, female, and whether she or he has obtained a partial or complete education at the secondary level or above.[16] In order to examine the claims of the ethnic voting literature, the vector also includes a dummy variable for whether a respondent's first language falls within the Bemba ethnolinguistic group, which is the same as the incumbent Michael Sata.[17]

To test the claims of the vote-buying literature, I also include a dummy variable for whether a respondent observed parties offering handouts in his or her neighborhood during the 2008 campaign. Such handouts often occur in the form of money, food, drinks, T-shirts, and *chitenges,* which are brightly colored fabric. In all cases, the MMD was cited as the party most involved in handouts. In fact, 87 percent of respondents claimed the MMD provided handouts compared with 77 percent by the opposition. However, because the aim was to uncover whether opposition handouts affected voting behavior, handouts by the incumbent MMD were not included as a separate variable.

Instead, all the handouts by opposition parties are grouped together, but this does not necessarily prevent examining the specific effect of the PF's handouts. No one mentioned that the Heritage Party offered money or gifts, and this is consistent with popular views that the HP presidential candidate, Godfrey Miyanda, eschews giving the perception that he's buying peoples' votes (interview with Wazziah Phiri and Soko, 2008). By contrast, the PF was the most frequently mentioned opposition party involved in campaigning in respondent's neighborhoods. In particular, 90 percent of respondents claimed the PF campaigned in their neighborhood. Moreover, the PF was the most cited opposition party involved in offering handouts. If the UPND was also cited, then this party was also deemed to have offered handouts in addition to, not instead of, the PF.

As already noted, the school of thought around associational ties cannot be a relevant explanation for voting behavior in the Zambian case because so few respondents indicated that they belonged to associations. However, the role of retrospective assessments of the macroeconomy can be tested by incorporating into Z_i a dummy variable for whether a respondent believed that economic conditions worsened in the country

---

[16] Those who had no schooling or only primary schooling collectively were excluded as the reference category. The reason for doing this was that, unlike Senegal, only two respondents lacked any schooling. Therefore, using the no-schooling category as the sole reference category would have led to biased estimates.

[17] The languages within the Bemba language group are Bemba, Lunda, Lala, Bisa, Ushi, Chishinga, Ngumbo, Lamba, Kabende, Tabwa, Swaka, Mukulu, Ambo, Lima, Shila, Unga, Bwile, and Luano (CSO 2000). Due to high levels of collinearity, a similar dummy variable for those who belong to the Nyanja ethnolinguistic group, which is the same as Rupiah Banda, could not simultaneously be included.

during the prior year.[18] A more objective measure of respondents' personal economic conditions was proxied by how much they spend on a daily basis. Those who spent the equivalent of 30,000 Kwacha ($6 USD) or less a day were classified as belonging to a "low spending group."[19] This indicator also provides some measure of whether there is intra-class variation in voting patterns among this constituency.

In order to examine whether the PF's message had any congruence, I included dummy variables on two issues that Sata spoke about during his campaign. The first was whether a respondent had access to a water tap within his or her home. Convenient access to potable water is highly problematic in Lusaka, and the lack of it has contributed to a number of water-borne illnesses. In fact, the World Bank (2007a) notes that within Lusaka's informal settlements, residents rely on self-made shallow wells for water supply and on pit latrines, posing serious health challenges. Only 46 percent of survey respondents noted that they had access to a personal water tap. During interviews in the shanty compounds, water and sanitation were the top concerns that residents identified. Common complaints were that communal taps are timed and only open during specific times of the day, and that the quality of water was poor. The second indicator examined whether the respondent believed that the formerly ruling MMD performed poorly on employment creation. Of course, the rhetoric of providing more jobs was a central message to Sata's campaign. In the compounds, residents repeatedly noted that jobs were among the most important issues for them in elections. As a thirty-three-year-old Nyanja man from Misisi observed, he is most concerned about "jobs because there are too many people on the streets languishing without jobs, too many people living in shantytowns." Finally, given Sata's previous anti-Chinese rhetoric, I included a dummy variable capturing whether respondents believed that the growing presence of the Chinese was harmful to the country's economy.

---

[18] Of course, as noted in Chapter 2, prospective economic voting can also theoretically be a possible driver of political participation. However, during pretests of a survey question capturing respondents' views on whether they believed the economy would be improved by the same time the following year, a majority responded "Don't know." Given the lack of variation on this response, prospective economic voting could not be incorporated into the statistical analyses. More importantly, the inability of most people to analyze their country's future economic prospects implies that prospective assessments are clearly not a major driver of voting behavior for this sample.

[19] Respondents were asked about their expenditure behavior rather than their earnings due to the fact that the latter proved highly sensitive and resulted in few responses during pretests. Approximately 60 percent of respondents live in households with five or more people, and therefore, 30,000 Kwacha is extremely low when spent across household members.

Senegal

For the purposes of comparison, a very similar model was employed for the Senegalese case. In particular, the model for Senegal relies on the following specification:

$\Pr (V_i = 1 | S_i)$
$\Pr (V_i = 2 | S_i)$
$\Pr (V_i = 0 | S_i)$ base category

where V_i is equal to 1 if the individual voted for the incumbent, the PDS's Abdoulaye Wade; equal to 2 if the individual abstained; and the base category is set to those who voted for any one of the country's opposition parties. Unlike Zambia, no one opposition party obtained substantial support to be analyzed separately. As such, for statistical purposes, support for any opposition party needed to be collapsed into one category.

The vector S_i includes many of the same variables that are in Z_i, including a dummy variable capturing gender, those who are thirty years old or younger, perceptions of the economy, and whether respondents spend 3000 CFA ($6 USD) or less per day.[20] Again, I also included indicators on their perceptions of the incumbent's performance on job creation and whether they possessed access to water. As in Zambia, the latter two issues, along with better electricity provision, were identified by slum residents as the top improvements they wanted for their neighborhoods.

However, there are at least three notable differences between the two models. First, given that the education composition of voters in Senegal differs from that in Zambia, dummy variables were included for whether respondents attended Koranic or language education, whether they had only a primary education, and whether their education is at the secondary level or above. Given that those with no schooling comprised a much larger category than in Zambia, they could constitute a distinct reference category. Secondly, I included in S_i whether a respondent belonged to an association because Table 5.5 indicated that, unlike in Zambia, many more Senegalese were involved in associational activities. Thirdly, the role of the Chinese in Senegal's economy was not a theme in any of the 2007 presidential candidates' messages and therefore is not an issue included in the Senegalese analysis.

---

[20] We can have greater confidence that 3000 CFA is an appropriate cutoff because a series of studies on poverty in Dakar by the Agence du Fonds de Développement Social (2004) found that in some of the city's poorest neighborhoods, household heads spend 2625 CFA per day on average.

Importantly, although the regression also includes a dummy variable for whether respondents obtained handouts from any of the main opposition parties (e.g., Rewmi, AFP, PS, LD-MPT, and AJ/PADS), far fewer respondents in Dakar than in Lusaka claimed that political parties offered handouts when they came to campaign in the respondents' neighborhoods.[21] Moreover, many more respondents in Dakar claimed that they never even received a campaign visit from any political party. For instance, whereas 65 percent of respondents noted that the PDS came to their neighborhood in the run-up to the 2007 elections, only 50 percent stated that the PS, AFP, or Rewmi arrived. This indicates that the Zambian opposition was much more active than its Senegalese counterparts in visiting the neighborhoods of the urban poor.

REGRESSION RESULTS AND INTERPRETATION

Table 5.7 presents the results from the two regression analyses. Importantly, very different dynamics influenced voting behavior in the two countries. First and foremost, those who believed that the incumbent MMD performed poorly on creating job opportunities proves the most statistically significant factor driving respondents to support Sata rather than Banda or abstaining. In fact, for someone who disapproves of the MMD's performance on job creation, the relative risk of supporting Banda over Sata is an extremely small 0.026 when all other variables are held constant.[22] In addition, those who lacked access to basic services in their homes, such as water, were also significantly less likely to support Banda than Sata. This highlights that Sata's message on creating more jobs and improving basic services held a great deal of resonance with the urban poor vis-à-vis Banda's message. At the same time, those who believed that the presence of the Chinese was harmful to the country's economy were not significantly more likely than those with more positive views to support Sata, indicating that his previous xenophobic rhetoric was not a key driver of support for his party in 2008.[23]

---

[21] Specifically, 43 percent identified the opposition as offering handouts; 59 percent claimed the PDS offered handouts.

[22] This is based on the calculation of the relative risk ratio, which is the ratio of choosing one category over the probability of choosing the reference category.

[23] To ensure that the subjective variables included in the models were not capturing the same underlying dynamic, I performed a Chronbach alpha test. The resulting scale reliability coefficients were 0.22 for Zambia and 0.58 for Senegal. Because these coefficients are less than 0.70, this indicates that the subjective variables in each model are not all measuring the same underlying variable dimension.

Table 5.7. *Multinomial Logit Regressions Analyzing Voting Behavior*

Independent Variables	Zambia (2008 Presidential Elections)[a]		Senegal (2007 Presidential Elections)[b]	
	Voted for Banda	Abstained	Voted for Wade	Abstained
Young (18–30 years old)	0.038	0.660	0.408	1.845***
	(0.744)	(0.588)	(0.565)	(0.641)
Female	-0.049	-0.247	0.988*	1.134*
	(0.572)	(0.492)	(0.528)	(0.676)
Wolof language group	–	–	0.117	0.297
			(0.574)	(0.665)
Bemba language group	-1.058*	-1.030**	–	–
	(0.630)	(0.480)		
Koranic or language education	–	–	-1.956***	-0.687
			(0.692)	(0.789)
Primary education	–	–	-1.392**	-1.106
			(0.687)	(0.823)
Secondary education or above[c]	-0.825	0.593	-1.381*	-0.474
	(0.676)	(0.553)	(0.725)	(0.844)
Observed opposition handouts in neighborhood campaign	-0.686	-0.763	0.056	-0.375
	(0.760)	(0.750)	(0.550)	(0.633)
Belong to any type of association	–	–	-0.443	-0.018
			(0.561)	(0.654)

(continued)

Table 5.7 Continued

Independent Variables	Zambia (2008 Presidential Elections)[a]		Senegal (2007 Presidential Elections)[b]	
	Voted for Banda	Abstained	Voted for Wade	Abstained
Believe economic conditions in country have worsened	0.396	-1.320**	0.809	-0.344
	(0.925)	(0.608)	(0.987)	(1.044)
Lack access to water within home	-1.192**	-0.515	-1.268	-0.966
	(0.563)	(0.515)	(1.668)	(1.694)
Believe incumbent (MMD/PDS) has performed poorly on employment creation	-3.668***	-2.590**	-0.444	0.722
	(1.213)	(1.198)	(0.826)	(1.039)
Low daily spending (Equivalent of $6 USD/day or less)	-0.188	0.122	1.467**	1.613**
	(0.642)	(0.625)	(0.578)	(0.692)
Believe that the growing presence of the Chinese is harmful to the country	-0.520	-0.397	–	–
	(0.614)	(0.569)		
Constant	4.744***	4.128***	2.148	-0.583
	(1.514)	(1.521)	(2.051)	(2.107)
N	189		191	
Pseudo R2	0.151		0.155	
Prob > chi2	0.003		0.001	

Source: Author's survey data.

Notes: Significance levels: ***$p < 0.01$; **$p < 0.05$; *$p < 0.10$. Standard errors are in the parentheses. The results are weighted.

[a] The base category is those who voted for Michael Sata.

[b] The base category is those who voted for any Senegalese opposition party.

[c] For Zambia, the excluded education reference category is those who have only primary or no schooling at all. For Senegal, the reference category is only those with no schooling.

Service delivery and views on job creation did not demonstrate an impact on voting behavior in Senegal. Instead, the results highlight that the poorest of the respondents (i.e., those who spend less than $6 USD a day) were significantly more likely to support the incumbent PDS or abstain rather than support the opposition. Women exhibited the same voting preferences. Moreover, those who were thirty years old or younger were more likely to abstain at substantively high rates. In fact, based on calculated relative risk ratios, they are more than six times likely to abstain than to vote for the opposition. Given the prevalence of youth unemployment in Senegal, which was highlighted in Chapter 4, the fact that this constituency preferred not to vote emphasizes the inability of Senegal's opposition parties in those elections to mobilize on this important socioeconomic issue.

In addition, education proves a powerful predictor of voting behavior in Senegal. Those with even just a little bit of schooling, such as Koranic or language training, were significantly less likely to support Wade over the opposition than those with no education at all. The same pattern prevails for those with primary and secondary education. This echoes survey findings by Vengroff and Magala (2001: 18), who examined voting behavior in the 2000 elections and discovered that those Senegalese with higher education demonstrated a greater propensity to support the opposition. This is not surprising given that Chapter 4 highlighted that Senegal's opposition de salon is perceived as elitist and intellectualistic. The better educated will be more exposed to the policy ideas or incendiary statements of the opposition in the printed press, which has more outlets for independent expression in Senegal than television or radio. This means that without actively campaigning in low-income neighborhoods and the workplaces of the urban poor, the activities of the opposition will remain largely unknown by, or unattractive to, the most uneducated among the urban poor.

In terms of the four alternative schools of thought on voting, two are found to be entirely wanting. These include the role of opposition vote buying and membership in civic and workplace associations. Retrospective perceptions of the macroeconomy demonstrate some salience in Zambia but only in terms of explaining respondents' decisions to vote for the opposition over abstaining. This highlights a more nuanced perspective on retrospective voting. When deciding to vote for the opposition over the incumbent, specific issues that affect the urban poor outweigh discontent with the broader national economy and are the primary drivers of voting behavior. However, if the choice is between abstaining rather than supporting the opposition, subjective perceptions of economic circumstances at the national level encourage citizens to go to the polls. In both cases, voters need to believe

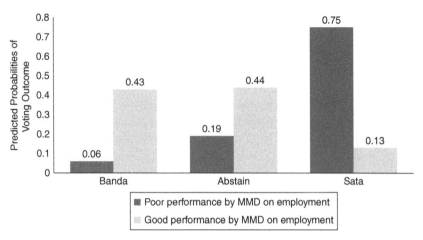

Figure 5.1 Predicted probabilities for respondents within the Bemba ethno-linguistic category.

that the opposition party is capable of addressing these issues, which is why the same patterns are not observed in Senegal.[24]

In the Zambian case, ethnolinguistic affinities appear to have the most salience among the alternative schools of thought. Those whose first language fell within the Bemba ethnolinguistic group were significantly more likely to vote for Sata than to either vote for Banda or abstain from elections. This suggests that ethnolinguistic identity cannot be dismissed as a factor shaping the voting preferences of the urban poor. However, it operates in conjunction with other considerations, including the policy message offered by political parties. This is highlighted in Figure 5.1, which presents the predicted probabilities of the three outcomes for members of the Bemba group according to whether they believe the MMD has performed well on job creation when all other variables are kept at their modal levels. Bemba members are more likely to support Sata than either abstaining or supporting Banda when they also believe that the MMD has performed poorly on job creation. Interestingly though, even when they believe that the MMD performed well on job creation, they are almost equally likely to abstain than to have voted for Banda.

Overall, Table 5.8 presents the table of predicted probabilities from the two models. These highlight that although the opposition PF is preferred to

---

[24] This pattern coincides with Posner and Simon's (2002) finding that declining economic conditions caused abstention in the 1996 Zambian elections when a weak opposition existed.

Table 5.8. *Predicted Probabilities Based on Model Results*

Predicted probabilities of …	Zambia	Predicted probabilities of …	Senegal
Voting for Banda	0.21	Voting for Wade	0.62
Voting for Sata	0.41	Voting for any opposition party	0.17
Abstaining	0.38	Abstaining	0.22

Source: Model results based on author's survey data.

abstaining in Zambia, the incumbent PDS and abstention are preferred to supporting the opposition in Senegal.

THE POWER OF *PABWATO* IN ZAMBIA

Further analysis emphasizes that Sata's populist strategy mobilized Zambia's urban poor via mechanisms of congruence and differentiation. Table 5.9 reveals that Sata was the favored candidate among those who labeled a candidate's party manifesto as the primary factor driving voting decisions, followed by whether the candidate promised a change. By contrast, of the total voters in the survey, those who cited "Other" as the main reason driving their voting decisions overwhelmingly supported Banda. When this category is examined more closely, it predominantly includes those who felt that the MMD should be allowed to complete its term in the wake of Mwanawasa's death.

These findings were consistent with results obtained through the shanty compound interviews. For instance, a twenty-two-year-old Nyanja-speaking housewife in Chaisa compound supported Sata because of his policies: "Sata has good policies on living and working conditions. If they were implemented, they would improve the conditions of Zambia. Under Mwanawasa, working conditions were bad and a few people were enriching themselves." In Kalikiliki, a forty-four-year-old uneducated Chewa-speaking man who works as a gardener claimed he supported the PF in 2008 "because of his [Sata's] promise to improve working conditions for informal workers and to have salaries start from 500,000 kwacha a month." In Misisi, a seventy-year-old Tumbuka-speaking woman who brews and sells beer within the compound voted for Sata because she liked the PF's policies, and added, "I thought Sata would provide roads, better houses, and would legalize Misisi."

However, explanations for why shanty residents voted for Banda are less consistent and tended to fall into three categories. The first was proxy

Table 5.9. *Primary Reason for Supporting Candidate in Zambia's 2008 Elections*

Primary Reason for Supporting a Candidate	Candidate Supported (% of all Voters)			Total (% of all Voters)
	Rupiah Banda (MMD)	Michael Sata (PF)	Hakainde Hichilema (UPND)	
Candidate's manifesto	1.6	27.6	4.9	34.1
Personal change in living conditions	2.4	2.4	0.0	4.9
Candidate promised a change	4.1	26.8	0.8	31.7
Candidate's experience	0.0	2.4	0.0	2.4
Candidate's personality	1.6	0.0	1.6	3.3
Candidate's ethnicity/ region of origin	0.0	0.0	0.0	0.0
Other reason	21.1	2.4	0.0	23.6
Total candidate share	30.9	61.8	7.3	100.0

Source: Author's survey data.
Notes: Cramér's V = 0.592; χ^2 = 86.180; p = 0.000; N = 123 of respondents who voted.

voting. For instance, a fifty-nine-year-old Tonga-speaking woman in Chaisa who sells fish in front of her home and a twenty-four-year-old Bemba woman in Kalikiliki who vends vegetables by the side of the road both admitted voting for Banda simply because they were told to do so by a family member or friend. The second explanation was that Banda was believed to be more likely to foster political stability than Sata. A forty-two-year-old Nyanja woman in Chaisa who sells groceries in the compound market represented an extreme example of this view, claim- ing that she worried a civil war would occur if Sata became president. Third, people wanted continuity with previous MMD policies. According to a forty-four-year-old Tumbuka man in Misisi who works as a security guard, "He [Banda] promised to give fertilizer in rural areas." Only two shanty compound residents supported Hichilema in 2008, one noting that she had no particular reason for voting for him, another claimed that she approved of his views on education and agriculture. Sata's policy message therefore played a critical role in the PF's ability to attract large segments of the urban poor; other candidate's appealed to voters according to much more ambiguous criteria.

Table 5.10. *Assessment of Opposition Parties*

Main Distinction Amongst Parties in Zambia	Opposition Parties Interested in Improving Living Conditions in Lusaka (% of all Respondents)						Total (% of all Respondents)
	PF	UPND	HP	UNIP	FDD	None	
Personality of party leaders	22.95	8.20	0.55	0	0.55	1.64	33.88
Positions on social and economic issues	32.79	11.48	0	0	0	3.28	47.54
Parties' links with a region of Zambia	2.73	0.55	0	0	0	0.55	3.83
No difference	2.73	1.09	0	0.55	0	7.65	12.02
Other	0.55	0	0	0	0	0	0.55
Don't know	1.09	0.55	0	0	0	0.55	2.19
Total share for party	62.84	21.86	0.55	0.55	0.55	13.66	100

Source: Author's survey data.
Notes: Cramér's V = 0.2719; $\chi2$ = 67.6221; p = 0.000; N = 183 due to the fact that the remaining respondents could not decide among one particular opposition party.

Table 5.10 focuses explicitly on survey respondents' views of the opposition parties. They were asked to identify which opposition party was most interested in improving living conditions in Lusaka as a proxy for determining which party they believed was most committed to addressing the city's development challenges. Their responses are compared to their opinions on the primary characteristic that distinguishes parties in Zambia.

A key observation from this table is that a majority of respondents, approximately 48 percent, identified "Positions on social and economic issues" as the main distinction among Zambian parties, followed by the "Personality of party leaders," and then "No difference." Overall, the PF was by far the opposition party believed to be most interested in improving living conditions in Lusaka, obtaining this distinction from 63 percent of respondents. The same merit was accorded to the UPND by only 22 percent of respondents. Likewise, a majority of those who identified the PF as the most interested in improving living conditions in Lusaka also claimed that social and economic issues distinguished parties, reflecting Sata's outspoken message on jobs and services. Due to Sata's charisma, it is not particularly surprising that 23 percent of respondents who supported the PF identified the personality of party leaders as the defining quality. Indeed, this table suggests that by using a populist strategy that combined charisma with a message that exhibited congruence with the lives of the urban poor, the PF provided greater differentiation from its counterparts. Furthermore, these results reinforce that parties such as Heritage, UNIP, and FDD, which were credible competitors in the 2001 elections, are no longer viable for the urban poor.

THE OPPOSITION THAT FAILS TO RESONATE IN SENEGAL

Although Sata's populist strategy mobilized Lusaka's urban poor, Senegal's lackluster opposition parties convinced many of Dakar's lower-class residents to remain loyal to an underperforming incumbent. The failure of the opposition to capitalize on the PDS's mistakes, to campaign on issues relevant to the urban poor, and even to enter many deprived neighborhoods during the campaign convinced poor Dakarois to stake their fortunes on the better-known incumbent, Abdoulaye Wade.

A significant indication of this is that a majority preferred Wade because he promised a change (see Table 5.11). This is unusual because, as an incumbent, Wade represented the least likely of all candidates to alter his own policies. Apparently, however, the incumbent who had done little for the urban poor represented a more credible agent of change than any of the opposition parties. Instead, most opposition parties obtained their votes because supporters simply recognized the name of a particular party from campaign materials. In stark contrast to Lusaka where almost 28 percent of Sata's supporters identified his party manifesto as their main reason for supporting him, almost no respondents in Dakar claimed to have picked an opposition candidate based on the candidate's platform.

A selection of more detailed views from opposition supporters in the survey further reveals the rationale driving their voting decisions. Seck supporters elaborated that the Rewmi leader "did not talk too much" and "seemed competent," and a third supporter claimed that he just wanted a change in regime. A male store vendor in Grand Yoff market noted that he supported Ousmane Tanor Dieng because he was "serious," and a women selling in the streets of Guele Tapée claimed that her life was better under the PS. The lone Landing Savané supporter admitted that she voted for him because that was what her husband had done, not because of his leftist orientation. In general then, opposition supporters attributed their voting behavior to candidates' personal characteristics or other idiosyncratic factors rather than candidates' positions on policy issues.

The low appeal of the opposition stems from a lack of differentiation among parties as well as the minimal degree of congruence between party

Table 5.11. *Primary Reason for Supporting Candidate in Senegal's 2007 Elections*

Primary Reason for Supporting a Candidate	Candidate Supported (% of all Voters)					Total (% of all Voters)
	Abdoulaye Wade (PDS)	Idrissa Seck (Rewmi)	Ousmane Tanor Dieng (PS)	Moustapha Niasse (AFP)	Other Party	
Candidate's platform	3.4	0.7	0	0.7	0	4.7
Recognized candidate's name	16.1	4	0.7	1.3	0.7	22.8
Personal change in living conditions	4	0	0.7	0	0	4.7
Candidate promised a change	46.3	3.4	0	1.3	0.7	51.7
Candidate's experience	0.7	0	0	0	0	0.7
Candidate's personality	0	1.3	0.7	0.7	0	2.7
Candidate's ethnicity/region of origin	0	0	0	0	0	0
Influenced by family member/friend	5.4	0	0.7	0	0.7	6.7
Other reason	4	2	0	0	0	6
Total candidate share	79.9	11.4	2.7	4	2	100

Source: Author's survey data.
Notes: Cramér's V = 0.279; χ^2 = 46.218; p = 0.017; N = 149 voters.

platforms and the priorities of the urban poor. Indeed, Table 5.12 examines whether respondents, including both voters and nonvoters, felt that any opposition parties were interested in improving living conditions in Dakar and what they believed constituted the main mode of differentiation among existing opposition parties. Approximately 53 percent of respondents claimed that they perceived no difference among parties; around thirty-three stated that the personality of party leaders represented the main mode of distinction. Only 2 percent of respondents claimed that positions on

Table 5.12. *Assessment of Senegal's Opposition Parties*

Main Distinction Amongst Parties in Senegal	Opposition Parties Interested in Improving Living Conditions in Dakar (% of all Respondents)						Total (% of all Respondents)
	Rewmi	*PS*	*AFP*	*LD-MPT*	*Other Party*	*None*	
Personality of party leaders	12.1	1.5	3.5	0.5	5.1	10.1	32.8
Positions on social and economic issues	1	0	0	0	0	0.5	1.5
Parties' links with a region of Senegal	1.5	0	0	0	0	0.5	2
No difference	2	1	0.5	0	1.5	48	53
Other	1.5	1	0	0	0	1.5	4
Don't know	1.5	0	0	0	0	5.1	6.6
Total share	19.7	3.5	4	0.5	6.6	65.7	100

Source: Author's survey data.
Notes: Cramér's V = 0.311; χ2 = 95.598; p = 0.000; N = 198 due to the exclusion of two respondents who could not identify just one party as interested in improving living conditions in Dakar.

social and economic issues distinguished parties. This presents a stark contrast with those surveyed in Lusaka, where most claimed that positions on social and economic issues represented the key axis of differentiation.

Moreover, almost 66 percent of respondents believed that no party was genuinely interested in improving living conditions within Dakar. Again, this is a dramatic difference from Lusaka, where only about 14 percent of those surveyed stated that no party was interested in addressing that city's problems. Of those who did identify a party, Rewmi stood out the most, whereas neither of the other heavy contenders nor the leftist LD-MPT was perceived as especially dedicated to improving conditions for Dakarois.

Interviews with slum dwellers in Dakar reflected these trends. When asked which opposition party appealed to them, twenty-one out of the thirty could not identify one particular opposition party. In HLM-Montagne, both a Serer-speaking laundress and an Ndiago-speaking male weaver captured the prevailing attitude by responding, "No one. They are all the same." A Serer-speaking unemployed woman in Cité Bissap also claimed that she saw all the opposition parties as being the same, adding, "They make promises that they don't keep." A young Wolof-speaking mason in Cité Bissap further noted that "you can't really judge an opposition party if it is not in power

Table 5.13. *Awareness of the Assises Nationales by Education Level*

Level of Education	Do you know what the Assises Nationales is? (% of Education Level)	
	Yes	No
Total	19	81
No schooling	6.9	93.1
Koranic/Language	20	80
Primary	25.5	74.5
Secondary	38.5	61.5
Postsecondary	75	25

Source: Author's survey data.
Notes: Cramér's V = 0.348; $\chi2$ = 24.063; p = 0.000; N = 200.

already." In Baraka, where nine out of ten residents voted for Wade in the 2007 election, a Pulaar-speaking housewife noted that she supported Wade simply because she did not recognize any of the other parties competing.

Finally, survey respondents were asked whether they were aware of the Assises Nationales, which, as noted in Chapter 4, was the opposition's grand project for addressing the challenges facing the country and critiquing Wade's governance. But Table 5.13 illustrates that a majority of respondents did not even know that such a vast opposition initiative was taking place. The significance of education is again highlighted here given that only 7 percent of those without schooling knew about the Assises Nationales compared with almost 39 percent of those with some secondary schooling. Likewise, in the slums, only two people knew about the Assises Nationales, and they were the two with the highest levels of education. In general, this highlights that the opposition was either not properly marketing its activities or its activities were not viewed by the urban poor as the most effective means for improving their immediate living and working conditions.

CONCLUSIONS

One of the major contributions of this chapter is the introduction of a novel set of primary data that examines the political behavior of the urban poor in Dakar and Lusaka. By probing the views of market workers and residents of slum and shanty compounds, this chapter accomplished two objectives.

First, the four hypotheses introduced in Chapter 2 regarding the voting behavior of the urban poor were tested. Vote buying in the form of money and/or gifts by the opposition during the election period was not found to be a major explanation for disparate voting patterns. This is not to say that parties did not try to engage in vote buying, but rather demonstrates that such practices on their own do not shape the voting decisions of the urban poor. Likewise, the influence of associational ties on voting behavior was not confirmed. Associational life is by no means absent, especially in Senegal. However, the work, microfinance, and religious organizations that the urban poor participate in lack formal linkages to political parties and therefore do not exhibit a large impact on voting.

The chapter uncovered mixed evidence regarding the role of ethnic voting as well as retrospective economic voting. In Zambia, those belonging to the same ethnolinguistic group as the Sata were significantly more likely to support him. However, the predicted probabilities illustrated that Bemba speakers were most likely to support Sata when they were disappointed with issues, such as jobs, that he directly addressed in his campaigns. At the same time, negative, subjective perceptions of the economy encouraged Zambian voters to avoid abstention and support the opposition. Specific issues, including performance on jobs and water provision, proved to be more immediate motivations than the economy for voters' decisions to support the PF over the incumbent. The same pattern is not observed in Senegal because the opposition did not represent a viable alternative for improving the economy. In fact, the analysis revealed that those Senegalese with objectively lower incomes, as measured by spending ability, were actually more likely than those with higher expenditure patterns to support Wade.

Uncovering key relationships between party strategies and voter mobilization represented a second goal of the chapter. I illustrated that an opposition party that employs a populist strategy, such as the PF, appeals most to the urban poor by offering both greater congruence and greater differentiation than alternative party linkage approaches. In Lusaka, Sata was the overwhelming favorite among market workers, a majority of whom pointed to policy promises on jobs and services as their primary motivation for supporting him. In addition, the PF was pinpointed by both voters and nonvoters as the main opposition party interested in improving living conditions in Lusaka, and most PF supporters identified positions on social and economic issues as the main distinction among Zambia's political parties. The regression analyses further highlighted that many of the issues Sata emphasized in his campaign were significantly associated with his electoral success. By promising to ameliorate inequalities through the creation of jobs and the improvement of basic services, Sata's message adhered closely to the policy priorities of the urban poor. This in turn helped distinguish him from his other opposition competitors, specifically the UPND and HP, which eschewed the populist strategy in favor of alternative linkage approaches.

The appeal of an opposition party relying on a populist strategy becomes even more apparent when compared with perceptions of the Senegalese party scene. In Dakar, the urban poor directly claimed that they voted for Wade not because they approved of his past performance in office but more because he promised to change his policies. By relying on personalistic or programmatic linkages, the opposition was unable to capitalize on disillusionment with Wade's first seven years in office. Programmatic leftist parties were the least successful in obtaining any votes, and those who supported Rewmi, AFP, or PS predominantly did so because of the party leader's personality. Furthermore, more than half of survey respondents claimed that they could discern little difference among the existing opposition parties, and almost two-thirds stated that no party was interested in improving conditions for Dakarois. With less than 50 percent of respondents claiming that an opposition party even visited his or her neighborhood during the 2007 campaign, these parties clearly demonstrated that the urban poor were not their key constituency base in the same way they were for Zambia's PF. Furthermore, widespread ignorance among the urban poor of the opposition's main forum for critiquing Abdoulaye Wade, the Assises Nationales, proved that this initiative was largely divorced from the realities of the everyday lives of most Senegalese.

Thus, although Chapters 3 and 4 discussed the political party landscape in Senegal and Zambia and highlighted the various linkage strategies to the urban poor employed by disparate parties over time, this chapter focused on how the urban poor react to such strategies. Chapter 6 examines how populist strategy can be combined with appeals to rural voters, whose support is still needed to obtain national electoral majorities.

SIX

Beyond the City

Building Coalitions with Rural Voters

Thus far, this study has shown that Africa's urban poor are most likely to support an opposition party when they are mobilized by a populist strategy. Yet in most African countries, rural votes are still necessary for a candidate to win national elections. As such, this chapter examines how the strategies used by opposition parties with the urban poor influences their mobilization of rural voters.

This chapter argues that parties reliant on a populist strategy with the urban poor can simultaneously mobilize a sizable share of rural voters through clientelistic linkages based on appeals to a politically salient, ascriptive identity cleavage, such as ethnicity, religion, language, or race. Given their resource limits, opposition parties reliant on populist strategies would ideally target only enough rural voters who, in tandem with the urban poor, would help them win national office without requiring extensive campaigning in remote rural areas. Consequently, such an opposition party can forge what E. Gibson (1997) referred to as coalitions comprised of "metropolitan" and "peripheral" members. In other words, the urban poor constitute the base of the coalition and rural voters provide the necessary votes to obtain national majorities.

Opposition parties that rely on personalistic linkages do not face the same trade-offs as those with populist strategies. However, by not specifically targeting the urban poor with a populist strategy, such opposition parties cannot be assured they will obtain significant votes in urban areas. When there is not a sizable share of the rural population that the candidate can easily target with identity appeals, then she or he will have to campaign more broadly within rural areas and again rely on personalistic linkages.

Michael Sata was able to orient his populist strategy around the policy priorities of Zambia's urban poor using clientelistic linkages with his co-ethnic Bembas in the rural provinces of Northern and Luapula. But a similar strategy remained unavailable for his main opposition competitor, Hakainde Hichilema, who belongs to the numerically inferior Tonga ethno-linguistic group. Instead, Hichilema relied on personalistic linkages and a broad campaign strategy in Zambia's countryside. In Senegal, the politically salient identity cleavage is Sufi brotherhood. Prior to the 2000 elections in Senegal, Abdoulaye Wade's populist strategy was combined with clientelistic appeals to leaders of the Mouride Sufi brotherhood. Prior to the 2007 elections, Wade continued not only to co-opt leaders of the Mouride brotherhood but also one sect of the Tidiane brotherhood. Senegalese opposition parties therefore lacked the ability to credibly use religious appeals for significant rural votes. Like Hichilema, Idrissa Seck, Ousmane Tanor Dieng, and Moustapha Niasse needed to campaign broadly among rural voters rather than specifically targeting their Tidiane coreligionists.

The next section elaborates on the costs of using a populist strategy alone to win national votes and discusses why appeals to ascriptive identity cleavages through clientelistic linkages is a useful approach for opposition parties to gain a segment of rural votes. This section also highlights why such dual appeals to the urban poor and a segment of rural constituents are surprisingly compatible. Subsequently, the chapter discusses politically relevant cleavages in Senegal and Zambia. By drawing on elite interviews, local newspapers, census, and campaign data, the chapter proceeds to illustrate whether and how opposition parties in each country mobilized such identities in rural areas. Finally, nationally disaggregated election data reveals the success of the PF in creating metropolitan and peripheral coalitions in 2008 as well as emphasizes the Senegalese opposition's inability to do the same in the 2007 elections.

THE CHALLENGE OF MOVING BEYOND THE CITY

Although a populist strategy best mobilizes an increasingly growing constituency – the urban poor – this approach simultaneously poses large trade-offs by alienating other important voters. For instance, middle- and upper-class voters, who are often needed to finance the campaigns of resource-deprived opposition parties, may fear that populist promises to ameliorate living conditions for the urban poor could result in excessive taxation or other redistributive measures. Rural voters, whose votes are still necessary for a party to obtain national majorities, may find a focus on urban priorities antithetical to their own needs. Nelson (1979: 323) nicely summarizes this dilemma by noting that although the interests of the middle classes, organized labor, and peasants may coincide with those of the urban poor on some issues, they are often antagonistic to the urban poor in other respects.

The challenge of retaining a core constituency base while trying to expand support represents a common problem faced by political parties through-out the world. Most notably, Przeworski and Sprague (1988) introduced this problem in their discussion of the "Paper Stones" dilemma. They highlight that many Western European socialist parties of the mid-twentieth century faced the decision of retaining their working-class bases through a distinctly class ideology or appealing to a broader constituency through heterogeneous appeals. Whereas the latter strategy is important for gaining national sup-port, it also dilutes the salience of class appeals and creates the opportunity for other party competitors to mobilize the working class through particu-laristic appeals. Likewise, both Gibson (1997) and Moore (1997) focus on the challenge for political parties in Latin America and Sri Lanka, respectively, of implementing economic reforms in the 1990s that were predominantly beneficial to their core urban constituents without alienating large numbers of rural voters whose support was necessary for reelection.

Reconciling the trade-offs between retaining a core constituency among the urban poor and simultaneously mobilizing a substantial share of rural voters is particularly difficult for African opposition parties reliant on a populist strategy. The reasons for this are numerous. First, as noted by Bueno de Mesquita et al. (2003), incumbents always benefit from possessing greater credibility to deliver goods and services by virtue of already being in office. This credibility is reinforced by Olukoshi's (1998: 32) observation that ruling parties typically possess solid organizational structures on the ground in rural areas and thereby become the leading political force known to the rural population. The existence of fewer independent media outlets and lower literacy levels in rural areas further diminish the ability of oppo-sition parties to establish a presence beyond the city, particularly outside of campaign periods. Chapter 2 noted that even during campaign periods opposition parties typically possess fewer resources than the incumbent, and therefore they cannot campaign extensively in remote and less densely populated rural areas. Moreover, opposition parties reliant on a populist strategy naturally spend much more of their time campaigning in low-income urban areas and therefore are less well known in rural areas. All of these challenges interact strongly with a country's electoral rules, which stipulate how many votes and how nationally representative a candidate's support must be before winning the presidency.

How then can opposition parties make inroads with the rural populace and still employ a populist strategy with the urban poor? I argue that the only way to combine these two goals is by mobilizing an electorally "sizable" segment of the rural population through clientelistic linkages based on appeals to a politically salient, ascriptive identity. Sizable refers to having a share of the population that, when combined with vote shares in urban areas, provides enough votes to win the presidency according to the country's electoral rules. Following Chandra and Metz (2002: 10), I define an *ascriptive identity* as one that is inherited by birth (e.g., religion, ethnicity, first language, race, gender) rather than acquired over an individual's lifetime (e.g., occupation, subsequent languages, place of residence).[1] Importantly, the term "ascriptive identity" should not be confused with primordialist interpretations of the impact of such identities. Instead, as Chandra (2012) discusses, ascriptive identities can be nominal or activated. The former relates to the full menu of identity categories to which an individual can feasibly belong based on her particular attributes and heritage; the latter refers only to those categories to which an individual explicitly professes membership or "to which she is assigned membership by others" (Chandra 2012: 9). A *politically salient* ascriptive identity is one that has been historically activated through political competition within a particular country. Such identities might consistently feature in a country's historical voting patterns, electoral campaigning, and/or party building (see Posner 2004b). Appeals to ascriptive identities represent a subtype of clientelistic linkages between parties and voters because such identities offer a means of determining who should receive selective benefits (Hardin 1995; Kitschelt 2000; Roniger 1994).

As described in Chapter 2, there is a vast literature about the role of such identities, particularly ethnolinguistic background, in African politics. Without repeating the observations from that literature here, it is important to note that opposition parties have been found to be more likely to use narrow sectional appeals along identity lines (Cheeseman and Ford 2007; van de Walle 2007). The benefits for opposition parties of appealing to such identities are twofold. First, if voters believe that a candidate with a similar ascriptive identity is more likely to provide selective benefits, then appeals to such identities might help opposition parties overcome the credibility problem created by incumbents in rural areas. Secondly, unlike in cities, certain identities are geographically concentrated in Africa's rural areas (Barkan 1995; Kimenyi 2006), and therefore campaigns based on identity do not require extensive travel throughout a country to garner sufficient support. An opposition candidate can

---

[1] In the remainder of this chapter, the term "identity" only refers to ascriptive identities.

therefore simultaneously conserve scarce resources by focusing on only a small number of rural areas.

But what prevents these dual appeals from simultaneously alienating, rather than mobilizing, the heterogeneous urban poor and rural residents? The key factor is whether politicians combine populism with inclusive, rather than exclusive, identity appeals (see Madrid 2008). An exclusive identity subsumes all others that a person may possess as a member of society. Because such identities can become more intense due to the appeals of political entrepreneurs who personally benefit by advancing an us-versus-them worldview, exclusive identity appeals are therefore divisive and potentially destabilizing. One example is the discourse of *Ivoirité*, which was used by Henri Bédié in Côte d'Ivoire during the 1990s to promote Christian Southerners over their Muslim counterparts and became the source of resentment between these two groups that ultimately led to that country's civil war (see Crook 1997). The ideology of "Hutu power" promoted by Rwanda's Hutu extremists and the National Party's promotion of white supremacy in apartheid South Africa also represent exclusive identity appeals because they were used to define who was a legitimate citizen, deserving of the benefits and protections of the state. Mudde and Kaltwasser (2013) argue that much of the right-wing populism in Europe is exclusionary populism precisely because it is based on denying certain groups, particularly immigrants and ethnic minorities, welfare assistance and political rights that they receive from the state.

Inclusive identities are mutually compatible and reflective of a person's multiple roles in society. In turn, inclusive identity appeals draw on one of these identities to mobilize voters without alienating those who do not share the same identity. In other words, inclusive identity appeals do not degenerate into ethno-nationalist appeals. Although such appeals may imply that a party leader's tenure in office will coincide with benefits to those with similar backgrounds, they do not explicitly suggest that other ethnolinguistic, religious, or racial groups will not receive those same benefits. Moreover, inclusive appeals rely on implicit overtures to a specific identity through the use of local languages, cultural symbols, and a shared history of real or imagined political and economic marginalization. This latter dimension is particularly important because perceptions of marginalization will coincide with frustrations also experienced by the urban poor about their lack of opportunities. For example, in Bolivia, Evo Morales relied on inclusive-identity appeals to indigenous peoples by espousing support for indigenous grievances and campaigning in both the Quechua and Aymara languages in rural areas. But he also advocated the importance of improving the conditions for Bolivia's ethnically diverse urban poor, and his party, the Movimiento al Socialismo, recruited members from all races to run for local and legislative offices (see Madrid 2008).

Opposition parties that are not reliant on populist strategies with the urban poor face a different challenge. Specifically, they are much less likely to capture many votes in urban areas, especially when competing against a populist party or others with personalistic linkages. As such, they can only depend on ascriptive identity appeals in rural areas if they belong to a particular demographic that is sizable enough to provide electoral majorities in the absence of large-scale urban support. If not, or if the leaders of other opposition parties have the same ethnic, linguistic, or religious background, then they will be forced to campaign very broadly in rural areas to ensure a larger range of support. However, their ability to spend a great deal of time across broad swathes of the countryside will still be overshadowed by better-endowed incumbent parties.

Overall then, parties reliant on a populist strategy in urban areas can create a coalition between metropolitan members who are the constituency base (i.e., the urban poor) and peripheral members among rural voters who can provide national majorities. Such coalition building allows the opposition to conserve scarce resources on campaigning in rural areas and also increase its credibility to deliver on campaign promises. Importantly, the clientelist linkages forged with rural voters through appeals to ascriptive identities must rely on an inclusive discourse that in many ways complements the concerns of the urban poor. Without the possibility of large-scale support from urban voters, and depending on the backgrounds of their competitors and the actions of the incumbent party, opposition parties that are not reliant on populist strategies are likely to engage in less targeted campaigning in rural areas. The following two sections apply this argument to the cases of Zambia and Senegal.

ETHNOLINGUISTIC APPEALS IN RURAL ZAMBIA

In Zambia, ethnolinguistic cleavages have long represented the most politically salient ascriptive identities. Indeed, Posner (2005) illustrates that in multiparty national elections, political cleavages tend to be aligned according to the country's four main ethnolinguistic groups: Bemba, Nyanja, Tonga, and Lozi. Under Kenneth Kaunda's UNIP, it appeared that Nyanja speakers, particularly from his home base of Eastern Province, were favored in political positions. In fact, during the historic 1991 elections, the only region that UNIP retained was Eastern Province (see Bratton 1994). Under

Chiluba, the MMD became perceived as a Bemba party, which only fueled the desire of Tongas and Lozis for greater political representation in the central government (Burnell 2001).[2] According to Burnell (2005: 122), "Zambia's politicians continue to factor ethnic and provincial considerations into their strategies for mobilizing support at local levels."

Importantly, however, overt ethnic appeals are rare (Posner 2005: 181), and there are no ethnic parties in the manner defined by Chandra (2004: 3) "as a champion of the cause of one particular ethnic category or a set of categories *to the exclusion* of others" [emphasis added]. Rather, ethnic appeals follow a pattern of implicit mobilization, meaning that they are coded in a manner that targets specific constituents without necessarily naming a particular ethnic identity (Chandra 2009). Based on interviews conducted in 2000, Scarritt (2006) found most politicians admitted that ethnopolitical mobilization occurred during campaigns but not in an exclusionary manner that threatened national unity.

For national politicians, one of the advantages of focusing on ethno-linguistic identity is that these identities are territorially concentrated, especially in rural areas. According to Zambia's 2000 census, the Bemba ethnolinguistic group remains the largest nationally, with 31.7 percent of the population identifying with this group. The Tonga and Nyanja groups comprise about 18.9 and 17.4 percent of the population, respectively. Along with English, the Lozi, Mambwe, Northwester, and Tumbuka ethnolinguistic groups make up the remainder of the population.[3] But as seen in Table 6.1, almost all provinces have one particular ethnolinguistic group that constitutes the majority of the population for that province. Map 6.1 highlights where these provinces are located.

The combined population of Zambia's major urban centers, including Lusaka City and a variety of cities on the Copperbelt, was approximately 23.5 percent of Zambia's total population in the 2000 census (CSO 2003b). Even though Zambia has a First-Past-the-Post voting system, which allows candidates to win with just a plurality of votes, politicians do not know ex ante how many votes other candidates will win and therefore will not know

---

[2]   Under British colonial rule, the proximity of Bemba-speaking groups to the Copperbelt meant that they supplied much of the labor to the copper-mining operations, which placed them in a more advantageous position vis-à-vis other groups at the time of independence (Taylor 2006).

[3]   The language groups encompass a number of different dialects. However, these dialects are mutually intelligible among ethnic groups within each language group. For example, the Chewa, Ngoni, and Nsenga tribes all speak a language that falls within the broader Nyanja language group.

Table 6.1. *Distribution of Zambian Ethnolinguistic Groups by Province*

Province	Share of Province Population That Is Rural (%)	Predominant First Language Group	Share of Provincial Population Belonging to Language Group (%)
Central	76.0	Bemba	47.7
Copperbelt	22.1	Bemba	79.5
Eastern	91.2	Nyanja	67.9
Luapula	87.0	Bemba	88.5
Lusaka	18.2	Nyanja	55.9
Northern	85.9	Bemba	64.2
Northwestern	87.7	Northwestern	81.9
Southern	78.8	Tonga	72.8
Western	88.0	Barotse/Lozi	70.0

Notes: The designation of the ethnolinguistic groups follows the procedure used by Zambia's Central Statistical Office.
Source: Calculations based on the 2000 Zambian census.

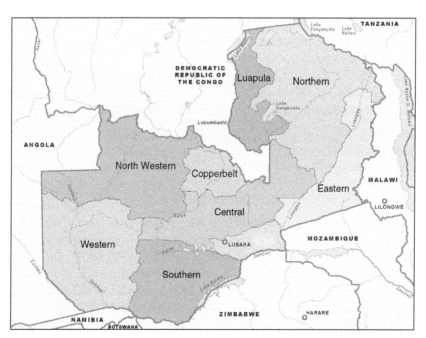

Map 6.1 Map of Zambian Provinces. Copyright © 2007 by World Trade Press. All rights reserved.

how much of a plurality is needed. As such, a presidential candidate will aim to expand votes beyond these two areas to increase the chances of winning national majorities. If the candidate is from a sizable ethnolinguistic group and can rely on support from the urban poor, then she or he will prefer to concentrate scarce campaign resources in those rural areas where members of her or his ethnolinguistic group are most concentrated. If not, then the candidate will have to campaign more broadly in rural areas or form a coalition with candidates from other ethnolinguistic groups.

Sata's Peripheral Coalition in the Bemba Heartland

In both the 2006 and 2008 presidential elections, Michael Sata followed the former approach and coupled his populist strategy in urban areas with ethnolinguistic appeals in Bembaphone rural areas. The approach was predicated first and foremost on the fact that the Bemba language group is the country's largest. At the same time, using ethnolinguistic appeals was the one way Sata could compete with the many numerous advantages possessed by the incumbent MMD. Indeed, the PF Vice President, Guy Scott, noted that this reflected the challenges of rural mobilization: "That's part of the problem, that the rural areas do vote along tribal lines. Or, in default, they vote for the government. That's kind of the strategy of the rural voter" (interview with Scott, 2009).

The MMD had at least two major advantages with rural voters. First, the former incumbent party possessed greater access to resources to campaign in remote rural areas. According to the BBC correspondent in Zambia:

What tends to happen, the ruling party, MMD, they tend to use state money, government public funds; that is indisputable. They use that, they use public money, they use Zambia air force planes to cover and get to every part of the country. They use government cars, they have free access to the media, they don't pay for their adverts. (Interview with Chibamba, 2009)

Secondly, the MMD engaged in high-profile agricultural policies. The MMD's manifesto for 2007–2011 ranked agriculture as its number-one priority for the country's economic development agenda (MMD 2006). The party mainly accorded attention to this sector via the Fertilizer Support Program (FSP) and the Food Reserve Agency (FRA). Launched in the 2002–2003 farming season, the FSP provides subsidized fertilizer to households in rural areas. The FRA, which was established in 1995, aims to ensure the country has a strategic reserve of food by buying smallholder maize and cassava and thereby guaranteeing farmers that they will have a market for their output.

The MMD's Rupiah Banda used the FSP and FRA to his advantage in the 2008 elections. At the inception of the campaign, the government announced that the FRA would increase the cost it paid farmers for their maize from 45,000 Kwacha to 55,000 Kwacha.[4] During his campaign rallies, Banda promised to expand the FSP from 120,000 to 220,000 families, and that the government would increase the share of the fertilizer that it subsidized from 60 to 75 percent (Miti 2008). Around the same time, the government announced that the budget for the FSP 2008–2009 year would be increased to 485 billion kwacha (*Times of Zambia* 2008b). The PF complained that the MMD also strategically timed the distribution of its annual fertilizer deliveries not during the proper planning season but rather in the months just before the 2008 elections (interview with Scott, 2009). Even the MMD's national campaign manager, Mbita Chitala, admitted that his party tried to control rural areas via fertilizer distribution (interview with Chitala, 2009).

By drawing on these programs as well as the fact that it already occupied the presidential office, the MMD claimed that it could more credibly implement projects and fulfill campaign promises than any of the opposition candidates. This was the common message during Rupiah Banda's campaign tour across the country's nine provinces. For example, in Southern Province, he promised to continue promoting agricultural growth through the FSP and warned residents "against being hoodwinked by other presidential candidates whom he [Banda] said could not deliver on their promises because they were out of the system while he was in Government" (Moonga 2008: 1). In Eastern Province, Banda emphasized that only he possessed enough members in parliament to form a strong government (Ntanda and Lungu 2008: 1). In Northwestern Province, he fortuitously announced the allocation of 100 million kwacha for the rehabilitation of the main market in the town of Solwezi (*Times of Zambia* 2008e).

Given these advantages for the MMD in rural areas, Sata and other opposition candidates lacked few alternative modes of credibly appealing to rural voters other than based on ethnolinguistic appeals in specific geographic areas. As the Zambian political analyst Dr. Neo Simutanyi explains:

You know, Sata's political strategy has been very simple. It's based on demographics … the strategy has been that if the Bemba group is consolidated and it votes as a bloc and then gets sympathy, in other words gets support from non-Bembas

---

[4]   In response, the PF unsuccessfully filed for a court injunction to force the FRA either to wait until after the elections before paying the new price or to compensate farmers who had already sold their maize at the cheaper price (*Times of Zambia* 2008d).

Table 6.2. *Distribution of Campaign Rallies in Majority Rural Provinces (%)*

Province	Candidates (Party)			
	Banda (MMD)	Sata (PF)	Hichilema (UPND)	Miyanda (HP)
Central	5.6	16.0	0.0	50.0
Eastern	16.7	0.0	31.6	0.0
Luapula	13.9	16.0	10.5	0.0
Northern	16.7	48.0	10.5	25.0
Northwest	11.1	4.0	10.5	25.0
Southern	16.7	4.0	31.6	0.0
Western	19.4	12.0	5.3	0.0
Total	100 (N = 36)	100(N = 25)	100 (N = 19)	100 (N = 4)

Source: Calculated from news reports in *The Times of Zambia* newspaper between the 2008 presidential campaign period of September 26–October 29.

who are in the group of the working class and the poor and so forth, then it should be possible for this bloc vote to help him win the presidency. (Interview with Simutanyi 2009).

The clearest evidence of this strategy emerges by observing where Sata spent most of his time campaigning in 2008. Table 6.2 illustrates the share of rallies that each candidate held within provinces outside of the urban provinces of Lusaka and the Copperbelt. These figures were derived from counting the number of separate rallies held by each presidential candidate and reported in the newspaper *Times of Zambia* during the official campaign period, which started on September 26 and ended on October 29, 2008.[5] Newspaper reports offer a useful approximation of candidates' geographic focus given that more extensive data regarding political campaigns remains unavailable. Admittedly, this approach can be problematic for at least two reasons. First, the number of rallies will inevitably be underreported because newspaper space cannot be solely devoted to reports on candidates' campaign activities. Godfrey Miyanda in particular argued that the lack of media coverage of his rallies conveyed to the public that he did not engage in much campaigning in rural areas (*Times of Zambia* 2008f). However, this bias is more likely to exclude smaller rallies and therefore will only serve to further emphasize which constituencies a candidate accorded the most attention. Secondly, rallies that were held by parties but

[5] September 26, 2008, marked the day when presidential candidates needed to submit their official nomination forms to the Zambian High Court.

not attended by the actual presidential candidate are excluded. But one would assume that those constituencies that are deemed most important by the party are those most likely to receive a visit from the actual presidential contender.

Due to the MMD's access to campaign resources, Banda conducted more rallies than any of the other candidates. Notably, Banda distributed his rallies relatively evenly amongst the provinces, spending marginally more time in Western Province, which, as will be discussed later in this section, was designed to deprive Lozi votes from the UPND. By contrast, Sata concentrated a majority of his time in the two majority Bemba-speaking rural provinces, Luapula and Northern. Eastern Province, which is Banda's stronghold, received no visits from Sata, who presumably felt that it was a waste of resources to campaign in the incumbent's main area of influence.[6] Both the Tonga-speaking Southern Province and those in Northwestern Province also obtained minimal attention from Sata.

Sata mobilized fellow Bemba speakers through implicit, rather than explicit, appeals that were centered on their shared identity. In other words, he represented the PF as an inclusionary party that would seek to cater to all groups, simultaneously claiming that non-Bemba candidates did not have this constituency's best interests at heart. For example, during one of his visits to the Lozi-speaking Western Province, he stressed in a radio interview that the PF was a national party and not just for Bembas (*Times of Zambia* 2008g). Furthermore, key members of the PF Party hierarchy at the time were relatively diverse. For instance, the vice president (Guy Scott) is a white Zambian, the former PF spokesperson and minister of foreign affairs (Given Lubinda) is mixed race, and the former chairperson for mines and current minister of lands and natural resources (Wilbur Simuusa) is Tonga. At the same time, however, the UPND leader, Hakainde Hichilema, believes Sata purposely discouraged Bembas from supporting him: "I went to campaign in Luapula Province. And Sata told the people there not to vote for me because I was Tonga and they are Bemba. How can you campaign like that? I never go to Southern Province and say, 'Don't vote for Sata because he's Bemba.' No" (interview with Hichilema, 2009).

Two other key campaign tactics he used in these rural areas was language and a story of shared exclusion. Specifically, the PF's slogan of Pabwato, which is Bemba, was never translated into any other indigenous languages in campaign materials. This presumably reinforced for rural voters, who were

---

[6]   Banda's popularity in Eastern Province is due to the fact that his father was Chewa and his mother Ngoni, both of which are members of the Nyanja language group that is dominant in this area of Zambia.

less likely to relate to a message of "Lower taxes, more jobs and more money in your pockets," that Sata was a Bemba candidate. Moreover, King Cobra relied on Bemba to address his rallies in Northern and Luapula provinces. His promises at these rallies, which were nationally broadcast on independent radio stations, were about issues even non-Bembas would appreciate, including improving the road network and the distribution of fertilizers as well as helping widows and orphans (see *Times of Zambia* 2008h; *Times of Zambia* 2008i). Even during his closing rally in the majority Nyanja-speaking Lusaka, Sata resorted to Bemba when exhorting supporters not to engage in violence if the election outcome did not favor the PF: "Kabiyeni, mwilalwa kabili mwila tukana" ["Go, but do not fight and insult"] (cited in *Times of Zambia* 2008j).

In addition, Sata drew on the fact that the late President Mwanawasa had deliberately pursued corruption cases against notable Bemba politicians, including Chiluba. Mwanawasa, whose father was from the Lenje tribe and therefore part of the Tonga ethnolinguistic group, was famously quoted as saying to the allegedly corrupt politicians, "Just leave the party because you are stinking and dirty" (cited in Malido 2003: 1). Mwanawasa had also reversed many of Chiluba's appointments and thereby removed Bembas from top positions within the government hierarchy (Sishuwa 2011). This in turn encouraged Sata to proclaim on the campaign trail that the MMD deliberately sought to marginalize the Bemba and viewed Bembas as "stinking and dirty" (interview with Simutanyi, 2009).

Table 6.3 illustrates how Sata's campaign strategy affected voting outcomes. Specifically, the PF's base of support centered on Zambia's most urban and cosmopolitan areas in Lusaka and the Copperbelt, as well as the Bemba-speaking Luapula and Northern Provinces. In these two rural provinces, Sata obtained 66 and 65 percent of the vote in 2008, respectively.[7] This contrasts starkly with the PF's vote shares in the 2001 elections when he failed to campaign at all outside urban areas. At that time, he obtained 3 and 8 percent of the votes in Luapula and Northern Provinces, respectively. Table 6.3 further illustrates that the UPND's support base remains predominantly concentrated in the Tonga-speaking Southern Province. The MMD's 2008 results emphasize that this ruling party, which originally emerged in urban areas, has now become predominantly rural.

Afrobarometer public-opinion survey data further confirms that these regionally patterned election results are actually related to ethnolinguistic

---

[7] Notably, within Northern Province, the PF only lost to the MMD in non–Bemba-speaking areas (Simutanyi 2009).

Table 6.3. *Vote Share (%) by Province in 2008 Zambian Presidential Elections*

Province	Banda (MMD)	Sata (PF)	Hichilema (UPND)	Miyanda (HP)
Central	56.0	22.5	20.8	0.7
Copperbelt	35.7	58.2	5.5	0.6
Eastern	74.5	18.7	5.8	1.0
Luapula	26.0	65.8	1.3	0.3
Lusaka	30.3	54.5	14.6	0.6
Northern	32.4	64.7	1.3	0.4
Northwestern	57.6	4.4	37.1	0.8
Southern	20.5	4.8	73.3	1.5
Western	68.4	10.1	20.4	1.1
Total	40.6	38.6	20.0	0.8

Source: Electoral Commission of Zambia.

Table 6.4. *Party Affinities by Ethno-linguistic Group (%)*

Ethnolinguistic Group	Rural Zambians (N = 429)					Urban Zambians (N = 221)				
	MMD	PF	UPND	HP	Other	MMD	PF	UPND	HP	Other
Bemba	38	54	8	1	0	19	71	5	3	2
Tonga	31	1	66	0	2	40	14	44	0	2
Northwestern	66	3	29	0	2	30	49	15	0	6
Lozi	57	20	22	0	0	38	24	37	0	0
Nyanja	64	9	21	0	6	33	62	6	0	0
Mambwe	51	38	2	2	6	32	49	19	0	0
Tumbuka	65	16	11	0	9	23	66	8	0	4
Others	32	0	68	0	0	34	66	0	0	0
Total	47	22	29	0	2	27	57	13	0	3

Notes: For both rural and urban Zambians, the cross-tabulation between ethnolinguistic group and party affinity is significant at the 1 percent level. The proportions are only for those respondents who admitted feeling close to one of Zambia's political parties. The results are weighted.
Source: Afrobarometer Round 4.

identities in rural areas. Table 6.4 uses the Round 4 data, which were collected in Zambia only eight months after the 2008 elections. Among those Zambians who admitted that they felt close to a particular party, 54 percent of rural Bemba supported the PF; 66 percent of rural Tonga and 64 percent of rural Nyanja felt closest to the UPND and the MMD, respectively. In urban areas, Bembas were just as likely to support the PF. However, 64 percent of urban Nyanja speakers also expressed the greatest affinity to Sata's party. In addition, a higher proportion of other ethno-linguistic groups in urban areas expressed an affinity to the PF than their counterparts in rural areas.

The success of Sata in Bembaphone provinces is difficult to attribute to other factors besides ethnolinguistic appeals. Due to his focus on his metropolitan coalition of the urban poor, he had not spoken much about agriculture during the campaign. Indeed, one disgruntled Zambian wrote that "his [Sata's] political vision is in town alone, talking about making fly-over bridges, sweeping the markets, etcetera. Coming to issues that affect the rural multitudes, he has nothing to offer or talk about. Ask him about agricultural policies and you will get nothing from him" (Daka 2008: 5). In fact, Cheeseman and Hinfelaar (2010: 23 and 24) point out that some of Sata's promises to the urban poor, such as reducing food prices, were directly antithetical to the interests of rural producers. They further observe that Sata insulted rural producers during the 2008 campaign by claiming that their farm practices were from the "stone age."

Another alternative explanation, which is that Bembaphone rural voters were disillusioned with MMD policies, can also be questioned. For instance, Govereh et al. (2009) show that the PF's Bemba strongholds disproportionately benefitted from the FSP. In addition, they note that the FRA also favored Northern and Luapula Provinces over other cassava-producing regions, such as Northwestern and Western Provinces. As such, support for Sata in these provinces could not necessarily be traced to farmers' disappointment with the MMD's agricultural policies.

Sata's dualistic mode of coalition building explains why such disparate views exist over how best to characterize the PF. Not surprisingly, other parties attempt to portray the PF as a distinctly Bemba party. The MMD's campaign manager in 2008, Dr. Mbita Chitala, claims, "He [Sata] is basically a very tribal gentleman, if you look at his party, the whole leadership is Bemba, the Northern people, the Bemba" (interview with Chitala, 2009). Likewise, the research director for the UPND, Dr. Choolwe Beyani believes that "there are ethnic considerations to voting patterns. There is what you may call a Bemba voting bloc that has voted PF, which has been seen as a Bemba party.... You see, if there's any party that is ethnically associated, it's PF" (interview with Beyani, 2009).

But for PF members, the accusations of tribal affiliation appear unfounded. The PF's Director of Research, Dr. Chileshe Mulenga, states, "In cities which are metropolitan, where you have mixed populations, people from different parts of the country living side by side, we have a lot of support" (interview with Mulenga, 2009). He echoes the PF's former spokesman and MP for Lusaka's Kabwata constituency, Given Lubinda, who observes, "Now, we have been criticized as a tribal party but you will see that the areas where we win votes are the most cosmopolitan" (interview with Lubinda, 2009). Other independent observers point to the PF's victories in a multilingual city such as Lusaka as contradictory to the party's categorization as a Bemba entity (interviews with Chifuwe and Chibamba, 2009). Scholars of the Zambian political scene, such as Gould (2007: 8) and Larmer and Fraser (2007: 632), also dismiss the PF as an ethnic party precisely because of its populist appeal in key cities. These conflicting perspectives reflect Sata's success at creating a coalition between the urban poor and Bemba-speaking rural voters.

Sata ultimately lost the presidency in 2008 by only two percentage points, and this was most likely due to the refusal of the Electoral Commission to register new voters who had become eligible to vote since the previous election. Given Sata's popularity among the urban youth, the decision not to reopen the electoral register most likely created an advantage for the MMD (Cheeseman and Hinfelaar 2010). Otherwise, Sata's dual coalition more than likely would have proved victorious.[8]

Hichilema's Dilemma

Having eschewed the use of a populist strategy to mobilize the urban poor, Hichilema did not face the same potential trade-offs as Sata when trying to obtain national electoral majorities. Indeed, his personalistic linkages with the urban poor could be easily combined with similar linkages to rural voters. But because Hichilema lacked a clear constituency in urban areas and his ethnolinguistic group was too small demographically to deliver national majorities, the UPND leader required a broad campaign strategy in rural areas.

Specifically, both Hichilema and his predecessor, the late Andrew Mazoka, are from the Tonga ethnolinguistic group. But first-language Tonga speakers are only approximately 19 percent of the rural population. Moreover, Table 6.1 highlighted that they are only the majority group in Southern Province, which, according to the Central Statistical Office (2003b), only

---

[8] Chapter 8 notes how Sata's ultimate victory in the 2011 elections was predicated the continuation of his dual approach of combining a populist strategy in urban areas with identity appeals in rural areas.

contains 12 percent of the national population. In the past, the UPND has been able to create multiethnic coalitions, particularly with the Lozis of Western Province. In fact, in 2001, Mazoka obtained 49 percent of the vote there, compared with Mwanawasa's 27 percent. However, after Mazoka's death and the appointment of Hichilema as the party's leader, the vice president of the UPND, Sakwiba Sikota, defected and formed the United Liberal Party. Sikota, who is a Lozi, threw his weight behind the MMD in 2008 and campaigned vigorously on Banda's behalf, especially in Western Province.

Given these circumstances, Hichilema attempted to portray the UPND as a national rather than Tonga party in order to obtain votes from other rural voters in 2008. This was apparent in two key respects. First, in contrast to the PF, the UPND's slogan was printed on the party's campaign materials in seven indigenous languages, including Nyanja, Bemba, Tonga, Lozi, and a language of the Northwestern linguistic group (see UPND 2008). During campaign rallies, Hichilema also attempted to speak local languages, rather than English, when addressing the audience. For instance, at his rally in Chipata, the capital of Eastern Province, he spoke entirely in Nyanja (*Times of Zambia* 2008k). He also affirmed the role of traditional chiefs from all ethnolinguistic groups, pledging on the campaign trail to renovate chiefs' palaces, provide them with better allowances, and offer them new cars if he were elected president (Lungu 2008). Overall, Hichilema spent more time campaigning in Eastern Province and the PF's strongholds than Sata spent in the UPND's strongholds or Eastern Province. This indicates that Hichilema recognized a peripheral coalition could not be secured by focusing on Southern Province alone in the same manner that Sata could concentrate on Bembaphone provinces.

Secondly, outside of Tonga-speaking areas, Hichilema engaged in a concerted effort to appeal to rural voters by addressing agricultural concerns. For example, at his October 7, 2008, rally in Katete, Eastern Province, Hichilema stressed the importance of revitalizing the agricultural sector and pledged to provide farmers with free inputs during the first three years of his tenure (*Times of Zambia* 2008k). In the town of Isoka, Northern Province, Hichilema promised that as president, he would cancel the Presidential Emoluments Bill and the Constitutional Office Holders' Bill, both of which aimed to increase salaries for the president, vice president, speaker of parliament, ministers, and deputy ministers. Instead, the money for such salary increases would be reallocated to buy fertilizers and other agricultural inputs that would be distributed to farmers free of charge (Mulowa 2008). However, such promises were not necessarily different from what the MMD was already offering through the FSP and FRA.

Consequently, Hichilema did not obtain substantial electoral majorities outside of Southern Province.

RELIGIOUS BROTHERHOODS IN THE
SENEGALESE COUNTRYSIDE

Unlike Zambia, ethnolinguistic differences are not politically relevant identity cleavages in Senegal. In fact, ethnic cleavages have never been a part of the Senegalese landscape (Mamadou Diouf 1994). For example, the former President, Abdou Diouf, who belongs to the Wolof ethnic group, received some of the highest votes from the Pulaar-speaking Toucouleur. His predecessor, Leopold Senghor, was from the Serer ethnic group and obtained high levels of support in regions containing non-Serers (Beck 2008).[9]

One reason for the low salience of ethnic identity is because, like some other West African societies, many ethnic groups in Senegal are structured by caste. For example, the Wolof, Serer, and Pulaar-speaking Toucouleur are all caste societies (A. Diop 1964; Markovitz 1970).[10] Members of the same caste across different ethnic groups may have more in common than they do with their co-ethnics. Traditionally, marriage practices encouraged endogamy within castes rather than within ethnic groups (Ross 2008). In addition, Wolof is almost equivalent to a lingua franca because approximately 70–80 percent of Senegalese speak it as either their first or second language (Ross 2008).

Instead, Sufi brotherhoods (*confrèries, tariqa*) represent Senegal's most politically salient identity cleavage for the approximately 95 percent of the population who are Muslim. As Villalón (1999) notes, the brotherhoods have an extraordinary presence in the everyday lives of the Senegalese, ranging from businesses, transport, government offices, and schools. There are four main brotherhoods: the Tijaniyya, Mouridiyya, Qadiriyya, and Layène. Based on Senegal's 2002 census, the Tijaniyya and Mouridiyya are the country's two largest brotherhoods, and they represent 49 and 32 percent of the population, respectively.

---

[9] For example, Posner (2004b) constructed a Politically Relevant Ethnic Group (PREG) index that determines how many ethnic groups have actually been engaged in political competition. According to the PREG index, Senegal received a score of only 0.14 out of a possible 1, indicating that ethnicity plays a negligible factor in competition over policy in the country. The equivalent figure for Zambia was 0.71.

[10] Historically, for instance, the Wolof caste structure included the nobility, commoners, artisans, *griots*, and slaves (Markovitz 1970). Within each caste stratum, there were even further subdivisions.

All of the brotherhoods are hierarchically structured, with authority filtering downward from the Khalifa Général, or leader of the brotherhood, to multiple religious leaders known as marabouts, to *talibés* or disciples (O'Brien 1971).[11] The Mouride brotherhood, which was established in Senegal during the early 1900s by Cheikh Amadou Bamba Mbacké, believes that a marabout's intercession on behalf of his talibé is necessary for the latter's redemption (Beck 2008). The Mouridiyya is very centralized, recognizes only one Khalifa Général, and is centered on the town of Touba in the region of Diourbel. Despite being smaller than the Tijaniyya, the Mouridiyya historically controlled Senegal's main export crop, peanuts. In addition, the brotherhood is notable for promoting a Muslim variety of the Protestant work ethic, and it incorporates most Wolof-speaking Senegalese (Le Vine 2004).

In the Tidiane brotherhood, which originated in Morocco, disciples view their marabouts as religious guides with mystical powers. Due to internal rivalries and family disputes, the Tijaniyya are much more fragmented than the Mourides. As highlighted in Table 6.5, the Malikiyya branch established by Al-Hajj Malik Sy is located in Tivaouane in the region of Thiès; the Niassène sect, which was founded by Al-Hajj Abdoulaye Niass, is headquartered in the region of Kaolack (Ross 2008; Loimeier 2007).

The remaining two brotherhoods are much smaller. The Qadiriyya order originally emerged in Baghdad and attracts many of Senegal's minority ethnic groups, such as migrants from Mauritania, Bambara from Mali, and the Mandika of Casamance. The Layène was established in a suburb of Dakar, and its membership is generally limited to the Cap Vert Peninsula (Ross 2008).

Jostling between brotherhoods for influence has ebbed and flowed since the 1960s. At independence, demographers were not allowed to collect census data on the brotherhoods because the government feared that revealing which group was actually numerically larger could be politically explosive (O'Brien 2003). In the late 1970s, the Mourides were viewed by the other brotherhoods as excessively proselytizing, particularly toward urban youth who were attracted to the Mourides's political and economic connections. This resentment ultimately resulted in riots in Dakar between the Mourides and Tidianes in both 1978 and 1980, and led to warnings of potential civil war by the Tidiane leadership (O'Brien 2003).

---

[11] In the version of Senegalese Islam, marabouts possess the power to grant salvation to their disciples, who are in turn required to obey and pay homage to their spiritual leader (Boone 1992: 41).

Table 6.5. *Description of Sufi Brotherhoods*

Brotherhood (sects, *subsects*)	Founder	Spiritual Center	Share of Population Belonging to Brotherhood
Tijaniyya	–	–	
Malikiyya	El Hajj Malik Sy	Tivaoune, Thiès	
Moustarchidine	Moustapha Sy		49
Niassène	Al-Hajj Abdoulaye Niass	Kaolack	
Mouridiyya	Cheikh Amadou Bamba Mbacké	Touba, Diourbel	
			32
Baye Fall	Ibrahima Fall		
Qadiriyya	Cheikh Bou Kounta	Ndiassane, Thiès	8.5
Layène	Mouhamadou Seydina Limamou Laye	Dakar	0.6

Sources: Population shares based on the 2002 Senegalese census, accessed from the Minnesota Population Center (2011). They do not total to 100 because 5 percent of Senegalese are Christian and another 5 percent are Muslim but do not adhere to a Sufi brotherhood.

The Mourides in particular have exerted a strong influence on Senegal's political sphere. A broad range of scholarship classifies the Mourides as "influential brokers" (Beck 2008) who encourage disciples to support specific political candidates depending on the economic benefits the brotherhood receives from the ruling regime (e.g., Coulon 1981; O'Brien 1971). Their ability to bestow politicians with legitimacy remains strong in rural areas, prompting Boone (2003: 91) to observe the following:

So it is that even after the groundnut era the regime has continued to invest in sustaining the material bases of the Mouride order, and thus to provide the economic linkages by which religious prestige and legitimacy were transformed into worldly political clout. Senegal's opposition politicians in the 1990s courted the marabouts almost as assiduously as Lamine Guèye and Léopold Senghor did in the 1950s.

Importantly, however, Loimeier (2007) argues that the Mourides were forced to engage in explicit demands for political concessions precisely because most government offices have traditionally been held by Tidianes. By contrast, the Mourides were conspicuously missing from the upper echelons of politics: "Murids have thus had to ask for 'their goods' rather 'loudly.' …

Table 6.6. *Distribution of Senegalese Sufi Brotherhoods by Region*

Region	Share of the Population that is Rural (%)	Predominant Sufi Brotherhood	Share of Region's Population Adhering to Brotherhood (%)
Dakar	2.8	Tijaniyya	49.8
Diourbel	84.1	Mouridiyya	89.5
Fatick	87.3	Tijaniyya	42.3
Kaolack	77.0	Tijaniyya	64.8
Kolda	86.7	Tijaniyya	60.8
Louga	81.7	Mouridiyya	43
Matam	85.75	Tijaniyya	89.1
St. Louis	63.6	Tijaniyya	79
Tambacounda	83.2	Tijaniyya	58.1
Thiès	57.5	Mouridiyya	45.6
Ziguinchor	53	Tijaniyya	30.1

Notes: Ziguinchor is predominantly Catholic, which is why the share of Sufi affiliation is so low. At the time of the 2007 elections, there were only eleven regions. Since then, three more have been created.

Sources: Calculations based on the 2002 Senegalese census, accessed from the Minnesota Population Center (2011).

Tijanis were not forced to resort to 'Murid' strategies as long as they were 'in power' or close to it" (Loimeier 2007: 71).[12]

Declining patronage resources due to structural adjustment certainly contributed to the Mouride marabouts' decision not to issue an *ndigel* instructing disciples to vote for the Tidiane candidate, Abdou Diouf, in the 2000 elections (Diop et al. 2002). However, their support for a Mouride candidate instead, Abdoulaye Wade, also reflected a sense of disappointment with their long-standing exclusion from the structures of state bureaucracy and authority (Loimeier 2007). By contrast, one of the heads of the Tidiane brotherhood in Tivaoune, Chiekh Tidiane Sy, publicly instructed his followers to support Diouf in the same elections (Villalón 2004).

As seen in Table 6.6, one brotherhood is more predominant than another in some rural regions; in others – such as Thiès, Louga, and Fatick which are shown in Map 6.2– they have relatively equal followings. Although most urban dwellers are devout Muslims, a number of observers have emphasized

---

[12] Murid and Tijan are alternative spellings for adherents to these two particular brotherhoods.

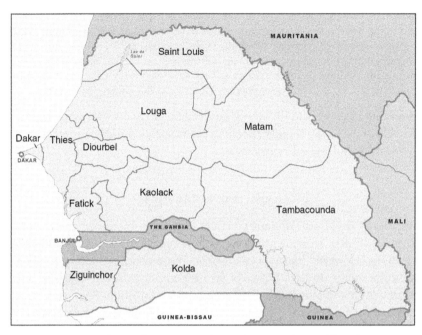

Map 6.2 Map of Senegalese Regions. Copyright © 2007 by World Trade Press.

that religious brotherhoods take on different manifestations in rural than urban areas (e.g., Dahou and Foucher 2004). In urban areas, the marabouts tend to play a prominent role in facilitating social and business networks (Beck 2001: 605).[13] However, they have less influence over secular matters such as politics (Gellar 2005: 111). In rural areas, however, loyalty to religious leaders has historically been much higher than in urban centers (Beck 2008). Moreover, Senegal's relatively high level of administrative decentralization accords religious leaders, particularly in regions where the seat of the brotherhoods are based, a substantial level of authority over local development and therefore makes them important intermediaries for the central government (see Beck 2001). Recognizing that local development depends on a community leader's assessment of continued government beneficence can play a powerful role for voting-age residents:

---

[13] For instance, daaras, or religious solidarity associations and Koranic schools, exist in urban areas to assist migrants financially with their adjustment to city life, and they are often controlled by a particular marabout (Beck 2001; Guèye 2001).

When you go into rural areas, if you have in your party the leader of the village who serves the community, etcetera, you are sure to win there because he dominates the region economically, etcetera. When the leader says vote for something, then it's of course necessary for the people to vote for that person.... But, in large cities, the people can position themselves more as they personally wish; they are less conditioned psychologically by the *marabouts*. (Interview with Badara Diop, 2008)

Engaging in appeals to local religious leaders in rural areas, especially the Khalifa of the brotherhoods, therefore offers party candidates an important mode of mobilization in rural areas.

Gorgui and the Mourides

As already discussed, Abdoulaye Wade focused primarily on the use of a populist strategy with the urban poor in the run-up to the 2000 presidential elections. However, like Sata in Zambia, Wade could not afford to alienate rural voters. Indeed, Senegal's primary urban center, Dakar, still only represents about one-quarter of the country's population. Because Senegal has a two-round electoral system, candidates typically aim for a plurality of votes in the first round to advance to the second round. But as in Zambia, politicians do not know what other candidates will receive, and their first preference will be to win 50 percent of the vote to avoid a runoff with other candidates in a second round. However, relying on Senegal's urban poor alone is not sufficient for this strategy. As Beck (2001) points out, Wade would never have won national office in 2000 without receiving both urban and rural support.

Consequently, Wade began focusing on stressing his Mouride identity during the 2000 campaign. According to the Tidiane religious leader Serigne Moustapha Sy, "In 1993, no one knew that Wade was a Mouride. We [Tidiane marabouts] helped him and protected him" (cited in A. Diouf 2007). However, the Mourides, who had until 1993 supported the PS by issuing ndïgels to their disciples to vote for the party, were increasingly disappointed with Diouf's policies and the dwindling patronage resources they received from the state. Upon returning in October 1999 from a year of self-imposed exile in France, Wade received an endorsement from the Mourides (Englebert 2000) and proclaimed that he would be "their" president (Loimeier 2007: 72). The approach helped him out-compete his closest opposition competitor in the first round of the 2000 elections, Moustapha Niasse, within Mouride strongholds. For instance, Wade received 26,483 votes in the Mouride stronghold of Diourbel in the first round compared with 12,111 for Niasse. By the second round of elections, Wade also defeated

Diouf in this region, obtaining 62.6 percent of the vote compared with 37.6 percent for the former president.[14]

As Villalón (2004: 66) notes, "Wade provoked what can only be described as a major uproar in Senegal by seeming to violate the implicit understanding of the PS years that no preferential treatment would be accorded along confessional lines." His most controversial move was to immediately travel to Touba on the day of the 2000 elections to be photographed kneeling before the Mouride Khalifa Général. Hundreds of copies of the photograph were subsequently distributed widely throughout the country. In an interview shortly after his election, Wade emphasized that his personal identity is closely intertwined with his Mouridism (cited in Villalón 2004: 66). As P. Mbow (2009: 5) notes, "One thing is certain, the exploitation of Touba provided him [Wade] with a coherent base and allowed him to free himself from the allies who had helped him come to power."

But even though most Dakarois are Tidiane, Wade's focus on his Mouride identity was not incompatible with his populist strategy in urban areas. Indeed, as noted in Chapter 4, the urban poor, especially youth, had become inspired by the Baol Baol model of socioeconomic mobility, which is intimately linked to the Mouride brotherhood. Moreover, Wade's approach coincided with a period of generational change within the brotherhoods, demonstrated by the emergence in the late 1990s of a series of young, popular Mouride marabouts as vocal political agents in urban areas (Villalón 1999). These trends reinforced the notion that the Mouride identity signified advancement for the youth and a deviation from the status quo, which was a message that resonated well with Wade's Sopi rallying cry.

Broad Opposition Campaigning in the Senegalese Countryside

In the 2007 elections, the opposition could not follow the same targeted approach as Wade did in 2000 to garner votes in the countryside. Personalistic parties, such as Rewmi, the PS, and the AFP were relying on vague messages in urban areas, and all emphasized the importance of addressing rural poverty. As already shown, none of these three parties viewed the urban poor as their main constituents and all three parties launched their campaigns outside of Dakar. Rural votes were essential for these parties to obtain national majorities. Yet, like the MMD in Zambia, the PDS focused heavily on agricultural issues. For instance, soon after entering office, Wade announced the launching of the Loi d'Orientation

---

[14] Election data provided by the Ministry of Interior.

Agro-Sylvo-Pastorale, and stressed that Senegal needed a grand vision for its agricultural sector. In all, the PDS spokesman Babacar Gaye claims that between 2006 and 2008 1,000 tractors were delivered to rural areas to help with the modernization of agriculture and both seeds and fertilizer were heavily subsidized (interview with Gaye, 2008).[15]

Theoretically, each of the main opposition parties could have focused solely on targeting coreligionists in order to gain rural votes. However, in reality, this was not possible for two reasons. First, Seck, Dieng, and Niasse were all from the same brotherhood, the Tidiane. Secondly, Wade had forged clientelistic linkages in rural areas with not only members of the Mourides but also sections of the Tidiane sect.

Specifically, during Wade's first term, his relationship with the Mouride leadership became even more pronounced, fueled by what Galvan (2009: 4) describes as "implicit patronage promises and overt gestures." Wade engaged in frequent visits to Touba, which is the holy town of this brotherhood. In fact, his trips became so regular that he became mocked for only engaging in the 3Ts: *tukki, télé, Touba*, meaning "traveling overseas, going on television, and visiting Touba" (Dahou and Foucher 2004). Among other patronage promises, Wade oversaw the construction of a new road from Touba to Mbacké, which is where the leader of the Mouridiyya, Cheikh Saliou Mbacké, resides (Le Vine 2004). He also promised to build an airport there to facilitate religious pilgrimages (Gervasoni and Guèye 2005). Furthermore, prominent Mourides received special favors, such as being issued diplomatic passports that are usually only reserved for public officials (P. Mbow 2008). Unlike previous presidents who have possessed a retreat in a beach community south of Dakar, Wade decided to build his own vacation home at Touba (Vengroff and Magala 2001:150). Shockingly, he also claimed during his first term that he would not engage in any project within the country without first consulting with his personal marabout, Cheik Saliou (Gervasoni and Guèye 2005: 633). Tellingly, unlike in the 2000 elections when Wade focused his campaign in Dakar, he launched his 2007 one in Touba (Schwartz 2007).

Such actions provoked a great deal of tension among the brotherhoods and created especially difficult relations between the Tidjani branch at Tivaoune and Wade's government during his first term in office (Villalón 2004). Nevertheless, Wade remained committed to his Mouride coreligionists. When he launched his 2007 presidential campaign in Mbacké,

---

[15]   In the wake of food riots in 2008, Wade then announced yet another agricultural initiative, known as the Great Agricultural Offensive for Food and Abundance.

Wade announced to the assembled crowd, "I have constructed mosques and churches. I have helped all religions. But, I will say clearly that I am a Muslim and a Mouride" (cited in Faye 2007a: 4). According to the journalist who accompanied Wade on the campaign trail, the president gave out 50 million CFA and a 4 × 4 car to all of the most important families within the Mouride brotherhood (Faye 2007b). Such efforts ultimately proved fruitful for Wade, as Cheikh Saliou Mbacké issued a declaration for his disciples to support Wade and appeared on television to lobby on behalf of the incumbent on the eve of the elections (P. Mbow 2008). At the same time, Cheikh Mbacké had tried to convince Idrissa Seck not to compete in the elections (M. Sow 2006).

For Aiwa Wade, the representative for the LD-MPT, these clientelistic relations were a critical factor in explaining the PDS's support in rural areas: "The PDS is supported by the *marabout* bourgeoisie, who are compradors, and you know that in Senegal, there are the *marabouts* who say to their supporters 'vote for this person' and then their supporters will vote for that person" (interview with Wade, 2008). Indeed, interviews conducted with Mouride followers in the region of Diourbel revealed that although many preferred Idrissa Seck of Rewmi, they supported Wade because they did not want to disobey Cheikh Mbacké (see Faye 2007b). Wade also forged close ties with other influential Mouride marabouts in urban areas, such as Cheikh Bethio Thioune, whose disciples violently attacked members of Idrissa Seck's campaign team (Mane 2007c).

However, Wade also attempted to co-opt portions of the Tidiane leadership. Specifically, he split the Tidianes by favoring one segment of the brotherhood, the Niassène branch at Kaolack, over the traditionally more influential one, which is the Malikiyya branch headquartered in Tivaoune (P. Mbow 2008). Wade did so by inviting a high-ranking Niassène marabout, Serigne Mamoune Niasse, to the presidential palace in the months immediately preceding the 2007 campaign and offered him 1.5 million Euros in cash in exchange for his support (S. Diop 2007). In November 2006, Wade also promoted Serigne Niasse, who is illiterate in French, to the position of minister of state without portfolio and appointed him as a national senator. In addition, Wade appointed Ahmed Khalifa Niasse, who is one of the sons of the Niassène Khalifa Général, as his minister in charge of a new capital, which was a newly created ministry intended to oversee the construction of a new Senegalese capital between Dakar and St.Louis (Kane and Anne 2007).

Such actions were strategic in thwarting the opposition candidates. Indeed, given the backgrounds of Abdou Diouf and Dieng, the PS's main constituency base has always focused on the Tidiane (interview with Ibrahima Sall,

2008). Moreover, co-opting the Niassène branch of the Tidiane brotherhood undermined Moustapha Niasse, who belongs to this branch of the brotherhood and traditionally relied on Kaolack as his stronghold. Serigne Mamoune Niasse was also formerly an organizer for the AFP in the regions of Kaolack, Fatick, and Diourbel.

Wade's actions provoked anger among the Tivaoune branch of the Tidiane co-fraternity. A subsect of this branch, known as the Moustarchidine, threw their support behind Idrissa Seck, who is the mayor of Thiès, which is the department where the subsect is based.[16] Cheikh Tidiane Sy of the Moustarchidine encouraged Seck to compete in the elections and affirmed his close ties with the Rewmi leader by stating that he had baptized Seck when the latter was an infant (M. Sow 2006). Ultimately, the influential son of Cheikh Sy, Cheikh Moustapha Sy, issued a ndïgel for all Moustarchidine adherents to vote for Seck in the 2007 elections. Mbaye (2007) speculates that this ndïgel created the impression among Mourides that Seck was a distinctly Tidiane candidate, and in turn actually spurred more Mourides to vote for Wade.

Due to Wade's maneuvering as well as overlapping religious affinities among some of the main opposition candidates, no opposition leader could rely on targeting specific regions with religious appeals. Rather, they needed to campaign more broadly in the countryside. To demonstrate this, campaign data was collected from the newspaper *Sud Quotidien* between the official presidential campaign period of February 4–23, 2007. This newspaper is one of the most important independent newspapers in Senegal, and it dedicated a specific section of the paper to following the campaign trail for every day of the campaign period.

Importantly, the mode of campaigning is different in Senegal than in Zambia. Perhaps influenced by Wade's once-novel blue marches, candidates tend to travel through towns and stop occasionally to tour a neighborhood. Although rallies do occur, especially at the launch and ending of a campaign, they are not the overriding method of campaigning in the same manner as they are in Zambia. As such, the number of villages and towns visited by each of the main candidates were recorded. Then, the village names were matched with the 2002 census, which indicates the administrative region

---

[16] According to Villalón (1999), the Moustarchidine is a movement that was founded in 1980 as a result of a succession crisis within the Tivaouane Tijaniyya order. When Cheikh Ababacar Sy died in 1957, his successor as caliphate was fought over by his son, Cheikh Tidiane Sy, and his brother, Cheikh Abdoul Aziz. The latter ultimately obtained a majority of family support, and Tidiane Sy established the Moustarchidine as a parallel power base. The movement stresses the importance of genealogy as the source of legitimacy for its leadership, and has been active in hosting political activities aimed at targeting disillusioned youth.

Table 6.7. *Distribution of Total Campaign Visits Outside Dakar by Key Candidates in the 2007 Presidential Elections*

Region	Main Candidates (Party), % of Campaign Visits				
	Wade (PDS)	Seck (Rewmi)	Niasse (AFP)	Dieng (PS)	Bathily (LD-MPT)
Diourbel	5.3	10.3	3.4	16.7	0.0
Fatick	10.5	0.0	0.0	0.0	6.3
Kaolack	5.3	13.8	13.8	11.1	12.5
Kolda	2.6	10.3	3.4	5.6	6.3
Louga	5.3	10.3	17.2	11.1	12.5
Matam	7.9	3.4	0.0	5.6	0.0
St. Louis	34.2	17.2	10.3	5.6	6.3
Tambacounda	5.3	6.9	10.3	16.7	25.0
Thiès	10.5	20.7	27.6	22.2	18.8
Ziguinchor	13.2	6.9	13.8	5.6	12.5
Total	100 (N = 38)	100 (N = 29)	100 (N = 29)	100 (N = 18)	100 (N = 16)

Source: Calculated from news reports in *Sud Quotidien* newspaper between February 4–23, 2007.

where each locality can be found. Subsequently, the share of places visited within each region was calculated as the share of total places visited.

Table 6.7 reveals that like Zambia, the incumbent was the only candidate to have visited all regions outside of Dakar. This included the most remote regions, such as Matam, where Wade lost badly in the 2000 elections and religious leaders have increasingly been instructing residents how to vote (see Dabo 2007b). In St. Louis, where President Wade concentrated many of his visits, these mostly occurred in the remote department of Podor, along the northern border with Mauritania. Unlike the PF in Zambia, the opposition politicians spread out their rural campaign activities more broadly. Dieng and Seck spent most of their time in Thiès, followed closely by St. Louis and Louga, respectively. In contrast to Sata's concentration in those rural areas with large numbers of co-ethnics, Niasse allocated only 14 percent of his time in Kaolack, which is where he has the greatest affinity with the populace along religious lines. He concentrated rather more of his visits in Louga, which has a Mouride majority, and in Thiès, where the other Tidiane sect is located. Bathily conducted eleven campaign visits in Dakar because the LD-MPT's message about advancing the rights of salaried workers is only relevant to a small group of urban professionals. However, he is also

Table 6.8. *Distribution of Vote Shares in Senegal's 2007 Presidential Elections, Outside Dakar*

Regions	Selected Candidates (Party), % of Votes					Others	Total
	Wade (PDS)	Seck (Rewmi)	Niasse (AFP)	Dieng (PS)	Bathily (LD-MPT)		
Diourbel	73.5	10.4	2.2	8.3	1.0	4.6	100
Fatick	55.9	6.5	9.9	16.9	3.6	7.2	100
Kaolack	44.8	6.6	23.1	18.0	2.2	5.3	100
Kolda	68.1	4.4	4.5	5.6	3.2	14.2	100
Louga	59.1	14.2	2.8	15.4	2.5	6	100
Matam	67.1	3.7	11.4	5.2	5.9	6.7	100
St. Louis	59.5	12.2	3.4	17.1	2.5	5.3	100
Tambacounda	60.0	7.0	4.3	10.6	6.8	11.3	100
Thiès	38.6	32.9	2.6	19.9	1.2	4.8	100
Ziguinchor	55.9	4.9	2.4	2.2	2.1	32.5	100

Source: "Résultats Provisoires de la Commision Nationale de Récensement des Votes," *Sud Quotidien*, March 2, 2007, p.3.

a Tidiane and therefore faced the challenge of campaigning broadly in the few areas outside of Dakar that he did visit.

When campaigning, these opposition candidates were careful to espouse broad messages and appeal to various religious authorities, which underscores that they were not specifically relying on identity appeals. For instance, Niasse focused a great deal on agricultural issues, noting, for example, in Tambacounda that he wanted to end the rural exodus as well as frontier banditry caused by the stealing of cows (Thiam 2007). Seck and Dieng assiduously courted religious leaders. In Diourbel, Seck requested an audience with Saliou Mbacké in order to pray for peace in Senegal (Mane 2007d). Yet, when he was in Kaolack, Seck made sure to court the hierarchy of the Niassène sect (Mane 2007b). In Matam, Dieng confirmed that he wanted to maintain a strong relationship with the Tidiane marabout leader in the region, Thierno Mouhamadou Samassa (Dabo 2007b). At the same time, during his visit to Diourbel, Dieng emphasized to Saliou Mbacké that he believed religious cities should be treated differently than other Senegalese cities and towns (Dabo 2007a).

Regardless of where the opposition candidates campaigned, Table 6.8 highlights that they all received their greatest electoral support in their home regions. The one exception was Wade, who is originally from Louga.

Instead, the explicit support of the Mouride Khalifa Général helped Gorgui achieve his highest victories in the overwhelmingly Mouride region of Diourbel, even though Wade did not spend much physical time in that region during the two-week campaign period. His lowest share of votes was in the region of Thiès, where Seck was certainly assisted by his support from the Moustarchidine. Dieng, who was born in the department of Mbour within Thiès, also obtained the highest share of his votes in this region. Collectively, Seck's and Dieng's votes in Thiès exceeded those obtained by Wade, indicating that having two candidates with ties to this region caused a split in support. Bathily's highest level of support in rural Senegal came from his home region of Tambacounda. The relatively high results for "Other" candidates in Kolda and Ziguinchor can be attributed to Savané and Sagna, who are originally from these two regions, respectively.

For Niasse, Kaolack was by far the region in which he was most popular. However, Wade's ties to the Niassène marabouts there surely dampened some of Niasse's support. Indeed, in the first round of the 2000 presidential elections, Niasse received 32 percent of the votes in the region of Kaolack; Wade received only 14 percent.[17] The tables were turned by 2007, when Niasse received only 23 percent of the vote compared with Wade's 45 percent. As such, Wade's actions in the interim encouraged the Niassène leadership and its disciples that the incumbent was a better choice than their coreligionist.

The Afrobarometer survey data again offers a complementary perspective on the role of religion and party affinity. Although the survey data were taken a year after the 2007 presidential elections, previous campaigning should still have had an impact on party affinities among those who expressed that they were close to a particular party. Table 6.9 looks specifically at Muslim voters who either self-identify as solely Muslim or who see their identity as particularly tied to one of the four Sufi brotherhoods. Notably, we see that in both rural and urban areas, those who self-identify as Mouride overwhelmingly express an affinity to the PDS vis-à-vis the other political parties. Reflecting Wade's ability to co-opt one portion of the Tidiane leadership, rural Tidianes also demonstrated a greater closeness to the PDS than to any of the opposition parties. However, this profile changes dramatically in urban areas, where the PS gains much more support from this brotherhood. In fact, the combined share of support from urban Tidianes for all the opposition parties exceeds that which the PDS obtained.

---

[17] Data was provided by Macoumba Coumé at the Ministry of the Interior in Dakar on October 2, 2008.

Table 6.9. *Party Affinities by Religious Affiliation (%)*

Religion	Rural Senegalese (N = 392)					Urban Senegalese (N = 240)				
	PDS	Rewmi	PS	AFP	Others	PDS	Rewmi	PS	AFP	Others
Mouride	84	8	4	0	4	71	7	9	4	9
Tidiane	57	10	13	7	13	38	13	30	5	14
Qadir	42	9	3	13	34	70	0	14	0	17
Layène	100	0	0	0	0	0	0	0	0	100
Muslim	56	6	16	14	9	60	17	7	5	11
Other[a]	51	11	22	6	10	40	15	11	13	21
Total	60	8	13	9	10	53	13	16	5	13

[a] "Other" refers to self-identified Christians.
Notes: For both rural and urban Senegalese, the cross-tabulation between religion and party affinity is significant at the 1 percent level. The results are weighted and only include those who expressed an affinity to any political party.
Source: Afrobarometer Round 4.

CONCLUSION

Most African opposition parties first gain their political foothold in urban areas. This chapter examined how the strategies used by opposition parties to mobilize the poor in urban areas affect how they can in turn mobilize rural voters. I argued that parties reliant on populist strategies face important trade-offs because they may alienate rural voters, who remain important for national electoral victories in most African countries. At the same time, such parties face the risk of losing part of their support base, the urban poor, if they deviate from their main message in order to capture rural votes. By appealing to a sizable share of rural voters based on politically salient ascriptive identities, which is a type of clientelist linkage, opposition candidates can create a sizable coalition consisting of metropolitan and peripheral elements.

If an opposition party avoids making exclusionary identity appeals, this approach allows it to retain the support of the urban poor and remain competitive vis-à-vis the incumbent party in rural areas and concentrate scarce resources on campaigning. In 2008, Sata combined his populist strategy with the urban poor with appeals to Bemba-speaking rural Zambians who are concentrated in Northern and Luapula Provinces. In 2000, Wade mobilized Dakar's poor, drawing on his Mouride background

Table 6.10. *Summary of Mobilization Approaches across Cases*

Approach with the Urban Poor	Approach with Rural Voters	Examples
Populist strategy	Clientelistic linkages based on politically salient ascriptive identity	PF (2006, 2008); PDS (2000)
Personalistic linkages	Clientelistic linkages based on handouts (e.g., fertilizer subsidies, cars, money)	MMD (2008); PDS (2007)
Personalistic linkages	Personalistic linkages	UPND (2008); Rewmi (2007); PS (2007); AFP (2007)
Programmatic linkages	Personalistic linkages	LD-MPT (2007)

in rural areas. In both instances, the opposition candidates benefitted from the fact that no other serious opposition competitor drew on the same identity appeals.

The ability of opposition parties with populist strategies to specialize in different campaign techniques in urban and rural areas is emphasized by the inability of personalistic opposition parties to do the same. Without a core constituency among the urban poor, Hichilema, Seck, Niasse, and Dieng all needed to campaign relatively broadly in the countryside to improve their chances at national victory. In Zambia, however, Hichilema belongs to a relatively small ethnolinguistic group, the Tonga, which alone could not provide a national victory. In Senegal, all of the candidates from the heavy-contender opposition parties belonged to the numerically superior Tidiane Sufi brotherhood. However, Wade had already co-opted the Niassène sect of the Tidiane brotherhood, which precluded these parties from engaging in geographically targeted rural campaigns. Table 6.10 summarizes the patterns that emerged in this chapter.

Overall, this chapter confirms Hagopian's (2007) observation that parties can mix their strategies in order to mobilize different constituents within the same electoral cycle. I showed that opposition parties reliant on a populist strategy with the urban poor often simultaneously exploit politically salient cleavages along identity lines in order to form unlikely coalitions. This finding contradicts the typical urban-rural dichotomy, which portrays Africa's rural residents as divorced from political affairs (e.g., Hyden 1980) and supportive of the status quo (see Harding 2010); urbanites are typically much more politically engaged and less supportive of incumbents (see Bratton and van de Walle 1997). In fact, Bienen and Herbst (1996: 36) go so far as to claim that "elections have least affected the urban-rural divide" in Africa. But by disaggregating voters within the urban and rural domains, this chapter revealed when and why certain sectors of society in both milieus might share similar political party preferences, albeit for different reasons.

SEVEN

Political Parties and Populist Strategies in Other African Democracies

Thus far, this study's case studies demonstrated that opposition parties reliant on a populist strategy are more likely to mobilize the urban poor than their competitors, and that such a strategy is often combined with appeals to ascriptive identity cleavages to mobilize a segment of rural voters. This chapter tests the external validity of the argument by examining additional African case studies beyond Senegal and Zambia. Specifically, I look at both opposition and incumbent party strategies in key elections in Botswana, Kenya, and South Africa. All three countries are faced with severe challenges in urban areas, including high levels of inequality, unemployment, and slum housing. As noted in Chapter 2, these conditions contribute to both objective and subjective grievances that are susceptible to populist strategies.

However, the three cases simultaneously provide variation on the study's main dependent variable, which is opposition success at mobilizing the urban poor. Moreover, they all have different electoral rules for presidential contests, which ex ante should influence their approaches for appealing to rural voters. In Kenya, the opposition ODM obtained a majority of urban votes during the country's last elections in 2007 based on a populist strategy spearheaded by Raila Odinga. At the same time, the ODM targeted its rural campaigns in provinces where either Odinga's co-ethnics or minority groups reside. In Botswana, the opposition BNF controlled the capital of Gaborone for more than a decade as a result of Kenneth Koma's populist strategy. The party concurrently appealed to non-Tswana tribal groups in rural areas who have felt culturally, politically, and economically marginalized. But in the wake of Koma's disappearance from the political scene, the incumbent BDP has finally regained control of Gaborone by adopting elements of the BNF's populist strategy. In South Africa, the incumbent ANC faced its most competitive elections ever in 2009 as well as growing apathy by disappointed citizens. The party's leader, Jacob Zuma, reinvigorated support for the party through a populist strategy in urban areas, focusing on appeals to ethnolinguistic identities in rural areas, especially his home province of Kwa-Zulu Natal.

Collectively, the cases emphasize three points about a populist strategy. First and foremost, it is a winning strategy for mobilizing a heterogeneous group of urban poor. Secondly, it is almost always predicated on a dual coalition that consists of the urban poor and a segment of rural voters who are mobilized according to a politically salient identity cleavage. Thirdly, a populist strategy is not just the reserve of the opposition but can also be used successfully by incumbent parties to rejuvenate their party's image among the urban poor. Indeed, as Barr (2009) suggests, populist figures can arise even within established political parties to pose a challenge to existing ruling factions.

THE ODM, POPULISM, AND KENYA'S URBAN POOR

During Kenya's 2002 presidential elections, Mwai Kibaki and his opposition coalition the NARC finally ousted the long-ruling Kenyan African National Union (KANU). In those elections, Kibaki obtained approximately 76 percent of the votes in the capital of Nairobi. Similar to Levy Mwanawasa's first term in office in Zambia, Kibaki's first five years as president were characterized by good stewardship of the macroeconomy. By privatizing failing state enterprises, enforcing tax regulations, and improving Kenya's business environment, the budget deficit declined substantially and tax revenue doubled (Chege 2008). Between 2003 and 2007, economic growth increased from 3.4 to 7 percent, and Kibaki also delivered on his presidential promise to provide universal primary education (Chege 2008; Gibson and Long 2009).

However, urban poverty and inequality actually increased during roughly the same period. Over the last decade, Kenya has experienced rapid urbanization, growing at 4.4 percent in recent years (UN-Habitat 2003). Between 1997 and 2006, two poverty studies conducted under the auspices of the Kenya Integrated Household Budget Survey Bureau revealed that the share of the urban population considered "food poor" increased from 38 to 41 percent (Oxfam 2009). In Nairobi Province, the poverty incidence is 44 percent (World Bank 2009), and the Gini coefficient is 0.59 (UN-Habitat 2010b). According to UN-Habitat (2008), an estimated 60 percent of the city's population lives in slums that occupy only 5 percent of the capital's land area. Moreover, whereas total unemployment fell between 1998 and 2006, urban unemployment increased from 18.5 to 20 percent and youth unemployment in urban areas rose from 60 to an astounding 72 percent (World Bank 2009).

Moreover, the Kibaki regime's treatment of the urban poor was relatively harsh. For instance, in February 2004, the government threatened to evict 300,000 people from Kibera, which is considered Africa's largest slum, because houses had been built by railway tracks, under electricity pylons, or in areas marked for road construction. Between 2004 and 2006, government authorities also bulldozed and set fire to hundreds of homes in dozens of Nairobi's other informal settlements (COHRE 2006: 21–23). Even more controversially, gang violence within the slums resulted in heavy-handed police intervention that was resented by residents. A raid on gangs in Nairobi's Mathare slum in mid-2007, which resulted in the deaths of more than 100 people, left the urban poor particularly incensed over Kibaki's inability to control the police (Kagwanja 2009: 371).

Raila Odinga was well placed to capitalize on the urban poor's disenchantment. Nicknamed Agwambo, or "the mysterious one," Odinga is a well-established Kenyan politician. During the early 1990s, Odinga belonged to a party known as the Forum for the Restoration of Democracy (FORD).[1] When that party split into two, he became leader of the FORD-Kenya faction. After losing internal elections to lead this faction, he left to form the National Democratic Party, from which he contested the 1997 presidential elections. Subsequently, he became a member of the Liberal Democratic Party, which in turn joined Kibaki's NARC coalition in the 2002 elections. Odinga was appointed the minister of roads under Kibaki's government. But in 2005, in the aftermath of Kibaki's failed referendum on strengthening presidential powers, a number of cabinet ministers, including Odinga, were purged. Odinga subsequently formed the ODM, and Kibaki changed the name of his own party to the Party of National Unity (PNU).[2]

Despite traversing so many parties, Odinga's constituency base is undoubtedly tied to the urban poor. Since 1992, he has been consistently reelected as the MP for Nairobi's Langata constituency, which contains the large slum of Kibera, estimated to house from 750,000 to 1 million of Nairobi's population. Residents have cited unemployment, poor housing, insufficient water

---

[1] Raila Odinga's father, Jaramogi Oginga Odinga, had been vice president to Jomo Kenyatta during the 1960s and a stalwart of KANU until he left the party and founded FORD.

[2] The origins of the ODM's name come from the 2005 referendum, when an orange represented the symbol of those who opposed greater executive powers and a banana was the symbol for those who did not.

and sanitation facilities, and insecurity as some of their main concerns (*The Nation* 2007). The ODM also has an unofficial office located in a part of the slum known as Gatwikira (De Smedt 2009).

Highly charismatic and politically ambitious, Odinga is a rich businessman who gave up his adherence to socialist ideology in exchange for flamboyant outfits and his expensive Hummer car. During the 2007 campaign, he would improvise riddles and alter song lyrics in order to highlight the Kibaki government's failings, and he notably once emerged from his car's sunroof to exclaim, "This government needs a hammer ... it needs to be hammered out" (cited in Bosire 2007). Such tactics attracted large crowds to his urban rallies. In fact, his motorcade was mobbed with adoring supporters during his opening rally in Nairobi's Uhuru Park, where the crowd forced people onto trees and rooftops to find space to hear his message (Odula 2007). As Lynch (2006: 255) observes, "Raila is a man who stirs up the strongest of emotions – be it 'Railamania' or 'Railaphobia.'"

A discourse firmly targeted at ameliorating inequalities and catering to the needs of the urban poor proved central to Odinga's 2007 campaign. The interests of slum dwellers in particular have long represented one of his priorities. Back in 2001, Odinga had appealed to then-President Daniel Arap Moi to lower the rents in Kibera (De Smedt 2009). In 2005, when speculators were trying to obtain private ownership of land in Nairobi's Kiambiu slum, Odinga gave a speech on behalf of protecting the slum residents' interests and argued that the Kibaki government should more actively upgrade slums in both the capital and elsewhere in the country (*The East African* 2005). Symbolically, Odinga spent the day before the 2007 elections holding a series of rallies in the slums of Langata constituency (Barasa 2007).

When accepting the presidential nomination by the ODM in September 2007, Odinga promised to end Kenya's "economic apartheid" and ensured his young supporters jobs, free schooling, and cash for the poor (Chege 2008). In a subsequent rally, Odinga announced, "Kibaki says that the economy is better, but the situation on the ground shows that inflation has grown high. Sixty percent of Nairobi residents live in informal settlements because of government mismanagement. We want to improve the economic power of the people. We want a social movement" (cited in Odula 2007). Whereas Kibaki focused on emphasizing his government's economic achievements, Odinga placed job creation as the first priority in his party manifesto and countered that growth under Kibaki only resulted in widening income gaps. As such, Odinga promised the following: "I give you a cast-iron guarantee that I will be a champion of social justice and social emancipation – a champion of the poor, the dispossessed and the disadvantaged in our nation.

I will redress the imbalance between the powerful and the weak, between the rich and the poor, between the satisfied and the hungry" (Odinga 2007: 7). Odinga also launched attacks on government corruption, which only strengthened his focus on inequality because Kibaki himself was one of the world's highest-paid heads of state at the time (see Bosire and Peytermann 2007).

Given the lack of large-scale associations or unions that represent the urban poor in Kenya, Odinga's campaign relied on unmediated ties with this constituency.[3] Chege (2008: 135) observes that the ODM's lively and colorful campaign oriented around exclusion proved much more entertaining than the PNU's bland and businesslike one, which tried to appeal to voters on the basis of dry statistics. Lynch (2006) also claims that, despite being sixty years old at the time, Odinga portrayed himself as a modern and youthful leader, which undoubtedly aimed to endear him to Nairobi's restless and relatively young population. In fact, Cheeseman (2008) notes that young people saw Odinga's candidacy as a counterweight to corrupt and aging politicians. Moreover, the ODM's orange campaign T-shirts espoused that Odinga was the "People's President" (see Odula 2007) and provided yet another example of the candidate's attempt to convey that he was a man of the people rather than a wealthy politician. Rumors that Odinga has for years paid the rent for some Kibera tenants (De Smedt 2009: 595) also suggests that he has at times engaged in the distribution of selective benefits to his constituents.

By contrast, Odinga was not particularly well liked by the country's business community. The PNU's economic record appealed to the business class, and when share prices on the Nairobi Stock Exchange fell in early 2007, the ruling party argued that this was the consequence of international fears over an Odinga win (Chege 2008). Privately, financial actors admitted to preferring Kibaki to Odinga because the former offered continuity (Bosire and Peytermann 2007). Beyond economic stability, some Kenyans feared that Odinga conveyed a "street-brawling image," which was only reinforced by his support from young and unemployed "street thugs" in the slums (Clayton 2007).

Nevertheless, given the predominance of poor people in Nairobi compared with middle- and upper-class voters, Odinga's populist strategy proved successful in the capital. An exit poll conducted by the IRI

---

[3] For instance, the main labor confederation, known as the Central Organization of Trade Unions, represents only 4 percent of Kenya's labor force (Pollin, we Githinji, and Heintz 2007).

Table 7.1. *Poverty and Votes in Kenya's 2007 Parliamentary Elections*

Divisions	Number of Poor People	Share of ODM Votes (%)	Share of PNU Votes (%)
Nairobi District	881,265	41.9	28.8
Central	91, 559	42.2	40.9
Dagoretti	106,177	38.1	47.7
Embakasi	170,165	32.9	26.4
Kasarani	152, 825	48.5	20.8
Langata	110,504	69.7	28.1
Makadara	108,100	32.5	33.9
Westlands	60,705	45.3	31.1

Notes: The poverty data is based on an urban-specific poverty line, pegged at 2,648 Kenyan shillings per adult per month for an urban household. This was equivalent to about $35 in 2003 prices, which was when the survey was conducted. Official results in the eighth division, Kamukunji, were contested and went to court. The results were never declared but a PNU MP was appointed in August 2008. *Sources:* Poverty data calculated by Ndeng'e et al. (2003). Election data from the Electoral Commission of Kenya, www.eck.ke, (accessed March 13, 2008).

during the elections found that in Nairobi, Odinga obtained 54.6 percent of the vote in the 2007 elections compared with Kibaki's 33.1 percent (see Gibson and Long 2009).[4] Table 7.1 also presents the parliamentary results in Nairobi's constituencies. Parliamentary results are used instead of the presidential ones given widespread evidence that the latter were rigged (Gettleman 2007). The more credible parliamentary results reveal that ODM candidates received the majority of votes in five of these divisions, and Odinga did exceptionally well in Langata, where he ran again as MP.

Constructing a Pentagon Alliance with Rural Kenyans

However, the urban poor were not Odinga's only constituency base. He also forged a coalition with a segment of rural voters who were either his Luo co-ethnics or belonged to other minority groups. Of all potential cleavages, ethnicity certainly has proved the most salient in Kenya's political history (see Barkan and Chege 1989; Hulterström 2004; Miguel 2004; Oyugi 1997). Indeed, according to Posner's (2004b: 856) PREG index, Kenya possesses

---

[4]   This exit poll was nationally representative and relied on a survey sampling frame based on the voter's registry. See Gibson and Long (2009) for more details.

a relatively high rating of 0.57. Perceived political domination and wealth accumulation by the Kikuyu has been a key concern among other ethnic groups. The Luo were largely excluded from power during both the previous regimes of Jomo Kenyatta and his successor, Daniel Arap Moi. Moreover, groups such as the Luhya and Kamba often felt that their political representation was not commensurate with their share of the voting population (Branch and Cheeseman 2008). Although the victory of the multiethnic NARC in 2002 hinted of ethnicity's potentially declining salience, a debate over constitutional reform in 2005 reinvigorated it as opposing camps largely divided along ethnic lines (Lynch 2006).

Although Nairobi is a very diverse city, some of Kenya's rural provinces demonstrate a greater degree of concentration by certain ethnic groups.[5] For instance, Table 7.2 reveals that Central Province is almost entirely comprised of Kikuyu; the Luo represent almost 58 percent of the population in Nyanza. However, given Kenya's electoral rules at the time of the 2007 elections, Odinga could not portray the ODM as solely an ethnic party oriented around the Luo.[6] Specifically, a presidential candidate needed to obtain not only a national plurality of votes but also 25 percent of the vote in at least five of the eight provinces and win the parliamentary seat in his or her own electoral constituency. By explicitly focusing only on the Luo, Odinga would not have won in the country's other rural provinces.

As such, Odinga constructed a "pentagon alliance" with five leaders representing not only his Luo co-ethnics but also groups such as the Luhya, Kalenjin, and Coast peoples. These leaders included Musalia Mudavadi, William Ruto, Joseph Nyagah, Najib Balala, and Charity Ngilu. Furthermore, his rhetoric was often couched in class terms with ethnic implications, blaming the president and his "Mount Kenya mafia" for creating massive disparities between Kikuyu-dominated areas and the rest of Kenya.[7] The ODM's campaign focused on Kikuyu domination in banking, government, commercial farming, and education (Chege 2008) as well as their influx into the Rift Valley, which was historically the home of the Kalenjin and Maasai (Kagwanja 2009: 374). This storyline was reinforced by the ODM's campaign symbol, which was an orange divided into eight equal pieces. According to Odinga's manifesto, this symbolism represented that Kenya's

---

[5] Although the Kikuyu are the ethnic group with the largest representation in Nairobi, they comprise only 32 percent of the city's population, followed by the Luo at 18 percent and the Luhya at 16 percent (Butler 2002).

[6] In 2010, Kenya adopted a new constitution with new electoral rules.

[7] Mount Kenya clan refers to those politicians in Kibaki's inner circle and who hail from predominantly Kikuyu areas in Central and Eastern Province (*Africa Confidential* 2003: 2).

Table 7.2. *Distribution of Ethnic Groups in Kenya*

Province	Dominant Ethnic Group		Share of Province in Kenya's Population (%)
	Name	*Share of Ethnic Group in Province's Population (%)*	
Central	Kikuyu	93.8	11.4
Coast	Mijikenda	54.4	8.6
Eastern	Kamba	53.9	14.7
Nairobi	Kikuyu	32.4	8.1
North-eastern	Ogaden	36.0	6.0
Nyanza	Luo	57.9	14.1
Rift Valley	Kalenjin	46.4	25.9
Western	Luhya	86.2	11.2

Sources: 1989 Kenyan Census; 2009 Kenyan Census (Accessed at the Kenyan National Bureau of Statistics, http://www.knbs.or.ke/).

eight provinces would receive equal resources under his administration (Odinga 2007: 4). The implication was that under Kibaki, interprovincial disparities prevailed.

At the same time, one of Odinga's policy themes in the 2007 elections was an advocacy of *majimbo*, which means "regions" in Swahili. Specifically, majimbo refers to the devolution of power from the central government to the provinces in a manner similar to federalism. First advocated at independence by the Kenya African Democratic Union, this idea has a long legacy in Kenya (see D. Anderson 2005). For non-Kikuyu groups, this held appeal because it implied that regardless of who won power at the central level their particular region would have greater autonomy. In turn, Kibaki argued that Odinga was fostering tribalism because majimbo would divide the country along ethno-regional lines. Odinga countered such claims by stressing the importance of decentralization for local representation and accountability, which are themes that hold widespread appeal across ethnic groups (Gibson and Long 2009).

Due to scarce resources compared with the PNU, Odinga also geographically targeted his 2007 campaign rallies in the Rift Valley and Western Provinces. According to Horowitz (2009), Odinga only visited the Kikuyu-dominated Central Province once. He never visited Eastern Province, from where the Kamba leader of the ODM-Kenya party, Kalonzo Musyoka, hailed.[8]

---

[8] The ODM-Kenya party broke off from the ODM shortly before the 2007 elections.

Table 7.3. *Distribution of Parliamentary Seats Won by Party in 2007 Kenyan Elections*

Province	Dominant Ethnic Group	Number of Seats				Total
		ODM	*PNU*	*ODM-K*	*Other*	
Central	Kikuyu	0	18	0	11	29
Coast	Mijikenda	**12**	3	1	5	21
Eastern	Kamba	2	7	13	14	36
Nairobi	Kikuyu	**5**	2	0	0	7
North-eastern	Ogaden	5	0	0	5	10
Nyanza	Luo	**25**	0	0	7	32
Rift Valley	Kalenjin	**32**	11	1	4	48
Western	Luhya	**18**	2	0	4	24
Total		*99*	*43*	*15*	*50*	*207*

Notes: The results for one seat in Nairobi were contested and the results were never publicized. As such, the results for only seven, rather than eight, seats are indicated here.

Source: Office of Government Spokesperson: Election Results 2007, http://www.communication. go.ke/elections/province.asp (accessed January 19, 2010).

The Impact of Odinga's Approach

As Table 7.3 highlights, these targeted campaigns and implicit appeals to eth-nolinguistic identity proved conducive to mobilizing ethnic groups beyond Odinga's Luo base. Parliamentary results are used to ensure consistency with those that were presented in Table 7.1 and because, once again, they are considered more accurate than their presidential equivalents. The results show that Musyoka's party only achieved a majority of seats in Eastern Province; the PNU was most successful in Central Province. Similarly, the ODM's biggest wins, highlighted in boldface, occurred in the four provinces where the Luo and minority ethnic groups were located as well as in Nairobi.

Moreover, the exit polls conducted by IRI revealed that 48 percent of those concerned with employment and 85.8 percent of those who supported majimbo voted for Odinga. The comparable figures on these issues for Kibaki supporters were 35 percent and 9.2 percent, respectively. Instead, those who were most concerned with economic growth and education supported the incumbent. Moreover, these polls revealed that although 94 percent of Kikuyus voted for Kibaki, 98 percent of Luos, 75 percent of Luhya, 88 percent of Kalenjin, and 72 percent of Mijikenda supported Odinga (see Gibson and Long 2009).

Consequently, Odinga created a peripheral coalition oriented around Luo co-ethnics and other minority ethnic groups employing a populist strategy to mobilize most of the poor in Nairobi, which notably contains a Kikuyu majority. Well-documented vote rigging caused Odinga to lose his presidential bid, despite the ODM's parliamentary victory and exit polls showing him winning 46.1 percent of the national vote compared with Kibaki's 40.2 percent (Gibson and Long 2009). Subsequently, violence not only erupted among ethnic groups in rural provinces but also spilled out of the city's slums, where disappointed Odinga supporters threatened "No Raila! No Peace!" for weeks thereafter (De Smedt 2009). The violence represented an unfortunate testament to the emotional resonance of a campaign discourse that consistently focused on rectifying various manifestations of inequality.

THE RISE AND DECLINE OF THE BNF'S POPULIST
STRATEGY IN BOTSWANA

With approximately 57 percent of its population living in urban areas (World Bank 2009), Botswana has an even higher urbanization rate than Kenya. Well-managed diamond mines have ensured high economic growth rates over the last few decades, but little of the diamond wealth translated into significant poverty reduction. In the capital of Gaborone, 47 percent of the population lives below the poverty line (UNFPA 2007). Official unemployment has increased from 13.9 percent in 1991 to its current level of around 24 percent (Good 1996; OECD 2006). Youth unemployment is especially high, standing at 40.9 percent by the time of the 2001 census (UNDP-IPC 2005). Moreover, between 1994 and 2003, the country's Gini coefficient increased from 0.6 to 0.65 (UNDP-IPC 2005), and inequality in Botswana's cities is considered to be some of the highest in Africa (UN-Habitat 2009). These circumstances, combined with Botswana's long history of democracy, help explain why the country represents one of the earlier examples of an opposition party relying on a populist strategy to win votes from the urban poor.

Botswana's political system is often classified as one-party dominant because the ruling BDP has never been ousted from the presidency (e.g., Bogaards 2000; Doorenspleet 2003). Established by cattle elites, the BDP possesses strong roots in rural areas and has long adhered to a free-market orientation (Good and Taylor 2008). Yet, between 1984 and 2009, the opposition BNF won substantial support among the urban poor in the capital city of Gaborone, and its bastion of support centered in the city's slum of Old Naledi.

Founded in 1965, the BNF's leader was Dr. Kenneth Koma, an intellectual trained in the former Soviet Union who inherited considerable wealth from his father (Makgala 2005). Like Senegal's pôle de gauche opposition, Koma long espoused a programmatic message centered on socialism that held little appeal to the urban poor (van Bingsbergen 1994). For instance, Koma argued that Botswana's masses were being exploited by an African bureaucratic bourgeoisie and in the BNF's "Pamphlet No.1," he stated that "the neo-colonialist regime of the Democratic party (BDP) is much more reactionary than the classical colonial administration which preceded it" (cited in Polhemus 1983:406). He further stated that his party did not believe that "the profit motive, individual material incentives, money, capital and private entrepreneurs are indispensable pre-requisites to development" (cited in Polhemus 1983:408). Koma promised to instead make Botswana a society dominated by workers and a place where no one class would exploit the labor of another (Selolwane 2002). Pointing to this rhetoric, the BDP often generated fear among rural peasants that the BNF would nationalize their land and enforce communal ownership of cattle (Molomo 2000).

As a result of this discourse, the BNF long posed little threat to the BDP. Yet, the BNF gradually shifted away from its programmatic orientation and began adopting a populist strategy. This first became apparent in the 1984 elections when the BNF developed an increasingly coherent electoral appeal (Charlton 1993). As seen in Table 7.4, the BNF's vote shares began increasing at that time, and reached their zenith in 1994 when the party won almost 40 percent of the national vote.

Part of the BNF's growing electoral success during this period can be attributed to the waning popularity of the BDP. The BDP's image became tarnished by a range of corruption scandals by high-level politicians as well as its resistance to electoral reforms, such as lowering the voting age from twenty-one to eighteen years of age and creating an independent electoral commission, which were otherwise broadly popular measures (Tsie 1996; Wiseman 1998). According to observers, the BDP had cultivated "an image of arrogance, greed, corruption, insensitivity, and indifference" (cited in Good 1996: 66).

At the same time, Koma gradually created a populist strategy characterized by a number of key features. First, Koma had always been a highly charismatic leader who fostered a personality cult around him and within the party (Mokopakgosi and Molomo 2000; Somolekae 2005). When he was first elected as an MP for Gaborone South constituency in 1984, after defeating the vice president for the seat, a BNF colleague noted that "fame surrounded [Koma], and his ingress into Parliament

Table 7.4. *Seats Won by Party in Botswana (% of National Votes)*

Party	1969	1974	1979	1984	1989	1994	1999	2004	2009
Botswana Democratic Party (BDP)	24 (68.6)	27 (76.6)	29 (75.2)	29 (68)	31 (64.8)	27 (54.6)	33 (57.2)	44 (50.6)	45 (53.3)
Botswana National Front (BNF)	3 (13.5)	2 (11.5)	2 (12.9)	4 (20.4)	3 (27)	13 (37.1)	6 (26)	12 (25.5)	6 (21.9)
Botswana People's Party (BPP)	3 (12.1)	3 (6.6)	1 (7.5)	1 (6.6)	0 (4.4)	0 (4.6)	–	0 (1.9)	0 (1.4)
Botswana Progressive Union (BPU)	–	–	–	0 (1.3)	0 (0.9)	0 (1.2)	–	–	–
Botswana Independence Party (BIP)	1 (6)	1 (4.8)	0 (3.8)	0 (4.2)	0 (2.5)	0 (0.5)	–	–	–
Botswana Congress Party (BCP)	–	–	–	–	–	–	1 (11.9)	1 (16.3)	4 (19.2)
Botswana Alliance Movement (BAM)	–	–	–	–	–	–	0 (4.7)	0 (2.8)	1 (2.3)
Total Seats	31	32	32	34	34	40	40	57	57

Notes: The dashed line indicates that the party did not compete in those elections.
Sources: African Elections Database (http://africanelections.tripod.com/); Danevad (1995); Mokopakgosi and Molomo (2000).

was hailed almost like the arrival of a messiah by his followers" (cited in Makgala 2005: 309).

Secondly, although he was relatively affluent and very well educated, Koma was viewed as a modern Moses by Gaborone's poor, and his appearance in crumpled clothes and use of colloquial Setswana helped him forge unmediated ties with this constituency (see Makgala 2005; Motlogelwa 2009). His direct relationship with poor urbanites was reinforced by his lack of formal horizontal ties with other major civil society organizations, such as the Botswana Federation of Trade Unions, and his view that unions in particular were not credible representatives of urban laborers (Holm et al. 1996). Instead, as Holm, Molutsi, and Somolekae (1996: 59) note, "Koma said unequivocally that citizens should support parties as 'individuals' and not through groups."

Thirdly, his main constituency base was firmly centered on the urban poor. His support and position as MP in Gaborone South was notable given that the country's largest slum, Old Naledi, is located there. Koma referred to the slum as his "political bunker," and by the mid-1990s, residents of the slum indicated their loyalty to Koma by threatening to remove any politicians from the incumbent BDP who campaigned there (Motlogelwa 2009). Prior to the 1994 elections, Koma launched his campaign in Gaborone with a motorcade of 600 cars that included the party's entire slate of parliamentary candidates (Good 1996). By contrast, the BDP held no mass rallies in the capital city during those elections (Wiseman and Charlton 1995).

However, the most important characteristic of the BNF was its ability to finally offer a discourse that resonated with the priorities of the urban poor. According to Wiseman (1998), the sense of relative deprivation in urban areas among recently arrived rural migrants who failed to find jobs contributed to the rise of the BNF and the concurrent decline of the BDP during this period. Grievances included the shortage of accommodation in the city, high prices for consumer goods, the BDP's refusal to grant voting rights to those younger than twenty-one, and the general lack of social amenities for the poor (see Garekwe and Moloi 1994; Good 1996). As Tsie (1996: 31) explains:

A substantial section of the electorate supports it [the BNF] because its political message seems to be relevant to the socio-economic conditions of contemporary Botswana. The issues which it has stressed in its campaigns such as affordable housing, employment creation, better working conditions and the revamping of the education system resonate with more conviction amongst urban and peri-urban dwellers than amongst the peasantry.

Likewise, Molomo (2000: 72) observes that the BNF's message assisted the party in differentiating it from both the BDP and other opposition competitors: "It was a message focused on defining a niche for themselves [and that emphasized] defending the interests of the unemployed and the poor, largely those who stand on the losing side of rapid economic development." Among other claims, Dr. Koma argued that foreign investors should not be allowed to exploit Botswana's resources if Batswana were not receiving any profits in return (Molomo 2000), and he advocated for tax exemptions for people living below the subsistence level (Aguilar and Pacek 2000). In contrast to the BDP's campaign on a bland message of continuing its achievements, Koma ended his urban campaign rallies with "*a le chencheng*," Setswana for "let's make a change" (Good 1996).

The BNF Courts Minority Tribes

At the same time, the BNF combined its populist strategy in urban areas with appeals to tribal identities in rural areas. This approach was necessary given that Botswana's electoral rules require that the president is elected indirectly by more than half of the elected members of parliament. As such, the BNF needed its candidates to win in just more than half of the country's forty electoral constituencies at the time.[9] Gaborone only represented four parliamentary seats, therefore the BNF could not rely on support from the capital alone.

The BNF faced a disadvantage in rural areas however because the ruling BDP targeted many of its social welfare programs there. For instance, the BDP supported farmers through the Accelerated Rainfed Arable Program and the Arable Lands Development Program as well as established a Drought Relief Program (DRP) (Charlton 1993; Osei-Hwedie 2001). Picard (1987) had found that the drought relief money was funneled through rural chiefs with the understanding that this was help in exchange for BDP support. According to Molutsi (1989: 128), the DRP was critical to the BDP's support in rural areas: "Through this project, where many people are fed, subsidized, employed and assisted in so many ways, the ruling party has successfully resisted inroads to its popularity, especially in the rural areas." Solway (1994) also suspected that the program intended to forestall migration to urban areas and thereby prevent growth in the BNF's support base.

In turn, appealing to tribal identities in rural areas was one way to gain constituency seats in a manner that circumvented the BDP's incumbent advantages. Although Botswana is frequently deemed ethnically

---

[9]   Today, Botswana has fifty-seven electoral constituencies.

homogeneous, communal tensions are not rare (see Solway 2002), and the most politically salient identity cleavage has revolved around tribal affiliation. Until very recently, articles 77, 78, and 79 of Botswana's constitution stipulated that only members of the eight Tswana tribes were allowed to be members of the House of Chiefs, which is a legislative chamber of government that makes all decisions related to culture and tradition (Nyamnjoh 2002). In effect, this has meant that eight chiefs ruled over the country's thirty-eight other tribes whose chiefs are not recognized (Nyati-Ramahobo 2008). As a consequence, non-Tswana tribes felt that their culture and languages had been marginalized by the Tswana (Wiseman 1998). There is also evidence that major income, education, and service-delivery disparities exist in rural areas of the country that are dominated by non-Tswana-speaking residents (Nyati-Ramahobo 2008).

Although Botswana's government does not collect census data by ethnic and tribal group, it is estimated that minority groups collectively comprise approximately 60 percent of the population (Nyati-Ramahobo 2008). Because these minority groups represent a numerical majority, Charlton (1993) notes that Botswana's political parties have an incentive to appeal to them by addressing ethnic interests and emotions. As early as 1988, the BNF recognized this and attempted to establish grassroots structures in remote rural areas with large numbers of minority groups, such as the districts of Boteti, Ghanzi, Ngami, and Kgalagadi (Wiseman 1998).

The minority San, who are concentrated in Ghanzi and Kgalagadi, have historically been Botswana's most marginalized and poorest citizens. The BNF's electoral strategy coincided with greater collection action among the San in the early 1990s, who argued that they were treated as an underclass (Good 1996). The BNF further sought to draw attention to the plight of the San, and in the 1994 district council elections the party fielded a full slate of San candidates in Ghanzi (Good 1996; Wilmsen 1996). Solway (2004: 142) quotes one San as saying:

Then I saw the BNF pamphlet and on page 16, Koma said he was indebted to all the minorities for paying taxes so that he could study and to the Sarwa who herded his cattle while he was at school. Then, from 1979 to 1994, I spent up to 65 percent of my time campaigning for the BNF in western Kweneng.[10]

Beyond the San, the BNF also attracted the Bayei in the Okavango area (Rule 2000), as well as the Kalanga-speaking group who reside in the country's Northeast District and have long resented the country's

---

[10] *Sarwa* is the Setswana word for "San."

Tswana- and English-only language policies (Du Toit 1995). Notably, in the 1994 national elections, one of the BNF's main campaign issues was the amendment of those sections of the constitution related to the House of Chiefs. This strategically drew on the desire of many minority tribes who wanted chiefly representation at the national level, which would indicate that their tribe was as legitimate and important as the Tswana tribes (Solway 1994).

At the same time, however, the BNF was also popular among some disaffected Tswana tribes. In rural areas, the BDP has traditionally been supported by the two largest Setswana-speaking groups, the Bangwato and the Bakwena. However, the BNF has proved popular among the Batlokwa tribe (*Africa Confidential* 2004) as well as the Bangwaketse tribe who live in the country's Southern District. The chief of the latter tribe joined the BNF early on in 1969 because he believed the BDP-led government had neglected his region (Lemon 2007).

The Impact of Koma's Dual Appeals

Using identity appeals and promising to reform the House of Chiefs in the 1994 campaign and simultaneously capitalizing on widespread disillusionment with inequality and unemployment in urban areas caused the BNF to achieve its most successful election results in the party's history. As seen in Table 7.5, the BNF obtained thirteen out of forty parliamentary seats in the 1994 elections. Koma's party was clearly the winner in all four of Gaborone's constituencies, as well as the country's other major urban areas such as Francistown, Lobatse, and Selebi-Phikwe. In addition, the BNF won six rural constituency seats: Okavango (Ngamiland District), Kanye (Southern District), Kglateng East and West (Kglateng District), Mogoditshane (Kweneng District), and Ngwaketse South (South East District). Although the party still did not capture the constituency seat in Ghanzi, the party increased its share of the vote there from 34 percent in 1989 to 46 percent five years later (Wiseman 1998). Although the BDP still retained its seat in the North East, Tsie (1996) notes that the incumbent party only just obtained enough votes to win there.

An important element of this approach was that Koma was actually also a member of the Setswana-speaking Bangwato tribe (Makgala 2005), and this probably explains why his inroads into minority-dominated rural areas were not as large as they could have been. Yet given that no other opposition party leaders were from minority groups, Koma effectively tapped into discontent over tribal issues in a manner that coincided with the urban

Table 7.5. *Distribution of Constituency Seats by District in 1994 Elections*

Urban Constituencies	BDP	BNF
Gaborone	0	4
Francistown	1	1
Lobatse	0	1
Selebi-Phikwe	0	1
Rural Constituencies	**BDP**	**BNF**
Southern	1	1
South East	2	1
Kweneng	4	1
Kgatleng	0	2
Central	14	0
North East	1	0
Ngamiland	1	1
Chobe	1	0
Ghanzi	1	0
Kgalagadi	1	0
Total	*27*	*13*

Sources: Tsie (1996); Wiseman and Charlton (1995); and EISA (http://www.eisa.org.za/WEP/bot1994election.htm).

poor's despair over economic inequalities. As Solway (2002: 726) explains, the BNF was not an ethnic party, but its support of minority goals helped extend its base into rural areas. At the same time, the core of its voter coalition remained urban areas: "In spite of definite progress in the rural areas amongst non-Tswana ethnic groups, the major strength of the BNF remains its urban support base. Here the appeal of the BNF is essentially based on class rather than ethnicity" (Wiseman 1998: 257).

In the subsequent 1999 elections, the BNF, whose populist strategy most struck a chord with unemployed urban youth, further benefitted from a 1997 referendum that finally lowered the voting age from twenty-one to eighteen (Molomo 2000). In those elections, the BNF retained its dominance in Gaborone where the young are concentrated, still failing to mobilize older voters (see Garekwe and Moloi 1994). Observers again noted that the win reflected "a potentially dangerous polarization between the urban poor who benefit little from the country's diamond wealth, the Batswana elite, and the rural people whose cash incomes are somewhat appeased by a sense of community and government handouts" (*Africa Confidential* 1999: 4).

However, the BNF's vote shares never returned to their 1994 level, and this is attributed to the manner by which Koma managed the party. As is typical of charismatic leaders, Koma displayed authoritarian tendencies and tolerated little dissension within the BNF or interparty debate (Makgala 2005; Molomo 2000). The BNF was viewed as having very little institutionalization beyond Koma, and the party was effectively synonymous with him (Somolekae 2005). As one party insider noted, "*Party ke Koma*," meaning "Koma is the Party" (cited in Mokopakgosi and Molomo 2000). He repeatedly refused to have the BNF overshadowed by participating in a larger opposition coalition, known as the Botswana Alliance Movement (BAM) (*Africa Confidential* 1999). The lack of internal democracy ultimately culminated in a particularly virulent fight in 1998, known as the Battle of Palapye, between Koma and the party's Vice President, Michael Dingake. Subsequently, Dingake left the BNF and formed the Botswana Congress Party (BCP), and eleven of the BNF's thirteen MPs defected to this new party. Then, after Koma's retirement from politics and the arrival of Otsweletse Moupo as the BNF's new leader, the party experienced additional infighting and subsequent splintering (see Poteete 2012). For example, at least ten new parties have emerged that are led by previous members of the BNF (Molefhe 2009).

Internal problems, coupled with recent attempts by the BDP to re-brand its image, have caused the BNF to lose its appeal among the urban poor. One factor has been that Moupo lacks the same popular touch with the electorate, and BNF elites are now found to espouse a less coherent message on issues of social redistribution and public spending (van Eerd 2011). At the same time, the BDP decided to start echoing the BNF's rhetoric and adopting its own populist stance. When Ian Khama took over as leader of the BDP in April 2008, he began a series of fireside chats and surprise town tours intended to demonstrate an understanding and affinity with the challenges faced by the urban electorate (see Molefhe 2009). Right before the 2009 general elections, Khama uncharacteristically rode a bicycle into the slum of Old Naledi to address a rally, prompting Mooketsi (2009) to observe that he had a common touch with the "grassroots." Ultimately, the BDP grabbed the BNF's constituency seats in Gaborone for the first time in more than a decade, and it captured the majority of votes in Old Naledi. To symbolize the importance of the urban poor to the BDP's re-branding, Khama returned to the slum to hold his party's victory rally (Motlogelwa 2009).

A POPULIST FACTION WITHIN SOUTH AFRICA'S ANC

The Botswana case illustrates that an incumbent party can just as easily adopt a populist strategy to win over new constituents as the opposition, and this point becomes even clearer by examining South Africa's ANC in the country's 2009 elections. South Africa represents one of Africa's most urbanized democracies, with almost 60 percent of its population living in urban areas as of 2005 (World Bank 2009). The country's largest city, Johannesburg, currently has around 3.4 million residents (De Wet et al. 2008). By 2015, Gauteng Province, in which both Johannesburg and Pretoria are located, is estimated to contain approximately 14 million people (De Wet et al. 2008).

However, the legacy of apartheid has left massive inequalities both between rural and urban areas as well as within cities. For instance, based on surveys from 2005, there is a Gini coefficient of 0.75 percent in Johannesburg, 0.67 percent in Cape Town, and 0.72 in both Durban and Pretoria (UN-Habitat 2009). Racial disparities also still persist, as approximately 25 percent of the country's black population is unemployed, compared with only 4 percent of the white population (Statistics South Africa 2009a). Declines in the manufacturing sector and low demand for both unskilled and semiskilled labor has not only contributed to this unemployment but also depressed wages for those with a job (see Beall, Crankshaw, and Parnell 2000). Moreover, a quarter of the population still lives in shacks rather than safe and durable housing (Blair 2009).

In the mid-1990s, under President Nelson Mandela, the ANC and its tripartite alliance partners, COSATU, and the South African Communist Party (SACP), developed the Reconstruction and Development Program (RDP) to address the inequalities created by apartheid. The RDP focused on achieving growth through redistribution by advocating a strategic role for the public sector, land reform, better training and a living wage for workers, and the provision of houses, electricity, and water to poor communities (Lodge 2002). But without substantial foreign investment, the growth needed for these policies never emerged.

Thabo Mbeki, the country's second democratically elected president from the ANC, facilitated the shift to a more free-market economic program known as GEAR (Saunders 2005). During his tenure, South Africa experienced substantial GDP growth, which averaged 4.6 percent between 2002 and 2008 (Statistics South Africa 2009b). However, Mbeki's neoliberal policy orientation prompted growing rifts within the ruling tripartite alliance. Both COSATU and SACP opposed the ANC's abandonment of its dirigiste principles in favor of a plan that, among other things, emphasized privatization, tariff reductions, and productivity-linked wage rates (Lodge 2002; Saunders, 2005). In fact, the two alliance partners began claiming that the ANC was becoming a "bourgeois nationalist political party" (Pillay 2008: 18).

At the same time, Mbeki's policies prompted widespread discontent among the poor. Whereas a small number of extraordinarily wealthy black business tycoons benefitted from the ANC's Black Economic Empowerment initiative (Gumede 2008), most of the poor were still grappling with insufficient service delivery. In fact, between 2004 and 2006, the number of protests over substandard services in poor townships and informal urban settlements increased from 5,800 to more than 10,000 (Alexander 2010; Gumede 2008). Although water and electricity infrastructure were extended to millions of customers after the end of apartheid, the policies of cost recovery, which required customers to pay the full cost of these services, meant that hundreds of thousands of residents effectively could not afford them (see Khunou 2002; Pape and McDonald 2002). Illegal reconnections of electricity subsequently became the source of violent conflict between the police and members of poor communities (Bassett and Clarke 2008). Moreover, although the ANC increased the number of people living in proper housing, the rate of progress disappointed many slum and squatter dwellers. Movements such as Abahali baseMjondolo ("shack dwellers") in Durban organized marches under the banner of "No Land, No House, No Vote" (Pithouse 2006), and shack dwellers outside Johannesburg admitted losing faith in the ANC (Georgy 2007). By 2008, much of this disappointment over substandard housing, poor services, and lack of jobs erupted into xenophobic riots within Johannesburg's townships and then spread to townships in Durban and Cape Town. After 20 days of violence, 62 people were dead, 670 were wounded, and up to 100,000 people were internally displaced (Misago, Landau, and Monson 2009).

Concurrently, the ANC faced an internal power struggle that ultimately benefitted a long-time party insider, Jacob Zuma. From 1999 until 2005, Zuma was South Africa's vice president, until he was forced by Mbeki to resign because of involvement in a fraud case. Yet in December 2007, when the ANC held its first internal party elections since 1958, Zuma benefitted from both popular disillusionment with the ANC and inter-alliance squabbling. With the help of leftist allies, Zuma unseated Mbeki as president of the ANC, and therefore as president of South Africa, by obtaining 2,329 delegate votes to Mbeki's 1,505 (Foster 2009).[11] Notably, observers claimed

---

[11] South African scholars dubbed the victory the Zuma tsumani, or Zunami (see Lodge 2009; Southall 2009).

that many of the delegates who supported Zuma were unemployed or belonged to the labor movement; Mbeki's delegates tended to have a more middle-class background (e.g., Alexander 2010). The vice president at the time, Kgalema Motlanthe, subsequently took over as interim president until the next general elections could be held in April 2009. Furthermore, all of Mbeki's supporters were removed from the National Executive Committee, which is the party's main decision-making body (Bassett and Clarke 2008). Mbeki's followers eventually split from the ANC and left to form a more economically conservative and business-friendly opposition party, named the Congress of the People (COPE).

Subsequently, the ANC adopted a populist strategy in preparation for the 2009 elections. The need for a different strategy was necessary for at least two reasons. First, the 2009 elections would be more competitive than any the ANC faced since coming to power in 1994. Indeed, due to the formation of COPE, these were the first elections where the ANC would encounter a credible black opposition party. Simultaneously, the country's other main opposition party, the Democratic Alliance (DA), was gradually gaining support beyond its white constituency base and attracting the votes of the colored community, particularly in the Western Cape.[12] The leader of the DA, Helen Zille, had been elected mayor to Cape Town a few years previously, and her party was creating a reputation for successfully delivering services, including to the poor township of Khayelitsha in the southern part of that city.

Even more dangerous to the ANC's prospects, however, was that neglect of the poor and marginalized had contributed to growing voter apathy overall and specifically with the party (Pillay 2008). Between 1999 and 2004, overall turnout decreased by more than 13 percent. Even though the voting-age population had increased by about 5 million in the interim, only approximately 2 million registered to vote in 2004. For the ANC in particular, only 39 percent of the eligible voting-age population supported the party in 2004 compared with 54 percent a decade earlier (Schulz-Herzenberg 2008). Many young South Africans aged between eighteen and twenty-nine, who are the country's fastest-growing cohort, are considered the country's "post-apartheid" generation and demonstrate lower levels of partisanship to the ANC than their older counterparts (Schulz-Herzenberg 2008; see also A. Butler 2009). These two trends, growing opposition competition and increased voter apathy, both posed a threat to the ANC's goal

---

[12] "Colored" is the term used in South Africa to refer to those who are mixed race or who have Khoisan ancestry.

in 2009 of gaining two-thirds of the parliament's 400, which is the necessary threshold for changing the constitution.

Zuma was central to the ANC's populist strategy to regain support. The candidate was both highly controversial and very charismatic. He was not only implicated in the corruption case that cost him the vice presidency, but also went on trial for rape in 2006. During his trial, masses of supporters gathered outside the supreme court each day to sing Zuma's signature song from his days in the liberation movement, "Bring Me My Machine Gun," as well as other songs that Gunner (2008) claims symbolized the marginalization of the poor and the distance of the ruling elite. During the 2008 xenophobic riots in the townships, a number of the violent perpetrators sang this liberation song and often left graffiti on demolished shacks with pro-Zuma slogans (Gunner 2008). Known by his clan name of Msholozi, which means "dancer" in Zulu, Zuma was famous for singing and dancing on stage during his campaign rallies (Foster 2009). According to Southall (2009: 326), Zuma is "a master of political theatre which appeals to 'the masses,' his rallies a colorful mixture of homilies, parables, dancing and song."

During the campaign period before the 2009 general elections, Zuma wandered around urban townships, promising to finally deliver to the masses. Although job creation was a central part of his message, he also emphasized the importance of providing housing, social benefits, and services such as electricity (Hunter 2011). This message complemented the ANC's election manifesto, which was launched in January 2009 and focused on five development issues. The priority issue was "more jobs, decent work, and sustainable livelihoods" (ANC 2009). To achieve these goals, the manifesto promised within the following five years to, among other things, create a new national youth development agency aimed at helping young people find jobs, engage in a massive public works program, focus on creating more labor-intensive industries, expand unemployment insurance, and accelerate the country's national housing program (ANC 2009). Unlike the opposition, the ANC could not credibly campaign on an overt message of change. However, an underlying message of the party's campaign was that the ANC's past failings were a deviation and linked to political machinations that occurred during Mbeki's presidency (A. Butler 2009). In other words, the incumbent party was in effect promising that despite its long tenure, it was now much more attuned to the needs of South Africans.

Zuma's direct ties with the poor and his man-of-the-people persona facilitated the impression that the ANC was changing its image. Although COSATU had been highly instrumental in pushing for Zuma to replace

Mbeki at the head of the ANC during the Polokwane conference, this trade union confederation has few ties to the urban poor. In fact, COSATU is primarily an organization for those who are employed and in formal jobs. Even then, COSATU only represents 19 percent of those employed in the formal sector. Attempts to organize the unemployed and informal sector workers have not been very successful (Pillay 2008). In some cases, COSATU's aims are antithetical to the unemployed, such as its goal of tightening labor laws to increase the difficulty of firing workers (Commey 2008).

Instead of mediated relationships through other civil society associations, Zuma was able to endear himself to the poor by focusing on his background as a goat herder with no formal education. In this way, he presented a stark contrast to the "*amamodel C*" group, which derisorily refers to the small group of African men and women who became middle class by studying at former white "model-C" schools after the end of apartheid (Hunter 2011). Consequently, he appeared more approachable than the well-educated and aloof Mbeki. As Gumede (2009) notes, "Zuma successfully portrayed himself as 'poor,' identifying his personal marginalization by former president Thabo Mbeki with the marginalization of the poverty-stricken masses. He successfully distanced himself from the failures of the ANC government in the minds of poor voters, blaming them on Mbeki." Indeed, Hart (2007: 97 and 98) observes that Zuma held widespread appeal to the poor by simultaneously portraying himself as a liberation hero, a leftist, a traditionalist, and as an anti-elitist: "His [Zuma's] regular reference to himself as 'not educated' – but, by implication, extremely smart – is a direct attack on the technocratic elite surrounding Mbeki, often portrayed by Zuma supporters as arrogant and self-serving, and as not having served in the trenches of the revolutionary struggle." In a study of voters' intentions in the country's largest township of Soweto, Ceruti (2008: 322) further found that those who supported Zuma were more likely to be poorer in both objective and subjective terms. Their main reason for supporting him was that they viewed Zuma as someone "like them." Low-level factory workers further highlighted that they supported Zuma because he was a "listener" in touch with the everyday worker and concerned with offering greater representation to ordinary people (Beresford 2009). Foster (2009: 78) likewise observes that poor voters who attended Zuma's rallies saw the sixty-seven-year-old politician as a type of messiah who could revolutionize their lives. Similar to Michael Sata, Zuma also fostered vertical ties with an "open-door policy" and often faced long lines of people waiting to see him both outside his rural home in Kwa-Zulu Natal and his suburban home in Johannesburg (Russell 2009).

The ANC attempted to create more direct ties with township youth through two other measures. The first was recruiting the rambunctious and vitriolic leader of the ANC Youth League, Julius Malema, to extol Zuma's virtues and proclaim controversially that he would "kill" in order to get Zuma elected (Russell 2009). The second was by adapting a new form of campaigning called "Ride n' braai parties," especially in Gauteng. Specifically, the party targeted where young people socialize in the townships, which is usually near car washes.[13] High-level ANC politicians would arrive at car washes in convoys of 4 × 4 cars blasting *kwaito* music by popular DJs.[14] They would then distribute meat and beer to the growing crowds of curious onlookers and thereby encourage an impromptu party. The aim was to create the message that "It's really funky in the ANC" (cited in Butler 2009: 80). According to Hunter (2011), these tactics were successful at mobilizing greater numbers of young South Africans to register for the 2009 elections than in the previous ones.

By contrast, the DA's national campaign message was "Stop Zuma!," which aimed to create fears among voters about Zuma's potential antidemocratic behavior if the ANC reached its stated goal of obtaining a two-thirds majority in parliament and could thereby change the constitution. COPE focused mostly on corruption and cronyism within the ANC, and by highlighting Zuma's many court battles, argued that the party disrespected the judiciary, constitution, and rule of law (see Booysen 2009). According to Gumede (2009), neither tactic was especially powerful among the poor:

COPE was unable to counter the ANC's message that it [COPE] forms part of a rich black and white cabal which opposes the interests of the poor. It and the DA focused their campaigns on Zuma's compromised morals and attacks on democratic institutions. This may have resonated in the black and white middle classes, but it fell on stony ground among those living in shacks, without jobs or food, who cling to Zuma's promises of free healthcare, education and social grants.

Zuma Emphasizes His Zulu Heritage

However, the ANC did not just focus on the urban poor. In rural areas, Zuma appealed to voters based on ethnolinguistic identity which, along with race, has been an important feature of South Africa's history. Importantly, Zuma did not portray the ANC as an exclusionary party. In fact, unlike his predecessor, Zuma actively courted white Afrikaners during the campaign,

---

[13] *Braai* is the Afrikaans word for "grill" or "barbecue."

[14] *Kwaito* is a distinctive form of hip-hop music that emerged in Johannesburg's townships.

Table 7.6. *Distribution of Ethnolinguistic Groups in South Africa*

Province	Share of Province that is Rural (%)	Dominant Ethnolinguistic Group	Share of Ethnolinguistic Group in Province (%)	Share of Province in National Population (%)
Western Cape	9.1	Afrikaans	56.0	10.3
Eastern Cape	62.0	IsiXhosa	83.6	14.8
Northern Cape	16.5	Afrikaans	66.1	1.9
Free State	21.9	Sesotho	64.4	6.1
KwaZulu-Natal	55.3	IsiZulu	81.0	19.8
North West	58.9	Setswana	66.2	8.3
Gauteng	2.7	IsiZulu	21.9	19.5
Mpumalanga	57.4	Siswati	31.4	7.1
Limpopo	89.6	Sepedi	52.6	12.2

Notes: The ethnolinguistic groups are classified according to the definitions used by the South African statistics agency, Stats SA.
Source: 2001 South African Census, available from Minnesota Population Center. *Integrated Public Use Microdata Series, International: Version 6.1.* Minneapolis: University of Minnesota, 2011.

a community that at one time had included some of the most ardent supporters of apartheid policies (*Business Day* 2009). He called Afrikaners "the white tribe of Africa" and campaigned among the country's second-largest labor union, Solidarity, which consists mostly of Afrikaner members (Johnson and Macgregor 2009).

At the same time, however, Zuma unabashedly promoted his Zulu identity. He is originally from the village of Inkandla in one of South Africa's most rural provinces, Kwa-Zulu Natal. As seen in Table 7.6, Zulu is the overwhelming ethnolinguistic group in this region, and Kwa-Zulu Natal rivals only Gauteng as the country's most populous province. Furthermore, Zulu is the country's largest ethnolinguistic group with approximately 23 percent of the population, indicating this is their first language, followed by 18 percent for Xhosa speakers.[15]

As a polygamist who readily dons animal skins to participate in Zulu ceremonies, Zuma is proud of and comfortable with his heritage. In fact, whereas Mbeki rarely mentioned his Xhosa background, Zuma explained in an interview that he was "a South African who grew up here in KZN

[15] Their numbers are from the 2001 census.

[Kwa-Zulu Natal Province], who is a Zulu with Zulu traditions and Zulu values pushed into myself" (cited in Foster 2009: 75). This of course resonated with the Zulu community, which long felt excluded from political power because Mandela, Mbeki, and Motlanthe were all presidents from the Xhosa community, and Mbeki in particular had expanded the number of Xhosas in his cabinet during his tenure (Calland 2006; Johnson 2008).

Such Xhosa dominance in the ANC explained why many South Africans living in Kwa-Zulu Natal historically supported the Zulu-based Inkatha Freedom Party (IFP), led by Mangosuthu Buthelezi. Recognizing this, the ANC's campaign manager, Gwede Mantashe, noted that Kwa-Zulu Natal represented one of the regions that would be most aggressively targeted during the 2009 campaign (Butler 2009). This was particularly important given that COPE was dominated by Xhosa politicians and therefore expected to wrest votes away in the ANC's historical stronghold of the Eastern Cape.[16]

Zulu identity was promoted through campaign symbols and language. Notably, the ANC held one of its first campaign rallies in Kwa-Zulu Natal, where the main campaign message was "A vote for the ANC is a vote for Zuma" (Matshiqi 2008), and by extension, for the Zulu community. Zuma supporters wore T-shirts with the politician's face that stated "100 percent Zulu boy." He often threw Zulu phrases into his speeches, and his final campaign rally in Johannesburg was labeled the *Siyanqoba* rally, meaning "to conquer" in the Zulu language. In a country with eleven official languages, the use of Zulu for national rallies reinforced the impression that Zuma was not simply an ANC candidate but also a Zulu one. According to Russell (2009: 368), "Zuma had clearly led the ANC into a new era of politics in which tribal identity was no longer to be a taboo."

The Impact of Zuma's Strategy on the ANC's Electoral Fortunes

The impact of this strategy was notable in a number of respects. First, Zuma's populist promises on behalf of the poor threatened the business community and foreign investors who feared the country's macroeconomic fundamentals would be compromised. In early 2009, when Zuma's prospects of becoming the next president appeared inevitable, the currency considerably depreciated and the value of shares fell on the Johannesburg Stock Exchange (Gunnion 2009). Secondly, although voter turnout remained at the same level as in 2004, 3 million new people had registered in the interim, such

---

[16] During the Polokwane conference, Xhosa ANC delegates predominantly supported Mbeki in the leadership battle; Zulu delegates voted en masse for Zuma (Russell 2009).

Table 7.7. *Vote Shares of Selected South African Parties in Johannesburg, 2009 Elections*

Administrative Regions of Metropolitan Johannesburg	Selected Parties (% of Vote Within Region)			
	ANC	*COPE*	*DA*	*IFP*
Ennersdale	**67.1**	8.6	16.7	1.3
Inner City	**59.7**	10.9	21	4.6
Midrand	**69**	9.9	17.6	0.7
Northcliff Randburg	26.3	11.8	**53.4**	0.5
Roodeport	**48.3**	9.5	36.8	0.5
Sandton	**54.5**	10.2	29.7	2.1
Soweto	**84.1**	7.9	1.9	3.5

Source: Calculated by author based on election data from the Independent Electoral Commission (IEC).

that in absolute terms, a higher number of people voted. Thirdly, despite facing the most competitive opposition ever, the ANC received 1 million more votes than it obtained even a decade earlier. Fourthly, election results from South Africa's largest urban agglomeration, Johannesburg, highlight that the ANC won overwhelmingly in some of the city's regions with the most deprived neighborhoods, such as Soweto, Ennersdale, and Midrand (see Table 7.7). COPE fared less well in these poorer neighborhoods. However, Zuma's populist strategy proved less convincing to those in the wealthier areas of the city, such as Northcliff Randburg and Roodeport, where both white and black middle-class residents tended to lean more toward the DA.

Finally, at the provincial level, Table 7.8 highlights that the ANC was successful at wresting away voters from the IFP in Kwa-Zulu Natal. In 1999, the ANC only obtained 39 percent of the vote in Kwa-Zulu Natal Province compared with 42 percent for the IFP. In the 2009 elections, the ANC obtained 64 percent of the vote in Kwa-Zulu Natal, more than triple the IFP's 20.5 percent.[17] Notably, in the Eastern Cape, which is the Xhosa heartland of the ANC, the ruling party lost a share of its vote to COPE.

At the national level, the ANC was never at risk of losing the 2009 elections outright. However, at a time when many South Africans were

[17] Election results from South Africa's Independent Electoral Commission. Retrieved from http://www.elections.org.za/.

Table 7.8. *Share of Votes by Province for Selected Parties (%)*

Province	ANC	DA	COPE	IFP
Eastern Cape	69.7	10.0	13.3	0.1
Free State	71.9	12.1	11.1	0.2
Gauteng	64.8	21.3	7.8	1.5
KwaZulu-Natal	63.5	10.3	1.6	20.5
Mpumalanga	85.8	7.6	2.9	0.5
Northern Cape	61.1	13.1	15.9	0.2
Limpopo	85.3	3.7	7.2	0.1
North West	73.8	8.7	8.4	0.2
Western Cape	32.9	48.8	9.1	0.1
Total (Parliamentary Seats Won)[a]	65.9	16.7	7.4	4.6
	(264)	(67)	(30)	(18)

[a] Nine other minor parties collectively won 21 of Parliament's 400 seats.
Source: Independent Electoral Commission of South Africa.

disappointed with the ANC's performance, the emergence of COPE and the growing success of the opposition DA did threaten to reduce the party's sizable parliamentary majority. Zuma's ability to reinvigorate the party's image by fusing a populist strategy toward the poor with appeals along identity lines demonstrates that this tactic of building dual coalitions is not only available to Africa's opposition parties but also to incumbents.

CONCLUSION

By examining three additional case studies, this chapter highlighted a number of similarities amongst parties that rely on populist strategies. The charismatic leaders in all three cases alternately were well educated or possessed little formal schooling, came from humble backgrounds or inherited wealth and prestige. Yet in every case, they portrayed themselves as men of the people who were comfortable wading into slums and townships and understood what it meant to be poor. With a message focused on job creation and service delivery, these populist leaders successfully forged direct ties with the poor living in diverse urban centers. They combined class appeals in diverse urban areas with overtures to ascriptive identities in rural areas that were targeted based on resource constraints and electoral demography. Both the urban poor and a segment of the rural population were mobilized with either a real or imagined story of exclusion from political and economic power structures. Thus, in terms of strategy and discourse, Odinga's, Koma's, and Zuma's campaigns contained many of the very same elements that characterized Michael Sata's 2006 and 2008 electoral bids and Abdoulaye Wade's 2000 electoral victory.

EIGHT

Conclusions, Contributions, and Implications

As the colonial era ended, African urban poverty was changing. The traditional poor were still there. Blind beggars still felt their way through the streets. Market-women still jostled for tiny profits.... But now new categories of poor joined them in the swollen towns. Unemployed youths sat on the kerbs awaiting the chance to unload a lorry.... Policemen with street urchins and old women with nothing sat in the shade awaiting the arrival of the social worker. Poverty in Africa has been a cumulative phenomenon

(Iliffe 1987: 192)

Iliffe's observations about the intersection between demographic and socio-economic trends in Africa continue to resonate today and, as this study has shown, can shape party strategizing and voting behavior within the region. Although Nelson (1979) argued more than thirty years ago that few African political parties accorded attention to the urban poor because the electorate was predominantly rural, Africa is now on the precipice of an urban "tipping point." Not only is Africa the fastest urbanizing region of the world, but also one where urbanization has resulted in a higher share of the region's poor living in urban areas. Substandard service delivery as well as high levels of unemployment and underemployment all provide grievances upon which opposition parties can capitalize for electoral gain. Yet, in the region's electoral democracies, opposition parties struggle to defeat incumbents at the national level, thereby hindering the attainment of democratic consolidation. Even at the subnational level, cross-country comparisons highlight that opposition parties are not uniformly popular among urban residents.

The puzzle of how and when different constituencies, especially the urban poor, are mobilized by certain political parties lies at the heart of this study. I compared the techniques of political parties, both opposition and incumbent, across countries and over time. I focused predominantly on the two case studies of Senegal and Zambia because the preferences of the urban poor for the opposition have diverged significantly across each country at various points in time since 2000. Despite this variation, the two countries are well-established multiparty democracies in Africa that contain growing numbers of economically marginalized urban dwellers concentrated into substandard housing on the peripheries of Dakar and Lusaka. Because neither country has a history of civil conflict, partisanship is not overwhelmingly shaped by affinities to a former rebel movement-cum-political party. Instead, due to either intraparty disputes or as a means of advancing the ambitions of particular individuals, both countries have a number of viable opposition competitors. Contemporary elections in each country therefore are not simply tantamount to endorsing a dominant ruling party or validating a rigid two-party system. The findings from these two countries were then supplemented by an analysis of the three shadow cases of Botswana, Kenya, and South Africa.

This concluding chapter summarizes the main findings with respect to the study's two main research objectives. The first and primary research objective was to understand when and why the urban poor support the opposition. A secondary objective was to illustrate how the tactics used by opposition parties to mobilize the urban poor affect their ability to gain support from rural voters. This final chapter also highlights the broader contributions of this study in at least four domains, including opposition parties and elections in Africa, party linkages and the sustainability of populist strategies, differences across regions in terms of the manifestations of populism, and democratic contestation and consolidation. I conclude by providing suggestions for further research.

POPULIST STRATEGIES AND THE URBAN POOR

This study began by considering four main hypotheses about the voting behavior of the urban poor (Chapter 2). These included the impact of vote buying by political parties during campaigns, ethnic affinities to candidates, retrospective economic voting, and associational ties. I demonstrated that each hypothesis on its own failed to provide a complete analysis of the urban poor's voting decisions.

Instead, I argued that the campaign strategies used by political parties to integrate the urban poor into the political arena were more likely explanations for this constituency's political behavior. Populist strategies in particular were believed to be more likely to mobilize the urban poor than personalistic, clientelistic, or programmatic linkages alone. Populist strategies were characterized by an antielitist discourse; a policy message of social inclusion focused on jobs, housing, and services; charismatic leadership; and the distribution of selective benefits. Populist strategies therefore fuse together the different modes of mobilization inherent in the three types of citizen-voter linkages. At same time, populist strategies target the same constituents as clientelistic linkages (i.e., the poor) and foster unmediated ties between leaders and voters in the same manner as personalistic linkages.

The main mechanisms facilitating the appeal of populist strategies are differentiation and congruence. Differentiation refers to the ability of a voter to determine distinctions among parties that extend beyond just the personality of the party leader. Congruence refers to the distance between the policies advocated by a party on the one hand and those desired by a constituency on the other hand. Because most African parties rely on personalistic linkages, a populist strategy provides greater differentiation. Simultaneously, by focusing on the priorities of the urban poor, populist strategies offer greater congruence with this constituency than either personalistic or programmatic linkages alone.

Subsequently, Chapters 3 and 4 relied on interviews with political elites and other local observers to illustrate the different manner in which parties interact with the urban poor in Zambia and Senegal. In Zambia, the PF's Michael Sata relied on personalistic linkages in the 2001 elections to little avail. In both the 2006 and 2008 presidential elections, he switched to a populist strategy that consisted of a campaign focused on improving urban services, reducing taxes, creating jobs, and ending harassment of marketeers and shanty compound residents. Along with controversial antics designed to attract attention, Sata targeted his urban campaigns in low-income areas of Lusaka. Despite being a long-time MMD loyalist, he reinvented himself as the antiestablishment candidate. This was facilitated by the creation of unmediated ties with the urban poor through the use of simplistic language that resonated with their plight and having an open-door policy to make him more available to constituents.

Despite the MMD's good economic record, this populist strategy provided Sata with a majority of votes in the ethnically diverse areas of the capital city of Lusaka. By contrast, both Hakainde Hichilema of the UPND and Godfrey Miyanda of the HP depended on more personalistic linkages with the urban poor. The inability of either of these candidates to garner a high number of votes in the capital city, and the fact that they obtained even fewer votes than the incumbent MMD, indicates that poor urbanites were not just pro-opposition but specifically pro-Sata.

In contrast with Sata, whose schooling only extended to grade four, the charismatic Abdoulaye Wade of the PDS was trained as a lawyer and

Table 8.1 *Party Strategies and Outcomes in the Case Study Countries*

	Senegal		Zambia	
	2000	*2007*	*2001*	*2006/2008*
Strategy by opposition party or parties	Populist strategy by PDS	Personalistic and programmatic linkages	Personalistic linkages	Populist strategy by PF
Outcome in largest city	Opposition PDS wins more than 50 percent of vote	Incumbent PDS wins more than 50 percent of vote	Vote is split amongst opposition parties and incumbent MMD	Opposition PF wins more than 50 percent of vote

economist. But he, too, successfully utilized a populist strategy to mobilize the urban poor during the country's 2000 elections. Despite periods of cohabitation with the PS regime, he also portrayed himself as a political outsider and man of the people. He, too, focused on a message of social inclusion, such as creating jobs, addressing urban flooding, improving sanitation, and ending the demolition of illegal slums. Through the use of urban Wolof and his innovative blue marches through Dakar, he tapped into a growing urban identity concentrated around youth and informality.

However, Wade's first term in office resulted in few tangible benefits for this constituency. In Dakar, a majority of his attention was diverted toward large-scale construction projects that primarily benefitted the urban elite. In addition, Senegal's macroeconomy deteriorated substantially. Nevertheless, no opposition party could obtain sufficient vote majorities from the urban poor during the 2007 elections. Parties such as the PS, AFP, and Rewmi primarily forged personalistic linkages with the urban poor that were devoid of a clear policy message and mostly focused on the personalities of the party leaders. Leftist parties relied more on programmatic linkages, but their central messages were divorced from the everyday realities of the urban poor. Collectively, these parties have been dismissed as solely a "living room opposition" that is concerned more with exclusive policy dialogues rather than demonstrating solidarity with disgruntled urbanites. Table 8.1 summarizes the strategies used by opposition parties in these two countries during consecutive elections, as well as the impact on voting outcomes.

Two key points emerged by comparing parties across countries and over time. First, even when an incumbent fails to provide jobs, decent housing, and basic public services the opposition may still prove unable to capture the imagination of the urban poor if it does not employ a populist strategy with this constituency. Indeed, both Zambia's 2001 and Senegal's 2007 elections illustrated that even when the incumbent regime theoretically should be at a disadvantage, no opposition party may definitively win over the urban poor. Secondly, a populist strategy prevails with the urban poor not only due to the failed promises of the incumbent but also because other opposition parties are relying on personalistic or programmatic linkages that reduce their degree of differentiation and level of congruence with the policy priorities of the urban poor. Well-educated and potentially technocratic leaders, such as the UPND's Hichilema and AFP's Niasse, were disadvantaged by an intellectualism that created distance with the urban poor and by advancing broad messages intended to capture the votes of both urbanites and rural dwellers. By contrast, the success of Gorgui over the AFP and the pôle de gauche in the first round of Senegal's 2000 elections parallels that of King Cobra vis-à-vis the UPND and the Heritage Party in Zambia's 2006 and 2008 elections.

Chapter 5 utilized two surveys with informal market workers and slum dwellers to analyze the mechanisms of differentiation and congruence as well as to test alternative voting behavior theories. The chapter revealed that the populist PF was overwhelmingly viewed by respondents as the party most concerned about improving living conditions in Lusaka, and a majority of respondents believed that the main distinction among Zambia's political parties was their positions on social and economic conditions. By contrast, most respondents in Senegal did not perceive any difference among their country's political parties and believed that no opposition party was concerned with improving living conditions in Dakar. The econometric results confirmed that, among other factors, those respondents who lacked key services and were disappointed by job creation under the incumbent MMD were significantly more likely to support the opposition PF in Zambia. However, in Senegal, those who were least educated and objectively poorer still supported the incumbent, despite Wade's well-known lack of attention to the needs of the urban poor during his first term. In addition, younger people were significantly more likely to abstain from voting in the 2007 elections rather than support the opposition.

In addition, Chapter 5 further illustrated that two alternative explanations for voting behavior, associational ties, and vote buying were insufficient. Few survey respondents in either country were involved in any type of association. They either did not know that such organizations existed, or they felt that there was little benefit to their participation in them. Potentially, associational membership among the urban poor can at some point shape political affiliations or facilitate corporatist ties in the same way that formal trade unions have done in both other regions and at certain points in Africa's history. However, the existing results largely confirm the prevailing view that the diverse activities, time constraints, and heterogeneous backgrounds of the urban poor simply precludes their ability and desire to organize effectively and thereby create the critical mass necessary for political influence (see Amis 2004; Croucher 2007; Dietz 1998; Huntington and Nelson 1976; Nelson 1970, 1979; Thornton 2000).

Likewise, vote buying alone displayed no perceivable influence on the voting behavior of the urban poor in either Senegal or Zambia. Unlike in rural areas, where fewer opposition parties can extensively campaign, multiple parties may be engaged in vote buying in urban centers. This was clear in both case study countries where survey respondents reported that the incumbent party and most of the opposition parties offered gifts and sometimes even money to their communities during campaign periods. A voter may certainly be more likely to vote for any candidate who provides certain goods and services over one who does not. Indeed, Zambia's opposition candidate, Godfrey Miyanda, was known for abstaining from vote-buying practices and he received no support from the respondents surveyed in Lusaka. However, in a context where multiple parties are engaged in vote buying, this cannot be the main means of mobilizing the urban poor. This explains why, despite the high level of vote buying in both countries, this variable did not demonstrate a statistically significant effect in shaping respondents' support for Sata or Wade.

With regards to retrospective views of the macroeconomy, the findings are more nuanced. Negative sociotropic views of the macroeconomy did not play a statistically significant role in determining whether a survey respondent supported the opposition over the incumbent. However, in Zambia, it did influence the decision to vote for Sata over abstaining, highlighting that in some cases, those who are discontent with macroeconomic conditions are less likely to express voter apathy.

Because macroeconomic growth does not necessarily always filter down to the poor in developing countries (e.g., P. Lewis 2008; Thurlow and Wobst 2006), it can fail to address the urban poor's main concerns over jobs, housing, services, and food prices. Disappointment with incumbent performance with job creation and service provision proved a major impetus for supporting the opposition in Zambia. However, it provides less of an explanation for why voters supported the incumbent in Senegal. This in turn indicates that retrospective evaluations are necessary but not sufficient motivations to vote for the opposition, unless the latter specifically targets these issues in a compelling manner during campaigns.

Ethnicity did demonstrate an impact on voting behavior in the Zambian case, given that ethnolinguistic affinity has long been a factor in politics there. Bemba speakers among Lusaka's poor were more likely to vote for a co-ethnic leader Sata than for another candidate. Yet, a majority of the survey respondents who were non-Bemba also voted for him. Moreover, even after Bemba ethnolinguistic identity was controlled for in the statistical analyses; indicators capturing satisfaction with jobs and service delivery were also statistically significant predictors of a respondent's support for Sata.

These findings therefore question extreme views regarding the political influence of ethnic and other ascriptive identities among city dwellers. Urbanization does not overwhelmingly exacerbate ethnic differences, as Bates (1983) or Melson and Wolpe (1970) once speculated, nor does it entirely eradicate their salience, as Allport (1954) postulated. Instead, it allows the urban poor to adapt multiple identities – ascriptive, occupational, socioeconomic, demographic, and so forth – that can at times be mutually reinforcing.

IMPLICATIONS FOR THE MOBILIZATION OF RURAL VOTERS

Chapter 6 turned to the study's second research issue and examined how the strategies used by opposition parties with the urban poor affects their mobilization of rural voters that are still necessary for a candidate to win national elections in most African countries. I argued that African opposition parties generally face a number of constraints in campaigning outside major urban areas. These include the fact that their resources tend to be more limited and that the incumbent party usually exudes more credibility to rural voters by virtue of already being in government and having a greater presence in rural areas.

Opposition parties reliant on populist strategies with the urban poor also face an additional dilemma, which is that expanding their rural support may result in alienating their core base among the urban poor. I therefore argued that such a party could mobilize an electorally sizable segment of the rural population through clientelistic linkages based on appeals to a politically salient, ascriptive identity. Sizable referred to having a share of the population that, when combined with vote shares in urban areas, provides enough votes to win the presidency according to the country's electoral rules. This approach is advantageous given that identity appeals are a signaling mechanism to voters about the potential for selective benefits and because in rural areas, ascriptive identities tend to be geographically concentrated, thereby allowing a conservation of party resources. Importantly, however, such appeals must not imply that a party is exclusively for one identity group above all others.

Parties solely reliant on personalistic linkages can likewise rely on identity appeals in rural areas. However, without a base among the urban poor, they can be less assured of large-scale support in urban areas and therefore would need to target an even larger demographic group in rural areas. If this is not possible, due to either the identity of a party's presidential candidate or to multiple candidates sharing the same identity, then such parties will need to campaign much more broadly in rural areas, albeit at a shallower level than the incumbent.

The study showed that Zambia's populist candidate, Sata, concentrated his 2008 rural campaigning in Bemba-speaking provinces, and these were also the only rural provinces that he won during that election. Importantly, he relied on the use of implicit appeals to voters through Bemba language and symbols and a discourse about Bemba exclusion from politics. His main opposition competitor, Hichilema, could not adopt a similar approach given that he relied on personalistic linkages with the urban poor and is from a numerically inferior ethnolinguistic group. In Senegal, where Sufi brotherhood is the most politically salient identity, Wade combined his populist strategy with the urban poor in 2000 with overtures to his background as a Mouride. His appeals demonstrated a great deal of traction with Mouride voters in rural areas, especially in Diourbel, who felt that they were increasingly losing influence and power under Diouf's regime.

By contrast, in the 2007 elections, Senegal's personalistic opposition parties could not engage in the same coalition building with a combination of Dakar's poor and a segment of rural voters. The incumbent, Wade, had already co-opted the leaders of the Mouride brotherhood as well as those from the Niassène sect of the Tidiane brotherhood. Although Seck obtained support from a sect of the Tidiane brotherhood known as the Moustarchidines, this sect's following was not very sizable. Unable to rely on high levels of support in urban areas and mobilize sizable numbers of rural voters along identity cleavages, most of Senegal's opposition campaigned widely across the country, espousing broad messages of rural development.

OTHER CASES BEYOND SENEGAL AND ZAMBIA

By looking at three other democracies in Africa, Chapter 7 illustrated the external validity of the study's main arguments, also illustrating some of their logical implications. Specifically, I looked at Raila Odinga and the ODM in Kenya, Kenneth Koma and the BNF in Botswana, and Jacob Zuma and the ANC in South Africa. As with Senegal and Zambia, dynamics in these cases were examined over time to explain shifts in the voting preferences of the urban poor as a result of the choices offered by various political parties. These additional countries were selected as shadow cases because they possess the demand-side grievances discussed in Chapter 2 that facilitate the rise of populist strategies, including high levels of urbanization, urban poverty, unemployment, and inequality in major cities. Moreover, on the supply-side, the timing of the emergence of populist strategies can be linked to critical junctures within the party system. In both Botswana and South Africa, the appearance of such strategies was tied to growing disaffection with dominant parties in the mid-1990s and mid-2000s, respectively. In Kenya, greater fluidity in the party system emerged in 2005 as a result of intraparty and interparty disagreements related to proposed changes to the constitution. In each case, I illustrated that when a populist strategy emerged, the urban poor were mobilized to vote for the party that used it during key elections. In addition, such a strategy was always combined with appeals to politically salient identities in rural areas.

These cases further highlighted three other key points. First, variations in electoral rules and demography influence the breadth of rural voters that are targeted by parties reliant on populist strategies in urban areas. The requirement that Kenyan presidential candidates gain, among other things, 25 percent of the vote in at least five provinces meant that Odinga could not only focus on mobilizing his Luo co-ethnics in rural areas but also other minority groups who would be sympathetic to his implied message of exclusion under Kibaki's regime. Likewise, in Botswana, the need to win more than half the country's parliamentary seats to elect the president, and the fact that the BDP was the favored party among most Tswana tribes, meant that Koma needed to focus on mobilizing minority tribes located in different regions of the countryside. In South Africa, the multimember, single constituency, proportional representation system allocates national parliamentary seats based on the share of each province's contribution to the national population. As such, it was fortuitous that Zuma shared the same ethnolinguistic identity as those in the country's most populous province, Kwa-Zulu Natal.

Secondly, if a party such as the PF began gaining urban support upon using a populist strategy, then a party that ceases using this strategy should likewise lose votes from this constituency. The example of the rise and fall of the BNF demonstrates this exact trend, showing that with the loss of the party's charismatic leader and coherent message of social inclusion, the BNF gradually witnessed its support decline. Thirdly, although this study focused predominantly on the opposition, there is nothing that prevents incumbents from also using a populist strategy. This was demonstrated most clearly by the ANC during South Africa's 2009 elections when the ruling party faced fierce competition from both COPE and the DA as well as growing voter apathy. A populist strategy helped rejuvenate support among urban and unemployed youth, many of whom are too young to sympathize with the ANC's erstwhile role as a liberation movement.

RECENT DEVELOPMENTS IN ZAMBIA AND SENEGAL

The main arguments presented in this study have even greater weight when examined in light of more recent political developments in each country. In Zambia's 2011 elections, Michael Sata finally defeated Rupiah Banda and the MMD, becoming the country's fourth democratically elected president since the country's multiparty transition in 1991. This victory was particularly notable given that nine opposition parties competed in this election, increasing the expectation that the MMD would benefit from a split vote amongst the opposition. Instead, the PF's populist strategy continued to provide it with the necessary congruence and differentiation to outcompete the opposition and the incumbent. Moreover, this victory again contrasts starkly with events in Senegal's 2007 elections when no one opposition party could stand out among a crowded field of opposition competitors.

Although the MMD remained popular among wealthy city dwellers and the new middle classes in the 2011 elections (Redvers 2011a), Sata's populist strategy continued to mobilize the urban poor. He won 63 percent of the vote in the urban constituencies of Lusaka district and 68 percent in the Copperbelt. At the same time, Sata retained his base in Bembaphone heartlands of Northern and Luapula Provinces, where he won with 64 and 73 percent of the vote, respectively.[1]

There were two features of Sata's 2011 campaign that further reinforced some of this study's main claims. First, having been a staple of opposition politics for a decade, the PF has slowly increased its campaign resources, thereby allowing it to expand its campaigns in rural areas beyond the Bembaphone provinces. Notably, in 2011, Sata made inroads into the

---

[1] Election data is from the ECZ, Public Notice, 2011 Presidential Election Results, retrieved from http://www.elections.org.zm/media/28092011_public_notice_-_2011_presidential_election_results.pdf.

heavily rural, Lozi-speaking Western Province. Again, he relied on identity appeals to mobilize rural voters there by promising that if elected president, he would restore the Barotseland Agreement (*Africa Confidential* 2011). This agreement was signed in 1964 by the king of Barotseland, the British colonial secretary, and Kenneth Kaunda in order to bestow the king and the Barotse Royal Establishment with particular rights and privileges that were not awarded to other traditional leaderships. In exchange, the king was to cease overtures for secession and the formation of an independent Barotseland. Yet in 1969, Kaunda abrogated the Agreement, which the Lozi people have long viewed as an insult to their culture's past wealth and glory (Flint 2011). Sata's promise to restore the special rights and privileges of the 1964 Agreement therefore was especially appealing to Lozi voters and indicated that the PF was not simply just a Bemba party. As a result, his share of votes in Western Province increased from 10 to 23 percent between 2008 and 2011; those of Banda decreased by more than 30 percent.[2]

Secondly, a new PF campaign slogan appeared in urban areas during the 2011 campaigns, which was "Donchi kubeba" or "Don't tell" in Bemba. The implication of the slogan was that voters should accept the campaign hand-outs of the MMD but refuse to tell who they were planning to support in the elections. The slogan was turned into a song by a popular local artist, Dandy Krazy, which further increased the appeal of the PF's campaigns to disenchanted youth. Moreover, the slogan was accompanied by campaign photos of both Sata and Guy Scott with their finger in front of their lips, encouraging silence. As argued in Chapter 2, the slogan highlights that vote buying cannot directly explain urban voting behavior given that with a secret ballot, people can accept gifts from all parties but vote according to their conscience.

In Senegal's 2012 elections, an opposition leader, Macky Sall, also ousted an incumbent, Wade. But as would be expected from this study's main argument, the absence of a populist strategy in those elections did not lead to overwhelming support for Sall among the urban poor in the first round of those country's elections. Instead, those elections affirmed many of the characteristics of the country's opposition parties that have been described in previous chapters.

The ultimate victory of Sall over Wade after two rounds of elections reflected growing discontent with the latter rather than widespread support of the former. Since 2007, many of the urban poor have become increasingly discontent with Wade's inability to fulfill his original populist promises. In

[2]   Ibid.

November 2007, Wade provoked widespread protests in Dakar when he tried to remove street hawkers in preparation for the Organization of the Islamic Conference. The following year, Dakar experienced a series of riots over continuing electricity outages and the rise in food prices. In the midst of this growing misery, Wade also engaged in a series of controversial decisions. These included constructing a 164-foot-high African Renaissance monument overlooking the capital, which cost the government $27 million USD. In June 2011, Wade then attempted to pass legislation that would create the post of vice president and reduce the required voting threshold for winning a presidential election from 50 percent to 25 percent. Although the bill was ultimately rescinded, both provisions prompted massive protests throughout Dakar, particularly because many citizens suspected that the post of vice presidency would be given to Karim Wade, the president's son. The culmination of anti-Wade sentiment occurred in January 2012, when the country's Constitutional Council decided that Gorgui's bid to run for a third term was constitutional. Wade had long argued that he had not officially served two terms in office under the country's current constitution, which had been changed in 2001. The ensuing public demonstrations against the third-term bid resulted in the death of nine protesters.

Although such discontent should have galvanized the opposition, these parties were instead riddled by internal factions after having united within a broad opposition coalition called Benno Siggil Senegal (BSS). Although this coalition did not include Idrissa Seck, it did encompass thirty-five parties such as the AFP, PS, and Sall's new party, the APR. Sall, who had succeeded Seck as prime minister and coordinated Wade's 2007 election campaign, was ultimately dismissed by Wade from the PDS in 2008 and subsequently formed the APR. Despite an outpouring of solidarity in the wake of the protests on June 23, during which members of the BSS joined with other opposition parties and civil society groups to form the M23, the coalition began to crumble in the run-up to the elections. In January 2012, members of the BSS chose Moustapha Niasse as their presidential candidate for the elections. Despite originally agreeing to support a single candidate, Ousmane Tanor Dieng of the PS as well as Sall decided to run independently. Whereas all of these candidates, along with Seck, declared at the beginning of February 2012 that they would lead a joint anti-Wade campaign, Sall broke this promise three days later and began campaigning on his own behalf (Carayol 2012b). All the other candidates soon followed suit.

The ensuing election campaign highlighted a number of characteristics about the opposition. First, the pôle de gauche parties decided not to run separately and were completely subsumed within the BSS. Their absence from the political scene represented the most vivid evidence of the increasing irrelevance of their message to the electorate. Secondly, the living room opposition, which now included the APR, still remained unable to mirror the tactics of Wade when he had been in the opposition. One observer notes that "in launching slogans with a bellicose tonality but refusing a showdown in the street, the [opposition] movement is involved in a confrontation without engaging in the means of winning it" (Carayol 2012a). Likewise, one young disappointed PS member stated that the opposition's inability to sufficiently mobilize citizens was due to "the gap that separates political elites from the people" but also "the lack of combativeness among leaders of the opposition" (cited in Carayol 2012a). A widely popular rap group known as Y'en a marre ("Fed up"), which tried to encourage young, eligible Senegalese to vote, admitted that although it was anti-Wade, it did not support any particular opposition party (Nossiter 2011).

Sall in particular did not present a rousing opposition figure. Despite being Wade's former protégé, Sall did not use a populist strategy to mobilize the urban poor and this in turn required his use of broad campaigning in the countryside. Unlike Wade in 2000, Sall actually initiated his election campaign in rural areas rather than in Dakar (Gano 2012). He was actually the only opposition candidate who visited some of the most remote areas of the country, such as the Matam region on the northern border with Mauritania (Carayol 2012b). Moreover, Sall decidedly lacks the charisma inherent in a populist strategy. Nicknamed Niangal, which translates as "severe-faced" in Wolof, Sall was variously described during the campaign as "a relatively poor speaker" (Oxford Analytica 2011), "stolid, soft-spoken and deliberate" (Nossiter 2012: A4), and "an uncomfortable campaigner" (Akam 2012: 30). His campaign message was largely aimed at presenting himself as a contrast to Wade by promising a more technocratic style of governing, reducing expenditures on prestige projects, and limiting the presidential tenure to two terms (Nossiter 2012). In terms of economic policy, he promised both to protect urban consumers from high food prices with subsidies and invest heavily in agricultural production in rural areas. Yet, not only was this indistinct from Niasse's and Dieng's message on the campaign trail, it also ignored that subsidizing consumers can actually undermine agricultural production and reduce resources available for rural investment.

The lack of a populist strategy to mobilize the urban poor was clear in the outcome for the first round of the elections. In the urban region of Dakar, Sall only received 28 percent of the vote, lower than Wade's 49 and 54 percent in the city during the first rounds of the 2000 and 2007 elections, respectively.[3] Moreover, Sall was closely followed by Wade and Niasse, who won approximately 25 and 19 percent of the vote in the city, respectively.[4] Thus, in terms of differentiation, Sall was not the overwhelming favorite in the first round among Dakarois in the same way as Sata was in Lusaka. Most tellingly, despite the high levels of resentment against Wade, turnout only reached 48 percent in the capital, much lower than the 60 percent in 2000 and 70 percent in 2007. Notwithstanding the efforts of Y'en a marre, youth in particular abstained from the elections; even though 380,000 additional people registered to vote in 2012, more than 1 million young people had become newly eligible to vote since 2007 (see EU, U.S. Embassy, Germany Embassy 2011).[5]

After Sall finished in second place in the first round of the elections, all of the erstwhile opposition parties rallied around the former prime minister in a new coalition known as Benno Bok Yakaar, which translates as "Together we Share the Same Hope." Sall was able to benefit from the votes of these former supporters in order to substantially defeat Wade in the second round and become elected Senegal's fourth postcolonial president. His victory, however, was not attributable to the use of a populist strategy. Thus, the 2012 elections highlight that although a populist strategy is more likely to increase the likelihood that an opposition party will win support among the urban poor, it is not the only reason an opposition party might achieve victory at the national level. Instead, Sall's victory is attributed to the nature of coalition politics, the continued absence of populist strategies by any other opposition parties, and Wade's violation of term limits and loss of credibility among those constituents who originally brought him to power in 2000.

BROADER CONTRIBUTIONS OF THE STUDY

Opposition Parties and Elections in Africa

At least four main contributions are provided by this study, which are relevant to research on voting behavior, party politics, and democratization in both Africa and beyond. First, this study focused on the interactive relationship between political parties and citizens in Africa, as well as the differentiation of opposition parties. Thus far, much of the Africanist

---

[3] Election data for the 2012 elections is from EUEOM (2012).
[4] Within Dakar's nineteen communes, Sall only won the plurality in eight; Wade and Niasse gained the most votes in six and five communes, respectively.
[5] In the second round of the 2012 elections, turnout only marginally increased to 53 percent in Dakar and 55 percent nationally.

scholarship on elections falls into at least three categories. Detailed public opinion data and innovative field experiments have motivated microlevel studies of voting behavior (e.g., Lindberg and Morrison 2008; Wantchekon 2003; D. Young 2009b). These studies reveal key influences on individual voting decisions. At the more macro-level, scholars have engaged in various classifications of party systems, such as multiparty, two-party, and dominant-party regimes (e.g., Bogaards 2000; Doorenspleet 2003; Giliomee 1998; Manning 2005). Such work often helps inform even larger themes within this literature regarding whether countries are experiencing democratic transitions, consolidation, or reversals (Bratton and van de Walle 1997; Fomunyoh 2001; Joseph 1998; Lindberg 2006a; Randall and Svåsand 2002; Von Doepp and Villalón 2005). This study, however, combines these micro and macro perspectives by highlighting how the preferences of the urban poor can inform party strategizing and consequently enable particular parties to obtain more votes from this sector of society.

Notwithstanding recent scholarship on opposition parties (e.g., Lindberg 2006b; Rakner and van de Walle 2009), there is also a tendency in the literature to discuss African opposition parties in monolithic terms, thereby portraying multiparty competition as simply a struggle between "the" opposition and the incumbent. By contrast, the present study actually distinguishes opposition parties according to the way in which they mobilize various constituents, such as the urban poor and rural dwellers. This is valuable for illustrating under what conditions an opposition party will be able to not just defeat an incumbent party but also why one opposition party proved more appealing than alternative competitors.

Party Linkages and the Sustainability of Populist Strategies

A second contribution is that this study provided a comparative analysis of party linkages and emphasized the feasibility of combining different linkages. As such, it began to address Kitschelt's (2000: 855 and 856) lament about the lack of comparative research on the rise and decline of different linkage strategies. This study did not just focus on linkages from the party perspective but also surveyed the political behavior of African informal sector workers to examine how well these modes of mobilization actually capture the sentiments and preferences of the urban poor. As such, it also begins to address Hagopian's (2007: 599) qualm that too little is known about the demand-side of the party-voter relationship.

Moreover, as detailed throughout the study, a populist strategy represents an amalgam of programmatic, personalistic, and clientelistic linkages.

Specifically, the programmatic element emerges through the advocacy of policies of social inclusion. Personalistic linkages manifest through a politician's charisma and the existence of vertical ties between a leader and his or her followers. The distribution of selective benefits and a constituency base oriented around subaltern groups are both key elements of clientelist linkages.

However, based on his observations of parties in Western Europe, Kitschelt (2000: 855) claims that these three linkages cannot be combined: "At low dosages, all linkage mechanisms may be compatible. As politicians intensify their cultivation of a particular type of linkage, however, they reach a production possibility frontier at which further intensifications of one linkage mechanism can occur only at the expense of toning down other linkage mechanisms." In his view, charisma is incompatible with programmatic linkages because the routinization of authority requires the abandonment of theatrical antics. Similarly, clientelistic linkages require the distribution of selective benefits that undercuts the credibility of a traditional programmatic message.

Because the populist strategies presented here rely on mobilization through policies that are not purely programmatic in the traditional sense, the three types of politician-citizen linkages are compatible. In fact, it is difficult to imagine the PF's appeal being just as robust without either Sata's charisma or his very pro-poor policy pronouncements. Likewise, Abdoulaye Wade's 2000 campaign would have proved less remarkable without the combination of theatrical antics and his targeted appeals to Dakar's youth and informal sector workers.

Furthermore, Kitschelt (2000) only examines the linkages forged by politicians with the general citizenry rather than different population groups. The present study, however, emphasizes that parties and politicians can employ different linkages with the urban poor than they may with rural constituents. For example, many of the parties in this study that have relied on populist strategies to mobilize the urban poor simultaneously used clientelistic linkages based on ascriptive identity cleavages to mobilize a segment of rural voters. In other words, the various linkages can be compatible when a party derives its credibility and support from different groups of constituents.

Importantly, however, the fusion of such linkages does appear much less feasible once a leader who was reliant on a populist strategy as a member of the opposition is ultimately elected to national office. Populism is a particularly short-lived mode of mobilization, and once in office, a former opposition party must respond to national issues, manage the macroeconomy, attract investors, and in the African case often court donors. As Weyland (2001: 14) notes, "Political success therefore transforms populism into a different type of rule that rests on nonpopulist strategies. Populist leadership therefore tends to be transitory. It either fails or, if successful, transcends itself." Furthermore, coalitions built on populist strategies cannot be sustained for indefinite periods if the urban poor fail to see any tangible improvements in their lives or experience policies that are directly antithetical to their own interests.

Cross-Regional Varieties of Populism

Thirdly, the study revealed comparisons and contrasts between populist strategies in Africa vis-à-vis those observed in other regions of the developing world, particularly Latin America. As discussed in Chapter 2, Africa has faced many of the same demand- and supply-side drivers of populist strategies as found in Latin America. These include rapid urbanization and informalization of the labor force, which generate a set of grievances on which populist strategies can thrive. Similarly, the high level of convergence among existing parties offers a window of opportunity for savvy leaders who present populist strategies as an alternative to the status quo.

Furthermore, Latin Americanist scholars have argued that the discourse inherent to a populist strategy can advance eclectic policy ideologies (e.g., Roberts 1995).This was also apparent across the African case studies. For instance, whereas Wade's party was associated with having an economically liberal orientation, Koma avidly favored distributive policies by the government. Sata wavered between antagonism to foreign investors, sometimes tinged by xenophobic rhetoric, and pledging to retain investment deals previously signed by the MMD. This volatility contributed to investor anxiety, reflected by the fact that the Zambian kwacha fell to a twelve-month low against the U.S. dollar when Sata was ultimately elected president in 2011 (Redvers 2011b).

At the same time, the party leaders in this study, who used populist strategies, fused liberal and leftist norms in their campaigns that privileged both individual prerogative and government intervention. Although they might have argued for the reduction of value-added tax on consumer goods and economic diversification as a means of generating jobs, they also promoted unemployment benefits and the delivery of water and sanitation as a human right rather than commodities to be purchased. Moreover, they have all challenged established government views on the illegality of slum housing and informal sector workers, advocating that such groups should not be harassed for their livelihoods but rather given upgraded accommodation or proper vending spaces in which to operate.

In addition, the fusion of a populist strategy toward the urban poor with appeals to ascriptive identities in rural areas is not unique to the African context. Indeed, as noted in Chapter 6, Evo Morales used a populist strategy in Bolivia to target a growing urban underclass, simultaneously drawing on his own background and employing symbolic rhetoric to empower indigenous rural communities. Other Latin American leaders, such as Hugo Chávez and Ollanta Humala of Peru, have also drawn on their mestizo heritage during their campaigns. However, this dual mobilization approach is likely even more pronounced in Africa due to the region's high levels of diversity and given that the rural dwellers are still an important constituency for politicians campaigning for a national office.

Nevertheless, there are also notable differences across the two regions. For instance, an important feature of Africa's populist strategies is their heavy focus on poor urban youth. The youth bulge in Africa makes this constituency difficult to ignore and particularly jarring when compared to the predominance of African leaders over sixty years old.[6] This demographic gap adds a highly paternalistic patina to the plebscitarian ties between the charismatic leaders employing populist strategies and their mass of urban followers. From Wade's blue marches to Zuma's Ride n' Braai parties and Sata's *Donchi kubeba* rap, these leaders have tried to create the impression that they can relate to the youth and understand their priorities. In doing so, they affirmed Schatzberg's (2001) observation about the prevalence of the "paternal metaphor" in Africa whereby leaders often portray themselves as the caretakers of a suffering population.

A final distinction between Africa's populist strategies and those elsewhere relates to the inauthenticity of these leaders' attempted portrayals as genuine outsiders to the established political structures they claim to oppose. In Latin America, many populist leaders gained credibility from their status as political outsiders (e.g., Madrid 2008; Roberts 1995, 2007). Unlike Morales's emergence from the coca growers union or Chávez's rise from the military ranks, many of the charismatic leaders at the center of Africa's populist strategies were insiders in their country's political scene for decades. Some were even key figures in the regimes they ultimately came to oppose. Nevertheless, they all succeeded in transforming themselves into

---

[6] The median age in Africa is nineteen years old compared with 26.4 years in Latin America (see UN-DESA 2010).

outsiders who loathed the existing political establishment for its alleged perpetuation of vast socioeconomic inequalities.[7]

Democratic Contestation and Consolidation

Finally, the study emphasized how demographic and socioeconomic dynamics in Africa are influencing voter preferences and party strategies. Such dynamics, in turn, hold important implications for democratic contestation and consolidation. For some scholars, urbanization driven by industrialization leads to a greater appreciation of democratic values and attitudes as well as a broad expansion in the political elite (Dahl 1989; Huber et al. 1993, 1997; Lipset 1959). This study highlighted that even urbanization driven by poverty can influence the democratization process by creating material grievances on which opposition parties can compete. This has important consequences given Dahl's (1971) emphasis on public contestation and inclusiveness as the two underlying dimensions of political democracy.

Thus far, however, the nature of opposition parties in Africa's young democracies rarely allows for genuine contestation in a manner that reflects a clear articulation of citizens' preferences. In fact, few have heeded Stepan's (1990: 44) advice that opposition parties can only defeat ruling regimes by providing a "credible democratic alternative." In turn, the lack of credible opposition alternatives has significant consequences for participation and inclusiveness. Indeed, if parties are irrelevant for voters, then parties' survival is threatened (Crisp 2000) and disillusionment with the democratic process could ensue. Hagopian (2005) further argues that if parties do not provide credible alternatives, this can lead to a diminished interest in politics and a decline in citizen participation. Likewise, according to Huntington and Nelson (1976: 158), "Standard theory argues that people must view politics as relevant and their own participation as potentially effective, as a prerequisite to political participation."

By targeting the preferences of the urban poor, parties that employ populist strategies present a viable alternative to the status quo for this particular constituency, thereby ensuring that their economic marginalization does not result in political exclusion. The policies espoused in such strategies do not correspond to a typical programmatic orientation along a left-right ideological spectrum, which tends to advocate greater or less government

---

[7] Importantly, Mudde (2004) notes that a number of right-wing European populists, such as Pim Fortuyn in the Netherlands and Jörg Haider in Austria, were also not outsiders but rather were well connected with sections of their countries' economic and political elites.

intervention in economic and social institutions. As noted in Chapter 2, such programmatic policies are rare in the African context. Moreover, the examples of the pôle de gauche in Senegal and the early days of Botswana's BNF highlight the inability of programmatic orientations aligned along traditional left-right ideological spectrums to attract the urban poor. However, populist strategies do nonetheless incorporate a policy discourse as one means of mobilizing the urban poor, and these policies tend to exhibit greater congruence to their contemporary working and living conditions than a traditional programmatic stance could.

In this way, populist strategies represent a new possibility for providing voters with meaningful choices when they go to the polls. The impact of these dynamics over time on African voters and party systems could be substantial. Political parties within the region may be encouraged to create greater alignment with the policy preferences of low-income citizens and offer programmatic appeals that involve an eclectic set of policy levers that collectively defy neat classification along a traditional left-right continuum. Moreover, the urban poor may benefit from having their policy priorities squarely brought into the political arena and becoming increasingly targeted by elites for votes. Indeed, the urban poor's growing importance as an electoral constituency may increasingly reduce the amount of harassment they face by state authorities who are hesitant to alienate this constituency base. Nelson (1979) even argues that sustained competition for the votes of the urban poor may ultimately educate the latter about their political options and help them draw links between complex policies and their own long-term interests.

Yet, against these potentially positive contributions must be weighed the pathologies of decision making that often pervade the parties and national governments run by leaders who effectively campaigned on populist strategies. Many, although not all, parties reliant on populist strategies typically lack mechanisms for internal democracy and are rarely institutionalized beyond their party's founder. For instance, Koma's autocratic tendencies ultimately resulted in the splintering of the BNF and the formation of at least ten new parties. Since Wade's loss in 2012, the PDS has virtually imploded as many long-time members defected to create new parties. Likewise, the succession of the PF remains highly uncertain in Zambia.

Moreover, the same charisma, antiestablishment views, and direct ties that enabled these leaders to forge close relationships with the urban poor can simultaneously make them resistant to supporting certain principles, laws, or institutions that could stifle their room for maneuver. As Mudde and Kaltwasser (2012: 20) observe from their comparisons of populism in

Latin America and Europe, "Populism is believed to increase participation by the *inclusion* of marginalized groups in society but limit (the possibilities for) contestation by *centralizing* power in the executive and *undermining* the power of counter-balancing powers." One example was Wade's amendment of the constitution in early 2012 to be able to run for a third term in office. In South Africa, Zuma has supported the passage of the Protection of Information Bill, which essentially curbs the freedoms of the private media to critique the ANC. After his own frequent conflicts in the courts, Zuma even questioned why the judiciary was given so much authority when its members were not even elected (see Vincent 2011), clearly attacking the importance of independent institutions. In Zambia, Sata's government removed three high court judges, attempted to de-register the MMD, and sued media outlets and opposition figures who were accused of insulting the president (see Redvers 2012). These examples caution that although populist strategies may reinvigorate Africa's party landscape, their impact on governance and democratic consolidation is more ambiguous.

AREAS FOR FURTHER RESEARCH

The contributions of the present study provide a useful starting point for considering at least three areas of further research. One area is related to whether development outcomes improve for the urban poor once a leader reliant on a populist strategy enters office. The existing evidence is not particularly positive for the urban poor. Wade's commitments to the urban poor remained unfilled after his twelve years as president. Shortly after Raila Odinga became Kenya's prime minister in 2008, he abandoned his position as protector of the poor and told Kibera residents that those who were illegally squatting in the slums would face legal action by the government (De Smedt 2009). Three months after Zuma was elected South Africa's president, riots over poor service delivery and lack of jobs flared up throughout the country's townships where residents felt the ANC failed to deliver promptly enough on its populist campaign messages (see Lindow 2009). In Zambia, King Cobra did increase mining royalty rates, but the frequency of power outages and level of food inflation in Lusaka remained very high a year after he entered the presidential office (see Redvers 2012). Further research in this area could examine how the availability of natural resource endowments and macroeconomic conditions intersect with a president's ability to deliver on populist campaign promises.

Secondly, how does the use of a populist strategy in one election condition the urban poor's expectations in future elections? Once voters become accustomed to a populist strategy, they may actually demand that the opposition adheres to this strategy in subsequent elections in order to gain their attention and support. This effect may have played an important role in the Senegalese case, where the populist campaigning of Wade as an opposition leader created an expectation about how the opposition should subsequently act in the 2007 elections. When the opposition failed to follow Wade's example, the urban poor chose to continue supporting the candidate who had won them over in 2000.

Thirdly, what does urbanization imply for the voting behavior of Africa's rural poor? Although some attention was given to rural voters in the present study, there is greater scope for analyzing whether rural voting behavior is influenced by how urban compatriots respond to opposition candidates and whether rural voting preferences are changing over time. In Zambia, Larmer and Fraser (2007) suggest that urbanites exhibit little influence over the voting behavior of their rural cousins largely because of the former's diminished ability to send back remittances and declining interest to retire in rural areas. As such, rural-urban linkages regarding voting behavior may vary according to the nature of a country's urbanization processes. In countries where rural-to-urban migration still drives urbanization, there may be greater latitude for feedback from urban residents to rural kin than in those countries where urbanization largely depends on natural population growth within the cities. Surveys focused on rural voting decisions across countries encountering disparate urbanization processes may help illuminate these issues.

CONCLUSION

Historically, the urban poor have been sidelined by governments in Africa. During colonial times, authorities viewed the poor urban masses as dangerous and violent (Cooper 1987), and they aimed to discourage African settlement in urban areas (Njoh 2003). The urban bias literature of the 1970s and 1980s stressed rural-urban cleavages, obscuring intra-urban disparities. Consequently, urban poverty was overlooked by both national governments and international donors as attention shifted to rural development. To ease population pressures, African governments have also at times encouraged the urban poor to return to the countryside (Pieterse 2010) or have built new capital cities instead of addressing chronic problems in the old ones.

However, rapid urbanization will continue to proceed apace in the years to come, particularly in those countries that are still predominantly rural.

Given the high concentration of young people in the region's urban areas, concern with unemployment and underemployment will persist as more and more students leave school. Crises in the provision of electricity and water, garbage collection, housing availability, and affordable food will likewise test the managerial capacities and priority-setting abilities of African governments. How well political parties respond to such challenges and effectively tap into popular discontent will certainly influence their fortunes at the ballot box, thereby ensuring that the urban poor will continue to represent a powerful force in African politics and democratization for the foreseeable future.

Share of Vote (%), Largest City in Recent National Elections

Country (Subnational unit containing largest city)	Election Type (Year)
Benin (Littoral Département)	*Presidential (2011)*
Adrien Houngbédji (PRD)	56.5
Boni Yayi (Independent)	37.9
A.B. Tchane (Independent)	3.0
Botswana (Gaborone Constituency)	*Parliamentary (2009)*
Botswana Democratic Party (BDP)	41.2
Botswana Congress Party (BCP)	36.8
Botswana National Front (BNF)	19.6
Ghana (Accra Metropolis District)	*Presidential (2012)*
John Dramani Mahama (NDC)	52.3
Nana A D Akufo-Addo (NPP)	46.9
Kenya (Nairobi Province)	*Parliamentary (2007)*
Orange Democratic Movement (ODM)	41.9
Party of National Unity (PNU)	28.8
Lesotho (Maseru Constituency)	*Parliamentary (2012)*
All Basotho Convention (ABC)	45.0
Lesotho Congress for Democracy (LCD)	25.5
Liberia *(Montserrado County)*	*Presidential (2011)*
Winston Tubman (CDC)	45.8
Ellen Johnson- Sirleaf (UP)	44.4
Malawi (Lilongwe City)	*Presidential (2009)*
Bingu wa Mutharika (DPP)	55.0
John Tembo (MCP)	43.0
Mozambique (City of Maputo)	*Presidential (2009)*
Armando Guebuza (FRELIMO)	80.7
Davíz Simango (MDM)	14.9
Alfonso Marceta Dhlakama (RENAMO)	4.4

continued

Country (Subnational unit containing largest city)	Election Type (Year)
Namibia (Khomas Province)	*Presidential (2009)*
Hifikepunye Pohamba (SWAPO)	64.2
Hidipo Hamtenya (Rally for Democracy & Progress)	21.1
Katuutire Kaura (DTA)	2.6
Sénégal (Dakar Region)	*Presidential (2012)*
Macky Sall	27.4
Abdoulaye Wade (PDS)	25.3
Sierra Leone (Western Area Urban District)	*Presidential (2007)*
Ernest Bai Koroma (APC)	60.5
Solomon Berewa (SLPP)	32.0
Charles Francis Margai (PMDC)	5.5
South Africa (City of Johannesburg)	*Parliamentary (2009)*
African National Congress (ANC)	63.2
Democratic Alliance (DA)	20.8
Congress of the People (COPE)	9.5
Tanzania (Dar es Salaam Region)	*Presidential (2010)*
Jakaya Kikwete (CCM)	50.7
Slaa Willibrod Peter (CHADEMA)	33.9
Zambia (Lusaka District)	*Presidential (2011)*
Michael Sata (PF)	56.3
Rupiah Banda (MMD)	31.0
Hakainde Hichilema (UPND)	11.4

Notes: The results of presidential elections are provided for countries with presidential systems. Parliamentary results are provided for the following four countries that are not purely presidential: Botswana (executive presidency linked to parliament), Lesotho (parliamentary, constitutional monarchy), and South Africa (executive presidency linked to parliament). The one exception to this rule is Kenya, which is a presidential system, but given the controversy over the 2007 elections, parliamentary results are provided here. For those countries with a two-round majority runoff system (TRS), the results of the first round are presented. Except for elections in Ghana, Senegal, and Sierra Leone, a second round was unnecessary for most TRS countries because one candidate was able to attain more than 50% of the votes in the first round.

Sources: Benin: Constitutional Court of Benin

Botswana : Independent Electoral Commission (IEC), http://www.iec.gov.bw/

Ghana: Ghana Electoral Commission, http://www.ghanaweb.com/GhanaHomePage/election2008/elections.results.runoff.php

Kenya: Kenya Electoral Commission, http://www.eck.or.ke

Lesotho: Lesotho Independent Electoral Commission, http://www.iec.org.ls/about/default.php

Liberia: National Elections Commission, http://www.necliberia.org/results2011/county_30_1.html

Malawi: Malawi Electoral Commission (MEC), http://www.mec.org.mw/

Mozambique: Center for Public Integrity (Centro de Integridade Publica), http://www.elections2009.cip.org.mz

Namibia: Electoral Commission of Namibia, http://www.ecn.na/

Senegal: http://www.sénélections.org

Sierra Leone: Sierra Leone National Election Commission, http://www.daco-sl.org/encyclopedia/7_
elect/7_1elections.htm
South Africa: Independent Electoral Commission, http://www.elections.org.za
Tanzania: The National Electoral Commission of Tanzania, http://www.nec.go.tz/
Zambia: Electoral Commission of Zambia, http://www.elections.org.zm

List of In-Depth Interviews

ZAMBIAN INTERVIEWEES

Bazin, Benoist. Social and Governance Sector Specialist, European Commission Delegation to the Republic of Zambia. March 17, 2009. Lusaka.

Beyani, Choolwe. Director of Policy and Research and Deputy Chairman for International Relations, United Party for National Development; Professor of History, University of Zambia. February 24, 2009. Lusaka.

Chibamba, Musonda. News Correspondent, British Broadcasting Corporation (BBC). January 28, 2009. Lusaka.

Chibwe, Winstone. Deputy Secretary General, United Party for National Development. February 17, 2009. Lusaka.

Chifuwe, Sheikh. Journalist, General Secretary of the Press Freedom Committee, *The Post* newspaper. January 29, 2009. Lusaka.

Chisenga, Edward. Publicity Director, Street Vendors Association. March 3, 2009. Lusaka.

Chitala, Mbita. Former Ambassador to Libya; Executive Campaign Manager, Movement for Multi-Party Democracy. January 29, 2009. Lusaka.

Chiwama, Sally. Journalist, Zambia Media Women's Association. January 21, 2009. Lusaka.

Henriot, Father Peter. Director, Jesuit Center for Theological Reflection. January 30, 2009. Lusaka.

Hichilema, Hakainde. President, United Party for National Development. February 17, 2009. Lusaka.

Kabimba, Wynter. Minister of Justice and Secretary General, Patriotic Front; Former Lusaka Town Clerk; Former Chairman for Local Government, Patriotic Front. February 5, 2009. Lusaka.

Kalumba, Katele. Former National Secretary, Movement for Multi-Party Democracy; Minister of Parliament for Chiengi Constituency; Former

Deputy Minister of Health, Minister of Health, Minister of Finance, Minister of Tourism, Minister of Home Affairs, and Minister of Foreign Affairs. March 5, 2009. Lusaka.

Lubinda, Given. Minister of Foreign Affairs and Tourism; Member of Parliament for Kabwata constituency; Party spokesperson for Patriotic Front; January 22, 2009. Lusaka.

Malido, Webster. Former editor and journalist, *The Post* newspaper. February 5, 2009. Lusaka.

Matawe, Bornwell. Deputy Director of Housing and Social Services, Lusaka City Council. April 8, 2009. Lusaka.

Mulenga, Chileshe. Director of Research and Deputy Secretary General, Patriotic Front. February 24, 2009. Lusaka.

Mumbwatasai, Morgan. Governance Advisor, UK Department for International Development. March 11, 2009. Lusaka.

Nchito, Wilma. Professor of Geography, Researcher on Urban Markets, University of Zambia. January 22, 2009. Lusaka.

Ncube, Nelson. Director, People's Process on Housing and Poverty in Zambia. February 17, 2009. Lusaka.

Palale, Patricia. Public Sector Management Specialist, World Bank. February 25, 2009. Lusaka.

Phiri, Rose. Director of Housing and Social Services, Lusaka City Council. April 8, 2009. Lusaka.

Phiri, Victor. National Coordinator and Organizer for Lusaka District, Workers Education Alliance of Zambia. February 25, 2009. Lusaka.

Phiri, Wazziah. Spokesman, Heritage Party. February 28, 2009. Lusaka.

Rubvuta, Elijah. Executive Director, Forum for Democratic Process (FODEP). February 11, 2009. Lusaka.

Sata, Michael. President of Zambia; President of Patriotic Front. January 28, 2009. Lusaka.

Scott, Guy. Vice President of Zambia; Vice President of the Patriotic Front. Member of Parliament for the constituency of Lusaka Central. January 21, 2009. Lusaka.

Sikota, Sakwiba. Member of Parliament for Livingstone Constituency; President of the United Liberal Party. March 31, 2009. Lusaka.

Simutanyi, Neo. Executive Director, Centre for Policy Dialogue. February 3, 2009. Lusaka.

Simuusa, Wilber. Minister of Lands, Natural Resources, and Environmental Protection; Member of Parliament for Nchanga Constituency. January 21, 2009. Lusaka.

Soko, Michael. Assistant Resident Representative/Governance Advisor, United Nations Development Program (UNDP). March 10, 2009. Lusaka.

Zulu, Brenda. Journalist, Zambia Media Women's Association. January 21, 2009. Lusaka.

SENEGALESE INTERVIEWEES

Abdoul, Mohammadou. Urban Development Researcher, Endapol of ENDA-Tiers Monde. October 3, 2008. Dakar.

Bâ, Abdoul Wahab. Team leader of Governance Unit, United Nations Development Program (UNDP). November 18, 2008. Dakar.

Balde, Demba. Social Development Specialist, World Bank. November 14, 2008. Dakar.

Coulibaly, Abdou Latif. Political analyst and journalist, *Sud Quotidien* newspaper. October 10, 2008. Dakar.

Coumé, Macoumba. Director of Information and Communication in the Office of Elections, Ministry of the Interior. October 2, 2008. Dakar.

Diop, Alioune Badara. Professor of Political Science, University of Gaston-Berger of St. Louis, Department of Juridical and Political Science. December 1, 2008. Dakar.

Diop, Mame Bou. Secretary General, *Union Nationale des Commerçants et Industriels du Sénégal* (UNACOIS). September 17, 2008. Dakar.

Diop, Momar Coumba. Professor of Sociology, University of Cheikh Anta Diop / West African Research Center. October 9, 2008. Dakar.

Fall, Abdou Salam. Professor of Sociology at the University of Cheikh Anta Diop; Director of the Laboratory for the Study of Poverty and Social Transformation, *Institut Fondamental d'Afrique Noire* (IFAN). August 28, 2008. Dakar.

Fall, Waly. Mayor of Dieuppeul-Derklé; Chargé for Communication for *Rewmi*. November 25, 2008. Dakar.

Faye, Ibrahima. Founder of Pressafrik.com; former journalist at *Sud Quotidien*. August 29, 2008. Dakar.

Gaye, Babacar. Spokesperson for the *Parti Démocratique Sénégalais* (PDS); former Director of the President's Political Affairs Cabinet. September 30, 2008. Dakar.

Guèye, Cheikh. Geographical Researcher, ENDA Tiers Monde. November 19, 2008. Dakar.

Martin, Nicolas. Governance team member, United Nations Development Program (UNDP). November 18, 2008. Dakar.

Mboup, Khalifa. Former Secretary General, Association of Senegalese Mayors. December 2, 2008. Dakar.

Sall, Aissata Tall. Chargé of communication for the *Parti Socialiste* (PS). September 15, 2008. Dakar.

Sall, Ebrima. Senior Program Officer, Head Department of Research. CODESRIA. September 9, 2008. Dakar.

Sall, Ibrahima. Former Minister of Planning under Abdou Diouf. *Parti Socialiste* (PS). November 11, 2008. Dakar.

Sall, Seydou Sy. Former Minister of Urbanization, member of *Ligue-Démocratique-Mouvement pour le Parti du Travail* (LD-MPT). September 23, 2008. Dakar.

Sarr, Omar. Spokesperson, *Rewmi*. November 11, 2008. Dakar.

Sène, Ibrahima. Chargé of economic and social affairs for *Parti de l'Indépendance et du Travail* (PIT). September 25, 2008. Dakar.

Sow, Malick. Director, Malick Sow & Associates. October 8, 2008. Dakar.

Tall, Serigne Mansour. Director, UN-HABITAT for Senegal. October 29, 2008. Dakar.

Thior, Mamadou. Chief News Editor, Radio Television Senegal (RTS). November 6, 2008. Dakar.

Thioub, Ibrahima. Professor of History, University of Cheikh Anta Diop. September 10, 2008. Dakar.

Tine, Helène. Spokesperson, *Alliance des Forces du Progrès* (AFP). September 16, 2008. Dakar.

Vasseur, Mathieu. Urban Development and Decentralization Specialist, *Agence France de Développement* (AFD). November 6, 2008. Dakar.

Vilane, Abdoulaye. Spokesperson, *Parti Socialiste* (PS). September 11, 2008. Dakar.

Wade, Aiwa. Spokesperson, *Ligue-Démocratique-Mouvement pour le Parti du Travail* (LD-MPT). September 21, 2008. Dakar.

Survey Questionnaires for the Markets
Lusaka, Zambia

I. Details concerning the interview
   A. Respondent Number:
   B. Date of interview:
   C. Time at which interview began:
   D. Market:

II. Details concerning the respondent
   A. Gender
      1. _____Female   2. _____Male
   B. What is your first language? (The language you first learned as a child)

1. _____Bemba	9. ____Lenje	16._____Ngoni
2. _____Bisa	10.____Lozi	17._____Nsenga
3. _____Chewa	11.____Lunda	18._____Nyanja
4. _____English	12.____Lungu	19._____Senga
5. _____Ila	13.____Luvale	20._____Tonga
6. _____Kaonde	14.____Mambwe	21._____Tumbuka
7. _____Lala	15._____Namwanga	22. _____Other
8. ____Lamba		

   C. How old are you?
      1. _____18–24 years   5. _____More than 40 years
      2. _____25–30 years   6. _____Don't know
      3. _____31–35 years   7. _____ Refuse to respond
      4. _____36–40 years
   D. What is the highest level of education you have attained?
      1. _____No schooling   8. _____ Don't know
      2. _____Primary, uncompleted
      3. _____Primary, completed

    4. _____Secondary, uncompleted

    5. _____Secondary, completed

    6. _____Post-secondary, uncompleted

    7. _____Post-secondary, completed

E. Do you currently live in Lusaka?

    1. _____Yes   2._____No

F. If so, in which constituency do you reside?

    1. _____Chawama   5. _____Mandevu

    2. _____Kabwata   6. _____Matero

    3. _____Kanyama   7. _____Munali

    4. _____Lusaka Central   8. _____Other

G. If so, in which ward do you reside?

H. In your opinion, what are the poorest wards in Lusaka?

 I. Were you born in Lusaka province?

    1. _____Yes   2. _____No

J. If you were not born in the province of Lusaka but currently reside here, in which province were you born?

    1. _____Central   6. _____Northwest

    2. _____Copperbelt   7. _____Southern

    3. _____Eastern   8. _____Western

    4. _____Luapula   9.Other

    5. _____Northern

K. If you were not born in the province of Lusaka, when did you move here?

    1. _____One year ago or less

    2. _____More than 1 year ago but no more than 5 years

    3. _____More than 5 years ago but no more than 10 years

    4. _____More than 10 years ago

L. If you were not born in the province of Lusaka, what was the main reason for why you decided to move here?

    1. _____A part of your family already lived here

    2. _____A lack of employment in the province where you were born

    3. _____To study

    4. _____Marriage

    5. _____Work transfer

    6. _____Husband or family members had a work transfer

    7. _____Brought by parents as a child

    8. Other reason

M. What is your main occupation?

1. _____Street hawker owner
2. _____Artisan
3. _____Sell merchandise in permanent stall
4. _____Sell merchandise in temporary structure
5. _____Sell merchandise in the street
6. _____Maid
7. _____Taxi driver
8. _____Professional, private sector
9. _____Professional, public sector

10._____Store/restaurant
11._____Student
12._____Unemployed
13._____Professor/Teacher
14. _____Beggar
15._____Other services (e.g. hairdresser, shoe-shiner, etc.)
16. _ _____Other non-services
17. _____ Trader

N. Approximately how much money do you spend per day?

1. _____Less than 10,000 ZMK
2. _____Between 10,000 and 30,000 ZMK
3. _____Between 30,000 ZMK and 50,000 ZMK
4. _____More than 50,000 ZMK
5. _____Refused to respond
6. _____Don't know

III. Living Conditions

A. In general, how would you describe *the economic conditions in Zambia* today compared with this same time last year?

1. _____Conditions are much better
2. _____Conditions are a little better
3. _____No change
4. _____Conditions are worse

B. If you believe that conditions became better or worse, what is the principal reason for this change?

1. _____Policies of the Zambian government
2. _____The global economy
3. _____The weather
4. Other_____
5. _____Don't know

C. In general, how would you describe *your own economic conditions today* compared with this same time last year?
  1. _____Conditions are much better
  2. _____Conditions are a little better
  3. _____No change
  4. _____Conditions are worse

D. If you believe that conditions have become better or worse, what is the principal reason for this change?
  1. _____Policies of the Zambian government
  2. _____The global economy
  3. _____The weather
  4. _____Your family situation
  5. Other reason
  6._____ Don't know

E. Do you have a water tap within your household?
  1. _____Yes   2. _____No

F. Do you have electricity within your household?
  1. _____Yes   2. _____No

G. How many people live in your home?
  1. _____2 or less   3. _____Between 5 and 6
  2. _____Between 3 and 4   4. _____More than 6

H. How many rooms are in your home?
  1. _____1 room
  2. _____2 rooms
  3. _____3 rooms
  4. _____ 4 or more rooms
  5. _____ Don't know

I. In your opinion, who should be responsible for the delivery of public services, such as water and electricity, in your neighborhood?
  1. _____The national government
  2. _____The Lusaka City Council
  3. _____Ward authorities
  4. _____National utility companies
  5. _____Don't know
  6. Other_____

J. In general, how would you describe the housing conditions in your neighborhood during the period in which you have lived there?
  1. _____Conditions are much better
  2. _____Conditions are a little better

3. _____No change
4. _____Conditions are worse

K. Within the last five years (or within the period that you have lived there, if less than five years), has your house or any houses in your neighborhood ever been demolished without warning by government authorities?

1. _____Yes   2. _____No
3. _____Refused to respond   4. _____Don't know

IV. Working Conditions and Associational Membership

A. Are you satisfied with your working conditions?
1. _____Yes, very much so
2. _____No, not at all
3. _____Sometimes/ A little bit

B. If you work in one of Lusaka's markets, have you or someone that you know ever been harassed by the government authorities?
1. _____Yes
2. _____No
3. _____Refused to respond

C. If so, which of the following have the government authorities done to you or someone that you know (check all that apply):
1. _____Destroyed stall(s) or merchandise
2. _____Forced you to work in a different place
3. _____Forced you to pay certain taxes or other fees
4. _____Arrested you
5. Other _____
6. _____Refuse to respond

D. If so, which level of government do you believe is responsible for such harassment?
1. _____The national government
2. _____The Lusaka City Council
3. _____Constituency-level authorities
4. _____Ward-level authorities
5. _____Market chairperson
6. _____Don't know

E. If so, how often does such harassment occur?
1. _____At least once every 6 months
2. _____At least once a year
3. _____At least once every 2 years
4. _____Very infrequently

F. Are you a member of any associations/organizations?
  1. _____Yes   2._____No
G. If so, which one(s)?
H. If yes, why did you decide to become a member of this organization?
  1. _____It has a good record of representing its members' interests
  2. _____It has a close relationship with the local authorities
  3. _____A friend convinced you to become a member
  4. _____A member of your family convinced you to become a member
  5. Other reason _____
I. If not, why have you decided not to join any organizations?
  1. _____The benefits of membership are not clear
  2. _____Membership fees are too high
  3. _____The existing organizations are too closely tied to the ruling party
  4. _____The existing organizations are too autocratic
  5. _____You didn't know that any organizations existed
  6. _____Other reason _____
  7. _____Don't know
J. Recently, the role of the Chinese in the Zambian economy has been controversial. What is your opinion of the growing Chinese presence in Zambia?
  1. _____Beneficial: They bring skills and resources that improve Zambia's development
  2. _____Harmful: They are taking away opportunities from Zambians
  3. _____Mixed: They bring both benefits and disadvantages
  4. _____No opinion

V. Presidential Elections
  A. Did you vote in the 2006 presidential election?
    1. _____Yes   2. _____No
  B. If no, why not?
    1. _____ None of the candidates appealed to you
    2. _____You did not have enough time to vote
    3. _____You thought that the elections would not be fair and transparent
    4. _____You thought that your favorite candidate would not win

5. _____You did not know the manifestoes of the candidates
6. _____You thought that, no matter who wins, nothing will change
7. _____ You didn't have necessary documents (NRC, voter's card, or both)
8. _____You were too young to vote
9. _____You cannot vote for religious reasons (e.g., Jehovah's Witness)
10. _____Other

C. If yes, who did you support during the 2006 presidential election?
1. _____Levy Mwanawasa (MMD)
2. _____Michael Sata (PF)
3. _____Hakainde Hichilema (UDA)
4. _____Godfrey K. Miyanda (HP)
5. _____Winright K. Ngondo (APC)
6. Other candidate_ ___
7. _____Don't know
8. _____Refused to respond

D. What was the main reason you supported this candidate in the 2006 presidential election?
1. _____You recognized his name
2. _____You preferred the manifesto of this candidate
3. _____You had experienced a change in your own economic conditions
4. _____The candidate's ethnicity
5. _____The candidate's party campaigned in your neighborhood
6. _____The candidate promised a change
7. _____A member of your family voted for him
8. _____A neighbor/friend/acquaintance voted for him
9. _____This candidate had a lot of experience
10. _____You preferred the personality/characteristics of this candidate
11. Other reason _____
12. _____Don't know

E. Did you vote in the 2008 presidential election?
1. _____Yes   2. _____No

F. If no, why not?
1. _____ None of the candidates appealed to you
2. _____You did not have enough time to vote

3. _____You thought that the elections would not be fair and transparent

4. _____You thought that your favorite candidate would not win

5. _____You did not know the manifestoes of the candidates

6. _____You thought that, no matter who wins, nothing will change

7. _____ You didn't have necessary documents (NRC, voter's card, or both)

8. _____You were too young to vote

9. _____You cannot vote for religious reasons (e.g., Jehovah's Witness)

10. _____Other_____

G. If yes, who did you support during the 2008 presidential election?

1. _____Rupiah Banda (MMD)

2. _____Michael Sata (PF)

3. _____Hakainde Hichilema (UPND)

4. _____Godfrey K. Miyanda (HP)

5. Other candidate_____

6. _____Don't know

7. _____Refused to respond

H. What was the main reason why you supported this candidate in the 2008 presidential elections?

1. _____You recognized his name

2. _____You preferred the manifesto of this candidate

3. _____You had experienced a change in your own economic conditions

4. _____The candidate's ethnicity

5. _____The candidate's party campaigned in your neighborhood

6. _____The candidate promised a change

7. _____A member of your family voted for him

8. _____A neighbor/friend/acquaintance voted for him

9. _____This candidate had a lot of experience

10. _____You preferred the personality/characteristics of this candidate

11. Other reason _____

12. _____Don't know

VI. Perspectives on the ruling party (MMD)

A. Did the MMD campaign in your neighborhood during the 2008 presidential elections?

1. _____Yes 2. _____No 3. _____Don't know

B. If yes, did the MMD give a speech in your neighborhood?

    1. _____Yes   2. _____No   3. _____Don't know

C. If yes, did the MMD hang up signs in your neighborhood?

    1. _____Yes   2. _____No   3. _____Don't know

D. If yes, did the MMD give out gifts, such as T-shirts, hats, etc., in your neighborhood?

    1. _____Yes   2. _____No   3. _____Don't know

E. If yes, did the MMD give out money in your neighborhood?

    1. _____Yes   2. _____No   3. _____Don't know

F. Do you agree or disagree with the following statement:

    «*The MMD has improved the availability of electricity in Lusaka* »

    1. _____Yes   2. _____No   3. _____Don't know

G. Do you agree or disagree with the following statement:

    «*The MMD has improved the cost of electricity in Lusaka* »

    1. _____Yes   2. _____No   3. _____Don't know

H. Do you agree or disagree with the following statement:

    «*The MMD has improved the availability of water in Lusaka* »

    1. _____Yes   2. _____No   3. _____Don't know

I. Do you agree or disagree with the following statement:

    «*The MMD has improved the cost of water in Lusaka* »

    1. _____Yes   2. _____No   3. _____Don't know

J. Do you agree or disagree with the following statement:

    «*The MMD has improved the cost of transport in Lusaka* »

    1. _____Yes   2. _____No   3. _____Don't know

K. Do you agree or disagree with the following statement:

    «*The MMD has done a lot to improve the conditions of the poor in Lusaka* »

    1. _____Yes   2. _____No   3. _____Don't know

L. Do you agree or disagree with the following statement:

    «*Thanks to the MMD, unemployment has declined* »

    1. _____Yes   2. _____No   3. _____Don't know

M. Why did the MMD win the 2008 presidential elections?

    1. _____The MMD has had good policies for improving the living conditions of many Zambians

    2. _____The opposition parties were not competitive enough

    3. _____The election was not fair

    4. _____The MMD gave money and/or other goods to certain voters in order to obtain their support

    5. _____Sympathy for the loss of Levy Mwanawasa

6. Other reason _____
7. _____Don't know

VII. Perspectives of the opposition parties
  A. Which opposition parties campaigned in your neighborhood during the 2008 presidential elections?
    1. _____Patriotic Front (PF)
    2. _____United Party for National Development
    3. _____Heritage Party
    4. Other party_____
    5. _____None
    6. _____ Don't know
  B. Did any of these opposition parties give a speech in your neighborhood?
    1. _____Yes   2. _____No   3. _____Don't know
  C. Did any of these opposition parties hang up signs in your neighborhood?
    1. _____Yes   2. _____No   3. _____Don't know
  D. Did any of these opposition parties give out gifts, such as T-shirts and hats, in your neighborhood?
    1. _____Yes   2. _____No   3. _____Don't know
  E. Did any of these opposition parties give out money in your neighborhood?
    1. _____Yes   2. _____No   3. _____Don't know
  F. Which opposition parties do you think are the most interested in improving the living conditions of those living in Lusaka? (check all that apply)
    1. _____Patriotic Front (PF)
    2. _____United National Independence Party (UNIP)
    3. _____United Party for National Development (UPND)
    4. _____Forum for Democracy and Development (FDD)
    5. _____Heritage Party (HP)
    6. Other party_____
    7. _____None
  G. In your opinion, what is the major difference between Zambia's political parties?
    1. _____The personalities of the party leaders
    2. _____The parties' positions on important social and economic issues
    3. _____The parties' links with a particular region of Zambia

4. _____There is no difference

5. Other factor_____

6. _____ Don't know

H. If elections took place tomorrow, would you support the MMD?

1. _____Yes

2. _____No

3. _____Don't know

4. _____Refused to respond

5. _____Not Applicable (e.g., Jehovah's Witness, etc.)

I. How would you define what a "political party platform/manifesto" is?
Time that interview ended:

DAKAR, SENEGAL (*Translated from French*)

I. Details concerning the interview

A. Respondent number:

B, Date of interview:

C. Time at which the interview began:

D. Market:

II. Details concerning the respondent

A. Gender

1. _____Female 2. _____Male

B. What is your first language?

1. _____French	5. _____Serer
2. _____ Jola	6. _____Soninke
3. _____Mandinka	7. _____Wolof
4. _____ Pulaar	8. Other

C. How old are you?

1. _____18–24	5. _____40 and over
2. _____25–30	6. _____Don't know
3. _____31–35	7. _____Refused to respond
4. _____36–40	

D. What is the highest level of education that you obtained?

1. _____ No schooling

2. _____ Koranic schooling

3. _____ Language training

4. _____Primary school

5. _____Secondary school

6. _____Post-secondary school

7. _____Don't know

E. Where you born in the region of Dakar?
    1. _____Yes 2. _____No

F. If no, when did you move to Dakar?
    1. _____Less than one year ago
    2. _____More than a year ago but less than five years
    3. _____More than five years ago but less than ten years
    4. _____More than ten years ago

G. If you are not originally from Dakar, which region are you from?
    1. _____Diourbel   7. _____Saint Louis
    2. _____Fatick   8. _____Tambacounda
    3. _____Kaolack   9. _____Thiès
    4. _____Kolda   10._____Casamance
    5. _____ Louga   11.Other
    6. _____Matam

H. If you are not originally from Dakar, what was your primarily reason for moving here?
    1. _____A part of your family already lived here
    2. _____A lack of employment in the region where you are from
    3. _____To study
    4. Other reasons_____

I. What is your primary occupation?
    1. ____Street hawker   9. ____ Shop owner
    2. ____Artisan   10.____ Student
    3. ____Sell merchandise in a
        store   11. ____Fisherman/woman
              12. ____Unemployed
    4. ____Sell merchanise in the street 13. ____ Professor or teacher
    5. ____Maid   14. ____Beggar
    6. ____Taxi driver   15. ____ Other services
        profession
    7. ____Private sector employee   16. ____Other non-services
        profession
    8. ____ Public sector employee

J. Approximately how much money do you spend per day?
    1. _____ 1,000 CFA or less
    2. _____More than 1,000 but less than 3,000 CFA
    3. _____More than 3,000 but less than 5,000 CFA
    4. _____More than 5,000 CFA
    5. _____Refused to respond
    6. _____Don't know

III. Living Conditions
   A. In which département do you live?
      1. _____Dakar
      2. _____Pikine
      3. _____Guédiawaye
      4. _____Rufisque
      5. Other_____
   B. In which commune do you live?
   C. In which neighborhood do you live?
   D. In your opinion, which are the poorest neighborhoods in Dakar?
   E. In general, how would you describe Senegal's economic conditions today compared with the same time a year ago?
      1. _____Conditions are much better
      2. _____Conditions are a little better
      3. _____There is no change
      4. _____Conditions are worse
   F. If you believe conditions have become better or worse, what is the primary reason you attribute for this change?
      1. _____Policies of the Senegalese government
      2. _____The global economy
      3. _____The weather
      4. Another reason_____
      5. _____At least two of the above are responsible
      6. _____Don't know
   G. In general, how would you describe your own economic conditions today compared with the same time last year?
      1. _____Conditions are much better
      2. _____Conditions are a little bit better
      3. _____There is no change
      4. _____Conditions are worse
   H. If you believe that conditions have become better or worse, what is the principle reason for this change?
      1. _____Policies of the Senegalese government
      2. _____The global economy
      3. _____Weather
      4. _____Your family circumstances
      5. Another reason_____
      6. _____ Don't know
   I. Do you have water taps in your home?
      1. _____Yes   2. _____No

J. Do you have electricity in your home?
    1. _____Yes   2. _____No

K. How many people are there in your home?
    1. _____2 or less
    2. _____Between 3 and 4
    3. _____Between 5 and 6
    4. _____More than 6

L. How many rooms are there in your home?
    1. _____1 room
    2. _____2 rooms
    3. _____3 rooms
    4. _____ 4 or more
    5. _____ Don't know

M. In general, how would you describe the housing conditions in your neighborhood during the period in which you have lived there?
    1. _____Conditions are much better
    2. _____Conditions are a little bit better
    3. _____There is no change
    4. _____Conditions are worse

N. In your opinion, who should be responsible for the delivery of public services, such as water and electricity, in your neighborhood?
    1. _____The national government
    2. _____The municipal government
    3. _____The commune government
    4. _____SENELEC/SDE/Other utility companies
    5. _____Don't know
    6. Other_____

IV. Working Conditions
    A. Are you satisfied with your working conditions?
        1. _____Yes, very much so
        2. _____No, not at all
        3. _____Sometimes/a little bit
    B. Are you a member of UNACOIS?
        1. _____Yes   2. _____No
    C. If yes, why did you decide to become a member of UNACOIS?
        1. _____ UNACOIS has a good reputation
        2. _____ UNACOIS has close ties with the ruling party
        3. _____A friend convinced you to become a member

4. _____A member of your family convinced you to become a member

5. Other reason_____

D. If no, why not?

    1. _____The membership fees are too high

    2. _____The benefits of membership are not clear

    3. _____ UNACOIS has close ties with the ruling party

    4. _____ UNACOIS is too autocratic

    5. _____You did not know that UNACOIS existed

    6. Other reason_____

    7. _____Don't know

E. Are you a member of any other association?

    1. _____Yes   2. _____No

F. If yes, which one?

V. The 2007 Presidential Elections

A. Did you vote during the last presidential election?

    1. _____Yes   2. _____No

B. If not, why not?

    1. _____ None of the candidates appealed to you

    2. _____You didn't have enough time to vote

    3. _____You thought that the elections would not be fair

    4. _____You thought that your favorite candidate would not win

    5. _____You did not know the candidates' platforms

    6. _____You thought that no matter who wins, nothing will change

    7. _____You did not have your identity documents/electoral card

    8. _____You were too young to vote

    9. Other reason

C. If yes, who did you support during the last presidential election?

    1. _____Abdoulaye Wade, (PDS)

    2. _____Ousamane Tanor Dieng (PS)

    3. _____Moustapha Niasse (AFP)

    4. _____Idrissa Seck (Rewmi)

    5. _____Robert Sagna (Démocratie-Solidarité)

    6. _____Talla Sylla (APJ-JJ)

    7. _____Abdoulaye Bathily (LD-MPT)

    8. _____Refused to respond

    9. Other candidate/party_____

    10. _____Don't know

D. Why did you support this candidate?
1. _____Recognized candidate's name
2. _____Preferred the party platform of this candidate
3. _____Experienced a change in your own economic conditions
4. _____The candidate's ethnicity
5. _____The candidate campaigned in your neighborhood
6. _____The candidate promised a change
7. _____ Religious reasons
8. _____A member of your family voted for him
9. _____Friends/neighbors voted for him
10. _____The candidate had a lot of experience
11. _____Prefered the personality of the candidate
12. _____Other reason_____
13. _____Don't know

VI. Perspectives of the ruling party (le PDS)
A. Did the PDS campaign in your neighborhood during the 2007 presidential elections?
1. _____Yes   2. _____No   3. _____Don't know
B. If yes, did the PDS give a speech in your neighborhood?
1. _____Yes   2. _____No   3. _____Don't know
C. If yes, did the PDS hang up posters in your neighborhood?
1. _____Yes   2. _____No   3. _____Don't know
D. If yes, did the PDS give out gives (such as T-shirts, hats, etc.) in your neighborhood?
1. _____Yes   2. _____No   3. _____Don't know
E. If yes, did the PDS give out money in your neighborhood?
1. _____Yes   2. _____No   3. _____Don't know
F. Do you agree or disagree with the following statement:
   « The PDS has improved the availability of electricity in Dakar »
   1. ____Agree   2. _____ Disagree   3. _____Don't know
G. Do you agree or disagree with the following statement:
   « The PDS has improved the cost of electricity in Dakar »
   1. ____Agree   2. _____ Disagree   3. _____Don't know
H. Do you agree or disagree with the following statement:
   « The PDS has improved the availability of water in Dakar »
   1. ____Agree   2. _____ Disagree   3. _____Don't know
I. Do you agree or disagree with the following statement:
   « The PDS has improved the cost of water in Dakar »
   1. ____Agree   2. _____ Disagree   3. _____Don't know

J. Do you agree or disagree with the following statement:
    « *The PDS has improved the transport system in Dakar* »
    1. ____Agree   2. _____ Disagree   3. _____Don't know

K. Do you agree or disagree with the following statement:
    « *The PDS has done a lot of things to improve the living conditions of the poorest Dakarois* »
    1. ____Agree   2. _____ Disagree   3. _____Don't know

L. Do you agree or disagree with the following statement:
    « *Thanks to the PDS, unemployment has declined* »
    1. ____Agree   2. _____ Disagree   3. _____Don't know

M. Do you agree or disagree with the following statement:
    « *The PDS is only engaged in projects that benefit the rich* »
    1. ____Agree   2. _____ Disagree   3. _____Don't know

N. Do you agree or disagree with the following statement:
    « *The PDS has become more repressive towards the media* »
    1. ____Agree   2. _____ Disagree   3. _____Don't know

O. Do you agree or disagree with the following statement:
    « *The change to the presidential mandate from 5 to 7 years is good for Senegal's democracy* »
    1. ____Agree   2. _____ Disagree   3. _____Don't know

P. In your opinion, why did the PDS win the 2007 presidential elections?
    1. _____The PDS had good policies to improve living conditions for the Senegalese people
    2. _____The opposition parties were not competitive enough
    3. _____The election was not fair
    4. _____The PDS gave money to important communities in exchange for support
    5. Other reason_____
    6. _____Don't know
    7. _____The PDS candidate promised a change

Q. Last year, the government tried to forcibly remove street hawkers. What do you think of this initiative by the government?
    1. _____It was a good idea; street hawkers are a problem in Dakar
    2. _____It was a bad idea; the government should leave street hawkers alone
    3. _____The government should have instead found a permanent space for the street hawkers to vend

4. _____No opinion

VII. Views on opposition parties
A. Which opposition parties campaigned in your neighborhood during the 2007 presidential elections?
1. _____Parti Socialiste (PS)
2. _____Alliance des forces de progrès (AFP)
3. _____Rewmi
4. _____Alliance pour le progrès et la justice –Jëf-Jël (APJ-JJ)
5. _____Ligue démocratique – Mouvement pour le parti du travail (LD-MPT)
6. _____Démocratie-Solidarité
7. _____None
8. Other parties_____
9. _____ Don't know

B. Did any of these opposition parties give a speech?
1. _____Yes   2. _____No   3. _____Don't know

C. Did any of these opposition parties hang up signs?
1. _____Yes   2. _____No   3. _____Don't know

D. Did any of these opposition parties give out gifts (such as T-shirts, hats, etc.)?
1. _____Yes   2. _____No   3. _____Don't know

E. Did any of these opposition parties give out money?
1. _____Yes   2. _____No   3. _____Don't know

F. Which opposition parties do you think are most interested in improving living conditions in the region of Dakar? (You can choose more than one party)
1. _____Parti Socialiste (PS)
2. _____Alliance des forces de progrès (AFP)
3. _____Rewmi
4. _____Alliance pour le progrès et la justice –Jëf-Jël (APJ-JJ)
5. _____Ligue démocratique – Mouvement pour le parti du travail (LD-MPT)
6. _____Démocratie-Solidarité
7. _____No political parties
8. Another party_____

G. According to you, what is the main factor that distinguishes Senegal's political parties?
1. _____The personalities of the party leaders
2. _____Their policy positions on important economic and social issues

3. _____Their close ties with a particular region of Senegal
4. _____There is no difference among parties
5. _____ Other factors_____
6. _____ Don't know

H. If elections took place tomorrow, would you support the PDS?
1. _____Yes   3. _____Don't know
2. _____No   4. _____You can't vote (e.g., because of religion, etc.)

I. In your view, what is a political party platform?
J. Do you know what the *Assises Nationales* is?
1. _____Yes 2. _____No
K. If yes, what do you think of this initiative?
1. _____It's a good idea and it will change the Senegalese political
scene
2. _____It's a good idea but nothing will change
3. _____It's not necessary
4. _____No opinion
5. Other opinions_____
Time at which the interview ended:

Bibliography

Aarts, Kees, and Bernard Wessels. 2005. "Electoral Turnout." In Jacques Thomassen (ed.), *The European Voter: A Comparative Study of Modern Democracies*. Oxford: Oxford University Press, 64–83.

Adejumobi, Said. 2007. *Political Parties in West Africa: The Challenge of Democratization in Fragile States*. Stockholm: International Institute for Democracy and Electoral Assistance (IDEA).

Africa Confidential. 1999. "All His own Work." 40 (21): 4–5.

2003. "Facing Mount Kenya," 44 (19): 2.

2004 "Khama's Coming." 45 (23): 7.

2006. "Zambia: The Titanic Sails at Dawn." 47 (21): 4–5.

2007. "Wading In." 48 (23): 8.

2008. "Banda, the Successor." 49 (23): 4–5.

2011. "Sata Rises in the West." 52 (12): 4.

African Economic Outlook. 2009. Paris: African Development Bank and Organization for Economic Cooperation and Development (OECD).

African National Congress (ANC). 2009. *African National Congress 2009 Manifesto: Working Together We Can Do More.* Retrieved from: http://www.anc.org.za/elections/2009/manifesto/policy_framework.html.

Agence du Fonds du Développement Social. 2004. "Evaluation Participative de la Pauvreté: Rapport d'Analyse, Version Finale [Région de Dakar, Département de Pikine, Commune d'arrondissement de Yeumbeul Sud, Quartier Médina Yeumbeul]." Dakar, Sénégal: Ministère du Développement Social.

Agence France Presse (AFP). 2005. "Senegal's President Wants Vote Postponed to Pay for Flood Damage," August 29.

Agence Nationale de la Statistique et de la Démographie (ANSD). 2005. "Situation Economique et Sociale: Région Dakar, Edition 2005." Dakar, Sénégal: Ministère de l'Economie et des Finances.

2006. "Rapport National de Présentation: Résultats du Troisième Récensement Général de la Population et de l'Habitat." Dakar, Sénégal: Ministère de l'Economie et des Finances.

2007a. "Enquête de Suivi de la Pauvreté au Sénégal." Dakar, Sénégal: Ministère de l'Economie et des Finances.

2007b. "Situation Economique et Sociale: Région Dakar Année 2006." Dakar Sénégal: Ministère de l'Economie et des Finances.

Aguilar, Edwin E., and Alexander C. Pacek. 2000. "Macroeconomic Conditions, Voter Turnout, and the Working-Class/Economically Disadvantaged Party Vote in Developing Countries." *Comparative Political Studies* 33 (8): 995–1017.

Akam, Simon. 2012. "Après Moi, Mon Fils." *New Statesman* 21 (May): 29–31.

Alexander, Peter. 2010. "Rebellion of the Poor: South Africa's Service Delivery Protests – A Preliminary Analysis." *Review of African Political Economy* 37 (123): 25–40.

Allport, G. W. 1954. *The Nature of Prejudice*. Reading, MA: Addison-Wesley.

Amis, Philip. 2004. "Regulating the Informal Sector: Voice and Bad Governance." In N. Devas (ed.), *Urban Governance, Voice, and Poverty in the Developing World*. London: Earthscan, 145–163.

Anderson, Christopher. 2007. "The End of Economic Voting? Contingency Dilemmas and the Limits of Democratic Accountability." *Annual Review of Political Science* 10: 271–296.

Anderson, David. 2005. "'Yours in Struggle for *Majimbo*': Nationalism and the Party Politics of Decolonization in Kenya, 1955–1964." *Journal of Contemporary History* 40 (3): 547–565.

André, Pierre, and Jean-Luc Demonsant. 2009. "Koranic Schools in Senegal: An Actual Barrier to Formal Education?" School of Economics Working Papers, Guanajuato, Mexico: Universidad de Guanajuato.

Annez, Patricia, Robert Buckley, and Jerry Kalarickal. 2010. "African Urbanization as Flight? Some Policy Implications of Geography." *Urban Forum* 21: 221–234.

Ariga, Joshua, Thomas S. Jayne, and James Nyoro. 2006. "Factors Driving the Growth in Fertilizer Consumption in Kenya, 1990–2005: Sustaining the Momentum in Kenya and Lessons for Broader Replicability in Sub-Saharan Africa." Working Paper 24/2006. Nairobi, Kenya: Tegemeo Institute of Agricultural Policy and Development.

Arriola, Leonardo R. 2009. "Patronage and Political Stability in Africa." *Comparative Political Studies* 42 (10): 1339–1362.

Audrain, Xavier. 2004. "Du 'Ndigël Avorté' au Parti de la Vérité." *Politique Africaine* 96 (December): 99–108.

Auyero, Javier. 1999. "'From the Client's Point(s) of View': How Poor People Perceive and Evaluate Political Clientelism." *Theory and Society* 28 (2): 297–334.

Aziz Tall, Abdoul. 2008. "Enjeux Poliques et Capacité d'Adaptation: Quelle Opposition Face au Régime Actuel?" *Le Quotidien* Décembre 3: 9.

Ba, Diadie. 2007. "Senegal Migrant Crisis Clouds Wade Second Term Bid." *Reuters New Service*. Retrieved from: http://www.bdnews24.com/Reuters.

Baker, Pauline. 1974. *Urbanization and Political Change: The Politics of Lagos, 1917–1967*. Berkeley: University of California Press.

Banégas, Richard. 1998. "Marchandisation du Vote, Citoyenneté et Consolidation Démocratique au Bénin." *Politique Africaine* 69 (March): 75–87.

Banks, Arthur S., Thomas C. Muller, and William R. Overstreet, eds. 2008. *Political Handbook of the World 2008*. Washington, DC: Congressional Quarterly Press.

Barasa, Lucas. 2007. "Raila Backers Keep an Eye on Langata as He Traverses Country." *The Nation* December 17.

Barkan, Joel D. 1995. "Elections in Agrarian Societies." *Journal of Democracy* 6 (4): 106–116.

Barkan, Joel D., and Michael Chege. 1989. "Decentralising the State: District Focus and the Politics of Reallocation in Kenya." *Journal of Modern African Studies* 27 (3): 431–453.

Barr, Robert R. 2009. "Populists, Outsiders, and Anti-Establishment Politics." *Party Politics* 15 (29): 29–48.

Bassett, Carolyn, and Marlea Clarke. 2008. "The Zuma Affair, Labour and the Future of Democracy in South Africa." *Third World Quarterly* 29 (4): 787–803.

Bates, Robert. 1981. *Markets and States in Tropical Africa: The Political Basis of Agricultural Policies*. Berkeley: University of California Press.

1983. "Modernization, Ethnic Competition and the Rationality of Politics in Contemporary Africa." In D. Rothchild and V. A. Olorunsola (eds.), *State versus Ethnic Claims: African Policy Dilemmas*. Boulder, CO: Westview, 152–171.

1991. "The Economics of Transitions to Democracy." *PS: Political Science and Politics* 24 (1): 24–27.

Beall, Jo, Owen Crankshaw, and Susan Parnell. 2000. "Local Government, Poverty Reduction and Inequality in Johannesburg." *Environment and Urbanization* 12 (1): 107–122.

Beck, Linda J. 2001. "Reining in the Marabouts? Democratization and Local Governance in Senegal." *African Affairs* 100: 601–621.

2008. *Brokering Democracy in Africa: The Rise of Clientelist Democracy in Senegal*. New York: Palgrave Macmillan.

Beresford, Alexander. 2009. "Comrades 'Back on Track?' The Durability of the Tripartite Alliance in South Africa." *African Affairs* 108 (432): 391–412.

Beteille, Andre. 1970. "Caste and Political Group Formation in Tamil Nadu." In R. Kothari (ed.), *Caste in Indian Politics*. New Delhi: Orient Longman, 259–298.

Bienen, Henry, and Jeffrey Herbst. 1996. "The Relationship between Political and Economic Reform in Africa." *Comparative Politics* 29 (1): 23–42.

Blair, David. 2009. "Zuma Prepares to Lead a Country Beset by Squalor." *The Daily Telegraph*, April 17, 16.

Bleck, Jaimie, and Nicolas van de Walle. Forthcoming. "Valence Issues in African Elections: Navigating Uncertainty and the Weight of the Past." *Comparative Political Studies*.

Bogaards, Matthijs. 2000. "Crafting Competitive Party Systems: Electoral Laws and the Opposition in Africa." *Democratization* 7 (4): 163–190.

2004. "Counting Parties and Identifying Dominant Party Systems in Africa." *European Journal of Political Research* 43: 173–197.

Boone, Catherine. 1992. *Merchant Capital and the Roots of State Power in Senegal 1930–1985*. New York: Cambridge University Press.

2003. *Political Topographies of the African State: Territorial Authority and Institutional Choice*. New York: Cambridge University Press.

Booysen, Susan. 2009. "Congress of the People: Between Foothold of Hope and Slippery Slope." In Roger Southall and John Daniel (eds.), *Zunami! The 2009 South African Elections*. Auckland Park, South Africa: Jacana Media Ltd, 85–113.

Bosire, Bogonko. 2007. "Raila Odinga, Kenya's Mercurial Political Ogre." *Agence France Presse*, December 24.

Bosire, Bogonko, and Lucie Peytermann. 2007. "Kenya Economy Set to Defy Polls." *Agence France Presse*, December 24.

Branch, Daniel, and Nicholas Cheeseman. 2008. "Democratization, Sequencing, and State Failure in Africa: Lessons from Kenya." *African Affairs* 108 (430): 1–26.

Bratton, Michael. 1989. "Beyond the State: Civil Society and Associational Life in Africa." *World Politics* 41 (3): 407–430.

    1994. "Economic Crisis and Political Realignment in Zambia." In J. Widner (ed.), *Economic Change and Political Liberalization in Sub-Saharan Africa*. Baltimore: Johns Hopkins University Press, 101–128.

    1998. "Second Elections in Africa." *Journal of Democracy* 9 (3): 51–66.

    2006. "Poor People and Democratic Citizenship in Africa." *Afrobarometer Working Paper No. 56.*

Bratton, Michael, and Nicolas van de Walle. 1992. "Popular Protest and Political Reform in Africa." *Comparative Politics* 24 (4): 419–442.

    1997. *Democratic Experiments in Africa: Regime Transitions in Comparative Perspective.* New York: Cambridge University Press.

Braun, Michael. 2003. "Errors in Comparative Survey Research." In J. A. Harkness, F. J. R. Van de Vijver, and P. P. Mohler (eds.), *Cross-Cultural Survey Methods*. Hoboken, NJ: John Wiley & Sons, 137–142.

Breuillac, Brigitte. 2000a. "Le Sénégal à l'Heure du Changement dans la Continuité ou la Rupture." *Le Monde*, February 28.

    2000b. "Portrait: Le lièvre Abdoulaye Wade, ou la Ténacité Récompensée." *Le Monde*, March 22.

British Broadcasting Company (BBC). 1999. "Senegal: Former Minister Urges Cut in Presidential Term," June 16.

Brockington, David. 2009. "It's about the Benefits: Choice Environments, Ideological Proximity, and Individual Participation in 28 Democracies." *Party Politics* 15 (4): 435–454.

Bryan, Shari, and Denise Baer, eds. 2005. *Money in Politics: A Study of Party Financing Practices in 22 Countries*. Washington, DC: National Democratic Institute.

Bueno de Mesquita, Bruce, Alastair Smith, Randolph M. Siverson, and James D. Morrow. 2003. *The Logic of Political Survival*. Cambridge, MA: The MIT Press.

Bupe, Florence. 2006. "Lusaka Residents Protest Zesco's Power Outages." *The Post* 20 (July): 9.

Burnell, Peter. 2001. "The Party System and Party Politics in Zambia: Continuities Past, Present, and Future." *African Affairs* 100: 239–263.

    2002. "Zambia's 2001 Elections: The Tyranny of Small Decisions, 'Non-Decisions,' and 'Not Decisions.'" *Third World Quarterly* 23 (6): 1103–1120.

    2005. "From Low-Conflict Polity to Democratic Civil Peace: Explaining Zambian Exceptionalism." *African Studies* 64 (2):107–133.

Business Day. 2009. "South Africa: ANC Aims to Bring Afrikaners Back into Laager," April 6.

Butler, Anthony. 2009. "The ANC's National Election Campaign of 2009: Siyanqoba!" In Roger Southall and John Daniel (eds.), *Zunami! The 2009 South African Elections*, Chapter 4. Auckland Park, South Africa: Jacana Media Ltd.

Butler, Tramayne M. 2002. "Nairobi." In M. Ember and C. R. Ember (eds.), *Encyclopedia of Urban Cultures: Cities and Cultures around the World* Volume 3. Danbury, CT: Grolier Publishing Co., Inc, 70–77.

Buvinić, Mayra, and Andrew Morrison. 2000. "Living in a more Violent World." *Foreign Policy* 118: 58–72.

Calland, Richard. 2006. *Anatomy of South Africa: Who Holds the Power?* Cape Town, South Africa: Zebra Press.

Calvo, Ernesto, and Maria Victoria Murillo. 2004. "Who Delivers? Partisan Clients in the Argentine Electoral Market." *American Journal of Political Science* 48 (4): 742–757.

Camara, Sadio. 2000. "A propos de la floraison des partis politiques." *Le Soleil*, September 26.

Cameron, Maxwell. 1991. "The Politics of the Urban Informal Sector in Peru: Populism, Class, and 'Redistributive Combines.'" *Canadian Journal of Latin American and Caribbean Studies* 16 (31): 79–104.

1994. *Democracy and Authoritarianism in Peru: Political Conditions and Social Change.* New York: St. Martin's Press.

Canache, Damarys. 2004. "Urban Poor and Political Order." In J. L. McCoy and D. J. Myers (eds.), *The Unraveling of Representative Democracy in Venezuela.* Baltimore: The Johns Hopkins University Press, 33–49.

Canovan, Margaret. 1981. *Populism.* New York: Harcourt Brace Jovanovich.

1999. "Trust the People! Populism and the Two Faces of Democracy." *Political Studies* XLVII: 2–16.

Carayol, Rémi. 2012a. "Le saut dans l'inconnu." *Jeune Afrique* 2667 (February 19–25): 22–29.

2012b. "Wade touché, pas encore coulé. " *Jeune Afrique* 2669 (March 4–10): 10–12.

Centeno, Miguel Angel, and Alejandro Portes. 2006. "The Informal Economy in the Shadow of the State." In P. Fernández-Kelly and J. Shefner (eds.), *Out of the Shadows: Political Action and the Informal Economy in Latin America.* University Park, PA: The Pennsylvania State University Press, 23–48.

Central Statistical Office (CSO). 1995. "1990 Census of Population, Housing, and Agriculture." Lusaka, Zambia: Ministry of Finance and National Planning.

2000. "*Enumerator's Instructions Manual: Zambia 2000 Census of Population and Housing.*" Lusaka, Zambia: Central Statistical Office.

2003a. "*Migration and Urbanization: 2000 Census Report.*" Lusaka, Zambia: Central Statistical Office.

2003b. "Summary Report for the 2000 Census of Population and Housing." Lusaka, Zambia: Central Statistical Office.

2004. "*2000 Census of Population and Housing: Lusaka Province Analytical Report.*" Lusaka, Zambia: Central Statistical Office.

2006. "*The Non-Farm Informal Sector in Zambia, 2002–2003.*" Lusaka, Zambia: Central Statistical Office.

2007. "*Labourforce Survey Report 2005.*" Lusaka, Zambia: Labour Statistics Branch, Central Statistical Office.

Centre on Housing Rights and Evictions (COHRE). 2004. "Housing Rights in West Africa: Report of Four Fact-Finding Missions." Geneva, Switzerland: COHRE.

2006. "Forced Evictions: Violations of Human Rights-Global Survey 10." Geneva, Switzerland: COHRE International Secretariat.

Ceruti, Claire. 2008. "Who Thought Zuma Should be President in Soweto, 2006: Teasing the Social Bases of a Politician's Following from a Quantitative Dataset." *South African Review of Sociology* 39 (2):317–360.

Chandra, Kanchan. 2004. *Why Ethnic Parties Succeed: Patronage and Ethnic Head Counts in India*. New York: Oxford University Press.

2009 "A Constructivist Dataset on Ethnicity and Institutions (CDEI)." In R. Abdelal, Y. Herrera, A. I. Johnston, and R. McDermott (eds.), *Measuring Identity: A Guide for Social Scientists*. New York: Cambridge University Press, 250–276.

2012. "Introduction." In Kanchan Chandra (ed.), *Constructivist Theories of Ethnic Politics*. Oxford: Oxford University Press.

Chandra, Kanchan, and Daniel Metz. 2002. "A New Cross-National Database on Ethnic Parties," Paper presented at the Annual Meeting of the Midwest Political Science Association, Chicago, IL.

Charlton, Roger. 1993. "The Politics of Elections in Botswana." *Africa* 63 (3): 330–370.

Cheeseman, Nicholas. 2008. "The Kenyan Elections of 2007: An Introduction." *Journal of Eastern African Studies* 2 (2): 166–184.

Cheeseman, Nicholas, and Robert Ford. 2007. "Ethnicity as a Political Cleavage," *Afrobarometer Working Paper No. 83*.

Cheeseman, Nicholas, and Marja Hinfelaar. 2010. "Parties, Platforms, and Political Mobilization: The Zambian Presidential Election of 2008." *African Affairs* 109 (434):1–26.

Chege, Michael. 2008. "Kenya: Back from the Brink?" *Journal of Democracy* 19 (4):125–139.

Chellah, George, and Patson Chilemba. 2006. "Levy Condemns PF Cadres' Behavior." *The Post* (September 21): 1 and 4.

Chellah, George, and McDonald Chipenzi. 2006. "HH Co-Opts Non-Tongas … to Remove Tribal Tag, Forestall Defections." *The Post* (July 21): 1 and 4.

Chellah, George, and Lwanga Mwilu. 2006. "Zambia Needs a New Order – Sata." *The Post* (September 28).

Chhibber, Pradeep. 1999. *Democracy without Associations: Transformation of the Party System and Social Cleavages in India*. Ann Arbor, MI: University of Michigan Press.

Chibamba, Musonda. 2009. "Hollow Victory." *BBC Focus on Africa* (January–March): 34–35.

Chibuye, Felina. 1992. "Squatters get Council Ultimatum." *The Weekly Post* 2 (August): 14–20.

Chibuye, Miniva. 2011. "Interrogating Urban Poverty Lines: The Case of Zambia." *Poverty Reduction in Urban Areas Working Paper No. 30*. London: International Institute for Environment and Development (IIED).

Chifuwe, Sheikh. 1993. "No Trade Restrictions for the 'President's Men." *The Weekly Post* (November 12): 10 and 11.

2000. "Mazoka Accuses Chiluba of Misusing Tax Payers' Money." *The Post* (May 5): 4.

Chilaizya, Joe. 1993. "Sellers without Buyers." *The Weekly Post* (December 17): 13.

Chilemba, Patson. 2008. "'Pabwato' Greets Rupiah at Lusaka City Market." *The Post* (September 19): 1 and 4.

Chitenje, Elias. 1993. "Where the Rich and Poor Live." *The Weekly Post* (February 26–March 4): 12.

Clark, Terry N., and Seymour Martin Lipset. 2001. *The Breakdown of Class Politics: A Debate on Post-Industrial Stratification*. Baltimore: Johns Hopkins University Press.

Clayton, Jonathan. 2007. "Wind of Change is Shaking Tribal Loyalties." *The Times* (December 26): 37.

Cohen, Abner. 1969. *Custom and Politics in Urban Africa*. London: Routledge & Kegan Paul.

Cohen, Jeffrey. 2004. "Economic Perceptions and Executive Approval in Comparative Perspective." *Political Behavior* 26 (1): 27–43.

Collier, Paul, and Pedro Vicente. 2009. "Votes and Violence: Evidence from a Field Experiment in Nigeria." Working Paper, Oxford: Department of Economics, Oxford University.

Collignon, René. 1984. "La lutte des pouvoirs publics contre les 'encombrements humains' à Dakar." *Canadian Journal of African Studies* 18 (3):573–582.

Commission Electorale Nationale Autonome (CENA). 2006. "Code Electoral." Dakar, Sénégal: Ministère de l'Interieur et des Collectivités Locales.

Commission for Africa. 2005. *Our Common Interest: An Argument*. London: Penguin Books.

Conniff, Michael. 1981. *Urban Politics in Brazil: The Rise of Populism, 1925–1945*. Pittsburgh: University of Pittsburgh Press.

1982. "Introduction: Toward a Comparative Definition of Populism." In M. Conniff (ed.), *Latin American Populism in Comparative Perspective*. Albuquerque, NM: University of New Mexico Press, 3–30.

Cooper, Frederick. 1983. "Urban Space, Industrial Time, and Wage Labor in Africa." In F. Cooper (ed.), *Struggle for the City: Migrant Labor, Capital, and the State in Urban Africa*. Beverly Hills: Sage Publications, Inc, 1–50.

1987. *On the African Waterfront: Urban Disorder and the Transformation of Work in Colonial Mombasa*. New Haven, CT: Yale University Press.

2002. *Africa since 1940: The Past of the Present*. New York : Cambridge University Press.

Coppedge, Michael. 1997. *Strong Parties and Lame Ducks: Presidential Partyarchy and Factionalism in Venezuela*. Palo Alto, CA: Stanford University Press.

Coulibaly, Abdou Latif. 2003. *Wade, un opposant au pouvoir: L'Alternance piégée?* Dakar, Sénégal: Les Editions Sentinelles.

Coulon, Christian. 1981. *Le Marabout et le Prince: Islam et Pouvoir au Sénégal*. Paris: Editions A. Pedone.

Creevey, Lucy, Paul Ngomo, and Richard Vengroff. 2005. "Party Politics and the Different Paths to Democratic Transitions: A Comparison of Benin and Senegal." *Party Politics* 11 (4):471–493.

Crisp, Brian. 2000. *Democratic Institutional Design: The Powers and Incentives of Venezuelan Politicians and Interest Groups*. Stanford: Stanford University Press.

Crook, Richard C. 1997. "Winning Coalitions and Ethno-Regional Politics: The Failure of the Opposition in the 1990 and 1995 Elections in Côte d'Ivoire." *African Affairs* 96: 215–242.

Croucher, Richard. 2007. "Organizing the Informal Economy: Results and Prospects: The Case of Ghana in Comparative Perspective." In G. Wood and C. Brewster (eds.), *Industrial Relations in Africa*. New York: Palgrave Macmillan, 209–218.

Crowder, Michael. 1962. *Senegal: A Study in French Assimilation Policy*. London: Oxford University Press for Institute of Race Relations.

Dabo, Bacary. 2007a. "Ousmane Tanor Dieng à Touba." *Sud Quotidien* (February 14): 8.

2007b. "Ousmane Tanor Dieng à Matam." *Sud Quotidien* (February 17–18): 6.

Daddieh, Cyril Kofie. 2009. "The Presidential and Parliamentary Elections in Ghana, December 2008." *Electoral Studies* 28: 642–673.

Dahl, Robert A. 1971. *Poyarchy: Participation and Opposition*. New Haven, CT: Yale University Press.

1989. *Democracy and Its Critics*. New Haven, CT: Yale University Press.

Dahou, Tarik, and Vincent Foucher. 2004. "Sénégal 2000–2004: L'Alternance et ses Contradictions." *Politique Africaine* 96 (December): 5–21.

Dalton, Russell J. 1985. "Political Parties and Political Representation: Party Supporters and Party Elites in Nine Nations." *Comparative Political Studies* 18 (3):267–299.

2000. "The Decline of Party Identification." In R. J. Dalton and M. P. Wattenberg (eds.), *Parties without Partisans: Political Change in Advanced Industrial Democracies*. New York: Oxford University Press, 19–36.

2008. "The Quantity and Quality of Party Systems: Party System Polarization, its Measurement, and its Consequences." *Comparative Political Studies* 41(7): 899–920.

Danevad, Andreas. 1995. "Responsiveness in Botswana Politics: Do Elections Matter?" *The Journal of Modern African Studies* 33 (3): 381–402.

Davis, Mike. 2006. "Planet of Slums." *New Left Review* 26: 5–34.

Decalo, Samuel. 1997. "Benin: First of the New Democracies." In J. F. Clark and D. E. Gardinier (eds.), *Political Reform in Francophone Africa*. Boulder, CO: Westview Press, 41–61.

Demmers, Jolle, Alex E. Fernández, and Barbara Hogenboom, eds. 2001. *Miraculous Metamorphoses: The Neoliberalization of Latin American Populism*. New York: Palgrave Macmillan.

De Smedt, Johan. 2009. "'No Raila, No Peace!' Big Man Politics and Election Violence at the Kibera Grassroots." *African Affairs* 108 (433): 581–598.

De Wet, Thea, Leila Patel, Marcel Korth, and Chris Forrester. 2008. *Johannesburg Livelihoods and Poverty Study*. Johannesburg, South Africa: Center for Social Development in Africa, University of Johannesburg.

Diaw, Aminata, and Mamadou Diouf. 1998. "The Senegalese Opposition and its Quest for Power." In A. O. Olukoshi (ed.), *The Politics of Opposition in Contemporary Africa*. Uppsala, Sweden: Nordiska Afrikainstitutet, 113–143.

Dietz, Henry A. 1998. *Urban Poverty, Political Participation, and the State: Lima, 1970–1990*. Pittsburgh: University of Pittsburgh Press.

Dione, Babacar. 2006. "Présidentielle 2007: La Caution Fixée à 25 Millions de FCFA." *Le Soleil* (August 29).

Diongue, Momar, Mandiaye Thiobane, and Babacar Dione. 2007. "Interview de Moustapha Niasse, Secrétaire Général de l'AFP." *Nouvel Horizon* (Février).

Diop, Abdoulaye. 1964. *Société Toucouleur et Migration*. Dakar, Sénégal : Institut Fondamental d'Afrique Noire (IFAN).

Diop, Momar-Coumba. 2002. "Réformes Économiques et Recomposition Sociales." In C. O'Brien, M.-C. Diop, and M. Diouf (eds.), *La Construction de l'Etat au Sénégal*. Paris: Editions Karthala, 63–82.

2006. "Le Sénégal à la Croisée des Chemins." *Politique Africaine* 104 (Décembre): 103–126.

Diop, Momar-Coumba, and Mamadou Diouf. 1990. *Le Sénégal sous Abdou Diouf: Etat et Société*. Paris: Karthala.

Diop, Momar-Coumba, Mamadou Diouf, and Aminata Diaw. 2002. "Le Baobab a Été Déraciné: L'alternance au Sénégal." *Politique Africaine* 78 (Juin): 157–179.

Diop, Souleymane Jules. 2007. *Wade: L'avocat et le Diable*. Paris: L'Harmattan.

Diouf, Amadou. 2007. "Accusé d'Avoir Soutenu Idy Contre de l'Argent: Serigne Moustapha Sy Fusille Wade et Charge Abdoulaye Diop." *Wal Fadjri* (April 2), 2.

Diouf, Makhtar. 1994. *Sénégal: Les Ethnies et la Nation*. Paris: L'Harmattan.

Diouf, Mamadou. 1996. "Urban Youth and Senegalese Politics: Dakar 1988–1994." *Public Culture* 8: 225–249

Division de la Prévision et de la Statistique (DPS). 1993. "Recensement Général de la Population et de l'Habitat de 1988." Dakar, Sénégal: Ministère de l'Economie, des Finances et du Plan.

2003. "*Le Secteur Informel dans l'Agglomeration de Dakar: Performances, Insertion et Perspectives.*" Dakar, Sénégal: Ministère de l'Economie et des Finances.

2004. "Rapport de Synthèse de la Deuxième Enquête Sénégalaise auprès des Ménages (ESAM-II), Draft." Dakar, Sénégal: Ministère de l'Economie et des Finances.

Dixit, Avinash, and John Londegran. 1996. "The Determinants of Success of Special Interests in Redistributive Politics." *Journal of Politics* 58 (4): 1132–1155.

Dixon, Robyn. 2007. "Dissatisfied Senegalese Look Forward to Election," *Los Angeles Times* (February 24): A3.

Doorenspleet, Renske. 2003. "Political Parties, Party Systems, and Democracy in Sub-Saharan Africa." In M. A. M. Salih (ed.), *African Political Parties: Evolution, Insitutionalism, and Governance*. London: Pluto Press, 169–187.

Drake, Paul W. 1982. "Conclusion: Requiem for Populism?" In M. Conniff (ed.), *Latin American Populism in Comparative Perspective*. Albuquerque, NM University of New Mexico Press, 217–245.

Du Toit, Pierre. 1995. *State-Building and Democracy in Southern Africa: A Comparative Study of Botswana, South Africa, and Zimbabwe*. Pretoria, South Africa: Human Sciences Research Council.

The East African. 2005. "Nairobi Slum Appeals to President Kibaki," August 2.

Eckstein, Susan. 2001. "Poor People versus the State and Capital: Anatomy of a Successful Community Mobilization for Housing in Mexico City." In S. Eckstein (ed.), *Power and Popular Protest: Latin American Social Movement*. Berkeley, CA: University of California Press, 329–350.

The Economist. 2006. "The Technocrat and the Populist," October 5.

2009. "If Words Were Food, Nobody Would go Hungry," November 19.

Economist Intelligence Unit (EIU). 1999. "Country Report: Senegal, The Gambia, Mauritania, 4th Quarter." London: The Economist Intelligence Unit Limited.

2000. "Country Report: Senegal, The Gambia, Mauritania, 1st Quarter." London: The Economist Intelligence Unit Limited.

2007a. "Country Report: Zambia, March." London: The Economist Intelligence Unit Limited.

2007b. "Country Report: Senegal, August." London: The Economist Intelligence Unit Limited.

2007c. "Country Report: Senegal, May." London: The Economist Intelligence Unit Limited.

2007d. "Country Report: Kenya, December." London: The Economist Intelligence Unit.

2008. "Country Report: Zambia, October." London: The Economist Intelligence Unit Limited.

2011. "Country Report: Zambia, August." London: The Economist Intelligence Unit Limited.

Electoral Commission of Zambia (ECZ). 2008. "Public Notice: Voters' Card Replacement Exercise 2008." Retrieved from: http://www.elections.org.zm/ (accessed March 13, 2009).

Englebert, Pierre. 2000. "Senegal: Recent History." In I. Frame (ed.), *Africa South of the Sahara 2001*. London: Europa Publications Limited, 960–969.

2008. "Senegal: Recent History." In I. Frame (ed.), *Africa South of the Sahara 2009*. London: Europa Publications Limited, 984–993.

European Development Fund (EDF). 1996. "The Development of a Master Plan to Rehabilitate and Rationalise the Urban Markets of Lusaka, Kitwe, and Ndola." Rome: Studio Bichara s.r.l.

European Union Electoral Observer Mission (EUEOM). 2012. "*Rapport Final: Election Présidentielle Sénégal 2012*." Brussels: European Union. Retrieved from: http://www.eueom.eu/senegal2012/rapports.

European Union, U.S. Embassy, and Germany Embassy. 2011. "Mission d'Audit du Fichier Electoral, Rapport Final." Retrieved from: http://www.dakar.diplo.de/contentblob/3106718/Daten/1212067/_de_Wahl2012SEN_dok.pdf.

Eyoh, Dickson. 2007. "Politics of Urban Identity in Anglophone Africa." In D. Eyoh and R. Stren (ed.), *Decentralization and the Politics of Urban Development in West Africa*. Washington, DC: Woodrow Wilson International Center for Scholars, 117–134.

Fall, Abdou Salam, Cheikh Guèye, and Serigne Mansour Tall. 2005. "Changements Climatiques, Mutations Urbaines et Stratégies Citadines à Dakar." In A. S. Fall and C. Guèye (eds.), *Urbain-Rural: L'Hybridation en Marche*. Dakar, Senegal: Enda-Tiers Monde, 191–231.

Faubert, Serge. 2008. "Y a-t-il un Pilote dans l'Avion?" *Jeune Afrique* Novembre 30.

Fay, Marianne, ed. 2005. *The Urban Poor in Latin America*. Washington, DC: The World Bank.

Faye, Ibrahima Lissa. 2007a. "Abdoulaye Wade lors due Démarrage de sa Campagne à Mbacké." *Sud Quotidien* February 5: 4.

2007b. "Election Présidentielle du 25 Février : Les Raisons de la Victoire de Wade à Mbacké." *Sud Quotidien* February 27: 3.

Faye, Modou Mamoune. 2008 "Cité Bissap: Un Bidonville en Sursis ou Condamné à Disparaître?" *Le Soleil* April 10.

Ferguson, James. 1999. *Expectations of Modernity: Myths and Meanings of Urban Life on the Zambian Copperbelt*. Berkeley: University of California Press.

Ferree, K. 2011. *Framing the Race in South Africa: The Political Origins of the Racial Census*. New York: Cambridge University Press.

Flint, Lawrence. 2011. "Contradictions and Challenges in Representing the Past: The Kuomboka Festival of Western Zambia." *Journal of Southern African Studies* 32 (40): 701–717.

Fomunyoh, Christopher. 2001. "Democratization in Fits and Starts." *Journal of Democracy* 12 (3): 36–50.

Foster, Douglas. 2009. "Jacob's Ladder." *The Atlantic* (June): 72–80.

Foucher, Vincent 2007. "'Blue Marches': Public Performance and Political Turnover in Senegal." In J. Strauss and D. C. O'Brien (eds.), *Staging Politics: Power and Performance in Asia and Africa*. New York: I.B. Tauris & Co Ltd, 111–132.

Fournier, Patrick, André Blais, Richard Nadeau, Elizabeth Gidengil, and Neil Nevitte. 2003. "Issue Importance and Performance Voting." *Political Behavior* 25 (1): 51–67.

Fox, Jonathan. 1994. "The Difficult Transition from Clientelism to Citizenship: Lessons from Mexico." *World Politics* 46 (2):151–84.

Freedom House. 2010. *Freedom in the World 2010: Erosion of Freedom Intensifies*. Landham, MD: Rowman and Littlefield Publishers, Inc.

Freund, Bill. 2007. *The African City: A History*. New York: Cambridge University Press.

Galvan, Dennis. 2001. "Political Turnover and Social Change in Senegal." *Journal of Democracy* 12 (3): 51–62.

2009. "The Presidential and Parliamentary Elections in Senegal, February and June 2007." *Electoral Studies* xxx: 1–5.

Gano, Souleymane. 2012. "New Alternative in Senegal after Wade Defeat," Inter-Press Service, March 28.

Gaotlhobogwe, Monkagedi. 2009. "Botswana: Old Naledi – From 'Paradise Lost to Paradise Regained.'" *Mmegi*, May 22.

Garekwe, Marx, and Ernest Moloi. 1994. "Botswana Politics Shaken by Scandal." *The Post* (April 19): 8.

Geddes, Barbara. 1999. "What do we Know about Democratization after Twenty Years?" *Annual Review of Political Science* 2: 115–144.

Gellar, Sheldon. 2005. *Democracy in Senegal: Tocquevillian Analytics in Africa*. New York: Palgrave Macmillan.

Georgy, Michael. 2007. "South Africa's squatters lose faith in ANC." *Mail and Guardian* December 10.

Gervasoni, Olivia, and Cheikh Guèye. 2005. "La Confrérie Mouride au Centre de la Vie Politique Sénégalaise: Le "Sopi" Inaugure-t-il un Nouveau Paradigme?" In M. Gomez-Perez (ed.), *L'Islam Politique au Sud du Sahara: Identités, Discours et Enjeux*. Paris: Editions Karthala, 621–639.

Gettleman, Jeffrey. 2007. "Dispute Vote Plunges Kenya into Bloodshed." *The New York Times* (December 31), http://www.nytimes.com/2007/12/31/world/africa/31kenya.html?pagewanted=all&_r=0.

Ghorbal, Samy. 2001. "Besoin d'Air." *Jeune Afrique* (December 18): 10.

Gibson, Clark, and James Long. 2009. "The Presidential and Parliamentary Elections in Kenya, December 2007." *Electoral Studies* 30(1): 1–6.

Gibson, Edward L. 1997. "The Populist Road to Market Reform: Policy and Electoral Coalitions in Mexico and Argentina." *World Politics* 49 (3):339–370.

Giliomee, Hermann. 1998. "South Africa's Emerging Dominant-Party Regime." *Journal of Democracy* 9 (4): 128–142.

Gisselquist, Rachel M. 2005. "Ethnicity, Class, and Party System Change in Bolivia." *T'inkazos* (May): 18.

Good, Kenneth. 1996. "Towards Popular Participation in Botswana." *The Journal of Modern African Studies* 34(1): 53–77.

Good, Kenneth, and Ian Taylor. 2008. "Botswana: A Minimalist Democracy." *Democratization* 15 (4):750–765.

Gould, Jeremy. 2007. "Zambia's 2006 Elections: The Ethnicization of Politics?" *News from the Nordic Africa Institute.* 1 (January): 5–9.

Govereh, Jones, Emma Malawo, Tadeyo Lungu, Thom Jayne, Kasweka Chinyama, and Pius Chilonda. 2009. "Trends and Spatial Distribution of Public Agricultural Spending in Zambia: Implications for Agricultural Productivity Growth." Lusaka, Zambia: Food Security Research Project.

Graham, Carol. 1994. *Safety Nets, Politics, and the Poor.* Washington, DC: The Brookings Institution.

Groves, Robert M., Floyd J. Fowler Jr. Mick P. Couper, James M. Lepkowski, Eleanor Singer, and Roger Tourangeau. 2004. *Survey Methodology.* Hoboken, NJ: John Wiley & Sons, Inc.

Guèye, Cheikh. 2001. "Touba: The New *Dairas* and the Urban Dream." In A. Tostensen, I. Tvedten and M. Vaa (eds.), *Associational Life in African Cities: Popular Responses to the Urban Crisis.* Stockholm: Nordiska Afrikainstitutet, 107–123.

Gumede, William M. 2008. "South Africa: Jacob Zuma and the Difficulties of Consolidating South Africa's Democracy." *African Affairs* 107 (427): 261–271.

2009. "The Power of the Poor." *Mail and Guardian,* April 25. Retrieved from http://www.mg.co.za/article/2009-04-25-the-power-of-poor.

Gunner, Liz. 2008. "Jacob Zuma, The Social Body, and the Unruly Power of Song." *African Affairs* 108 (430): 27–48.

Gunnion, Stephen. 2009. "Rand Hits Low as Bourses Slump." *Business Day,* January 13.

Gunther, Richard, and Larry Diamond. 2001. "Types and Functions of Parties." In L. Diamond and R. Gunther (eds.), *Political Parties and Democracy.* Baltimore: Johns Hopkins University Press, 3–39.

Gutkind, Peter C. W. 1973. "From the Energy of Despair to the Anger of Despair: The Transition from Social Circulation to Political Consciousness among the Urban Poor in Africa." *Canadian Journal of African Studies* 7 (2): 179–198.

Haddad, Lawrence, Marie T. Ruel, and James L. Garrett. 1999. "Are Urban Poverty and Undernutrition Growing? Some Newly Assembled Evidence." *World Development* 27 (11): 1891–1904.

Hagopian, Frances. 2005. "The Rising Quality of Democracy in Brazil and Chile." In L. Diamond and L. Morlino (eds.), *The Quality of Democracy: Improvement or Subversion?* Baltimore: Johns Hopkins University Press, 123–162.

2007. "Parties and Voters in Emerging Democracies." In C. Boix and S. C. Stokes (eds.), *The Oxford Handbook of Comparative Politics.* New York: Oxford University Press, 582–603.

Hagopian, Frances, Carlos Gervasoni, and Juan Andres Moraes. 2009. "From Patronage to Program: The Emergence of Party-Oriented Legislators in Brazil." *Comparative Political Studies* 42 (3): 360–391.

Hahs-Vaughn, Debbie. 2005. "A Primer for Using and Understanding Weights with National Datasets." *The Journal of Experimental Education* 75 (3): 221–248.

Hampande, Douglas. 2000. "Ibex Hill Illegal Land Occupants Resist Eviction." *The Post* (August 24): 3.

Hansen, Karen Tranberg. 2002. "Lusaka, Zambia" In M. Ember and C. R. Ember. (eds.), *Encyclopedia of Urban Cultures: Cities and Cultures Around the World, Volume 1.* Danbury, CT: Grolier Publishing Co., 80–85.

2004. "Who Rules the Streets? The Politics of Vending Space in Lusaka." In K. T. Hansen and M. Vaa (eds.), *Reconsidering Urban Informality: Perspectives from Urban Africa.* Uppsala, Sweden: Nordiska Afrikainstitutet, 62–80.

2007a. "The Informalization of Lusaka's Economy: Regime Change, Ultra Modern Markets, and Street Vending, 1972–2004." In J. B. Gewalt, M. Hinfelaar, and G. Macola (eds.), *One Zambia, Many Histories: Towards a Post-Colonial History of Zambia.* Leiden, The Netherlands: J. Brill, 213–239.

2007b. "Changing Youth Dynamics in Lusaka's Informal Economy in the Context of Economic Liberalization." Presented at the Informalizing Economies and New Organizing Strategies in Africa Conference, Nordic Africa Institute, Uppsala, Sweden: April 20–22.

Hansen, Karen Tranberg, and Mariken Vaa. 2004. "Introduction." In K. T. Hansen and M. Vaa (eds.), *Reconsidering Informality: Perspectives from Urban Africa.* Uppsala, Sweden: Nordiska Afrikainstitutet, 7–24.

Hardgrave, Robert L. 1970. "Political Participation and Primordial Solidarity: The Nadars of Tamilnad." In R. Kothari (ed.), *Caste in Indian Politics.* New Delhi: Orient Longman, 102–128.

Hardin, Russell. 1995. *One for All.* Princeton, NJ: Princeton University Press.

Hart, Gillian. 2007. "Changing Concepts of Articulation: Political Stakes in South Africa Today." *Review of African Political Economy* 34 (111): 85–101.

Havard, Jean-François. 2001. "Ethos 'Bul Faale' et Nouvelles Figures de la Réussite au Sénégal," *Politique Africaine* 82 (Juin): 63–77.

2004. "De la Victoire du 'Sopi' à la Tentation du 'Nopi'?: Gouvernment de l'Alternance et Liberté d'Expression des Médias au Sénégal." *Politique Africaine* 96 (Décembre): 22–38.

Heritage Party. n.d. *The Heritage Party in Brief.* Lusaka, Zambia: Heritage Party.

Hibbs, Douglas. 1987. *The American Political Economy: Macroeconomics and Electoral Politics.* Boston: Harvard University Press.

Hickey, Sam. 2005. "Political Capital, Poverty and Livelihoods in Africa: The politics of Influencing Policy." In S. Jones and N. Nelson (eds.), *Practitioners and Poverty Alleviation: Influencing Urban Policy from the Ground Up.* London: ITDG Publishing, 71–84.

Hofstadter, Richard. 1969. "North America." In Ghita Ionescu and Ernest Gellner (eds.), *Populism: Its Meanings and Characteristics.* London: Weidenfeld and Nicolson, 9–27.

Holm, John, Patrick Molutsi, and Gloria Somolekae. 1996. "The Development of Civil Society in a Democratic State: The Botswana Model." *African Studies Review* 39 (2): 43–69.

Horowitz, Jeremy. 2009. "Ethnic Groups and Campaign Targeting in Kenya's 2007 Elections," paper presented at the Contemporary African Political Economy Research Seminar (CAPERS), New York: Columbia University, November 6.

Howard, Marc Morjé, and Philip Roessler. 2006. "Liberalizing Electoral Outcomes in Competitive Authoritarian Regimes." *American Journal of Political Science* 50 (2): 365–381.

Huber, Evelyn, Dietrich Rueschemeyer, and John D. Stephens. 1993. "The Impact of Economic Development on Democracy," *The Journal of Economic Perspectives*, 7(3): 71–86.

———. 1997. "The Paradoxes of Contemporary Democracy: Formal, Participatory, and Social Dimensions." *Comparative Politics* (April): 323–342.

Huber, John D., and G. Bingham Powell, Jr. 1994. "Congruence between Citizens and Policymakers in Two Visions of Liberal Democracy." *World Politics* 46 (3):291–326.

Hulterström, Karolina. 2004. *In Pursuit of Ethnic Politics: Voters, Parties, and Policies in Kenya and Zambia*. Uppsala, Sweden: Uppsala University.

Hunter, Mark. 2011. "Beneath the 'Zunami': Jacob Zuma and the Gendered Politics of Social Reproduction in South Africa." *Antipode* 43 (4): 1102–1126.

Huntington, Samuel P. 1991. *The Third Wave: Democratization in the Late Twentieth Century*. Norman, OK: University of Oklahoma Press.

Huntington, Samuel P., and Joan Nelson. 1976. *No Easy Choice: Political Participation in Developing Countries*. Cambridge, MA: Harvard University Press.

Ignazi, Piero. 1992. "The Silent Counter-Revolution: Hypotheses on the Emergence of Extreme Right-Wing Parties in Europe." *European Journal of Political Research* 22 (1–2): 3–34.

Ihonvbere, Julius. 1997. "From Despotism to Democracy: The Rise of Multi-Party Politics in Malawi." *Third World Quarterly* 18 (2): 225–247.

Iliffe, John. 1987. *The African Poor: A History*. New York: Cambridge University Press.

Inglehart, Ronald, and Pippa Norris. 2000. "The Developmental Theory of the Gender Gap: Women's and Men's Voting Behavior in Global Perspective." *International Political Science Review* 21 (4): 441–463.

International Labor Organization (ILO). 2002. *Decent Work and the Informal Economy*. Report VI, International Labor Conference 90th Session. Geneva: International Labor Organization.

Ionescu, Ghita, and Ernest Gellner, eds. 1969. *Populism: Its Meaning and National Characteristics*. New York: Macmillan.

Jere, Dickson. 2007. "Thousands Face Homelessness in Zambia Demolitions." *Agence France Presse*, March 8.

Jesuit Centre for Theological Reflection (JCTR). 2006. "The JCTR *Basic Needs Basket*: A Comprehensive Overview," Social Conditions Research Project. Lusaka, Zambia: JCTR.

Johnson, R. W. 2008. "Mosiuoa 'Terror' Lekota Threatens to Topple the ANC." *The Sunday Times*, (October 19). Retrieved from the Sunday Times website on January 21, 2010: http://www.thesundaytimes.co.uk/sto/news/world_news/article242712.ece

Johnson, Scott, and Karen Macgregor. 2009. "Bring Me My Machine Gun." *Newsweek* 153 (17): 32–33.

Johnson, Timothy, and Fons J. R. Van de Vijver. 2003. "Social Desirability in Cross-Cultural Research." In J. A. Harkness, F. J. R. Van de Vijver, and P. P. Mohler (eds.), *Cross-Cultural Survey Methods*. Hoboken, NJ: John Wiley & Sons, 195–206.

Joseph, Richard. 1998. "Africa, 1990–1997: From Abertura to Closure." *Journal of Democracy* 9 (2): 3–17.

Kabuswe, Chisenga. 2000. "LCC to Demolish 'New' Shanty Compounds." *The Post* (October 10): 5.

Kagwanja, Peter. 2009. "Courting Genocide: Populism, Ethno-Nationalism and the Informalisation of Violence in Kenya's 2008 Post-Election Crisis." *Journal of Contemporary African Studies* 27 (3): 365–387.

Kalaluka, Mwala, and Inonge Noyoo. 2008. "Sata Sees Light at the end of the Tunnel." *The Post* (September 26): 1 and 4.

Kaltwasser, Cristóbal Rovira. Forthcoming. "Explaining the (Re)Emergence of Populism in Europe and Latin America." In Carlos de la Torre (ed.), *Power to the People*. Lexington, KY: University of Kentucky Press.

Kane, Aguibou, and Ibrahima Anne. 2007. "Ahmed Khalifa Niasse, Ministre Chargé de la Nouvelle Capitale: 'La Nouvelle Capitale du Sénégal Sera Prête dans 36 Mois.'" *Wal Fadjri*, April 16.

Kanté, Babacar. 1994. "Senegal's Empty Elections." *Journal of Democracy* 5 (1): 96–108.

Kasara, Kimuli. 2007. "Tax Me If You Can: Ethnic Geography, Democracy, and the Taxation of Agriculture in Africa." *American Political Science Review* 101 (1): 159–172.

Katasefa, Zumani. 2008. "Marketeers are not Campaign Tools, AZIEA Tells Politicians." *The Post*, September 22: 7.

Kaufman, Robert, and Barbara Stallings. 1991 "The Political Economy of Latin American Populism." In R. Dornbusch and S. Edwards (eds.), *The Macroeconomics of Populism in Latin America*. Chicago: University of Chicago Press, 15–43.

Kersting, Norbert, and Jaime Sperberg. 2003. "Political Participation." In D. Berg-Schlosser and N. Kersting (eds.), *Poverty and Democracy: Self-Help and Political Participation in Third World Cities*. London: Zed Books, 153–180.

Kessides, Christine. 2006. *The Urban Transition in Sub-Saharan Africa: Implications for Economic Growth and Poverty Reduction*. Washington, DC: The World Bank.

Khunou, Grace. 2002. "'Massive Cutoffs': Cost Recovery and Electricity Service in Diepkloof, Soweto." In D. A. McDonald and J. Pape (eds.), *Cost Recovery and the Crisis of Service Delivery in South Africa*. Pretoria, South Africa: Human Sciences Research Council, 61–80.

Kimenyi, Mwangi S. 2006. "Ethnicity, Governance, and the Provision of Public Goods." *Journal of African Economies* 15 (Supplement 1): 62–99.

King, Gary, Christopher J. L. Murray, Joshua A. Salomon, and Ajay Tandon. 2004. "Enhancing the Validity and Cross-Cultural Comparability of Measurement in Survey Research." *American Political Science Review* 98 (1): 191–207.

King, Gary, and Jonathan Wand. 2007. "Comparing Incomparable Survey Responses: Evaluating and Selecting Anchoring Vignettes." *Political Analysis* 15: 46–66.

Kitschelt, Herbert. 2000. "Linkages between Citizens and Politicians in Democratic Polities." *Comparative Political Studies* 33 (6/7): 845–879.

Kitschelt, Herbert, and Steven I. Wilkinson. 2007. "A Research Agenda for the Study of Citizen-Politician Linkages and Democratic Accountability." In H. Kitschelt and S. I. Wilkinson (eds.), *Patrons, Clients, and Policies: Patterns of Democratic Accountability and Political Competition*. New York: Cambridge University Press, 322–343.

Klingemann, Hans-Dieter, and Bernard Wessels. 2009. "How Voters Cope with the Complexity of Their Environment." In Hans-Dieter Klingemann (ed.), *The Comparative Study of Electoral Systems*. Oxford: Oxford University Press, 237–265.

Larmer, Miles, and Alastair Fraser. 2007. "Of Cabbages and King Cobra: Populist Politics and Zambia's 2006 Election." *African Affairs* 106: 611–627.

Lawrence, Sophia, and Junko Ishikawa. 2005. "Trade Union Membership and Collective Bargaining Coverage: Statistical Concepts, Methods and Findings." *ILO Working Paper No. 59*. Geneva: International Labour Organization.

Lawson, Kay. 1980. "Political Parties and Linkage." In K. Lawson (ed.), *Political Parties and Linkage: A Comparative Perspective*. New Haven, CT: Yale University Press, 3–24.

Lemon, Anthony. 2007. "Perspectives on Democratic Consolidation in Southern Africa: The Five General Elections of 2004." *Political Geography* 26: 824–850.

Lerner, Daniel. 1968. *The Passing of Traditional Society: Modernizing the Middle East*. New York: Free Press.

Le Vine, Victor T. 2004. *Politics in Francophone Africa*. Boulder, CO: Lynne Rienner Publishers.

Levy, Paul S., and Stanley Lemeshow. 1999. *Sampling of Populations: Methods and Applications*, 3rd ed. New York: John Wiley & Sons, Inc.

Lewis, Oscar. 1959. *Five Families: Mexican Case Studies in the Culture of Poverty*. New York: Basic Books.

   1966. *La Vida: A Puerto Rican Family in the Culture of Poverty – San Juan and New York*. New York: Random House.

Lewis, Peter. 2008. "Poverty, Inequality, and Democracy: Growth Without Prosperity in Africa." *Journal of Democracy* 19 (4): 95–109.

Lewis-Beck, Michael. 1988. *Economics and Elections: The Major Western Democracies*. Ann Arbor, MI: University of Michigan Press.

Lewis-Beck, Michael, and Martin Paldam. 2000. "Economic Voting: An Introduction." *Electoral Studies* 19: 113–121.

Lindberg, Staffan I. 2006a. *Democracy and Elections in Africa*. Baltimore: Johns Hopkins University Press.

   2006b. "Opposition Parties and Democratization in Sub-Saharan Africa." *Journal of Contemporary African Studies* 24 (1): 123–138.

   2007. "Institutionalization of Party Systems? Stability and Fluidity among Legislative Parties in Africa's Democracies." *Government and Opposition* 42 (2): 215–241.

Lindberg, Staffan I., and Minion K. C. Morrison. 2008. "Are African Voters really Ethnic or Clientelist? Survey Evidence from Ghana." *Political Science Quarterly* 123 (1): 95–122.

Lindow, Megan. 2009. "South Africa's Outraged Poor Threaten President." *Time*, (July 24). Retrieved April 1, 2010 from http://www.time.com/time/world/article/0,8599,1912479,00.html.

Lipset, Seymour Martin. 1959. "Some Social Requisites of Democracy: Economic Development and Political Legitimacy." *The American Political Science Review* 53 (1): 69–105.

Lipton, Michael. 1977. *Why Poor People Stay Poor: Urban Bias and World Development*. London: Temple Smith.

Lodge, Tom. 2002. *Politics in South Africa: From Mandela to Mbeki*. Bloomington, IN: Indiana University Press.

   2009. "The Zuma Tsunami: South Africa's Succession Politics." *Representation* 45 (2): 125–141.

Loimeier, Roman. 2007. "Sufis and Politics in Sub-Saharan Africa." In P. L. Heck (ed.), *Sufism and Politics: The Power of Spirituality*. Princeton, NJ: Markus Weiner Publishers, 59–102.

Lund, Francie, and Caroline Skinner. 1999. "Promoting the Interests of Women in the Informal Economy: An Analysis of Street Trader Organisations in South Africa." In *Research Report No. 19*. Durban, South Africa: School of Development Studies, University of Kwa-Zulu Natal.

Lungu, Andrew. 2008. "HH Slams Chief Bright Nalubamba." *Times of Zambia* October 8: 3.

Lynch, Gabrielle. 2006. "The Fruits of Perception: 'Ethnic Politics' and the Case of Kenya's Constitutional Referendum." *African Studies* 65 (2): 233–270.

Macharia, Kinuthia. 1997. *Social and Political Dynamics of the Informal Economy in African Cities: Nairobi and Harare*. Lanham, MD: University Press of America, Inc.

MacKuen, Michael, Robert Erikson, and James Stimson. 1992. "Peasants or Bankers? The American Electorate and the U.S. Economy." *American Political Science Review* 86 (3): 507–611.

Madrid, Raúl L. 2008. "The Rise of Ethnopopulism in Latin America." *World Politics* 60 (3): 475–508.

Magaloni, Beatriz, Alberto Diaz-Cayeros, and Federico Estevez. 2007. "Clientelism and Portfolio Diversification: A Model of Electoral Investment with Applications to Mexico." In H. Kitschelt and S. I. Wilkinson (eds.), *Patrons, Clients, and Policies: Patterns of Democratic Accountability and Political Competition*. New York: Cambridge University Press, 182–205.

Magrin, Géraud. 2007. "Sopi or not Sopi?: A Propos des Élections Présidentielles de Février 2007 au Sénégal." *EchoGéo* Juillet–Septembre (3): 1–14.

Makgala, Christian John. 2005. "The Relationship Between Kenneth Koma and the Botswana Democratic Party, 1965–2003." *African Affairs* 104 (415): 303–323.

Malido, Webster. 2003. "'You Are Stinking, Dirty,' Levy tells MMD Rebels." *The Post* March 9: 1.

Mane, Bacary Domingo. 2007a. "Idy Entame sa Marche 'Dekal Yakar.'" *Sud Quotidien* February 5: 6.

2007b. "Caravane Orange à Kaolack et Guinguineo," *Sud Quotidien* February 10/11: 6.

2007c. "La Caravane Orange Attaque par des Talibés de Bethio." *Sud Quotidien* February 22: 4.

2007d. "A Touba, Mbacké et Darou Mousty." *Sud Quotidien* February 18: 6.

Manning, Carrie. 2005. "Assessing African Party Systems after the Third Wave." *Party Politics* 11 (6): 707–727.

Mapulenga, Amos. 2001. "Sata Haunts Madyenkuku out of Mulungushi MMD Convention." *The Post* May 1: 1.

2006. "UPND Blocks Sikota's Party from Joining UDA." *The Post* July 27: 1 and 4.

Mapulenga, Amos, and Brighton Phiri. 2001. "Anti 3rd Term Group is Doomed, Says Sata." *The Post* May 2: 1 and 4.

Markovitz, Irving Leonard. 1970. "Traditional Social Structure, the Islamic Brotherhoods, and Political Development in Senegal." *Journal of Modern African Studies* 8 (1): 73–96.

Mashiqi, Aubrey. 2008. "Zuma's Role in the ANC-IFP Crucible." *Business Day*, August 22. Retrieved from: http://www.businessday.co.za/Articles/Content.aspx?id=52455.

Matlosa, Khabele. 2007. *Political Parties in Southern Africa: The State of Parties and Their Role in Democratization*. Washington, DC: National Democratic Institute.

Mattes, Robert, and Michael Bratton. 2009. "Poverty Reduction, Economic Growth, and Democratization in Sub-Saharan Africa." *Afrobarometer Briefing Paper No.68*, retrieved from: http://www.afrobarometer.org/publications/afrobarometer-briefing-papers/262-bp-68.

Maxwell, Daniel, Carol Levin, Margaret Armar-Klemesu, Marie Ruel, Saul Morris, and Clement Ahiadeke. 2000. "Urban Livelihoods and Food and Nutrition Security in Greater Accra, Ghana." *IFPRI Research Report 112*. Washington, DC: International Food Policy Research Institute.

Mazonde, Isaac Ncube. 1996. "Old Naledi and Poverty in the City." *Pula: Botswana Journal of African Studies* 10 (2): 20–39.

Mbaye, Sadikh. 2007. "Touba ou Tivaoune? L'effet Ndiguel … en Question." *Sud Quotidien* February 28: 11.

Mbow, Lat Soucabé. 1993. "Urban Policies: Management and Development." In M.-C. Diop (ed.), *Senegal: Essays in Statecraft*. Dakar, Senegal: CODESRIA, 195–220.

Mbow, Penda. 2008. "The Return of Personalism." *Journal of Democracy* 19 (1): 156–169.

  2009. "Secularism, Religious Education, and Human Rights in Senegal." Working Paper No. 09–007, Institute for the Study of Islamic Thought in Africa (ISITA), Evanston, Illinois: Northwestern University.

McCulloch, Neil, Bob Baulch, and M. Cherel-Robson. 2000. "Poverty, Inequality, and Growth in Zambia During the 1990s." Working Paper, Institute for Development Studies, Sussex: University of Sussex.

McKenzie, Glenn. 2000. "International News." *Associated Press Worldstream*. March 22. Retrieved October 26, 2009, from LexisNexis Academic Database.

McLaughlin, Fiona. 2001. "Dakar Wolof and the Configuration of an Urban Identity." *Journal of African Cultural Studies* 14 (2): 153–172.

Mehretu, Assefa, and Chris Mutambirwa. 2003. "Cities of Sub-Saharan Africa." In S. D. Brunn, J. F. Williams, and D. J. Zeigler (eds.), *Cities of the World: World Regional Urban Development*. Lanham, MD: Rowman & Littlefield Publishers, 293–330.

Meillassoux, Claude. 1968. *Urbanization of an African Community: Voluntary Associations in Bamako*. Seattle, WA: University of Washington Press.

Melson, Robert, and Howard Wolpe. 1970. "Modernization and the Politics of Communalism: A Theoretical Perspective." *American Political Science Review* 64 (4): 1112–1130.

Mesple-Somps, Sandrine. 2007. "Programme de Lutte Contre la Pauvreté et Stratégie de Croissance au Sénégal: Les Deux Politiques se Completent-Elles?" *Document de Travail*. Paris, France Développement Institutions et Analyses de Long Terme (DIAL).

Meunier, Marianne. 2008. "Dakar, la Vie à Deux Vitesses." *Jeune Afrique* 2476: 38–39.

Michelitch, Kristin, Andrew Owen, and Joshua Tucker. 2012. "Looking to the Future: A Better Way to Study Prospective Economic Voting." *Electoral Studies* 31 (4): 838–851.

Miguel, Edward. 2004. "Tribe or Nation? Nation Building and Public Goods in Kenya versus Tanzania." *World Politics* (April): 327–362.

Misago, Jean Pierre, Loren Landau, and Tamlyn Monson. 2009. *Towards Tolerance, Law, and Dignity: Addressing Violence against Foreign Nationals in South Africa*. Pretoria, South Africa: International Organization for Migration.

Miti, Christopher. 2008. "Rupiah's Campaign Speech in Katete." *The Post* September 18: 2.

Mitlin, Diana. 2004. "Understanding Urban Poverty: What the Poverty Reduction Strategy Papers Tell Us." *Working Paper No. 13 on Poverty Reduction in Urban Areas.* London: International Institute for Environment and Development (IIED).

——— 2007. "New Directions in Housing Policy." In A. M. Garland, M. Massoumi, and B. A. Ruble (eds.), *Global Urban Poverty: Setting the Agenda.* Washington, DC: Woodrow Wilson International Center for Scholars, 151–180.

Mkandawire, Thandika. 1999. "Crisis Management and the Making of 'Choiceless Democracies.'" In R. Joseph (ed.), *State, Conflict, and Democracy in Africa.* Boulder, CO: Lynne Rienner Publishers, 119–136.

Mokopakgosi, Brian, and Mpho Molomo. 2000. "Democracy in the Face of a Weak Opposition in Botswana." *Pula: Botswana Journal of African Studies* 14 (1): 3–22.

Molefhe, Rampholo. 2009. "These Elections are about Candidate over Party." *Mmegi* March 13.

Molina, José. 2001. "The Electoral Effect of Underdevelopment: Government, Turnover and its Causes in Latin American, Caribbean and Industrialized Countries." *Electoral Studies* 20: 427–446.

Molomo, Mpho G. 2000. "Understanding Government and Opposition in Botswana." *Commonwealth and Comparative Studies* 38 (1): 65–92.

Molutsi, Patrick. 1989. "Whose Interests do Botswana's Politicians Represent?" In John Holm and Patrick Molutsi (eds.), *Democracy in Botswana: The Proceedings of a Symposium Held in Gaborone, 1–5 August 1988.* Gaborone: Botswana: Macmillan, 120–132.

Momba, Jotham. 2005. *Political Parties and the Quest for Democratic Consolidation in Zambia.* Johannesburg, South Africa: EISA.

Mooketsi, Lekopanye. 2009. "Saleshando Retains Gabs Central." *Mmegi,* October 19. Retrieved November 6, 2009 from http://www.mmegi.bw/index. php?sid=1&aid=66&dir=2009/October/Monday19

Moonga, Charity. 2008. "Rupiah Strong-Willed to Develop all Nine Provinces." *Times of Zambia* October 8: 1.

Moore, Mick. 1997. "Leading the Left to the Right: Populist Coalitions and Economic Reform." *World Development* 25 (7): 1009–1028.

Morgan, Jana. 2007. "Partisanship during the Collapse of Venezuela's Party System." *Latin American Research Review* 42 (1): 78–98.

Motlogelwa, Tshireletso. 2009. "The Symbolism of Khama in Old Naledi." *Mmegi,* October 23. Retrieved January 25, 2010 from http://www.mmegi.bw/index. php?sid=6&aid=198&dir=2009/October/Friday23

Mouzelis, Nicos. 1985. "On the Concept of Populism: Populist and Clientelist Modes of Incorporation in Semiperipheral Polities." *Politics & Society* 14 (3):329–348.

Movement for Multi-Party Democracy (MMD). 2006. *MMD Manifesto 2007–2011: For Growth and Empowerment.* Lusaka, Zambia: MMD National Campaign Committee.

Moynihan, Daniel. 1965. *The Negro Family: The Case for National Action.* Washington, DC: Office of Policy, Planning, and Research, United States Department of Labor.

Mthembu-Salter, Gregory. 2007. "Zambia: Recent History." In I. Frame (ed.), *Africa South of the Sahara 2008.* London: Europa Publications Limited, 1261–1268.

Mudde, Cas. 2004. "The Populist Zeitgeist." *Government and Opposition* 39: 542–563.

Mudde, Cas, and Cristóbal Rovira Kaltwasser. 2012. "Populism and (Liberal) Democracy: A Framework for Analysis." In Cas Mudde and Cristóbal Rovira Kaltwasser (eds.), *Populism in Europe and the Americas: Threat or Corrective for Democracy?* New York: Cambridge University Press, 1–26.

    2013. "Exclusionary versus Inclusionary Populism: Comparing Contemporary Europe and Latin America." *Government and Opposition* 48 (2): 147–174.

Mulenga, Chileshe. 2003. "The Case of Lusaka, Zambia." Lusaka, Zambia: Institute of Economic and Social Research, University of Zambia.

Mulowa, Anthony. 2008. "HH to Donate Salary to Vulnerable Youths." *Times of Zambia* October 15: 1.

Mumbati, Cheryl. 2000. "No Compensation for Squatters, Says LCC." *The Post* February 24: 2.

Munck, Gerardo L., and Jay Verkuilen. 2002. "Conceptualizing and Measuring Democracy: Evaluating Alternative Indices." *Comparative Political Studies* 35 (1): 5–34.

Mushinge, Gloria. 2007. "Lusaka Housing Demolitions Spell Doom for Poor Families." Women's International Perspective Web site (March 27), http://www.thewip.net/contributors/2007/03/lusaka_house_demolitions_spell.html (accessed March 10, 2009).

Mwanangombe, Lewis. 2007. "Zambian Government Begins Demolishing Illegal Shacks." *Associated Press*, March 11.

    2008. "3 Front-Runners Emerge in Zambia Presidential Race." *Associated Press*, October 2.

Mwape, Susan. 2007. "Poor City Planning Worries Youths in Lusaka." Women's International Perspective Web site (April 17), http://thewip.net/contributors/2007/04/poor_city_planning_worries_you.html (accessed March 10, 2009).

Mwiinga, Jowie. 1993. "Vendors Are Now a Law unto Themselves." *The Weekly Post*, March 26–April 1: 5.

    1994. "A Snake in the Grass Roots." *The Weekly Post* February 22: 7.

Myers, Garth A. 2005. *Disposable Cities: Garbage, Governance and Sustainable Development in Urban Africa*. Aldershot, UK: Ashgate.

Myers, Garth A., and Martin J. Murray. 2007. "Introduction: Situating Contemporary Cities in Africa." In M. J. Murray and G. A. Myers (eds.), *Cities in Contemporary Africa*. New York: Palgrave Macmillan, 1–30.

Nampito, Mukalya, and Shaka Gina. 1995. "Kanyama's Demolished Illegal Structures are Back after 2 Years." *The Post* August 4: 4.

The Nation. 2007. "Landslide Seems on the Cards for Raila in Lang'ata," July 29.

Nchito, Wilma. 2006. "A City of Divided Shopping: An Analysis of the Location of Markets in Lusaka, Zambia." Paper presented at the 42nd International Society of City and Regional Planners (ISoCARP). Istanbul, Turkey, September 14–18.

Ndeng'e, Godfrey, Collins Opiyo, Johan Mistiaen, and Patti Kristjanson. 2003. *Geographic Dimensions of Well-Being in Kenya: Where are the Poor?* Vol. 1. Nairobi, Kenya: Central Bureau of Statistics.

Ndiaye, Malick. 1996. *L'Éthique Ceddo et la Société d'Accaparement ou les Conduites Culturelles des Sénégalais d'Aujourd'hui*. Dakar, Sénégal: Presses universitaires de Dakar.

Nelson, Joan. 1970. "The Urban Poor: Disruption or Political Integration in Third World Cities?" *World Politics* 22 (3): 393–414.

1979. *Access to Power: Politics and the Urban Poor in Developing Countries*. Princeton, NJ: Princeton University Press.

Niasse, Moustapha. 2007. "Profession de Foi: Une Ambition pour le Sénégal." Dakar, Sénégal.

Nohlen, Dieter, Michael Krennerich, and Bernhard Thibaut. 1999. "Elections and Electoral Systems in Africa." In D. Nohlen, M. Krennerich, and B. Thibaut (eds.), *Elections in Africa: A Data Handbook*. Oxford: Oxford University Press, 1–40.

Nordin, Benita. 2004. "The Development of a GIS for an Informal Settlement." Presented at UN Expert Group Meeting on secure land tenure: New Legal Frameworks and Tools, Nairobi, Kenya.

Norris, Pippa, and Robert Mattes. 2003. "Does Ethnicity Determine Support for the Governing Party? The Structural and Attitudinal Basis of Partisan Identification in 12 African Nations." *Afrobarometer Paper No. 26*.

Nossiter, Adam. 2012. "Challenger Ahead in Vote in Senegal." *The New York Times* 26 (March): A4.

Noyoo, Inonge. 2008. "HH Warns MMD against Vote Rigging." *The Post* September 26: 3.

Ntanda, Maya, and Andrew Lungu. 2008. "I'll Rule for 3 Years – Banda." *Times of Zambia* October 23: 1.

Nugent, Paul. 2007. "Banknotes and Symbolic Capital: Ghana's Elections under the Fourth Republic." In Matthias Basedau, Gero Erdmann, and Andreas Mehler (eds.), *Votes Money, and Violence: Political Parties and Elections in Sub-Saharan Africa*. Uppsala, Sweden: The Nordic Africa Institute, 253–275.

Nyati-Ramahobo, Lydia. 2008. *Minority Tribes in Botswana: The Politics of Recognition*. London: Minority Rights International.

O'Brien, Donal Cruise. 1971. *The Mourides of Senegal: The Political and Economic Organization of an Islamic Brotherhood*. Oxford: Clarendon Press.

O'Brien, Donal Cruise. 2003. *Symbolic Confrontations: Muslim Imagining the State in Africa*. London: C. Hurst & Co.

Odinga, Raila. 2007. *Leadership Themes 2007*. Nairobi, Kenya: The Raila Odinga Centre.

Odula, Tom. 2007. "Kenya Opposition Kicks Off Campaign, Says 3 Supporters Shot." *Associated Press*, October 7.

Olson, Mancur. 1971. *The Logic of Collective Action: Public Goods and the Theory of Groups*. Cambridge, MA: Harvard University Press.

Olukoshi, Adebayo O. 1998. "Economic Crisis, Multipartyism, and Opposition Politics." In A. O. Olukoshi (ed.), *The Politics of Opposition in Contemporary Africa*. Uppsala, Sweden: Nordiska Afrikainstitutet, 1–38.

Organization of Economic Cooperation and Development (OECD). 2006. "African Economic Outlook 2005–2006: Botswana." Paris: OECD.

Osei-Hwedie, Bertha. 2001. "The Political Opposition in Botswana: The Politics of Factionalism and Fragmentation." *Transformation* 45: 57–77.

Ottaway, Marina. 1999. "Ethnic Politics in Africa: Change and Continuity." In R. Joseph (ed.), *State, Conflict, and Democracy in Africa*. Boulder, CO: Lynne Rienner Publishers, 299–317.

Oxfam. 2009. "Urban Poverty and Vulnerability in Kenya: Background Analysis for the Preparation of an Oxfam GB Urban Programme." Nairobi: Oxford GB.

Oxford Analytica. 2007. "Senegal: Electioneering Drives Economic Policy-Making." February 22.

2011. "Opposition Disunity Continues to Favor Wade." December 21.

Oyugi, Walter O. 1997. "Ethnicity in the Electoral Process: The 1992 General Elections in Kenya." *African Journal of Political Science* 2 (1): 41–69.

Pacek, Alexander C., and Benjamin Radcliff. 1995. "The Political Economy of Competitive Elections in the Developing World." *American Journal of Political Science* 39 (3): 745–759.

Panafrican News Agency. 2000. "Eight Presidential Candidates Kick Off Campaign." February 8. Retrieved from LexisNexis Academic Database September 24, 2009.

Pape, John, and David A. McDonald. 2002. "Introduction." In D. A. McDonald and J. Pape (eds.), *Cost Recovery and the Crisis of Service Delivery in South Africa.* Pretoria, South Africa: Human Sciences Research Council, 1–16.

Parsons, Talcott. 1975. "Some Theoretical Considerations on the Nature and Trends of Change of Ethnicity." In N. Glazer and D. P. Moynihan (eds.), *Ethnicity: Theory and Experience.* Cambridge, MA: Harvard University Press, 53–83.

Peffley, Mark, and Rohrschneider, Robert. 2003. "Democratization and Political Tolerance in Seventeen Countries: A Multi-Level Model of Democratic Learning." *Political Research Quarterly* 56 (3): 243–257.

Perlman, Janice. 1976. *The Myth of Marginality: Urban Poverty and Politics in Rio de Janeiro.* Berkeley: University of California Press.

Pfefferman, D., C. Skinner, D. Holmes, H. Goldstein, and J. Rasbash. 1998. "Weighting for Unequal Selection Probabilities in Multilevel Models." *Journal of the Royal Statistical Society* 60 (Series B): 23–40.

Picard, Louis. 1987. *The Politics of Development in Botswana.* Boulder, CO: Lynne Rienner.

Pieterse, Edgar. 2010. "Filling the Void: Towards an Agenda for Action on African Urbanization." In Edgar Pieterse (ed.), *Urbanization Imperatives for Africa: Transcending Impasses.* Cape Town, South Africa: University of Cape Town, Africa Centre for Cities, 6–27.

Pillay, Devan. 2008. "COSATU, SACP and ANC Post-Polokwane : Looking Left but does it Feel Right?" *Labour, Capital, and Society* 41 (2): 1–37.

Pison, Gilles, Kenneth H. Hill, Barney Cohen, and Karen A. Foote, eds. 1995. *Population Dynamics of Senegal.* Washington, DC: National Academy Press.

Pithouse, Richard. 2006. "Struggle is a School: The Rise of a Shack Dwellers' Movement in Durban, South Africa." *Monthly Review* (February): 30–51.

Polgreen, Lydia. 2007. "Senegalese Vote Hinges on Views of Economic Growth." *The New York Times*, February 26. Retrieved April 1, 2010 from http://www.nytimes.com/2007/02/26/world/africa/26senegal.html?pagewanted=all

Polhemus, James. 1983. "Botswana Votes: Parties and Elections in an African Democracy." *The Journal of Modern African Studies* 21 (3): 397–430.

Pollin, Robert, Mwangi we Githinji, and James Heintz. 2007. "Wage Cutting in Kenya Will Expand Poverty, not Decent Jobs." *One Pager* 46. Brasilia, Brazil: International Poverty Centre.

Posner, Daniel N. 2004a. "The Political Salience of Cultural Difference: Why Chewas and Tumbukas are Allies in Zambia and Adversaries in Malawi." *American Political Science Review* 98 (4): 529–545.

2004b. "Measuring Ethnic Fractionalization in Africa." *American Journal of Political Science* 48 (4): 849–863.

2005. *Institutions and Ethnic Politics in Africa*. New York: Cambridge University Press.

Posner, Daniel N., and David J. Simon. 2002. "Economic Conditions and Incumbent Support in Africa's New Democracies." *Comparative Political Studies* 35 (3): 313–336.

Posner, Daniel N., and Daniel J. Young. 2007. "The Institutionalization of Political Power in Africa." *Journal of Democracy* 18 (3): 126–140.

The Post. 2005. "Matero Turns out for Sata." November 28. Retrieved from LexisNexis Academic Database October 14, 2009.

Poteete, Amy. 2012. "Electoral Competition, Factionalism, and Persistent Party Dominance in Botswana." *The Journal of Modern African Studies* 50 (1): 75–102.

Potts, Deborah. 2007. "The State and the Informal in Sub-Saharan African Urban Economies: Revisiting Debates on Dualism." Paper read at Living on the Margins Conference, March 26–28 at Stellenbosch, South Africa.

Powell G. Bingham, Jr., and Georg Vanberg. 2000. "Election Laws, Disproportionality and the Left-Right Dimension." *British Journal of Political Science* 30 (3):383–411.

Jr., and Guy Whitten. 1993. "A Cross-National Analysis of Economic Voting." *American Journal of Political Science* 37 (2): 391–414.

Przeworski, Adam, and John Sprague. 1988. *Paper Stones: A History of Electoral Socialism*. Chicago: University of Chicago Press.

Putnam, Robert. 1993. *Making Democracy Work: Civic Traditions in Modern Italy*. Princeton: Princeton University Press.

Radcliff, Benjamin. 1994. "Turnout and the Democratic Vote." *American Politics Quarterly* 22 (3): 259–276.

Rakner, Lise. 2001. "The Pluralist Paradox: The Decline of Economic Interest Groups in Zambia in the 1990s." *Development and Change* 32: 521–543.

2003. *Political and Economic Liberalisation in Zambia, 1991–2001*. Uppsala, Sweden: The Nordic Africa Institute.

Rakner, Lise, Lars Svåsand, and Nixon Khembo. 2007. "Fissions and Fusions, Foes and Friends: Party System Restructuring in Malawi in the 2004 General Elections." *Comparative Political Studies* 40 (9): 1112–1137.

Rakner, Lise, and Nicolas Van de Walle. 2009. "Democratization by Elections? Opposition Weakness in Africa." *Journal of Democracy* 20 (3): 108–121.

Randall, Vicky, and Lars Svåsand. 2002. "Political Parties and Democratic Consolidation in Africa." *Democratization* 9 (3): 30–52.

Ravallion, Martin, Shaohua Chen, and Prem Sangraula. 2007. "New Evidence on the Urbanization of Global Poverty." *Population and Development Review* 33 (4): 667–701.

Rea, Louis, and Richard A. Parker. 2005. *Designing and Conducting Survey Research: A Comprehensive Guide*, 3rd ed., San Francisco: John Wiley & Sons, Inc.

Redvers, Louise. 2011a. "Personality Trumps Policy in Zambia's Election Battles." *Mail and Guardian*, September 2. Retrieved November 6, 2011 from http://mg.co.za/article/2011-09-02-personality-trumps-policy-in-zambias-election-battles

2011b. "The Puzzle that is Michael Sata." *Mail and Guardian*, September 30. Retrieved November 6, 2011 from http://mg.co.za/article/2011-09-30-the-puzzle-that-is-michael-sata

2012. "Zambians Lose Hope as 'King Cobra' Lives up to His Nickname." *Mail and Guardian*, June 14. Retrieved September 8, 2012 from http://mg.co.za/article/2012-06-14-zambians-lose-hope-as-king-cobra-lives-up-to-his-nickname

Remmer, Karen. 1991. "The Political Impact of Economic Crisis in Latin America in the 1980s." *American Political Science Review* 85 (September): 777–800.

Rencontre Africain pour la Défense des Droits de l'Homme (RADDHO). 2007. "Election Présidentielle du 25 Février 2007 au Sénégal: Rapport d'Observation de la RADDHO." Dakar, Sénégal: RADDHO.

Republic of Zambia. 2006. "Fifth National Development Plan: 2006–2010." Lusaka, Zambia: Ministry of Finance and National Planning.

Roberts, Kenneth M. 1995. "Neoliberalism and the Transformation of Populism in Latin America: The Peruvian Case." *World Politics* 48 (1): 82–116.

2006. "Populism, Political Conflict, and Grass-Roots Organization in Latin America." *Comparative Politics* (January): 127–148.

2007. "Latin America's Populist Revival." *SAIS Review* XXVII (1): 3–15.

2012. "Populism and Democracy in Venezuela under Hugo Chávez." In Cas Mudde and Cristóbal Rovira Kaltwasser (eds.), *Populism in Europe and the Americas: Threat or Corrective for Democracy?* New York: Cambridge University Press, 136–159.

2014. "Populism and Political Representation in Comparative Perspective," in Carlos de la Torre (ed.), *Power to the People*. Lexington, Kentucky: University of Kentucky Press.

Roberts, Kenneth M. Forthcoming. *Changing Course: Parties, Populism, and Political Representation in Latin America's Neoliberal Era*. New York: Cambridge University Press.

Roberts, Kenneth M., and Moises Arce. 1998. "Neoliberalism and Lower-Class Voting Behavior in Peru." *Comparative Political Studies* 31 (2): 217–246.

Roberts, Kenneth M., and Erik Wibbels. 1999. "Party Systems and Electoral Volatility in Latin America: A Test of Economic, Institutional, and Structural Explanations." *American Political Science Review* 93 (3): 575–590.

Roniger, Luis. 1994. "The Comparative Study of Clientelism and the Changing Nature of Civil Society in the Contemporary World." In L. Roniger and A. Günes-Ayata (eds.), *Democracy, Clientelism, and Civil Society*. Boulder, CO: Lynne Rienner Publishers, 207–214.

Ross, Eric S. 2008. *Culture and Customs of Senegal*. Westport, CT: Greenwood Press.

Rothchild, Donald, and E. Gyimah-Boadi. 1989. "Populism in Ghana and Burkina Faso." *Current History* 88 (May): 221–244.

Rueda, David. 2005. "Insider-Outsider Politics in Industrialized Democracies: The Challenge to Social Democratic Parties." *American Political Science Review* 99 (1): 61–74.

Ruel, Marie, James Garrett, Corinna Hawkes, and Marc Cohen. 2010. "The Food, Fuel, and Financial Crises Affect the Urban and Rural Poor Disproportionately: A Review of the Evidence." *The Journal of Nutrition* 140 (1): 170S–176S.

Rule, Stephen P. 2000. *Electoral Territoriality in Southern Africa*. Burlington, VT: Ashgate.

Russell, Alec. 2009. *Bring Me My Machine Gun: The Battle for the Soul of South Africa from Mandela to Zuma*. New York: Public Affairs.

Salih, M.A. Mohamed, and Per Nordlund. 2007. *Political Parties in Africa: Challenges for Sustained Multiparty Democracy*. Stockholm: International Institute for Democracy and Electoral Assistance.

Samuels, David. 2004. "Presidentialism and Accountability for the Economy in Comparative Perspective." *American Political Science Review* 98 (3): 425–436.

Satterthwaite, David. 2003. "The Millennium Development Goals and Urban Poverty Reduction: Great Expectations and Nonsense Statistics." *Environment and Urbanization* 15 (2): 179–190.

2004. "The Under-Estimation of Urban Poverty in Low- and Middle-Income Nations." *Working Paper on Poverty Reduction in Urban Areas 14*. London: International Institute for Environment and Development.

Saunders, Christopher. 2005. "South Africa: Recent History." In I. Frame (ed.), *Africa South of the Sahara*. New York: Routledge, 1088–1097.

Scarritt, James R. 2006. "The Strategic Choice of Multiethnic Parties in Zambia's Dominant and Personalist Party Systems." *Commonwealth and Comparative Studies* 44 (2): 234–246.

Schatz, Joseph J. 2007. "Opposition Leader Brings New, Combative Style to Politics in Copper-Rich Zambia." *Associated Press*, March 2.

Schatzberg, Michael. 2001. *Political Legitimacy in Middle Africa: Father, Family, Food*. Bloomington, IN: Indiana University Press.

Scheld, Suzanne. 2002. "Dakar." In M. Ember and C. R. Ember (eds.), *Encyclopedia of Urban Cultures: Cities and Cultures around the World, Volume 2*. Danbury, CT: Grolier Publishing Co., 85–93.

Schmitter, Philippe. 1974. "Still the Century of Corporatism?" *Review of Politics* 36 (1): 85–131.

Schwartz, Naomi. 2007. "Senegalese Presidential Contenders Tour Country." *Voice of America News*, February 6.

Schulz-Herzenberg, Collette. 2008. "A Silent Revolution: South African Voters during the First Ten Years of Democracy, 1994–2004." In Joelien Pretorius (ed.), *African Politics: Beyond the Third Wave of Democratisation*, chapter 6. Cape Town, South Africa: Juta and Co. Ltd.

Selolwane, Onalenna Doo. 2002. "Monopoly Politikos: How Botswana's Opposition Parties Have Helped Sustain One-Party Dominance." *African Sociological Review* 6 (1): 68–90.

Simler, Kenneth. 2007. "Micro-Level Estimates of Poverty in Zambia." Washington, DC: International Food Policy Research Institute.

Simon, David J. 2005. "Democracy Unrealized: Zambia's Third Republic under Frederick Chiluba." In L. A. Villalón and P. Von Doepp (eds.), *The Fate of Africa's Democratic Experiments: Elites and Institutions*. Bloomington: Indiana University Press, 199–220.

Simutanyi, Neo. 2009. "MMD's Narrow Electoral Victory." *Zambia Analysis* 8–9.

Sishuwa, Sishuwa wa. 2011. *The Making of an African Populist: Explaining the Rise of Michael Sata, 2001–2006*. MSc Dissertation, Oxford University.

Sisk, Timothy. 2004. "City Level Democracy in 21st Century Africa." In *Democracy at the Local Level in East and Southern Africa: Profiles in Governance*. Stockholm: International Institute for Democracy and Electoral Assistance (IDEA), 11–21.

Sixtine, Leon-Dufour. 2003. "La Jeunesse Entre Espoir et Désillusion: Malgré une Croissance de 5%, les Indices de Pauvreté Stagnent." *Le Figaro* Novembre 7: 2.

Smith, Benjamin. 2005. "Life of the Party: The Origins of Regime Breakdown and Persistence under Single-Party Rule." *World Politics* 57 (3): 421–451.

Le Soleil. 2003. "La Situation Nationale Vue par le CPC." March 29–30: 14.

Solway, Jacqueline S. 1994. "From Shame to Pride: Politicized Ethnicity in the Kalahari, Botswana." *Canadian Journal of African Studies* 28 (2): 254–274.

2002. "Navigating the 'Neutral' State: 'Minority' Rights in Botswana." *Journal of Southern African Studies* 28 (4): 711–729.

2004. "Reaching the Limits of Universal Citizenship: 'Minority' Struggles in Botswana." In Bruce Berman, Dickson Eyoh, and Will Kymlicka (eds.), *Ethnicity and Democracy in Africa*, chapter 8. Oxford: James Currey.

Somolekae, Gloria. 2005. *Political Parties in Botswana.* EISA Research Report No. 27, Johannesburg: EISA.

Southall, Roger. 2009. "Understanding the 'Zuma Tsunami.'" *Review of African Political Economy* 36 (121): 317–333.

Sow, Ibrahima. 2002. "Assises Politiques de l'Alternance: Nécessité et Urgence." *Le Soleil*, April 23, 2.

Sow, Moustapha. 2006. "Idy Plonge avec l'Aval de Cheikh Tidiane Sy 'Al Makhtoum.'" *L'Office*, April 10, 2.

Statistics South Africa. 2009a. *Quarterly Labour Force Survey.* Pretoria, South Africa.

2009b. *Gross Domestic Product: Annual Estimates 1993–2008, Regional Estimates 2000–2008, Third Quarter 2009.* Pretoria, South Africa.

Stepan, Alfred. 1990. "On the Tasks of a Democratic Opposition." *Journal of Democracy* 1 (2): 41–49.

Stokes, Susan C. 2001. "Introduction: Public Opinion of Market Reforms: A Framework." In S.C. Stokes (ed.), *Public Support for Market Reforms in New Democracies.* New York: Cambridge University Press, 1–34.

2005. "Perverse Accountability: A Formal Model of Machine Politics with Evidence from Argentina." *American Political Science Review* 99 (3): 315–325.

2007 "Political Clientelism." In C. Boix and S. C. Stokes (eds.), *The Oxford Handbook of Comparative Politics.* New York: Oxford University Press, 604–627.

Sud Quotidien. 2007. "Résultats Provisoires de la Commission Nationale de Recensement des Votes." March 2: 3.

Tacoli, Cecilia. 2001. "Urbanisation and Migration in Sub-Saharan Africa: Changing Patterns and Trends." In M. de Bruijn, R. van Dijk, and D. Foeken (eds.), *Mobile Africa: Changing Patterns of Movement in Africa and Beyond.* Leiden, The Netherlands: Brill Academic Publishers, 141–152.

Taylor, Scott D. 2006. *Culture and Customs of Zambia.* Westport, CT: Greenwood Press.

Thiam, Abdoulaye. 2007. "Un Département, un Hôtel, une Région, une Université.," *Sud Quotidien* February 6: 8.

Thiobane, Mandiaye. 2008. "Je t'Aime, Moi non Plus." *Nouvel Horizon* 648, November 21–27, 5–6.

Thioub, Ibrahima, Momar-Coumba Diop, and Catherine Boone. 1998. "Economic Liberalization in Senegal: Shifting Politics of Indigenous Business Interests." *African Studies Review* 41 (2): 63–89.

Thomas, Annie. 2001. "Senegalese President's Coalition well Ahead in Election." *Agence France Presse*, April 30.

Thornton, Douglas. 2000. "Political Attitudes and Participation of Informal and Formal Sector Workers in Mexico." *Comparative Political Studies* 33 (10): 1279–1309.

Thurlow, James, and Peter Wobst. 2006. "Not all Growth is Equally Good for the Poor: The Case of Zambia." *Journal of African Economies* 15 (4): 603–625.

Times of Zambia. 2007a. "Mwanawasa to Launch Keep Zambia Clean Campaign," June 22.

2007b. "Now PF MPs Block Expulsion," December 18.

2008a. "400 Market Stalls Demolished," June 21.

2008b. "State Ups Subsidy on Farming Inputs," September 18.

2008c. "Ruling Party Candidate Kicks Off Campaign," September 19.

2008d. "PF Applies for Injunction," September 30: 3.

2008e. "Solwezi Market Gets K100m," October 1: 7.

2008f. "600,000 Extra Ballots Rejected," October 11: 1.

2008g. "Sata Entices West on Barotse Agreement," October 21.

2008h. "Vote for Me, Appeals Sata," October 2: 3.

2008i. "My Vision to Lead Zambia Lives On – Sata," October 6: 1.

2008j. "Sata Calls for Peace," October 30. Retrieved via LexisNexis database December 7, 2009.

2008k. "Time's Up for Young Men to Lead Zambia, Says HH," October 7: 3.

Tolsi, Niren. 2008. "Shack Dwellers Take on Slums Act." *Mail and Guardian*, February 16. Retrieved May 10, 2009 from http://mg.co.za/article/2008-02-15-shack-dwellers-take-on-slums-act

2009. "Pooh-Slinging Slums Act Showdown at Con Court." *Mail and Guardian*, May 15–21, 3.

Tortora, Bob, and Jenny Marlar. 2010. "Sub-Saharan Africans Want Governments Focus on Agriculture, Jobs." April 15, Gallup Organization, retrieved from http://www.gallup.com/poll/127355/Sub-Saharan-Africans-Gov-Focus-Agriculture-Jobs.aspx.

Tostensen, Arne, Inge Tvedten, and Mariken Vaa. 2001. "The Urban Crisis, Governance and Associational Life." In A. Tostensen, I. Tvedten, and M. Vaa (eds.), *Associational Life in African Cities: Popular Responses to the Urban Crisis*. Stockholm: Nordiska Afrikainstitutet, 7–26.

Tripp, Aili Mari. 1997. *Changing the Rules: The Politics of Liberalization and the Urban Informal Economy in Tanzania*. Berkeley: University of California Press.

Tsie, Balefi. 1996. "The Political Context of Botswana's Development Performance." *Journal of Southern African Studies* 22 (4): 599–616.

Tufte, Edward. 1978. *Political Control of the Economy*. Princeton: Princeton University Press.

United Nations – Department of Economic and Social Affairs (UN-DESA). 2010. *World Population Ageing, 2009*. New York: UN-DESA.

2011. *World Urbanization Prospects: The 2011 Revision*. New York: UN-DESA.

United Nations Development Program (UNDP). 1998. *Zambia Human Development Report: Provision of Basic Services*. New York: UNDP.

United Nations Development Program-International Poverty Center (UNDP-IPC). 2005. *Poverty Status Report for Botswana: Incidence, Trends, and Dynamics*. Brasilia, Brazil: UNDP-IPC.

United Nations Human Settlements Programme (UN-Habitat). 2003. *The Challenge of Slums: Global Report on Human Settlements 2003*. London: Earthscan Publications Ltd.

2007. *Zambia: Lusaka Urban Sector Profile*. Nairobi: UN-Habitat.

2008. "UN-Habitat and the Kenya Slum Upgrading Programme Strategy Document." Nairobi, Kenya: UN-Habitat.

2009. *State of the World's Cities 2008/09: Harmonious Cities*. London: Earthscan Publications Ltd.

2010a. *State of the World's Cities 2010/2011: Cities for All: Bridging the Urban Divide*. London: Earthscan Publications.

2010b. *State of African Cities 2010: Governance, Inequality, and Urban Land Markets*. Nairobi: UN-Habitat.

United Nations Integrated Regional Information Networks (UN-IRIN). 2006. "Senegal: Utopian Plan Belies Dismal Reality for Flood Victims," December 19.

United Nations Population Fund (UNFPA). 2007. *State of the World Population: Unleashing the Potential of Urban Growth*. New York: United Nations Population Fund.

United Party for National Development (UPND). 2008. *Vision for Zambia*. Lusaka, Zambia: UPND.

Uppal, Yogesh. 2009. "The Disadvantaged Incumbents: Estimating Incumbency Effects in Indian State Legislatures." *Public Choice* 138: 9–27.

van de Walle, Nicolas. 2003. "Presidentialism and Clientelism in Africa's Emerging Party Systems." *Journal of Modern African Studies* 41 (2): 297–321.

2007. "Meet the New Boss, Same as the Old Boss? The Evolution of Political Clientelism in Africa." In H. Kitschelt and S. I. Wilkinson (eds.), *Patrons, Clients, and Policies: Patterns of Democratic Accountability and Political Competition*. New York: Cambridge University Press, 50–67.

van de Walle, Nicolas, and Kimberly Butler. 1999. "Political Parties and Party Systems in Africa's Illiberal Democracies." *Cambridge Review of International Affairs* 13 (1): 14–28.

Vengroff, Richard, and Michael Magala. 2001. "Democratic Reform, Transition, and Consolidation: Evidence from Senegal's 2000 Presidential Election." *The Journal of Modern African Studies* 39 (1): 129–162.

Venter, Denis. 2003. "Multi-Party Politics and Elections in Southern Africa: Realities and Imageries." In M. A. M. Salih (ed.), *African Political Parties: Evolution, Institutionalism, and Governance*. London: Pluto Press, 319–347.

Vernière, Marc. 1977. *Volontarisme d'État et Spontanéisme Populaire dans l'Urbanisation du Tiers-Monde: Formation et Évolution des Banlieues Dakaroises – le cas de Dagoudane Pikine*. Paris: Bibliothèque Nationale.

Vicente, Pedro. 2008. "Is Vote Buying Effective? Evidence from a Field Experiment in West Africa." Working Paper, Oxford: Department of Economics, Oxford University.

Vicente, Pedro, and Leonard Wantchekon. 2009. "Clientelism and Vote Buying: Lessons from Field Experiments in African Elections." *Oxford Review of Economic Policy* 25 (2): 292–305.

Villalón, Leonardo A. 1994. "Democratizing a (Quasi) Democracy: The Senegalese Elections of 1993." *African Affairs* 93 (371): 163–193.

1995. *Islamic Society and State Power in Senegal: Disciples and Citizens in Fatick*. New York: Cambridge University Press.

1999. "Generational Changes, Political Stagnation, and the Evolving Dynamics of Religion and Politics in Senegal." *Africa Today* 46 (3/4): 129–147.

2004. "ASR Focus: Islamism in West Africa-Senegal." *African Studies Review* 47 (2): 61–71.

Vincent, Louise. 2011. "Seducing the People: Populism and the Challenge to Democracy in South Africa." *Journal of Contemporary African Studies* 29 (1): 1–14.

Von Doepp, Peter, and Leonardo A. Villalón. 2005. "Elites, Institutions, and the Varied Trajectories of Africa's Third Wave Democracies." In P. Von Doepp and L. A. Villalón (eds.), *The Fate of Africa's Democratic Experiments: Elites and Institutions*. Bloomington, IN: Indiana University Press, 1–26.

Walicki, Andrzej. 1969. "Russia." In Ghita Ionescu and Ernest Gellner (eds.), *Populism. Its Meanings and Characteristics*. London: Weidenfeld and Nicolson, 62–96.

Walton, John. 1998. "Urban Conflict and Social Movements in Poor Countries: Theory and Evidence of Collective Action." *International Journal of Urban and Regional Research* 22 (3): 460–481.

Wantchekon, Leonard. 2003. "Clientelism and Voting Behavior: Evidence from a Field Experiment in Benin." *World Politics* 55: 399–422.

War on Want. 2007. "Time for a New Deal: Social Dialogue and the Informal Economy in Zambia." London: War on Want.

n.d. "Forces for Change: Informal Economy Organisations in Africa." London: War on Want.

The Weekly Post. 1992. "No Compensation for Kanyama Eviction Victims." March 27–April 2: 2.

Weyland, Kurt. 1999. "Populism in the Age of Neoliberalism." In M. Conniff (ed.), *Populism in Latin America*. Tuscaloosa, AL: University of Alabama Press, 172–190.

2001. "Clarifying a Contested Concept: Populism in the Study of Latin American Politics." *Comparative Politics* 34 (1): 1–22.

White, Howard. 1996. "Adjustment in Africa: A Review Article." *Development and Change* 27 (4): 785–815.

Widner, Jennifer. 1997. "Political Parties and Civil Societies in Sub-Saharan Africa." In M. Ottaway (ed.), *Democracy in Africa: The Hard Road Ahead*. Boulder, CO: Lynne Rienner Publishers, 65–82.

Wilkin, Sam, Brandon Haller, and Helmut Norpoth. 1997. "From Argentina to Zambia: A Worldwide Test of Economic Voting." *Electoral Studies* 16 (3): 301–316.

Wines, Michael. 2006. "Strong Challenge to Zambia's President." *The New York Times*, September 29. Retrieved April 1, 2009 from http://www.nytimes.com/2006/09/29/world/africa/29zambia.html?_r=0

Wiseman, John A. 1998. "The Slow Evolution of the Party System in Botswana." *Journal of Asian and African Studies* 33 (3): 241–264.

Wiseman, John, and Roger Charlton. 1995. "The October 1994 Elections in Botswana." *Electoral Studies* 14 (3): 323–328.

Woolcock, Michael, and Deepak Narayan. 2000. "Social Capital: Implications for Development Theory, Research, and Policy." *World Bank Research Observer* 15 (2): 225–249.

World Bank. 2007a. *Zambia Poverty and Vulnerability Assessment*. Washington, DC: International Bank for Reconstruction and Development.

2007b. "Sénégal: A la Recherche de l'Emploi – Le Chemin vers la Prospérité." *Country Economic Memorandum*. Washington, DC: International Bank for Reconstruction and Development.

2009. *World Development Report 2009: Reshaping Economic Geography*. Washington, DC: International Bank for Reconstruction and Development.

Yadav, Yogendra. 1996. "Reconfiguration in Indian Politics: State Assembly Elections, 1993–95." *Economic and Political Weekly* 31 (2/3): 95–104.

Young, Crawford. 1965. *Politics in the Congo: Decolonization and Independence*. Princeton: Princeton University Press.

Young, Daniel. 2009a. "Is Clientelism at Work in African Elections? A Study of Voting Behavior in Kenya and Zambia," *Afrobarometer Working Paper No. 106*.

2009b. "Support You Can Count On? Ethnicity, Partisanship, and Retrospective Voting in Africa," *Afrobarometer Working Paper No. 115*.

Zambian Confederation of Trade Unions (ZCTU). 2006. *Building a Better Zambia: Perspectives and Demands for the Zambia Congress of Trade Unions on the Next Government Ahead of the 2006 Tripartite Elections*. Lusaka, Zambia: ZCTU.

Zeleza, Paul Tiyambe, and Dickson Eyoh, eds. 2003. *Encyclopedia of Twentieth-Century African History*. New York: Routledge.

Zipp, John F. 1985. "Perceived Representativeness and Voting: An Assessment of the Impact of 'Choices' versus 'Echoes.'" *American Political Science Review* 79: 50–61.

Zolberg, Aristide. 1966. *Creating Political Order: The Party-States of West Africa*. Chicago: Rand McNally.

Index

Lightning Source UK Ltd.
Milton Keynes UK
UKHW01f2000080818
326976UK00001B/30/P